# THE ASSURANCE OF THINGS HOPED FOR

# THE ASSURANCE OF THINGS HOPED FOR

*A Theology of Christian Faith*

AVERY DULLES, S. J.

New York  Oxford
OXFORD UNIVERSITY PRESS
1994

## Oxford University Press

Oxford   New York   Toronto
Delhi   Bombay   Calcutta   Madras   Karachi
Kuala Lumpur   Singapore   Hong Kong   Tokyo
Nairobi   Dar es Salaam   Cape Town
Melbourne   Auckland   Madrid

and associated companies in
Berlin   Ibadan

## Copyright © 1994 by New York Province, Society of Jesus

Published by Oxford University Press, Inc.
200 Madison Avenue, New York, New York 10016

Library of Congress Cataloging-in-Publication Data
Dulles, Avery Robert, 1918–
The assurance of things hoped for : a theology of Christian
faith / Avery Dulles.
p.   cm.   Includes bibliographical references.
ISBN 0-19-508302-4 (alk. paper)
1. Faith.   I. Title.
BT771.2.D76 1994   234′.2—dc20
93-29720

1 3 5 7 9 8 6 4 2

Printed in the United States of America
on acid-free paper

*Faith—is the Pierless Bridge*
*Supporting what We see*
*Unto the Scene that We do not—*
*Too slender for the eye*

*It bears the Soul as bold*
*As it were rocked in Steel*
*With Arms of Steel at either side—*
*It joins—behind the Veil*

*To what, could We presume*
*The Bridge would cease to be*
*To Our far, vacillating Feet*
*A first Necessity.*

EMILY DICKINSON

# Contents

# Abbreviations

## Scripture

The abbreviations in the Revised Standard Version (New York: Oxford University Press, 1962), from which Scripture quotations are taken, have been followed.

## Documents of Vatican II

**AA** *Apostolicam actuositatem*—Decree on the Apostolate of the Laity

**AG** *Ad gentes*—Decree on the Church's Missionary Activity

**CD** *Christus Dominus*—Decree on the Bishops' Pastoral Office in the Church

**DH** *Dignitatis humanae*—Declaration on Religious Freedom

**DV** *Dei Verbum*—Dogmatic Constitution on Divine Revelation

**GS** *Gaudium et spes*—Pastoral Constitution on the Church in the Modern World

**LG** *Lumen gentium*—Dogmatic Constitution on the Church

**NA** *Nostra aetate*—Declaration on the Relationship of the Church to Non-Christian Religions

**OE** *Orientalium ecclesiarum*—Decree on Eastern Catholic Churches

**OT** *Optatam totius*—Decree on Priestly Formation

**PO** *Presbyterorum ordinis*—Decree on the Ministry and Life of Priests

**SC** *Sacrosanctum concilium*— Constitution on the Sacred Liturgy

**UR** *Unitatis redintegratio*—Decree on Ecumenism

## Other

**AAS** *Acta apostolicae sedis* (Rome, 1909ff.)

**ASS** *Acta Sanctae Sedis* (Rome, 1865-1908)

**CR** Corpus Reformatorum, ed. K. G. Kretschneider et al. (Halle and elsewhere, 1827 ff.)

**CSEL** Corpus Scriptorum ecclesiasticorum latinorum (Vienna, 1866 ff.)

**DB** *Enchiridion symbolorum;* ed. H. Denzinger, rev. by C. Bannwart; 30th ed. (Freiburg: Herder, 1955)

**DS** *Enchiridion symbolorum,* ed. H. Denzinger, rev. by A. Schönmetzer; 36th ed. (Freiburg: Herder, 1976)

**DTC** *Dictionnaire de théologie catholique* (Paris, 1930ff.)

**LW** Luther's Works, ed. J. Pelikan and H. Lehmann (Philadelphia and St. Louis, 1955ff.)

**LXX** Septuagint

**PG** Patrologiae cursus completus. Series graeca, ed. J. P. Migne (Paris, 1857ff.)

**PL** Patrologiae cursus completus. Series latina, ed. J. P. Migne (Paris, 1844ff.)

**SC** Sources chrétiennes (Paris, 1946ff.)

**WA** Martin Luther, *Werke* (Kritische Gesamtausgabe; "Weimarer Ausgabe"; Weimar: Böhlau, 1883 ff.)

# THE ASSURANCE OF THINGS HOPED FOR

# Introduction

The word "faith" might be described as *the* Christian word. More than any other religion, Christianity deserves to be called a faith. Among the terms that refer to the Christian movement, "faith" and its cognates occur with remarkable frequency in the Bible. In the New Testament the word "faith" *(pistis)* occurs 243 times; "believe" *(pisteuo)* likewise 243 times, and "faithful" *(pistos)* 67 times. By comparison, the noun "hope" *(elpis)* occurs 53 times; the verb "to hope," *(elpizo)* 31 times. "Charity" *(agape)* is used as a noun 116 times and as a verb *(agapao)* 143 times.[1] Thus in the triad of faith, hope, and charity, faith seems to outweigh hope and charity, not indeed in excellence (cf. 1 Cor 13:13) but in constitutive importance. It, more than anything else, is what makes the Christian. While the word count is not by itself decisive, it is instructive.

In Christian preaching and teaching throughout the centuries the biblical emphasis on faith has been retained, even reinforced. From the earliest years theology constantly pointed to faith as the necessary path by which human beings were to enter into a saving relationship with God. The Protestant Reformation, especially in its Lutheran form, insisted on "justification by faith alone." The Catholic Church, at the Council of Trent, called faith "the beginning of human salvation, the foundation and root of all justification, without which it is impossible to please God and to join the fellowship of God's children" (Session 6, chap. 8, DS 1532).

Theologians have taken faith to be the fundamental Christian virtue, the indispensable presupposition of hope, charity, and good works. In recommending the Scriptures, the sacraments, and the ministries of the Church, theologians have sought to show how all of them express and nurture faith. The dissemination of faith has been the prime motive for Christian mission. Theology itself revolves about faith. According to the classical definition of St. Anselm, which has been praised and echoed by many other writers, theology is "faith seeking understanding." It is often described as the study of God and of divine matters in the light of faith. It would be senseless to apply oneself to theology without some understanding of what faith is.

Not surprisingly, the literature about faith is immense. Nearly every theologian

3

of stature has written extensively on the subject. In the first half of the twentieth century the body of literature, both Protestant and Catholic, grew almost beyond human reckoning. About the middle of the century the Belgian priest Roger Aubert published in French a large and valuable, though somewhat selective, history of the theology of faith.[2] Catholic systematic reflection on faith was set forth in numerous manuals, generally written in Latin.

The works issued around the middle of the century, composed to meet the demands of their day, are no longer entirely satisfactory. The seminary manuals presupposed a specialized scholastic framework. The monographs written in continental Europe failed to deal adequately with literature in English. Catholic studies published before and during the Second Vatican Council generally gave insufficient attention to Scripture; they also neglected the Protestant literature, or handled it in too polemical a manner.

The Second Vatican Council (1962–1965), in my opinion, intensified the need for an updated theology of faith. It did not reject earlier Catholic theology, but it sought to supplement and correct Scholasticism, and especially modern Scholasticism, by introducing a theology of faith that was more experiential, more biblical, more historically conscious, and more ecumenical. While calling for a retrieval of earlier biblical and patristic models, Vatican II also sought to reach out to what was sound in the teaching of other Christan traditions, including the Protestant Reformation, for which faith had been a crucial theme. It recognized the need for the theology of faith to take account of the aspirations, expectations, and anxieties of the time in which we live.

As a teacher of theology, I have felt the difficulty of finding materials on faith, especially in English, that could be assigned or recommended to my students for reading and reference. I have heard other teachers complain of the same difficulty. The present work is written, in part, to fill that gap. But it is also my hope that this book may help reflective Christians of all traditions and walks of life to find out where theology has been, and is, in this important specialty.

Convinced that sound doctrinal developments must maintain continuity with Scripture and tradition, I have sought to keep these sources constantly in view. To me the history of the theology of faith is a fascinating story—a dialogue conducted over many centuries among great minds dealing with topics that were to them (and are to me) of utmost importance.

I recognize that theology can never be static. It is never sufficient just to repeat what has been said in earlier centuries. But the record seems to prove that the most creative advances in theology are made by thinkers who have appropriated the wisdom of the past. As the medieval axiom had it, they could see far because they sat on the shoulders of giants. Before proposing a personal theory, one would do well to find out whether it, or something like it, has been proposed and examined at some previous time. New theories that lack solid roots in Scripture and tradition may attract great attention when first proposed, but they often prove, on second thought, to be blind alleys.

I trust that, in sifting through the work of others, I may have succeeded in making some personal contribution, but my personal insights, such as they are, can be no more than a footnote to the work of others. This book will achieve its principal aim if it can help its readers to gain a sense of what the finest thinkers of the past and present have had to say about faith, thus equipping them to grapple with their own questions and to play their part in the unending quest whereby faith seeks to understand no less a thing than faith itself.

This book is not directly concerned with apologetical questions. It would be possible to present an almost endless series of difficulties against faith, some of them distinctive to our own time and culture. The most serious difficulties, I believe, are perennial. They stem from the limited capacity of the human mind in its outreach toward the divine and from the need to submit to a gracious word that comes from God.

While apologists do well to seek solutions to the objections, apologetics should be seen as a secondary discipline that depends on a prior theology of faith. The first requirement is to have a correct idea of what faith claims to be and is: a natural impossibility, a miracle of grace, a sheer gift from God for which one can only ask on one's knees. Faith is not an irrational act but it could be seen as such by those who fail to reckon with the initiatives of God. Faith is not a matter of human minds climbing up toward the divine, but of welcoming the gracious manifestation that God has given of himself. Faith itself is, in the words of Scripture, "the assurance of things hoped for, the conviction of things not seen" (Heb 11:1).

It remains for me to thank the many friends and colleagues who have assisted me in the production of this book. Chapters and major portions have been read and criticized, at various stages of development, by scholars including the following: Ewert H. Cousins, John R. Donahue, S.J., William V. Dych, S.J., Charles Homer Giblin, S.J., John Greco, René Latourelle, S.J., Joseph T. Lienhard, S.J., Gerald A. McCool, S.J., Louis Monden, S.J., Gerald O'Collins, S.J., and Vincent T. O'Keefe, S.J. I am grateful for their encouragement and suggestions. Finally, I must express a very special debt of gratitude to my able assistant, Dr. Anne-Marie Kirmse, O.P., without whose constant availability this work could hardly have come to completion.

## Notes

1. For statistics on the Greek New Testament I rely on Kurt Aland, *Vollständige Konkordanz zum griechischen Neuen Testament* (Berlin: Walter de Gruyter, 1978), vol. 2, *Spezialübersichten*.

2. Roger Aubert, *Le Problème de l'acte de foi: données traditionelles et résultats des controverses récentes*, 2d ed. revised and corrected (Louvain: E. Warny, 1950). The first edition had appeared in 1945. The third and fourth editions (1958, 1969) are simply reprints of the second.

# 1

## Biblical Foundations

It is characteristic of the biblical religions to give special emphasis to faith as the fundamental attitude that human beings should have in their relationship to God. In other religions, faith, in the sense of conviction based on personal allegiance, is less prominent and does not become a technical term in religious discourse.

Since New Testament times "faith" in a theological context has generally been taken to mean an acceptance of God's word or promises as true and trustworthy, and a commitment to live accordingly. This notion of faith has been constructed on the basis of a great variety of materials in the Old and New Testaments and is to some degree a systematization. The Christian theology of faith cannot be understood without constant reference to the biblical materials from which it is derived. In order to give the necessary background, a rapid survey will be here made of the most important passages from the Old and New Testaments.[1]

### The Old Testament

Like the term "Old Testament" itself, the Christian concept of faith in the Old Testament is constructed by reading the Hebrew Scriptures backwards, so to speak, in the light of the "New" Testament. Christians usually form their concept of faith from the New Testament and from the tradition of the Church, and then look to the Old Testament to find words or incidents that can ground or illustrate what they understand by faith.[2]

The Old Testament has no single term exactly corresponding to the New Testament term *pistis* and its cognates. The term *he'emin*, the hiphil of the verb *'mn*, is used to mean: he believed, he trusted, he relied on. . . . The Hebrew noun *'emunah*, which one would expect to be used to designate belief, trust, and the like, is rarely if ever so used in the Old Testament. (The most likely exception is Is 26:2, "Open the gates, that the righteous nation which keeps faith may enter in"; but even here the word "faith" does not necessarily mean belief or trust.) *'Emunah* means rather truth, honesty, loyalty. It is preeminently an attribute of God, who is faithful and will surely carry out his promises. "Know therefore that the Lord your God is God, the faithful God who keeps covenant and steadfast love with those who love him and keep his commandments, to a thousand generations . . ." (Dt 7:9).

God's faithfulness toward Israel is manifested in the developing covenant relationship. The proper response to the God who establishes and keeps his covenant is twofold. First, one must accept God's word or promises as true, and second, one must show energetic and persevering compliance. God's messengers, the prophets, are required to open themselves to God's word and to carry it out unswervingly, and thus to be, in both senses, persons of faith. The people, likewise, must be docile and steadfast in order that they may enter into the blessings of the covenant. The fidelity of the prophet or the true Israelite is an earthly replica of God's own enduring love. The Hebrew term *'amen*, which has found its way into many modern languages, expresses at once a passive acceptance of God's word as trustworthy and an active readiness to comply with it.

The great prototype of faith in the Old Testament is Abraham, who heard and faithfully executed all God's biddings. When God called him out of his homeland in Ur of the Chaldees and sent him forth as a nomad into the desert, he unhesitatingly obeyed (Gen 12:1–3). His trust in God's promise to make his descendants a great nation was sorely tested by the barrenness of his wife Sarah, but he nevertheless believed. When God repeated his promises in more specific terms, Abraham's belief, according to the author, was "reckoned to him as righteousness" (Gen 15:6). This means, minimally, that Abraham did the right thing in believing in God's promise. Abraham's confidence that nothing could be too difficult for the Lord stands in sharp contrast with the disbelief of Sarah, who laughs at the idea that she could still become pregnant (Gen 18:12). After the birth of his son Isaac, Abraham's faith is once again tested by God's command to offer up his only son as a sacrifice on Mount Moriah, but Abraham passes the test and is rewarded (Gen 22:1–19).

Abraham's qualities as the prototype of all believers are extolled in the later tradition. "Abraham was the great father of a multitude of nations, and no one has been found like him in glory. He kept the law of the Most High, and was taken into covenant with him; he established the covenant in his flesh, and when he was tested he was found faithful" (Sir 44:19–20). In the New Testament different authors derive different lessons from the stories about Abraham. For Paul, Abraham shows how it is possible to be justified by faith without circumcision and without observance of the law (Gal 3:6–14; Rom 4:3–25). The Letter to the Hebrews presents Abraham as one who by faith trusted in the promises of God even to the extent of being prepared to offer up his only son (Heb 11:4–12, 17–19). The Letter of James, unlike Paul, uses the example of Abraham to show that justification is accomplished not by faith alone but by works that complete faith—namely the offering of Isaac on the altar (Jas 2:20–24). Christian theologians such as Søren Kierkegaard will use the example of Abraham on Mount Moriah to give biblical grounding to their views on the relations between reason and faith, ethics and religion.[3]

The story of the Exodus illustrates the forces of belief and unbelief struggling for dominance in Moses, in the Egyptians, and in the people of Israel. When the Lord commissions Moses to ask for the release of the Israelites, Moses protests that people will not believe him. God responds by promising to convince them by signs and prodigies (4:1–9). Pursued by the great armies of Pharaoh, the Israelites temporarily lose confidence in Yahweh and Moses, but their trust is restored after they are miraculously rescued at the Red Sea (14:31). In these texts faith is understood both as belief in the divine message entrusted to God's representatives and as personal trust in the Lord, thanks to the signs and wonders that he works in favor of his messengers.

The writings of the prophets are yet another major source for the Old Testament theology of faith. They recall Israel to its original trust in Yahweh and insist on the need to obey God's commandments. The concept of faith is greatly enriched by Isaiah, who has been aptly termed the "prophet of faith." In a situation of grave crisis, when the survival of the Davidic monarchy was in jeopardy, Isaiah declared to King Ahaz, "If you will not believe, surely you shall not be established" (Is 7:9). The occurrence of the same verb (*'mn*) in two forms in this sentence indicates the close linking between faith and security in the Isaian theology. Faith gives security not simply because God rewards those who believe, nor because it gives psychological assurance, but because it grounds one's existence in its true source. The accent here is upon putting one's trust solely in the might of Yahweh, and of being thereby delivered from the fear of all human adversaries.

A similar lesson is conveyed in chapters 28 through 31, where Isaiah warns the rulers of Israel against putting their trust in the chariots of the Egyptians rather than in Yahweh alone. Isaiah 28:16 (quoted and applied to Jesus by Paul in Rom 9:33 and 10:11, and also in several other places in the New Testament) calls upon the people to have confidence that God is establishing his faithful people as "a stone in Zion." In all these Isaian texts faith is a basis for political decisions, but only in the sense that it dissuades believers from relying on human prudence or created forces and inculcates patient confidence that God will carry out his announced intentions.

The later chapters of the book of Isaiah, usually attributed to Deutero-Isaiah and his followers, inculcate a similar doctrine of faith under radically different circumstances. The prophet assures the despondent people exiled in Babylon: "They who wait for the Lord shall renew their strength" (Is 40:31). He who alone is God may be trusted to act for the salvation of his people. God's saving action in these passages is not conditioned upon the faith of Israel but is rather the ground upon which faith can be erected.

Writing shortly before the Babylonian exile, the prophet Habakkuk provides the statement, "the righteous shall live by his faith" (Hab 2:4), which Paul takes as meaning that faith, in the sense of trust or confidence, gives justification (Rom 1:17; Gal 3:11). Quite possibly, however, the text means that the righteous are those who live faithfully while awaiting vindication from God. This latter interpretation fits better with the application of the text in Hebrews 10:36–38, which speaks of the endurance needed to put up with persecutions, so as to "do the will of God and receive what is promised."

In the Book of Psalms faith is defined primarily through the ingredient of trust. The Psalmist extols the Lord as the shepherd whose goodness and mercy overcome every fear of evil (Ps 23:4–6). Some of the historical psalms recite the story of God's saving acts toward Israel in order to elicit confidence in the goodness and mercy of the Lord, who forgives the sins of his people, and does not destroy them, even when they fail to trust his saving power (Ps 78:22, 38). Often enough, faithfulness and trust are mentioned together as appropriate human responses to God's faithful mercies (Ps 26:1–3).

The Old Testament wisdom literature, generally speaking, does not attribute the same importance to faith as do the Pentateuch and the prophets. Wisdom is viewed as a gift of God, but also as the fruit of reflection on common human experience. Hebrew wisdom, unlike Hellenistic, is for the most part practical and this-worldly rather than speculative and theoretical. Several of the wisdom writers emphasize the inability of the human mind to find meaning in history or to know anything about future life. The Book of Job tells the story of a man whose faith is sorely tried by unmerited suffering, who has rebellious thoughts against God, and who at length is reconciled by experiencing the overpowering mystery of the divine.

In postexilic Judaism, partly as a result of the value placed on the Pentateuch, faith comes increasingly to be understood as fidelity to the law rather than as a personal relationship to God presently revealing himself in history. Hope no longer looks forward to the historical future of the people, but envisages eschatological events taking place beyond history. Salvation is not seen as the destiny of the nation but rather as a reward given to the pious who have faithfully observed the precepts of the law. Yet the element of trust remains. "He who believes the law gives heed to the commandments, and he who trusts the Lord will not suffer loss" (Sir 32:24).

With the New Testament we enter into a very different universe of thought, involving a shift of meaning in the term "faith." Possibly under the influence, in part, of the Greek rhetorical tradition, some New Testment authors see faith primarily as a matter of persuasion and conviction. The Greek term *pistis*, which was not prominent in Greek versions of the Old Testament, becomes central for many New Testament authors. Yet these authors speak of faith in a variety of ways and thus set the scene for the theological disputes about faith that have been waged in the history of the Church. Excellent studies have been published on almost every aspect of faith in the New Testament.[4] Here it may suffice to present a schematic summary, accenting what is specific to particular books and authors.


## The Synoptic Gospels

Although echoes of the preaching of the primitive Church can be detected in the Synoptic Gospels, these works also permit one to reconstruct to some extent the view of faith held by Jesus himself and the pre-Easter community.[5] In these Gospels faith comes up most frequently in connection with stories of healings and other miraculous events. Faith, however, is seen not only as a result of miracles but also, and perhaps predominantly, as a force that brings them about. On many occasions Jesus declares, "Your faith has made you well" (Mk 5:34 par; Mk 10:52 par; Lk 7:50; 17:19). Conversely, the lack of faith that Jesus encounters—at Nazareth, for instance—impedes him from working miracles (Mk 6:5; Mt 13:58; cf. 17:20).

Faith, then, is related to concrete situations of need, such as illness, danger, and death of one's loved ones. As a kind of hopeful expectation, faith is directed toward future well-being. The idea of salvation in a life beyond death rarely appears, at least in explicit form.

The term "faith" is often used absolutely, without any object being mentioned. God is the implied object. Because God is omnipotent, nothing is impossible for faith, which is, so to speak, a participation in the omnipotence of God. Faith as small as a grain of mustard seed is capable of moving mountains (Mk 9:23; 11:22; Mt 17:20).

The opposites of faith are fear and doubt, but faith sometimes coexists with its own opposite, as in the case of the anguished father of the epileptic boy who cries out, "I believe; help my unbelief" (Mk 9:24). The disciples, though they follow Jesus in faith, are often rebuked by him for their lack of faith (Mk 4:40 par) or for being "men of little faith" (Mt 14:31; 16:8; 17:20).

Jesus appears in the Synoptic Gospels as the awakener or catalyst of faith. Although it is possible to look upon Jesus as one who lives by faith, faith is not predicated of Jesus himself. Except in the undoubtedly secondary passage, Matthew 18:6, the Synoptic sayings (as contrasted with the Johannine) never present Jesus as explictly calling for faith in himself. Yet Jesus' urgent call for discipleship was implicitly a demand for faith in himself, as was his call to acknowledge him before the world (Mt 10:32–33). Jesus' peculiar use of the term "amen" as a guarantee of his own sayings, moreover, implies a claim to authority not paralleled in Jewish usage. Thus Jesus in his public ministry would seem to have laid the groundwork for the explicit faith in himself as Lord that would be demanded by the kerygma of the infant Church.

The believers are those who recognize the presence of God in the person and ministry of Jesus and who accept the good news of the kingdom that is being inaugurated in and through Jesus. As indicated from the very first verse (1:1), Mark's Gospel revolves about the personal identity of Jesus as Son of God, the title given to him in the centurion's confession of faith at the climactic moment of Jesus' death.[6] The power to recognize Jesus as Messiah or Son of God is attributed to the grace of the Father. Jesus gives thanks to the Father for the "little ones" who have received the gift of faith (Mt 11:25 par). Peter's confession of faith evokes from Jesus the response: "Blessed are you, Simon Bar-Jona! For flesh and blood has not revealed this to you, but my Father who is in heaven" (Mt 16:17). Jesus prays for Peter "that your faith may not fail" (Lk 22:31).

## The Post-Easter Community; the Acts

Since the Synoptic Gospels were composed by Christians for the use of the early Church, it is only natural that they should contain overtones of the post-Easter proclamation. It is not always easy to separate out what comes verbally from Jesus himself, who sometimes speaks in terms closely resembling the Church's kerygma. At the opening of his ministry Jesus is presented as calling upon people in general to "repent and believe in the gospel" (Mk 1:14). The use of the word "gospel" in this sentence seems to belong to Mark's own vocabulary. The appendix of Mark speaks for the early Church when it quotes the risen Jesus as declaring, "He who

believes and is baptized will be saved; but he who does not believe will be condemned" (Mk 16:16).

In the post-Easter situation the primary awakeners of faith are the apostles, the
witnesses divinely commissioned to preach the good news about the risen Christ.
The miracles of the apostles are divine signs accrediting their proclamation. The
hearers frequently accept the proclamation on the basis of the miracles (Acts 9:42;
13:12; 14:9). Faith begins to take on a more doctrinal content than it had in the
proclamation of Jesus. Its primary content is the apostolic message concerning
Jesus as Messiah and risen Lord (Acts 2:36). Frequently in the Book of the Acts,
faith is used in an objective sense to designate the content of the kerygma (Acts 6:7;
13:8; 14:22; 16:5).

Faith, however, is more than an intellectual assent to the Christian message.
To be a "believer," in the Book of Acts, is to have joined the Christian community
(Acts 4:32; 11:21). The apostles, when they proclaim the kerygma, regularly add an
exhortation to repent and be baptized. Thus Peter, at the conclusion of his Pente-
cost sermon, admonishes his hearers, "Repent, and be baptized every one of you
for the forgiveness of your sins" (Acts 2:38). Faith is virtually equated with baptism
and is regarded as remitting one's sins (Acts 4:12, 26:18). To believe in Jesus Christ
is a necessary condition for salvation (Acts 4:12; 16:31). In the Acts, close attention
is paid to the role of the Holy Spirit, who gives power to the apostolic preaching and
disposes the hearers to believe the gospel message.

## Paul

In Paul, as in the Book of Acts, faith generally means a response to the message
about Jesus the risen Lord.[7] The term "believers" is practically a synonym for
"Christians" (Rom 3:22; 1 Cor 1:21). Echoing an early creedal formulation, Paul
writes in Romans 10:9: "If you confess with your lips that Jesus is Lord and believe
in your heart that God raised him from the dead, you will be saved." Faith, as the
prerequisite of salvation, is something that "comes by hearing" (Rom 10:17), "and
what is heard comes by the preaching of Christ" (ibid.). The true content of faith is
the good news of God's saving action in Jesus Christ, "who was put to death for our
trespasses and raised for our justification" (Rom 4:25). This gospel message must
be zealously defended against every kind of falsification (Gal 1:6–9).

Intellectual assent to the gospel is not a blind or merely emotional venture. It
is solidly supported by signs and wonders (1 Th 1:5), by demonstrations of the
power of the Spirit (1 Cor 2:4), and especially by the well-attested appearances of
the risen Christ (1 Cor 15:1–8), which are part of the common teaching of all the
apostles (v. 11). Yet faith cannot be achieved without the help of grace. Since those
who are "unspiritual" cannot discern the things of the Spirit (1 Cor 2:12–15), faith
presupposes an inner call proceeding from God's free election (Rom 5:15; 8:30; Eph
2:8; 2 Th 2:13).

Faith admits of many degrees, corresponding to the measure which God is
pleased to bestow on each individual (Rom 12:3). The faith that "moves moun-

tains" (1 Cor 13:2) is a special charism freely bestowed upon some by the Holy Spirit, and is not essential to salvation. While destroying the proud claims of worldly wisdom, faith gives rise to a wisdom not of this world, founded upon Christ, whom God has constituted as our wisdom (1 Cor 1:30). Paul expects his converts to grow in knowledge and discernment, "to have all the riches of assured understanding and the knowledge of God's mystery, of Christ, in whom are hid all the treasures of wisdom and knowledge" (Col 2:2–3). As Christ dwells in their hearts through faith, believers are able to gain deeper knowledge of the love of Christ "which surpasses knowledge" (Eph 3:19). Yet so long as they remain on earth, they must continue to "walk by faith, not by sight" (2 Cor 5:7), "for now we see in a mirror dimly, but then [in the life to come] face to face" (1 Cor 13:12).

Faith, however, is far more than a merely intellectual act. Paul links it very closely with trust and obedience. By faith we open ourselves up to God the revealer and put our future in his hands (Rom 4:5). Like Abraham, who "in hope believed against hope" (Rom 4:18), the Christian looks forward trustfully, confident of being raised up one day together with Jesus (2 Cor 4:14). In many Pauline texts *pistis* and its cognates can be translated as "trust" no less accurately than as "faith." To believe in Christ is to put one's trust in him (Rom 10:11; Gal 2:16; Phil 1:29).

While it does involve the passive virtues of acceptance and trust, faith also calls for an active response. Belief leads to confession (Rom 10:9–10; 2 Cor 4:13). More generally, faith causes the life of the believer to be dominated by Christ. Paul can therefore speak of the "obedience of faith" (Rom 1:5) and attribute to faith the same predicates that he attributes to obedience (Rom 1:8 and 16:19).

Nothing is more characteristic of Paul than his doctrine of justification by faith. In Romans and Galatians he insists that we are justified freely by faith, and not by the works of the law (Rom 1:17; 3:28; Gal 2:16). Strictly interpreted, these passages refer to works of the Jewish law and not to good works as a whole. But it remains true that for Paul faith is freely given through God's grace and cannot be merited or effected by any merely human activity.

It is not easy to say whether Paul regards faith as sufficient for salvation. When he speaks of justification by faith in Romans and Galatians he seems to imply that faith is by itself salvific. But in First Corinthians he speaks of the gifts of faith, hope, and love as if all three were required. Faith without love, he says, is useless (1 Cor 13:3). The greatest and most important of the gifts is love (v. 13).

To harmonize these texts one may suggest that the faith that justifies and leads to salvation is a living, operative faith, which Paul elsewhere calls "faith working through love" (Gal 5:6). The works proceeding from faith and love are not without significance for salvation, for in the end God will render to everyone "according to his works" (Rom 2:6; cf. 2 Cor 5:10).

At the deepest level, faith is, for Paul, a new mode of existence. It is a new fellowship with Christ in the Spirit. Of this new life Paul can write that we "receive the promise of the Spirit through faith" (Gal 3:14). Faith makes it possible for a person to stand or walk in the Spirit (Rom 8:4; Gal 5:25). The Spirit of Christ effects an interpersonal union between the believer and Christ in the very act of faith itself. Thus Paul can write of himself that since he lives by faith in the Son of God "it is no longer I who live, but Christ who lives in me" (Gal 2:20). When Paul speaks of the life of faith in Christ, using expressions such as *pistis eis Christon* and *pistis Iesou Christou* he is saying something more than that faith has Christ as its object; Christ as subject is at work in the act whereby Christians believe in him. Paul's Christ-mysticism stands at the opposite pole from the kind of juridical or extrinsic doctrine of justification by faith that has sometimes been attributed to him.[8]

## John

Together with Paul, the other great New Testament theologian of faith is John.[9] Unlike the Synoptic writers, John (or, perhaps more correctly, the Johannine school) does not link faith with specific passing situations of need but rather with a total comprehensive decision leading to eternal life. His theology of faith also differs significantly from that of Paul. Whereas Paul focuses on belief in Jesus as crucified and risen Lord, John contemplates faith as it arises from encounters with the earthly Jesus, who goes to the Father and becomes, for others, the Way. He develops his theology of faith not in opposition to Jewish works-righteousness but rather against pride in human self-sufficiency. He may be consciously opposing Gnostic intellectualism.

In the Fourth Gospel and the Johannine epistles the verb "believe" (*pisteuein*) occurs 107 times (as against 54 times in Paul, including six times in the Pastoral Letters). But the substantive "faith" (*pistis*), which occurs 142 times in Paul, is never used in John's Gospel and only once in his Epistles (1 Jn 5:4). As this usage indicates, John is interested in faith as a dynamic process rather than as a state. In many stories he shows how the faith of the disciples rises above temptations and misunderstandings until at length it becomes firm and serene. The commentators distinguish four constructions that are characteristic of John. First, like Paul, he frequently uses the verb followed by "in" (*eis*) and the accusative—a construction peculiar to the New Testament, suggesting that faith brings the believer into a vital union with God and with Jesus. Second, the verb is sometimes used absolutely, with no expressed object, but generally with some claim of Jesus as its implied object. Third, John, alone among New Testament authors, uses the verb *pisteuein* in the sense of "believe" with an indirect object. The witness or the testimony adhered to is mentioned in the dative case. Finally, "believe" can be followed by a "that" (*hoti*) clause. In such cases faith is an acceptance of a Christological formula, to the effect that Jesus is the Christ, the Son of God, or some such title.

From this usage it is evident that John is deeply concerned with exploring the personal union with Jesus involved in faith, as well as the need for receptivity to the word of Christ or the Christian witness. Faith, in the Fourth Gospel, frequently issues in confessional statements on the part of persons such as Nathanael, Peter, the man born blind, Martha, and Thomas.

In the Johannine writings, as in Acts and Paul, faith is intimately connected with justification and salvation. It prevents a person from dying in a state of sin (8:24), liberates from judgment and condemnation (3:18; 5:24), and bestows eternal life (3:15–16, 36). Whereas Paul looks forward to salvation in a life beyond death, John teaches that eternal life is something already given (5:24; 6:47), though it is to be consummated on the last day, when the dead are raised to eternal life (5:29; 6:39–40).

In agreement with other New Testament authors, John insists that faith is a grace. We cannot by our own forces make the passage from death to life. To believe, a person must be drawn by the Father (6:44, 65), and it is precisely in responding to this attraction that one attains true freedom (8:32). Many texts in John emphasize the prevenience of grace, even to the point of insinuating predestinationism. Believers are those given to Jesus by the Father, his sheep, the ones who hear his voice (6:37; 8:47; 10:27; 18:37). If many disbelieve, it is because they are not "of God" (8:47). Yet they are culpable because their disbelief results also from moral defects (3:19–20; 5:44; 9:41), as does likewise the failure of believers to confess their faith (12:42–43).

Like Paul, John sees a very close link between believing and knowing—terms that are sometimes used by him almost as synonyms (6:69). By knowledge, John evidently means not a merely theoretical grasp of an objective kind, but an intimate personal relationship such as the familiar union existing between Jesus and his Father (10:14–15). Belief leads to knowledge (4:39–42; 10:38), but knowledge, conversely, leads to belief (16:30; 17:8; 1 Jn 4:16). Faith, indeed, may be described as a new mode of knowing.

Faith is supported by miracles and frequently takes its rise from them (2:11, 23; 4:53; 5:36–38; 10:38). Yet a faith that relies on miracles is only preliminary and inadequate (4:48; 6:26), inferior to faith that relies only on the word of Jesus (2:22; 14:10–11). The dialectic between seeing and believing resembles that between knowing and believing. Seeing can be an occasion for believing (20:8), but the faith of Thomas, who believes because of what he has seen, is less perfect than that of those who believe without seeing (20:29). While faith outstrips physical seeing, it brings with it a kind of spiritual vision (1:14, 11:40; 14:8–9).

During the earthly life of Jesus, the apostles frequently misunderstand his words and adhere to him without grasping the truth about him. Only after the resurrection do the disciples really understand the message of Jesus (2:22; 12:16). In this they are assisted by the Paraclete, the Spirit of truth, who has been sent to help them remember what Jesus has told them, to penetrate its meaning, to confirm their testimony, and to clarify in the course of time what Jesus could not communicate in his own ministry (14:26, 15:26; 16:12–15).

If Paul tended to contrast faith and works, John's tendency is to stress the unity between them. Those who do what is evil hate the light, whereas those who do what is true come to the light (3:20–21). Faith expresses itself in deeds of love. Those who abide in Jesus keep the commandments, especially the great commandment of love, and by their mutual love become a sign "so that the world may believe that thou hast sent me" (17:21; cf. 13:35; 15:8). Good works, therefore, lead to faith, and faith, conversely, is fruitful in good works. Good works without faith would in the end count for nothing, for the work that God requires above all else is to believe in Jesus as God's emissary (Jn 6:29). The great commandment involves both faith and love: "This is his commandment, that we should believe in the name of his Son and love one another" (1 Jn 3:23). God's love is the very object of faith: "So we know and believe the love that God has for us" (1 Jn 4:16). Empowered by God's love, faith is capable of overcoming the world, which lies in the power of the evil one (1 Jn 5:4–5,19).

## Other New Testament Writers

Ranking only after Paul and John as a theologian of faith is the anonymous author of the Letter to the Hebrews, who sets the consideration of faith in the perspective of a dynamic history of the people of God on pilgrimage toward the promised goal of eternal rest.[10] Faith, in Hebrews, frequently has the connotations of holding firm in one's confidence (3:14), perseverance, and endurance (10:36–39). The confidence of believers, says the author, has a great reward, provided that they remain in the company "of those who have faith and keep their souls" (10:39). The next chapter is entirely devoted to an encomium of the heroes of faith in the Old Testament, "who did not receive what was promised" and who were not to be perfected except through the new covenant (11:39–40; cf. 9:15). Having completed the long catalogue of saints, the author in chapter 12 admonishes his readers to look to Jesus "the pioneer and perfecter of our faith" (12:2).[11] The point here is not that Jesus himself was a believer—though this is perhaps implied—but rather that his example must inspire and sustain the faith of Christians, inasmuch as he endured the cross, heedless of the shame, and was consequently raised up to the right hand of God.

Several texts in Hebrews have become classic loci for subsequent theological discussion. Hebrews 11:1 proposes what has often been taken for a definition: "Faith is the assurance (*hypostasis*) of things hoped for, and the conviction (*elegchos*) of things not seen." In the context this sentence probably means that faith is both an assurance that the goods promised by God will be possessed in the future and a conviction that this assurance is reliably grounded in the saving action of Jesus Christ. In 11:3 the author goes on to say, "By faith we understand that the world was created by the word of God, so that what is seen was made out of things which do not appear." This verse seems to reflect a more Hellenistic and philosophical view of faith than the rest of the chapter, and it has sometimes been used to support the opinion that faith for the author is an intellectual assent rather than a matter of trust or confidence.

Hebrews 11:6a ("Without faith it is impossible to please him") is the biblical text most frequently quoted to prove the necessity of faith for salvation—a doctrine that, as we have seen, pervades the New Testament. Hebrews 11:6b gives a reason: "For whoever would draw near to God must believe that he exists and that he rewards those who seek him." In the mind of the author these two elements are probably inseparable; there is no question of believing in a God who would be unconcerned about human conduct. Many Christian theologians have seen here the minimum content of saving faith, required even from those who have no access to the biblical revelation.

Of great importance in the history of controversial theology is the Letter of James. Chapter 2, verses 14–26, contains a diatribe against the concept of justification by faith alone, without works. As previously mentioned, James takes Abraham to be an example of the necessity of joining works to faith. "As the body apart from the spirit is dead, so faith apart from works is dead" (2:26). This is perhaps the only passage in the New Testament in which faith is understood as intellectual assent rather than as a total adherence involving personal trust, communion with Jesus, and fidelity. Understanding faith in this restricted sense (which is surely not Pauline), James logically rejects the saving value of faith alone "without works." Martin Luther was greatly provoked by this passage, which seemed contrary to his own idea of justification by "faith alone." Whether or not his teaching is compatible with Luther's doctrine of justification, it would be hard to show that James is rejecting the true doctrine of Paul. He may be directing his criticism against some disciples of Paul who were oversimplifying their master's thought.

In the New Testament books to which most scholars give a relatively late date, such as Jude, the Apocalypse (Revelation), and the Pastoral Letters, the term "faith" is frequently used to denote the doctrinal content of church teaching. The author of Jude appeals to his readers "to contend for the faith that was once for all delivered to the saints" (v. 3) and to build themselves up on their "most holy faith" (v. 20). The author of the Apocalypse issues "a call for the endurance of the saints, those who keep the commandments of God and the faith of Jesus" (Rev 14:12; cf. 2:13). In the two letters to Timothy we find faith described as a trust or deposit to be preserved and defended (1 Tim 6:20; 2 Tim 1:14). Paul is portrayed as expressing his own satisfaction at having "kept the faith" (2 Tim 4:7). Many warnings are given against false teachers who "have made shipwreck of their faith" (1 Tim 1:19). The prescribed remedy is to abide faithfully in the doctrine of the Church, "the pillar and the bulwark of the truth" (1 Tim 3:15). Although the emphasis is no longer the same as in the Gospels and the great letters of Paul, the shift is at least partly warranted as an adaptation to the needs of a new generation.

## Conclusion

In both the Old and New Testaments the concept of faith is complex. It includes elements such as personal trust, assent to divinely revealed truth, fidelity, and obedience.

In the Old Testament faith is depicted as the appropriate response to God's faithfulness to his covenant promises. Although the element of belief is present by implication, the emphasis falls on trust or confidence in God as Lord. Faith is tested by obedience and fidelity. Security against hostile powers is the fruit of faith.

In the New Testament the cognitive element is more pronounced, partly for the reason that the hopes of Israel are held to have been surpassingly fulfilled in Christ. Salvation is linked to the memory of what God has done for his people in the death and resurrection of Jesus. But the element of trust continues to be central, especially perhaps in the Pauline letters. In the Letter to the Hebrews the ancient heroes of faith are extolled for their unshakable confidence in God's promises. In the Synoptic Gospels faith means personal trust in Jesus as the bearer of the kingdom. In John the accent falls rather on contemplative union with Jesus. The Letter of James insists on the need for faith to prove itself in good works.

In Acts and many of the New Testament letters faith is interpreted as acceptance of the apostolic proclamation. The intellectualization of faith is carried yet further in the Pastoral Letters, which exhibit a concern to hand down the Christian message as the objective content of faith. Trust, however, continues to be a theme, for Christians must always look forward to a future consummation in which salvation will be fully given.

The many facets of faith in the Old and New Testaments make it a foregone conclusion that the concept of faith in Christian theology will be rich, dynamic, and controverted. A great variety of views will be put forward, nearly all of them appealing to certain texts in Scripture.

## Notes

1. For general treatments of the subject of faith in the Bible the reader may consult Johannes Alfaro, "Fides in Terminologia Biblica," *Gregorianum* 42 (1961): 463–505; Hans-Jürgen Hermisson and Eduard Lohse, *Faith* (Nashville, Tenn.: Abingdon, 1981); standard dictionary articles such as those found in F. C. Grant and H. H. Rowley, eds., *Hastings' Dictionary of the Bible*, rev. ed. (New York: Scribner's, 1960), 288–90; Gerhard Friedrich and Geoffrey Bromiley, eds., *The Theological Dictionary of the New Testament*, vol. 6 (Grand Rapids, Mich.: Eerdmans, 1968), 174–228; *The Interpreter's Dictionary of the Bible*, vol. 2 (Nashville, Tenn.: Abingdon, 1962), 222–34; Supplementary Volume to *Interpreter's Dictionary* (Nashville, Tenn.: Abingdon, 1988), 329–35; *Sacramentum Verbi*, vol. 1 (New York: Herder and Herder, 1970), 243–57; *The Anchor Bible Dictionary*, vol. 2 (New York: Doubleday, 1992), 744–60; and James Michael Lee, ed., *Handbook of Faith* (Birmingham, Ala.: Religious Education Press), 99–122 (by Carroll Stuhlmueller) and 123–41 (by James L. Price, Jr.).

2. On the Old Testament concepts of faith see, in addition to the works listed in Note 1, Alfred Jepsen, "'aman," in *Theological Dictionary of the Old Testament*, vol. 1, ed. G. Johannes Botterweck and Helmer Ringen (Grand Rapids, Mich.: Eerdmans, 1977), 292–323. For the perspective of a distinguished Jewish thinker, see Martin Buber, *Two Types of Faith* (New York: Macmillan, 1951; reprint, Harper Torchbooks, 1961).

3. See Søren Kierkegaard, *Fear and Trembling* (Garden City, N. Y.: Doubleday Anchor, 1954), 64.

4. For general studies of the New Testament concepts of faith see, in addition to the literature mentioned in Note 1: Leander E. Keck, *The New Testament Experience of Faith* (St. Louis: Bethany Press, 1976); James L. Kinneavy, *Greek Rhetorical Origins of Christian Faith: An Inquiry* (New York: Oxford University Press, 1987); Otto Michel, "Faith," in *The New International Dictionary of the New Testament*, vol. 1, ed. Colin Brown (Grand Rapids, Mich.: Zondervan, 1986), 593–606.

5. On the views of faith reflected in the Synoptic Gospels see: Pierre Benoit, "Faith in the Synoptic Gospels," in his *Jesus and the Gospel*, vol. 1 (New York: Herder and Herder, 1973), 71–86; Gerhard Ebeling, "Jesus and Faith," in his *Word and Faith* (Philadelphia: Fortress, 1963), 201–46; Edward J. O'Connor, *Faith in the Synoptic Gospels* (Notre Dame, Ind.: University of Notre Dame Press, 1961).

6. A recent author summarizes Mark's conception of faith as follows: "Faith is believing confidence in Jesus inasmuch as he concretely embodies the saving action of God. In Mark's story, Jesus is, directly or indirectly, the sole mediator of the kind of faith required by the dawning kingdom. . . . The object of faith is, in a sense, quite specific: the presence of God's

eschatological power in the person of Jesus." See Christopher D. Marshall, *Faith as a Theme in Mark's Narrative*. Society of New Testament Monograph Series 65 (Cambridge, Eng.: Cambridge University Press, 1989), 231–32. This statement, as it stands, may not do justice to Mark's concern with the question of the personal identity of Jesus as Son of God.

7. On the Pauline concept of faith see Hermann Binder, *Der Glaube bei Paulus* (Berlin: Evangelische Verlagsanstalt, 1968); Marie-Émile Boismard, "La foi selon Saint Paul," *Lumière et Vie* 22 (1955): 489–514; Victor P. Furnish, *Theology and Ethics in Paul* (Nashville, Tenn.: Abingdon, 1968), especially 181–206; Leander E. Keck, *Paul and His Letters* (Philadelphia: Fortress, 1979), especially 49–55, 80–94; Otto Kuss, *Auslegung und Verkündigung*, vol. 1 (Regensburg: Pustet, 1963), 187–212; and Herman Ridderbos, *Paul* (Grand Rapids, Mich.: Eerdmans, 1975), especially 231–49.

8. In an interesting article, Greer M. Taylor holds that the *pistis Christou* is the faithful action by which he, as recipient of the inheritance in trust, disposes of the property so that aliens can inherit it after his death. See her "The Function of Πιστις χριστου in Galatians," *Journal of Biblical Literature* 85 (1966): 58–76. This interpretation, based on Roman law, brings out the role of Jesus as subject; it does not necessarily contradict the mystical identification of Christian believers with Christ emphasized by other authors.

9. On the Johannine concept of faith see: James Gaffney, "Believing and Knowing in the Fourth Gospel," *Theological Studies* 26 (1965): 215–41; Pierre Grelot, "Le problème de la foi dans le quatrième Évangile, *Bible et Vie chrétienne* 52 (1963): 61–71; Ferdinand Hahn, "Sehen und Glauben im Johannesevangelium," *Neues Testament und Geschichte. Oscar Cullmann zum 70. Gerburtstag*, ed. Heinrich Baltensweiler and Bo Reicke (Tübingen: Mohr, 1972), 125–41; Rudolf Schnackenburg, "The Notion of Faith in the Fourth Gospel," Excursus VII in *The Gospel According to Saint John* (New York: Herder and Herder, 1968), 558–75; Albert Vanhoye, "Notre Foi, oeuvre divine, d'après le quatrième évangile," *Nouvelle revue théologique* 86 (1964): 337–54.

10. On the theology of faith in Hebrews see Erich Grässer, *Der Glaube im Hebräerbrief* (Marburg: Elwert, 1965).

11. The word "our," in the Revised Standard Version, seems to be an interpolation not warranted by the better Greek texts. The New American Bible, Revised New Testament, renders the term "the leader and perfecter of faith."

# 2

# Patristic and Medieval Developments

## Ante-Nicene Fathers

In surveying the patristic period it seems best to select authors who have made significant contributions to the theology of faith and whose works on the subject still constitute valuable points of reference.[1] Specialized studies may be consulted by those who wish to pursue sections of the history in greater depth.

The apostolic fathers show no interest in formulating precise definitions of faith or speculative theories about the subject. Their concern is rather to motivate their readers to persevere and grow in the life of faith. Clement of Rome, in his First Letter to the Corinthians,[2] points out that Rahab was saved by faith and that her action in hanging a scarlet cord from her window prophetically indicates that all who believe and hope in Christ will be redeemed by his blood (no. 16; cf. Jos 2:18). Later he proposes Abraham and Isaac as models of faith shown forth in conduct (no. 31). Although justification is given by faith, not by works, believers are obliged to put their faith into action and must be "eager to perform every good work" (no. 33).

Ignatius of Antioch, in the seven letters attributed to him, regularly links faith and love.[3] Faith, he says, is the beginning of life, love is the end, "and when the two blend perfectly with each other, there is God" (*Ephesians*, 14). What makes for salvation is not the mere profession of faith, but perseverance to the end in faithful action (ibid.).

The apologists of the second century, seeking to relate Christian faith to Greek philosophy, made ingenious use of the Johannine doctrine of Christ as the incarnate Logos. According to Justin the intelligibility of creation is due to the eternal Logos, "the Word of whom all mankind partakes" (1 *Apology*, 46; cf. 2 *Apol.*, 8–10).[4] From this it followed that there could be no divorce between faith and reason, between religion and philosophy. The wisdom of Socrates was akin in its source to that of the prophets.

Irenaeus, late in the second century, transposes the Logos theology of his predecessors into a theology of salvation history.[5] For him Abraham was the father of believers because he was the first to follow the call of God's word (*Adv. haer.*, IV.5.3). "Abraham," says Irenaeus, "followed in generous faith freely and without ties and so became the friend of God" (*Adv. haer.*, IV.24.3). God revealed himself to Abraham "by means of the Word as by a ray of light" (*Demonstratio*, 24; SC ed. 62, p. 67). For us faith is the basis of salvation; it is the source of true understanding of things that truly are. God does not withhold his light from those who seek the truth (*Adv. haer.*, III.3.1).

Writing against the Gnostics, Irenaeus is particularly concerned to defend faith in the objective sense as the heritage received from the apostles (*Adv. haer.*, I.10.1), whose writings are "the ground and pillar" of our faith (*Adv. haer.*, III.1.1). The faith is one and the same throughout the Church, which believes as if it had but one mind and one heart (*Adv. haer.*, I.10.2).

The patriarchs and prophets had, through faith, a preview of Christ and the Church. In Christianity the Old Covenant is fulfilled; the faith is given in its plenitude. For those who stand firmly in the apostolic tradition, the faith remains always fresh and youthful. For, just as Christ "has fulfilled all things by his coming, he continues to fulfill the New Covenant in the Church until the end foretold by the law" (*Adv. haer.*, IV.56.1).

Tertullian, like Irenaeus, is concerned to defend the faith as a body of belief resting on the testimony of the apostles and maintained in the Church as a whole.[6] The "rule of faith," for him, is a summary of what was preached by Christ and taught by the apostles (*De praescriptione haereticorum*, 6 and 13; cf. *Apologeticus*, 47, referring to the "rule of truth.") Tertullian insists that the rule of faith is sufficient unto itself; it has no need to be supported or supplemented by philosophical investigation. "After Christ we have no need of speculation, after the Gospel no need of research."[7] He ridicules intellectuals who are always seeking and never arriving at belief. Those who do not have faith, he says, should seek faith, and when they find, believe. After coming into possession of the faith, one has no further need to seek (*Praescr.*, 10). For all that, Tertullian was not totally averse to philosophy. In his controversial writings he made use of philosophical arguments to support the teaching of faith about the existence of God, the creation of the world, and the nature of the soul. But he himself, as a Christian, did not wish to rely on these arguments, nor did he advise his fellow believers to rely on them.

Clement of Alexandria (140/50–c. 216) produced in his *Stromata*, Book II, what might be called the first Christian treatise on the theology of faith.[8] Basing his argument on a variety of biblical texts cited according to the Septuagint version (LXX), Clement rejects as inadequate the idea that faith is a mere opinion involving a certain risk of error. Even Aristotle, he remarks, held that the judgment that follows upon knowledge of a thing, whereby we affirm the truth of our knowledge, is faith (II, ch. 4, sec. 15, no. 5).[9] To rise above sensible things and know the invisible God, one must rely on God's own word and be docile to the Logos (II, ch. 4, sec. 16, no. 2). If the disciples of Pythagoras felt justified in assenting on the ground that "the master himself said so," Christians have far weightier reasons to submit to the master who is God (II, ch. 5, sec. 24, no. 3). The philosophers confirm the teaching of Scripture on this point:

> Does not the noble Heraclitus himself seem to blame those who do not believe? But the prophet said, "My just one will live by faith" [Hab 2:4]. And another prophet

adds, "If you do not believe, you shall not understand" [Is 7:9 LXX]. . . . Faith, which the Greeks calumniate because they judge it vacuous and barbaric, is a voluntary anticipation (*prolepsis*), a religious assent and, according to the divine apostle, "the guarantee of things hoped for, the proof of things not seen" [Heb 11:1]. . . . Others have defined faith as the assent that unites us to an invisible reality, just as demonstration is the assent given to the evidence of a hitherto unknown reality. . . . Indeed, anyone who has believed the divine Scriptures with a firm judgment, receives as an irrefutable demonstration the voice of God who has given them. Thus faith is no longer something that gains its force from a demonstration. "Blessed therefore are they who have not seen and have believed" (Jn 20:29). (II, ch. 2, sec. 8, no. 4 to sec. 9, no. 6.)

Clement's idea of a voluntary "prolepsis" is consciously borrowed from Epicurus. It means a kind of presentiment that arises spontaneously without study or deliberation (II, ch. 4, sec. 16, no. 3). By faith, as a freely given grace, the believer consents to the mystery of the hidden God and achieves union with the invisible (II, ch. 2, sec. 9, no. 1). In opposition to the Gnostic heretics, Clement insists that faith is freely received and that it can be refused. As a dynamic orientation of the human spirit to the truth, it is linked to moral activity (II, ch. 2, sec. 9, no. 2). The "prolepsis" tends to translate itself into a kind of knowledge (*gnosis*) that finds its ground and norm in the word of God (II, ch. 2, sec. 9, nos. 3–4). This knowledge does not emancipate itself from faith, but, as a deeper insight into the content of faith, rests on the word of God and defers to it (II, ch. 4, sec. 16, no. 2). "The gnostic is solidly established in faith" (II, ch. 11, sec. 51, no. 3). "Gnosis therefore remains faithful (*piste*) and faith becomes gnostic (*gnoste*) according to an order and reciprocity established by God" (II, ch. 4, sec. 16, no. 2). Faith is the seed, gnosis the fruit.

Against Philistine believers Clement defends the legitimacy of philosophical reflection, holding that it can be useful for defending the faith against assaults (*Stromata*, I, ch. 9, sec. 43, nos. 1–2). Against the Gnostics, on the other hand, Clement contends that simple faith is a shorter road to salvation than rationalized faith, and is not less secure (*Stromata*, VII, ch. 10, sec. 55).[10] Thus there are two kinds of faith, possessing equal worth in God's sight.[11]

In another work, the *Protreptikos*, an eloquent appeal to the pagans, Clement shows how true gnosis can be achieved by those who, after being initiated into the venerable mysteries of the Logos, dedicate themselves fully to discipleship. In his *Paidagogos* Clement shows how the Logos, having converted disciples to faith, instructs them in the paths of wisdom.

Clement's great successor as a catechetical teacher at Alexandria, Origen (c.185–c. 254), developed a theology of faith basically in line with that of Clement.[12] This teaching is scattered through many works, including his treatise on *First Principles*, his eight books *Against Celsus*, and his numerous biblical commentaries.

By the term *pistis,* Origen usually means an assent based on trust, though occasionally he speaks of trust itself as *pistis*. In trusting God one necessarily assents to God's word. Christ, the Word of God, speaks in Holy Scripture. His voice is heard not only in the New Testament but also in the Old, since both are forms of God's word. Critics such as Celsus have no right to object that it is unreasonable to believe in the word of God, for philosophers themselves see the need of submitting to teachers in order to learn. If it is reasonable to believe the founders of philosophical sects, it is far more reasonable to believe God and those who have preached God's message at great personal risk. For the multitude, who lack the talent and leisure for philosophical investigation, simple faith is a blessing. Such faith is no mere human achievement, for only the grace of the Holy Spirit can open human hearts to accept the Christian proclamation. The souls of believers are illuminated by Christ the true light.

Like Clement, Origen was concerned with the relationship between simple faith and "knowing faith" *(pisteuein egnokenai),* that is, faith grounded in reason or experience. Initially, as a "pistic," the Christian believes in the *name* of Christ, relying either on verbal testimony or on miraculous signs. But in advanced believers faith is sustained by an immediate interior perception achieved with the help of the spiritual senses. The soul feels within itself the presence of the Word and of the Father. In modern terminology, we might say that personal spiritual experience perfects and supplants merely propositional and "hearsay" forms of faith.

The interior appropriation of faith, in Origen's theology, never does away with the need to rely on the word of revelation. As Hans Urs von Balthasar explains, "The gnostic Christian [for Origen] does not outgrow the proclamation of the Church, but in the kerygma he finds, revealing himself, the Logos, who, in the most comprehensive sense, 'enlightens' the believer ever more clearly and, indeed, draws him, as John was drawn, to his breast ever more intimately and unites him interiorly with himself (*Commentary on John*, 32.20–21.)."[13] The progress from faith to knowledge is never complete in the present life. To be spiritual *(pneumatikos)* or perfect *(teleios)* is a limit-concept, indicating a direction rather than a state. Although all are called to be perfect, no one on earth attains perfection except in a mirror, dimly (cf. 1 Cor 13:12).

Speaking of justification, Origen holds that "faith suffices for righteousness, even if we have done nothing," but he adds that faith is destroyed by sins committed after justification. Good works done before faith, even if they seem to be correct, do not justify, "because they are not built on the proper foundation of faith."[14]

## Post-Nicene Greek Fathers

During the golden age of Greek patristic theology the Cappadocian fathers, Basil the Great (330–379), Gregory of Nazianzus (c. 329–390), and Gregory of Nyssa (c. 335–c. 394), combating the rationalism of Eunomius and other late Arians, moved toward a fideistic and mystical theology of faith. All three of them insist strongly on the limits of human reason and the need to rely on the word of God. Basil defines faith as "a whole-hearted assent to aural doctrine with full conviction of what is publicly taught by the grace of God."[15] Reason, he says, leads to knowledge of God's existence, but such knowledge enables us to rely in faith on God's word and thus to come to further knowledge. In the present life, however, our knowledge of divine things is fragmentary and incomplete.[16]

Gregory of Nazianzus, Basil's intimate friend who was bishop of Constantinople during part of the council of 381, set forth his views on faith and reason in his *Five Theological Orations* (nos. 27–31) delivered shortly before the council. He maintained that reason, carefully trained, could perceive its own limits and its need to be led by faith (Oration 28:28).[17] In an eloquent passage he explained that faith, far from nullifying reason, is needed to perfect reason:

> For when we abandon faith to take the power of reason as our shield, when we use philosophical enquiry to destroy the credibility of the Spirit, then reason gives way in the face of the vastness of the realities. Give way it must, set going, as it is, by the frail organ of human understanding. What happens then? The frailty of our reasoning looks like a frailty in our creed. Thus it is that, as Paul too judges, smartness of argument is revealed as a nullifying of the Cross. Faith, in fact, is what gives fullness to our reasoning (Oration 29:21).[18]

Basil's younger brother, Gregory of Nyssa, in his polemical works against the Eunomians, likewise contends that God, who is essentially incomprehensible, cannot be approached except through the medium of faith. Not even Moses, close though he was to God, was permitted to look on the divine countenance.[19] The mysteries of faith cannot be mastered by any human gnosis. Faith must therefore begin as a simple submission to the preaching of the gospel. As an instance in point Gregory refers to Abraham, who was deemed righteous because he relinquished false curiosity and believed in the word of God.[20] Simple faith, not gnosis, leads to justification.

Faith, for Gregory, is the presupposition for the mystical ascent of the soul to God. In his commentary on the Song of Solomon, Gregory depicts faith as a dynamic principle, an arrow, that directs the Bride to a nonconceptual encounter with God.[21] Again, in the life of Moses, Gregory writes that you must "in the impenetrable darkness draw near to God by your faith."[22]

In Gregory of Nyssa's dynamic spirituality, faith is closely connected with hope. He speaks of "the reasonings born of faith which confirm hope for the good things laid up for us" (*Life of Moses*, 266; p. 122). The end for which we hope is provisionally present in faith itself as "the substance of things hoped for."

The Antiochene bishop-theologian Theodoret of Cyrrhus (c. 393–c. 458) wrote a chapter on faith at the beginning of his apologetical summa, *The Cure of Pagan Maladies; or, The Truth of the Gospels Proved from Greek Philosophy.*[23] The analysis depends heavily on Clement of Alexandria, from whom it takes over the concept of faith as a voluntary assent whereby the mind contemplates invisible realities (I.91; SC ed. 57, p. 128; cf. Clement, *Stromata*, Bk. II, ch. 2, sec. 9, no. 1). Like Clement, Theodoret insists that anyone who wants to learn a trade or profession, or to become proficient in philosophy or religion, must begin by believing expert teachers. To understand divine things we must begin by believing "that God is and is a rewarder" (Heb 11:6). Just as the eye needs light to see bodily things, so the mind needs faith to perceive things that are divine (I.79; p. 124). Simple faith is made perfect by the addition of knowledge (I.116, p. 134).

In the sixth century, Greek patristic theology took a strong mystical turn, marked by Neoplatonic negative theology. Pseudo-Dionysius the Areopagite (c. 500), though he rarely uses the term *pistis*, obviously attaches great importance to faith as the foundation for mystical theology. "Faith," he writes, "is the unshakable basis of the faithful, whom it establishes in the truth and in whom it establishes the truth, so that they possess in an indissoluble unity simple knowledge of the things to be believed. For if knowledge unites things known with the knowers, and ignorance is a source of continual change and alienation from oneself, nothing, as the Scripture tells us, can move the person who possesses the true faith from the household founded on the true faith [cf. Eph 4:13], in which the permanence of its identity can be kept without change or variation."[24] Dionysius is chiefly celebrated for his mystical doctrine of the ascent to God by means of a grace-given ecstatic experience or connaturality (*patheia* or *sympatheia*), that informs the believer by means of a mysterious union, more passive than active, about mysteries that cannot be taught.[25]

Maximus the Confessor (c. 580–662) brought the mystical theology of Pseudo-Dionysius more firmly into the tradition of Alexandrian Platonism. For Maximus, faith is an unmediated union of the spirit with God.[26] It is the supreme act by which the spirit passes into what Dionysius had described as the "luminous darkness" of God. In opposition to theologians who regard faith as a mere point of departure for a journey toward genuine knowledge *(gnosis),* Maximus holds that *gnosis* is made perfect by faith. Thus he writes: "Earthly things are known by demonstration from the intelligible principles and causes into which they are by nature inscribed. With God, however, only his existence can be grasped by faith on the basis of principles that are in nature. Yet he enables the devout to believe and confess him truly and properly, with greater assurance than is given by any demonstration. Faith, in fact, is true knowledge *(gnosis)* that rests on indemonstrable principles, for it is the proof *(hypostasis)* of the things that are above intelligence and reason."[27]

For Maximus, then, faith is not an inferior type of knowledge. Surpassing natural knowledge, it stands at the highest level of human cognition attainable in this life. Like Pseudo-Dionysius, he understands the solidity of faith as an effect of a spiritual union with God achieved through self-surrender to the call of grace.[28]

## Post-Nicene Latin Fathers

Latin authors of the fourth century, such as Hilary, Marius Victorinus, and Ambrose, write of faith incidentally in connection with their polemical works against the Arianism of their day. Like Tertullian, they emphasize the value of faith as a simple submission to God's word as it comes to us through Scripture and apostolic tradition. Suspicious of philosophy, they regard faith as the only reliable path to true knowledge of God.

Among the Western fathers, Augustine of Hippo (354–430) holds a unique place because of his success in synthesizing the insights of Paul and John, as well as those of Tertullian and the Alexandrian and Cappadocian theologians, with his own religious experience, which was deep and complex.[29] His theology of faith has made a profound and lasting imprint on Western Christianity, both Catholic and Protestant.

Schematically, one may distinguish three periods in Augustine's thinking with regard to religious knowledge.[30] In his early writings, influenced by the Neoplatonists, he holds that the human mind is impeded from knowing God by its immersion in the realm of matter and sense-appearances. He prays with the Psalmist, "Create in me a clean heart" (Ps 51:10), and seeks purification through asceticism. After his ordination to the priesthood Augustine, in works such as the *Confessions*, speaks of pride rather than sensuality as the greatest obstacle. In order to know God the soul must humble itself through the obedience of faith. During this period Augustine is impressed by the statement of Peter that God cleansed the hearts of the Gentile converts "by faith" (Acts 15:9). In his later writings, such as the commentaries on John and the *City of God*, Augustine the bishop depicts faith primarily as a decision for the God who lovingly descends into the darkness of the world in order to rescue those in need of redemption. By allowing God's love to take possession of our hearts, so that we are moved to give and to serve, we can best overcome the false worldly loves that prevent us from truly knowing God. Thus Augustine's doctrine of faith comes to be enriched and completed, in his later works, by a stronger emphasis on charity. But he does not reject his earlier teaching on humility and obedience.

Faith, according to Augustine, is both possible and necessary because the light of divine truth shines in the darkness of the world. The darkness prevents us from grasping the light except through those who bear witness to the light. To accept such witnesses as "sent by God" (Jn 1:6) we must have faith (*De Trin.*, 13.1.2). To believe is to assent to the truth of what is said (*De spiritu et litt.*, 21:4).

According to another of Augustine's definitions, to believe is "to ponder with assent" ("cum assensione cogitare," *De praedest. sanctorum*, 2:5); it necessarily involves an exercise of thought or reason. Prior to faith we use our understanding to grasp the meaning of the proclamation and to consider the soundness of the reasons for assenting to it as true. "No one indeed believes anything unless he has first thought that it ought to be believed" (ibid.). People are moved to believe by proofs or signs, but that which moves one person may fail to move another *(De div. quaest. ad Simpl. libri 2)*. When Augustine seeks to give the reasons that he himself finds persuasive, according to the precept of 1 Pet 3:15, he generally mentions the miracles of Scripture but he dwells by preference on the wonderful expansion and catholic unity of the Church (*De fide rerum q. non vid.*, 7:10).

The rational approach to faith is for Augustine insufficient. Because faith is an act of consent, no one believes anything without wanting to believe. The will is directed by love: "It is love that asks; it is love that seeks; it is love that knocks; it is love that makes one adhere to revelation, and it is love that maintains the adherence once it is given" (*De moribus Ecclesiae*, Bk. I, ch. 17, n. 31). The faith that justifies, unlike the faith of the demons (Jas 2:19), is more than a submission to stringent evidence; it is a loving submission to Christ the Lord *(credere Christo)* and a movement of the soul that seeks union with Christ *(credere in Christum)*. Commenting on the text, "This is the work of God, that you believe in him whom he has sent" (Jn 6:29), Augustine asks: "What is to believe in him? Believing, to love; believing, to prize him highly; believing, to go to him and be incorporated in his members" (*In Joan. Evang.*, 29:6).

Especially in his later writings, directed against the Pelagians, Augustine strongly insists that faith is a pure gift freely bestowed by God. To believe in Christ we must be drawn to him, and this drawing is the work of the Father (Jn 6:44; *In Joan. Evang.*, 26:7). Augustine frequently quotes in this connection the Pauline text, "Not that we are sufficient of ourselves to think anything as coming from us; our sufficiency is from God" (2 Cor 3:5; *De praedest. sanct.*, 2:5). Since believing involves thinking, Augustine argues, believing cannot come from ourselves alone. In works of the apostolate, human beings may plant and water, but their work is useless unless God "gives the increase" (l Cor 3:7; *In Joan. Evang.*, 26:7). The noise of human words falling on our ears would avail nothing unless God, the interior teacher, were silently at work (ibid.).

Faith is necessary for justification, for the just live by faith (Hab 2:4; *In Psalm.*, 109:8). Justification is accomplished "not by the law of works but by the law of faith; not by the letter, but by the spirit; not by the merit of deeds, but by free grace" (*De spiritu et litt.*, 22). "Faith is the principle and origin of all merit," and conversely, as the Apostle says, "all that is not of faith is sin" (Rom 14:23; *Ep.*, 194.3.9).

Justifying faith, for Augustine, is always faith that comes through hearing, and more specifically through hearing of Christ the one Mediator. "All the righteous, that is to say, all true worshipers of God, whether before or after the Incarnation of Christ, neither did nor do live except by faith in the incarnation of Christ, in whom is the fullness of grace" (*Ep.* 190:8). "If Cornelius could have been saved without faith in Christ, the apostle Peter would not have been sent as the architect to build him up" (*De praedest. sanctorum*, 7:12).

The relations between faith and understanding are mutual. Prior to faith we must have some understanding, in order to make the judgment whether and what to believe. But there are many things that we cannot understand except by first believing them; otherwise the prophet would not have said, "Unless you believe you shall not understand" (Is 7:9 LXX; *In Psalm.*, 118, *Serm.*, 18.3; cf. *Ep.*, 70:l:3–4). Faith has its eyes by which it in some way perceives the truth of what is as yet unseen. When believing, we seek with a view to understanding, and we understand in order to seek still more (*De Trin.*, 9.1.1).

Faith prepares us for the vision of that which we do not see. Its merit consists in believing that which remains hidden, and its reward is the vision of that which is believed without being seen (*In Psalm.*, 109:8; *Serm.*, 43:1:1). Thanks to faith, we can already love the God in whom we believe (*De Trin.*, 8:4:6). In keeping the commandments out of love, we dispose ourselves to see. By faith we purify our hearts (Acts 15:9), and we must do so, since it is the pure of heart who will see God (Mt 5:8; *In Psalm.*, 109:8). Thus faith, although it occurs in time, has an eternal object and leads the believer to eternity (*De Trin.*, 14.1.3).

After the time of Augustine, Pelagianism in a moderate form (which later came to be called Semi-Pelagianism) continued to develop in Southern Gaul. In the second half of the fifth century, Faustus of Riez, a monk of Lerins, struggling against exaggerated predestinarianism, maintained that human nature, even after the Fall, retained the power to make an act of trustful adherence *(credulitatis affectus)* which, fortified by divine grace, could develop into a full-fledged life of faith. The Augustinians considered that this position gave too much credit to fallen nature. Some time after the death of Faustus, his doctrine on the "beginning of faith" was condemned by the Second Council of Orange (A.D. 529), a small gathering of bishops led by Bishop Caesarius of Arles, himself a moderate Augustinian. In canon 5 (DS 375) this council taught that the "beginning of faith" *(initium fidei)* or the "trustful adherence" *(credulitatis affectus)* by which we first enter into communion with God is not a product of our natural powers but is a gift of the Holy Spirit at work in our hearts.[31] In canon 7 the same council taught that it is impossible for anyone to assent to the saving message of the gospel "without the illumination and inspiration of the Holy Spirit, who gives to all [believers] ease (or: joy, *suavitatem*) in assenting to the truth and believing it" (DS 377).

The acts of the Council of Orange were lost during the Middle Ages, but, when they were recovered in the sixteenth century,[32] they were accepted by Catholics and by most Protestants as valid and decisive. Both the First and the Second Vatican Councils, as we shall see, quote Second Orange on the need for the grace of the Holy Spirit for any salutary act of faith. Even though Orange may have been using the term "faith" in a broad sense, more inclusive than that current in modern theology, its doctrine certainly does apply to faith in narrower sense of a believing response to revelation.

## Early Middle Ages

For some centuries the theology of faith in Western Europe remained heavily dependent on St. Augustine. Paschasius Radbertus (c. 790–c. 859) typifies the Augustinianism of the Carolingian Renaissance. His treatise *On Faith, Hope and Charity* (PL 120:1387–1490) follows the general lines of Augustine's *Confessions* and *De Trinitate*.[33] Like many of the fathers, he quotes Isaiah 7:9 according to the LXX, "Unless you believe, you shall not understand." Like many ancient theologians, he takes Hebrews 11:1 as a revealed definition of faith. He depicts faith as a kind of covenant with God, demanding trust and fidelity (PL 120:1391). He is convinced that the faith "that works by love" is a privilege of Christians, and that it alone leads to justification (PL 120:1402 and 1417–21).

John Scotus Erigena (c. 810–c. 877), with astonishing erudition, forged an original system influenced on the one hand by Ambrose and Augustine and on the other by Pseudo-Dionysius and Maximus the Confessor.[34] Denying that faith and reason could ever fall into conflict, he boldly applied dialectic reasoning to the patristic heritage. But he was not a rationalist in the modern sense of the word. Recognizing that human reason since the Fall stands in need of healing, he held that faith was necessary to help reason in its quest for truth. Faith kindles the light of speculation and points the way for philosophical understanding.

Anselm of Canterbury (1033–1109) continued to explore the relationships between faith and reason. He articulated the leitmotiv of his theology in the original subtitle of his *Proslogion*: "Faith Seeking Understanding."[35] In his various theological meditations he provides a classic instance of contemplative reason on pilgrimage between simple faith and the heavenly vision to which it aspires. Believing, for Anselm, is not a matter of intellect alone. The mind is inclined to believe by a heart that loves. By believing, one enters into the sphere of the divine inasmuch as it draws one to itself (*Monologion*, 75).

Faith, as Anselm uses the term, means a simple submission to the word of God presented by the testimonies of Scripture and tradition. Faith is a prerequisite for understanding. Anselm feels bound to believe that this is so, for it is written in Scripture that without belief it is impossible to understand (*Proslogion*, 1; cf. Is 7:9 LXX). In another text Anselm sets forth an argument: "For he who does not believe will not experience, and he who has not experienced will not know." Just as experience surpasses hearing, so knowledge by experience surpasses knowledge by hearsay (*Epist. de Inc. Verbi*, 1).

Anselm's effort to systematize the faith through a rigorous use of dialectics anticipates the Scholasticism of the high Middle Ages. Because of certain ambiguities in his work he has been variously interpreted as a fideist and as a rationalist. He can best be understood as seeking a middle path. While denying that the mysteries of faith can be mastered by the human mind, he is confident that they can be supported by "necessary reasons."

The tensions between the nascent Scholasticism of the eleventh century and the older monastic theology are dramatized in the conflict between Peter Abelard and Bernard of Clairvaux. Abelard (1079–1142), although he has a certain reputation of rationalism, always acknowledged that there are mysteries that "must be believed but cannot be explained" (*Theologia christiana*, III; PL 178:1226).[36] He did maintain, however, that Christians should show, against anyone who attacks the faith, that their beliefs are not demonstrably false (ibid., col. 1227). Arguing against Bernard that the "blind faith" of Abraham was a special grace, and could not be normative for Christians, Abelard cautioned against precipitate faith, quoting from the Ecclesiast, "One who trusts others too quickly is lightminded" (Sir 19:4).

Abelard held that reason without grace could achieve a beginning of faith ("primordia fidei"; *Introductio ad theologiam*, Bk. II, sec. 3; PL 178:1051). While granting that this achievement of reason is not meritorious, he contended that it is conducive to supernatural faith, which arises under the influence of grace and charity.

Reason, according to Abelard, always has a part in the assent of faith. At the very least, the believer must use reason to decide which of the many authorities is to be accepted. Furthermore one must use reason to understand what is preached and taught, and in this sense faith itself is an act of intelligence (*intellectus*). The understanding of faith, however, falls short of the knowledge *(cognitio)* of the blessed in heaven.

Like other theologians of his time, Abelard attempted to support his concept of faith from Hebrews 11:1, especially the second part of the verse, which read, in the Latin Vulgate, "argumentum non apparentium." Abelard interpreted this as a kind of intellectual analysis, which he called *existimatio* or *probatio*. In an important text he wrote, "Faith is called the argument *(existimatio)* of things that do not appear, whereas to know is to experience the things themselves through their presence" (*Introductio ad theologiam*, Bk. II, sec. 3; PL 178:1051). *Existimatio,* for Abelard, seems to mean a provisional and insufficient type of knowledge falling far short of the experience of vision.

Bernard of Clairvaux (c. 1091–1152) reflects the theological outlook of the monastic tradition.[37] In his sermons he developed a highly devotional Trinitarian theology, in which the three theological virtues are linked with the three divine per-

sons and with the three faculties of memory, reason, and will. Faith, he held, illuminates reason; hope raises up the memory, and charity cleanses the will. Three
species of faith are to be distinguished. By faith in signs, we believe in the divine
omnipotence; by faith in the promises, we rely on God to fulfill all that he has promised, and by faith in the precepts, we love the God in whom we believe and hope.
Faith without works is dead (Sermon 45; PL 183:667–69).

In his *De Consideratione*, the last and longest of his treatises, written at the
request of Pope Eugene III, Bernard distinguished between understanding, faith,
and opinion. Understanding relies on reason, faith on authority, and opinion on
resemblances. Opinion lacks certitude; faith has certitude in a veiled manner, and
understanding has certitude in a manifest manner (PL 182:790). Faith is defined as
a "voluntary and certain anticipation of truth that is not yet manifest" *(Fides est
voluntaria quaedam et certa praelibatio necdum propalatae veritatis)*. A faith that
lacks certainty is not really faith but rather opinion. What we already know
obscurely under the veils of faith will make us blessed when we know it by vision
(ibid., 791).

Although the disagreements between Abelard and Bernard were real and not
merely verbal, communication between them was impeded by difficulties in terminology. Whereas Abelard held that we have *intellectus* in this life and *cognitio*
only in the life to come, Bernard held that we already have *cognitio* but must await
for the future blessedness in order to have *intellectus*. Bernard understood Abelard's
*existimatio* as equivalent to *aestimatio* or *opinio*, and thus as merely probable
assent. He replied that according to Hebrews 11:1 faith is "the substance of things
hoped for." The term "substance," he remarked, designates something "fixed and
certain" (Letter 190 to Innocent II, *Tractatus de Erroribus Abelardi*, PL 182:1062).

In eleventh-century monasticism Bernard's type of affective and voluntaristic
theology faith was widespread. William of Saint Thierry (1080/85–1148/49), standing with Bernard against Abelard, emphasized the affective experience of faith, and
moved toward a kind of mystical gnosis.[38] The will, he insists, must draw reason to
assent to God's word, and the will, he adds, is powerless without grace. Faith relies
on the authority of God, attested by many and eminent human witnesses. Once one
does believe, true faith brings with it a certain experience or foretaste of the things
for which, according to Hebrews 11:1, we hope (*Expositio in Epist. ad Romanos*,
PL 180:655).

Another monastic theologian, Hugh of St. Victor (1098–1141), in the tenth
part of the first book of his *The Sacraments of the Christian Faith*, presents a small
treatise on faith, covering many of the standard questions.[39] Commenting on
Hebrews 11:1, he says that faith is properly called the "substance" of things hoped
for because it causes the future blessings for which we hope to be already present in
us, "and faith is their subsistence in us" (chap. 2, col. 328D; Deferrari trans., p. 165).
The formal element or substance of faith, according to Hugh, consists in affection
(or affectivity: *affectus*); but its material element is knowledge, for we cannot believe
unless the content to be believed is manifested to our minds (chap. 3, col. 331B;
Deferrari, p. 169). Faith is superior to opinion or conjecture but, considered as
knowledge, is inferior to science *(scientia)*; in merit, however, faith surpasses science (chap. 2; cols. 330D and 331A; Deferrari, p. 168). Faith can increase either

with respect to affection or with respect to cognition. As we advance in affection, we may receive greater visitations of grace and thus have a certain foretaste of the blessings toward which we are hastening (chap. 4; col. 333C; Deferrari, p. 170).

Peter Lombard (c. 1095–1160), who was trained in the school of St. Victor, develops his positions on faith primarily in Book III of his *Sentences*.[40] In a Scholastic style suited to a textbook of this sort, he treats faith less as an affection or movement of the soul than as a virtue, to be analyzed in the categories of philosophical psychology. Exploring the relations between the three theological virtues, Peter holds that faith is the presupposition of hope and charity. It is called the "substance of things hoped for" because faith makes the things we hope for subsist in our soul (Bk. III, Dist. 23, no. 9; col. 807). Faith provides the basis for hope; we cannot hope for what we do not believe in. So too, we cannot love what we do not believe in. Faith precedes charity, but faith without charity is not a virtue, for charity, as Ambrose taught, is the mother of all the virtues (Dist. 23, no. 3; col. 805). Charity, according to Peter, is not a merely created gift; it is the self-gift of the Holy Spirit, who is poured out in our hearts (Dist. 17, no. 6; col. 566; cf. Rom 5:5). Faith, insofar as it is a virtue, has its foundation in the Holy Spirit and in Christ, who lives by faith in our hearts. It is this living faith that justifies the sinner and incorporates the believer into the body of Christ (Dist. 23, no. 4; col. 805).

A more intellectualist or dialectical approach to faith may be found in Gilbert de la Porrée and Alan of Lille, who reflect on the relations between opinion, faith, and scientific knowledge. They agree with Hugh of St. Victor that faith is a firm assent, surpassing mere opinion, and that it falls short of scientific knowledge, since it does not rest on direct experience or cogent arguments.

## Golden Age of Scholasticism

In the high Scholasticism of the thirteenth century the philosophical grounding of faith was more systematically explored in the light of Aristotelian psychology and ethics, which were becoming available in newly discovered texts. Theologians debated whether "unformed" faith (i.e., faith not enlivened by charity) was a virtue, and whether the virtue of faith was radicated in the intellect, the will, or both. Much attention was devoted to the question of the intrinsic motive, or formal object, of faith. It came to be agreed that faith derives its certitude not from the rational arguments of credibility but from God alone, who is its motive. Many of the theologians recognized, and dealt with, the problem of how the firmness of the assent could be proportioned not to the force of the evidence, which was limited, but to God, whose word could contain no error.

William of Auxerre, in his *Summa aurea*, composed about 1225, treats the articles of faith as self-evident to those who see by the light of faith. William of Auvergne, who wrote his *Magisterium divinale* about 1228, adds that the supernatural light will be given only to those who are prepared to accept what appears improbable on the authority of God, who is Lord of the human intellect. Several years later Philip the Chancellor, in his *Summa de bono*, made the point that faith can be called "the evidence of things unseen" because it makes the truth appear, insofar as the human condition in this life allows, in the light of God, the "first truth."[41]

The early Franciscans, beginning with Alexander of Hales, attached great importance to the affective element in faith. St. Bonaventure (1221–1274), bringing Franciscan theology to its peak, described the object of faith as "salutary truth" or "truth according to devotion" ("veritas secundum pietatem," *In III Sent.*, Dist. 23, art. 1, q. 1, ad 2).[42] Quoting Bernard, Bonaventure called faith not only a virtue but the charioteer of all the virtues (*auriga omnium virtutum*, ibid., q. 1). While granting that faith, insofar as it is a stable quality *(habitus)*, is related in some sense to the speculative intellect, he connected faith especially with the practical intellect and the affections. Insofar as it is a virtue and a principle of merit, according to Bonaventure, faith has the free will (*liberum arbitrium*) as its subject (Dist. 23, art. 1, q. 2). He held that faith must be infallible, inasmuch as it judges according to the illumination of God's own knowledge (Dist. 24, a. 1, q. 1). While faith ranks below scientific knowledge in speculative certitude *(quoad certitudinem speculationis)*, it surpasses science in certitude of adherence *(quoad certitudinem adhaesionis)*, a certitude that depends on love (Dist. 23, a. 1, q. 4).

> If our intellect is to be well ordered in its belief, it must have a deeper faith in the supreme Truth than in itself; it must bring itself to the obedience of Christ. It must believe, then, not only what is accessible to reason, but even what exceeds reason and contradicts sense experience; otherwise it would fail to show due reverence to supreme Truth, preferring its own judgment to the teaching of eternal Light— which necessarily implies the puffing up of pride and of blameworthy conceit.[43]

For the affirmations of faith to be firm they must be supported by authoritative testimony. "Because authority is found primarily in Sacred Scriptures, all of which are inspired by the Holy Spirit for the sake of guiding the Catholic faith, true faith may never disagree with the Scriptures" (*Breviloquium*, no. 5; p. 209). The light of faith, as a presence of God in the soul, is a radiance of the light of the Holy Spirit. It gives full certainty to Christian revelation, enabling the believer to recognize the testimony of God in the inspired Scriptures. The interior grace of faith is the lamp that must guide the reader of Holy Scripture; it is the door that gives access to the true meaning of God's word (Prologue to *Breviloquium*, no. 2; p. 2).

All faith, for Bonaventure, is oriented toward Christ. The patriarchs, the prophets of the Old Testament, and even some pagan philosophers had implicitly Christian faith, since "After the Fall of Adam no one could be saved without faith in the Mediator" (*In III Sent.*, Dist. 25, a. 1, q. 2 resp.). By faith Christ dwells in the hearts of believers. The fullness of grace and truth, concentrated in Christ as head, flows down to the members of the body, binding them to one another and to him in a common faith (*Breviloqium*, IV, ch. 5, nos. 5–6; p. 159). The gift of faith orients the soul to the Word of God, the supreme Truth (ibid., V, chap. 4, no. 4; p. 194). The journey of faith is a progressive ascent to God, which may reach the point of mystical ecstasy as its culmination in the present life. By an extraordinary privilege of grace, St. Francis of Assisi was favored with a transforming union beyond all knowledge and intellectual operation.[44]

Albert the Great (1200–1280), though a Dominican and an Aristotelian, remained close to the earlier monastic and Scholastic traditions in his theology of faith.[45] He regarded it as an act of the "affective intellect," which consents because of the movement of the will (*In III Sent.*, Dist. 23, a. 2).[46] In comparison with his predecessors, Albert gave greater attention to the signs of credibility preparing the way to faith, thus laying a certain groundwork for what would later be called "fundamental theology."[47]

Albert's brilliant disciple, Thomas Aquinas (1225–1274), took generally traditional positions in his early commentary on the *Sentences* of Peter Lombard and in his relatively early *De veritate*, but as he matured he moved gradually to a more consistently Aristotelian synthesis.[48] The *Summa theologiae*, Part 2-2, in its first sixteen questions, may be taken as representing his definitive positions. Distinctive to his treatment is a strong emphasis on final causality and on the intellectual character of faith.

Like many medieval theologians, St. Thomas treats Hebrews 11:1 as an authoritative definition of faith. The "substance of things hoped for," as he interprets it, means a real beginning of eternal life, an anticipation of the beatific vision. The "evidence of things not seen" signifies, for him, the basis of intellectual conviction. In the case of faith, the authority of the divine intellect takes the place of rational demonstration, which gives conviction in the case of matters that can be made evident. Recasting the biblical text into the form of a strict Scholastic definition, St. Thomas defines faith as "that habit of mind *(habitus mentis)* whereby eternal life begins in us, causing the intellect to assent to things that are not manifest" (2–2.4.1).

The formal object or inherent motive of faith, according to St. Thomas, is God as "first truth," the one in whom intellect and being perfectly coincide. Like human faith, divine faith goes out first of all to the speaker and only secondarily to what the speaker says (2-2.1.1). In other words, faith is belief in God as witness *(credere Deo)*. Because faith occurs according to the conditions of this present life, it depends on hearing the word of God. In biblical times the prophets and apostles were privileged to hear the word of God immediately, whether through prophetic graces or through access to the person of Jesus. In the Christian community the word of God is mediated through preachers who are clothed with divine authority (2–2.6.1). For Christians, therefore, the formal object of faith is somewhat complex. "The formal object of faith is the first truth insofar as it is manifested in the holy Scriptures and in the doctrine of the Church, which derives from the first truth" (2-2.5.3).

Guaranteed by the divine veracity, faith surpasses in objective certitude all other forms of human knowledge, and is thus superior to scientific demonstration. But on the subjective side faith is less perfect than scientific knowledge, since the object believed is not evident. Commenting on Augustine's definition of believing as "to ponder with assent" *(cum assensione cogitare)*, St. Thomas remarks that the term "ponder" implies a kind of mental dissatisfaction or restlessness arising from the fact that the mind is not in possession of demonstrative evidence. Faith, therefore, is essentially imperfect; it tends toward a vision that eludes it so long as it is faith.

St. Thomas develops an extremely subtle psychological analysis of faith that cannot be presented here except in summary form. He wants to avoid suggesting, as Abelard seemed to do, that faith lacks certainty, but at the same time he seeks to retain the intellectual character of faith, which Hugh of St. Victor, the Franciscans, and even Albert seemed to compromise by their insistence on the role of the will and the affections. As an Aristotelian, St. Thomas maintains that faith is an act of the speculative intellect: its object is the uncreated truth, not some practical effect to be produced by human activity (2-2.4.2, ad 3). The firmness of faith is due to the divine authority, which is made present through divine grace. Grace inclines the mind to assent, not by making the object of faith evident, but by moving the will, which in turn commands the intellect to assent. Thus faith for St. Thomas is formally an act of the intellect, but one in which the intellect is swayed by the will, and the will, in turn, by divine grace. "To believe is an act of the intellect assenting to the divine truth by virtue of the command of the will as this is moved by God through grace" (2-2.2.9). The movement of the will, drawn by the prospect of eternal life, is prior to the assent of the intellect; but in some sense the priorities are mutual, since the will could not be attracted unless the intellect presented this prospect as attainable. In his treatise of faith, St. Thomas presumes his own doctrine of the relations between intellect and will as set forth in earlier parts of the *Summa theologiae* (e.g., 1.82.4 and 1-2.9.1).

The grace of God, while attracting the will, does not coerce it (2-2.2.9; cf. 1.82.2). Like other free acts, the act of faith is amenable to the norm of morality, which requires that the thing done be apprehended as good. To explain how a person can responsibly choose to believe something not evidently true, St. Thomas has recourse to the category of instinct. Animals have a spontaneous inclination, given to them by their creator, to do what is good for themselves and their species, and to avoid what is harmful (1.78.4). So, analogously speaking, grace implants in the human heart a spontaneous dynamism toward the eternal vision of God. This dynamism includes an inclination to embrace those things that are conducive to our eternal beatitude. In the light of this supernatural instinct we perceive that to believe the testimony of the first truth is suitable for us (2-2.1.4, ad 3).

This supernatural instinct of faith plays a crucial role both in the approach to faith and in the assent of faith itself. Among the factors leading to the act of faith, St. Thomas gives primary importance to this inner instinct. "One who believes has a sufficient inducement for believing, for he is led to faith by the authority of God's teaching confirmed by miracles and, still more powerfully, by the interior instinct of God inviting him to believe; thus he does not believe lightly" (2-2.2.9, ad 3). In his commentary on John 4:42 St. Thomas makes a clear distinction between the motives leading to faith and the motive of faith itself:

> Faith is right when it submits to the truth not because of something else but for its own sake, and for this reason the text tells us that they told the woman: Now we believe the truth not because of your word but because of the truth itself. There are three things that lead us to faith in Christ: first, natural reason (Rom 1:20) . . . ; second, the testimony of the law and the prophets (Rom 3:21) . . . , and, third, the preaching of the apostles and others (Rom 10:14). . . . But when someone believes after being led by these inducements, then he can say that he believes not because of any of these; neither because of natural reason, nor because of the testimony of the law, nor because of the preaching of others, but because of the truth itself. "Abraham believed God, and this was reckoned to him as righteousness" (Gen 15:5).[49]

In the *Summa theologiae* St. Thomas says, very concisely, "The assent, which is the principal act of faith, is caused by God moving us inwardly through grace" (2-2.6.1).

Modern authors have disagreed about whether St. Thomas admitted the possibility of "natural" or "scientific" faith, based on evidence accessible to unaided reason. From what he has to say about the faith of demons and heretics (2-2.5.1 and 2), it is clear that he holds that it is possible to become convinced of certain revealed truths on the basis of natural knowledge without accepting them precisely on the authority of God. But in the same passages he states that an acceptance of revelation on the grounds of human reasoning is not faith properly so called. Faith in the theological sense rests not on human inference but on the authority of God, mysteriously encountered in grace.

Faith does not exist without both a formal and a material object. The believer is convinced of something on the authority of the speaker, who is God, the formal object. The content or material object is what God says. There may appear to be a multitude of disparate items in the contents of revelation, but according to St. Thomas they form a unity of order insofar as all of them pertain to God and the way to God. The principal material object of faith is God himself. Faith is not only *credere Deo* (belief in God as witness) but also *credere Deum* (belief in God as attested to).

The essential content of faith, as St. Thomas understands it, is succinctly expressed in Hebrews 11:6, "Whoever would draw near to God must believe that he exists and that he rewards those who seek him." St. Thomas comments: "The existence of God comprises everything that we believe to be eternally true of God, and thus everything constitutive of our blessedness. Faith in God's providence, on the other hand, comprises everything that God provides in time for the salvation of human beings, and thus the whole way to blessedness" (2-2.1.7). The Church has grouped the data of revelation under certain headings, the articles of the creed. Although the object of faith is one and undivided in itself, the human mind cannot take it in except by expressing the various aspects in distinct propositions. The believer does not assent to the propositions for their own sake, but uses them as vehicles for assenting to the realities they signify. "The act of the believer does not terminate in the proposition but in the thing, for we do not form propositions except for the purpose of knowing things by means of them, whether in scientific knowledge or in faith" (2-2.1.2, ad 2).

Faith, for St. Thomas, is a dynamic perception. The mind, impelled by desire for union with the divine, cannot find its rest in propositions or created realities, but only in God himself. According to a traditional formula that St. Thomas attributes to Isidore of Seville, "an article of faith is a perception of the divine truth as something to which it tends" ("Articulus est perceptio divinae veritatis tendens in ipsam," 2-2.1.6, *sed contra*.) The first truth is, for the believer, the final end. For this reason, faith is not simply a belief on the authority of God *(credere Deo)*, or a belief in the existence and providence of God *(credere Deum)*, but also a belief that tends toward union with God *(credere in Deum,* 2-2.2.2).

Faith is living and active when it is animated by charity, that is to say, by a love that cherishes God for his own sake. Only where charity is present does faith rightly direct the believer to the divinely appointed end for which all human beings are destined. Yet it is possible for a believer to be lacking in this kind of love. In such a case the faith will be mutilated or dead (*fides informis, fides mortua*, 2-2.4.4; cf. Jas 2:26). Even unformed faith, defective though it be, is a gift of God, resting on God's revealing word, and has value in motivating one to turn away from sin and dispose oneself for grace (2-2.6.2).

In continuity with Scripture and the unanimous tradition, St. Thomas teaches that faith is necessary for salvation. Men and women cannot enter into the inheritance of eternal life without having oriented themselves toward it by faith in the present life (2-2.2.3). While admitting, as his predecessors had, the sufficiency of implicit faith for those living before the time of Christ, St. Thomas considers that it is necessary for Christians to believe explicitly in the triune God and in the incarnate Son of God. Unlearned believers, however, cannot be required to know the fine points of doctrine. It is enough for them to acknowledge the principal articles of faith, as set forth in the creed (2-2.2.5).

Among Christians who do not accept the full teaching of the Church, St. Thomas distinguishes two categories—those who are simply in error and those who pertinaciously reject what they are able to recognize as contained in the word of God. Only the second category of people are, properly speaking, heretics (2-2.2.6 ad 2). In spite of appearances, a heretic in this sense is not a believer at all. By disbelieving anything that is seen to be guaranteed by the infallible rule of faith people show that they do not accept even those truths to which they do adhere out of submission to the rule of faith—the authority of God who reveals—but from some other motive, such as their own powers of inference (2-2.5.3). St. Thomas does not dwell on the difficulties that a sincere believer might have in accepting some particular doctrine of the Church. Rather, he seems to presume that any well-instructed Christian will readily submit to the authority of the Church.

St. Thomas's treatise on faith deals principally with the virtue and with the interior act of faith. He does, however, include a brief question on the confession of faith. The same virtue that prompts us to believe, according to St. Thomas, prompts us to confess our faith before others. Such confession, therefore, is the external act of faith (2-2.3.1). We are required to confess our faith when failure to do so would bring dishonor upon God or jeopardize the salvation of other persons (2-2.3.2).

St. Thomas, at the height of medieval Scholasticism, achieved what many regard as the most successful synthesis ever made of the various elements of faith attested by Scripture and tradition. The balance and depth of his system were not broadly appreciated, however, until Cajetan and others wrote their commentaries in the sixteenth and seventeenth centuries.

## Later Middle Ages

John Duns Scotus (1265–1308) was interested, as Abelard and Albert had been, in the capacities of unaided reason.[50] The act of faith, he held, is impossible without a human preparation. Mysteries of faith such as the Trinity can be known only through the testimony of the community of believers, to whom the apostolic revelation has been committed. Faith has a logical foundation because the testimony, accredited by miracles, is fully credible. Regarding the apologetical arguments for Christianity as cogent, Scotus held that a person without supernatural grace can make an act of acquired faith in some or all of the articles of the Christian creed.

In the present order as willed by God, however, acquired faith is not sufficient for salvation. The salutary act of faith, as seen by Scotus, proceeds simultaneously from the habits of humanly acquired faith and supernaturally infused faith. Infused faith provides no new content and no new evidence, but it supplies the will with a stronger inclination to accept Christian doctrine in its entirety and renders the assent infallible. The motive of salutary faith, for Scotus, is not the supernaturally elevated will but rather the object of faith, God himself as true. The fact of revelation is not the cause of faith but only a condition.

As a Franciscan, Scotus was attentive to the role of the will and of love. Faith, he taught, is not a purely speculative act; it is a perfection of the practical intellect, since it is ordered toward love and toward fulfillment in the life of glory. Even infused faith does not suffice for salvation unless it is enlivened by charity in the will, which is an effect of the indwelling of the Holy Spirit. Faith without charity is unformed *(informis)* and thus deficient.

Duns Scotus did not minimize the necessity of grace, but his system tended to focus attention on the natural approach to faith through reason, and thus to make grace appear as a supplementary gift that was required only by reason of God's positive decree.

William of Ockham (c. 1285–1347), another Franciscan, carried the critical spirit of Duns Scotus to greater lengths.[51] Whereas Scotus had criticized the Thomistic proofs for God's existence, Ockham, with a passion for logical rigor, found fault with the Scotistic proofs as well. The existence and unicity of God, he concluded, were not strictly demonstrable. While seeking to minimize conflicts between reason and authority, he maintained that the claims of reason and experience were subordinate to the infallible authority of Scripture and of church teaching.

As a believer, Ockham was convinced on the basis of Scripture and the creeds that God, being omnipotent, could do anything not manifestly contradictory. Speculating on God's absolute power, Ockham advanced daring conjectures about what could presumably have been the case in some other possible world order. He saw no reason to deny the possibility that God, if he chose, could give merit and salvation to persons who observed the precepts of the moral law without sanctifying grace or infused faith. The very existence of infused faith, according to Ockham, is to be accepted simply because it is attested by the Bible and Church teaching. Infused faith is only a partial cause of the assent; thus it does not take the place of acquired faith, which is always needed as a concurrent cause of the act of faith.[52]

Gabriel Biel (c. 1415–1495) is historically important because of his prestige in Germany at the time of the Reformation.[53] He agreed with Ockham that faith, resting on the word of God, is more reliable than scientific knowledge. In his teaching on faith he spoke chiefly of acquired faith, which in his view comes from hearing. In a certain sense, he admitted, the demons themselves have this kind of faith, for they assent to the content of historical revelation on the basis of the signs of credibility. Their faith, however, is defective because they do not grasp the revelation as salutary for themselves. True faith accepts God's word as a message of salvation to the believer. While holding with Ockham that God could, if he so willed, give salvation to those who had only acquired faith, Biel agreed that infused faith is necessary by reason of God's positive decree.

In the Nominalist theology of the fourteenth and fifteenth centuries the harmonious synthesis of nature and grace, reason and faith, was undermined. Acquired faith was logically separated from infused faith. The former was made to rest on a purely rational basis—its certification by external signs of credibility. Great importance was attached to apologetical arguments, but these were, at the same time, weakened by an epistemology that insisted on the superiority of immediate experience and syllogistic deduction. Supernatural grace was held to be necessary in the present world order, but that necessity was attributed simply to God's positive decree as attested by the Bible and Church teaching, and was in no way grounded in experience.

Although Scotism and Nominalism were widespread in northern Europe throughout the fourteenth and fifteenth centuries, Thomas Aquinas continued to have a following, especially among the Dominicans.[54] John Capreolus (c. 1380–1444), the regent of studies at Toulouse, defended the doctrine of St. Thomas on the absolute necessity of infused grace against Scotus and others. Thomas de Vio, or Cajetan (1468–1534)—as he was commonly called from his birthplace, Gaeta—in his great commentary on the *Summa theologiae* (1517), followed the views of Capreolus on the motive of faith and produced the first systematic study of the question of credibility. He thereby set the stage for the issues about natural and supernatural credibility that were to be debated in post-Tridentine Scholasticism. Cajetan's mastery of the Thomistic doctrine on faith helped to equip him for the dialogue with Luther that he undertook on behalf of the Holy See in 1518. Because he revived Thomism in order to respond to the challenges of a new age, Cajetan belongs to the Catholic Reformation even more than to the history of medieval theology.

## Conclusion

Christian theology will remain forever indebted to patristic authors. In the ante-Nicene period Justin, Irenaeus, Tertullian, Clement of Alexandria, and Origen, among others, brilliantly defended the legitimacy of orthodox faith against the attacks of secular philosophy and Gnosticism. The Greek fathers of the post-Nicene period gave prominence to the mystical and unitive aspects of faith, which they saw as an immersion into the incomprehensibility of God. In the West, Augustine and his disciples gave a balanced account in which the sapiential and existential aspects of faith received their due. In general, the authors of the patristic age built bridges between the Bible and Hellenistic philosophy, making it possible for Christian believers to enter into constructive dialogue with philosophers in search of truth. Many of the patristic authors were bishops, laudably concerned with questions of practical import for the Christian life of the people entrusted to their care.

The early medieval writers fruitfully continued the Augustinian line of thought, stressing the priority of faith over reason and the importance of the will and the affections for the birth and maturation of faith. Scotus Erigena and the medieval mystics made the achievements of Pseudo-Dionysius and the Eastern mystics available to the Latin world. The monastic theologians fashioned an imposing spirituality in which prayer was the guardian and tutor of faith. Theirs was "a Christian thought perpetually residing in the interior of faith, never going beyond faith, never losing sight of faith, never departing from the practice of faith and at every level remaining an act of faith."[55]

The Scholastic theologians, reviving Aristotle's logic and psychology, clarified the relationship of faith to the faculties of intellect and will, and explored the connection between faith and other virtues, especially charity. Thomas Aquinas presented a masterly synthesis, integrating the biblical patrimony, Augustinian Platonism, and the Aristotelian legacy. His distinctive achievement is to have shown how grace gives rise to a supernatural instinct and to a connaturality with the divine, bestowing firmness and ease on the assent of faith.

In the fourteenth and fifteenth centuries university theology drove too deep a wedge between the natural and the supernatural orders. University theologians became heavily engaged in subtle questions about what might be possible in a hypothetical order of pure nature. The professors, absorbed in academic disputes, seemed to lose contact with ordinary Christian experience and with the original biblical heritage. The situation thus became ripe for a reaction on the part of Catholic humanists and Protestant Reformers in the fifteenth and sixteenth centuries.

## Notes

1. The following surveys are available: Ignacio Escribano-Alberca, *Glaube und Gottes-erkenntnis in der Schrift und Patristik,* Handbuch der Dogmengeschichte I/2a (Freiburg: Herder, 1974); Dieter Lührmann, "Glaube" in *Reallexikon für Antike und Christentum,* vol. 11 (Stuttgart: Hiersemann, 1979), 48–122. An up-to-date bibliography will be found in Stuart George Hall, "Glaube. IV. Alte Kirche," *Theologische Realenzyklopädie,* vol. 13 (Berlin: Walter de Gruyter, 1984), 305–8.

2. *The Epistles of St. Clement of Rome and St. Ignatius of Antioch,* ed. James A. Kleist, Ancient Christian Writers, vol. 1 (Westminster, Md.: Newman, 1949), 9–49.

3. Ibid., 60–69.

4. *The Writings of St. Justin Martyr,* ed. Thomas B. Falls, The Fathers of the Church, vol. 6 (New York: Christian Heritage, 1948), quotation from 83.

5. On the theology of faith of Irenaeus see Hans Urs von Balthasar, *The Glory of the Lord: A Theological Aesthetics,* vol. 2, *Studies in Theological Style: Clerical Styles* (San Francisco: Ignatius Press, 1984), 31–84. The works of Irenaeus will here be cited according to the Sources chrétiennes editions (Paris: Cerf). The *Adversus haereses* Book I appears in volume 263 (1979); Book II, in volumes 293 and 294 (1982); Book III, in volume 210 (1974); Book IV, in volume 100 (1965)), and Book V, in volume 152 (1969). The *Demonstratio praedicationis evangelicae* appears in volume 62 (1959).

6. On Tertullian see Harry A. Wolfson, *The Philosophy of the Church Fathers,* vol. 1, 3d ed. (Cambridge, Mass.: Harvard University Press, 1970), 102–6; Escribano-Alberca, *Glaube und Gotteserkenntnis,* 39–45.

7. Tertullian, "The Prescriptions against the Heretics" (*De praescriptionibus haereticorum*), 7; ET, S. L. Greenslade, *Early Latin Theology: Selections,* Library of Christian Classics, vol. 5 (London: SCM, 1956), 36.

8. On Clement of Alexandria see Thomas Camelot, *Foi et gnose: Introduction à l'étude de la connaissance mystique chez Clément d'Alexandrie* (Paris: Vrin, 1945); Raoul Mortley, *Connaissance religieuse et herméneutique chez Clément d'Alexandrie* (Leiden: Brill, 1973); Wolfson, *Philosophy of the Church Fathers*, 1:120–27; Escribano-Alberca, *Glaube und Gotteserkenntnis*, 50–63. References to Book II of the *Stromata* will be given according to the Sources chrétiennes edition, vol. 38 (Paris: Cerf, 1954).

9. Wolfson, *Philosophy of the Church Fathers*, 1:121.

10. Clement of Alexandria, *The Stromata, or Miscellanies*, in Ante-Nicene Fathers, 10 vols. (Buffalo: Christian Literature Publishing Co., 1885–1896), 2:539.

11. See Wolfson, *Philosophy of the Church Fathers*, 1:125–26.

12. On Origen, see Henri Crouzel, *Origène et la "Connaissance mystique"* (Bruges: Desclée De Brouwer, 1961); idem, *Origen* (San Francisco: Harper Row, 1989); Escribano-Alberca, *Glaube und Gotteserkenntnis*, 63–84.

13. Hans Urs von Balthasar, *The Glory of the Lord: A Theological Aesthetics*, vol. 1, *Seeing the Form* (San Francisco: Ignatius Press, 1982), 137.

14. Fragment of *Commentary on Romans*, quoted from Origen, *Spirit and Fire*, ed. Hans Urs von Balthasar (Washington, D.C.: Catholic University of America Press, 1984), no. 487, p. 198.

15. "Concerning Faith," in Saint Basil, *Ascetical Works*, ed. M. Monica Wagner, Fathers of the Church, vol. 9 (New York: Fathers of the Church, Inc., 1950), 57–69, at 59.

16. Basil of Caesarea, Letter 235 to Amphilochius, in *Nicene and Post-Nicene Fathers*, vol. 8 (New York: Christian Literature Co., 1895), 374–75.

17. ET, *Faith Gives Fullness to Reasoning: The Five Theological Orations of Gregory of Nazianzen*, ed. Frederick W. Norris (Leiden: Brill, 1991), 242.

18. Ibid., 260.

19. Gregory of Nyssa, *Life of Moses*, II, nos. 232–33 (New York: Paulist, 1978), 114–15.

20. Idem, *Contra Eunomium* II, nos. 92–93; in *Gregorii Nysseni opera*, ed. Werner Jaeger, vol. 1 (Leiden: Brill, 1960), 253–54.

21. Idem, *In Canticum canticorum*, Oratio VI, ed. W. Jaeger, vol. 6 (Leiden: Brill, 1960), 182–83.

22. Idem, *Life of Moses* II, no. 315; Paulist Press ed., p. 135.

23. Theodoret of Cyrrhus, *The Cure of Pagan Maladies*, ed. and trans. Pierre Canivet, Sources chrétiennes 57 (Paris: Cerf, 1958).

24. Pseudo-Dionysius, *De divinis nominibus*, chap. 7, no. 4; PG 3:872C–D.

25. Ibid., chap. 2, no. 9; PG 3:648B. These passages from Pseudo-Dionysius are discussed by René Roques, *L'Univers dionysien: Structure hiérarchique du monde selon le Pseudo-Denys* (Paris: Aubier, 1954), 129–30.

26. Maximi Confessoris, *Quaestiones ad Thalassium*, no. 34; Corpus christianorum, series graeca, vol. 7 (Turnhout: Prepols, 1980), 237; PG 90:377B.

27. Idem, *Capita ducenta ad theologiam . . . spectantia* 1:9; PG 90:1085; translation, *Two Hundred Chapters . . .* in Maximus Confessor, *Selected Writings* (New York: Paulist, 1985), First Century, no. 9, p. 130.

28. In terms reminiscent of Pseudo-Dionysius, Maximus can write: "The perfect mind is the one that through genuine faith supremely knows in supreme ignorance the supremely unknowable," *Centuria gnostica* 3:99; PG 90:1048; *Selected Writings*, 75. The relationship between these two authors is mentioned by Hans Urs von Balthasar, *Kosmische Liturgie: Das Weltbild Maximus des Bekenners*, 2d ed. (Einsiedeln: Johannes Verlag, 1961), 339.

29. On Augustine's doctrine of faith see Robert E. Cushman, "Faith and Reason in the Thought of Augustine," *Church History* 19 (1950): 271–94; Magnus Löhrer, *Der Glaubens-*

begriff des heiligen Augustinus in seiner ersten Schriften bis zu den Confessiones (Einsiedeln: Benziger, 1955); Roger Aubert, *Le problème de l'acte de foi*, 2d ed. (Louvain, E. Warny, 1950), 21–30; Eugène Portalié, *A Guide to the Thought of St. Augustine* (Chicago: Regnery, 1960), 114–24; Wolfson, *Philosophy of the Church Fathers*, 1:127–40; Escribano-Alberca, *Glaube und Gotteserkenntnis*, 116–25.

30. See Joseph Ratzinger, "Der Weg der religiösen Erkenntnis nach dem heiligen Augustinus," *Kyriakon: Festschrift Johannes Quasten* (Münster: Aschendorff, 1970), 553–64.

31. In modern theology this canon has been interpreted as teaching that it is impossible to dispose oneself for faith and justification without the grace of God. In the context of the fifth and sixth centuries, however, the term *initium fidei* probably meant not a movement toward faith but the first act of faith, and the *credulitatis affectus* probably meant not a desire for faith but a loving response of faith in movement toward the love of charity *(affectus caritatis)*. See Jean Chéné, "Que signifiaient 'Initium fidei' et 'Affectus credulitatis' pour les Semipélagiens?" *Recherches de science religieuse* 35 (1948): 566–88.

32. On the loss and recovery of the acts of this council see Henri Bouillard, *Conversion et grâce chez S. Thomas d'Aquin* (Paris: Aubier, 1944), 92–122.

33. On Paschasius see Elisabeth Gössmann, *Glaube und Gotteserkenntnis im Mittelalter,* Handbuch der Dogmengeschichte I/2b (Freiburg: Herder, 1971), 3–7.

34. On John Scotus Erigena, see Etienne Gilson, *History of Christian Philosophy in the Middle Ages* (New York: Random House, 1955), 113–15; Jaroslav Pelikan, *The Christian Tradition*, vol. 3, *The Growth of Medieval Theology (600–1300)* (Chicago: University of Chicago Press), 95–105; Gössmann, *Glaube und Gotteserkenntnis*, 7–9.

35. On Anselm see Avery Dulles, *A History of Apologetics* (New York: Corpus, 1971), 76–81; Jasper Hopkins, *A Companion to the Study of St. Anselm* (Minneapolis: University of Minnesota Press, 1972), 38–66; Klaus Kienzler, *Glauben und Denken bei Anselm von Canterbury* (Freiburg: Herder, 1981); von Balthasar, *The Glory of the Lord*, 2:211–59; Gilson, *Christian Philosophy in the Middle Ages*, 128–39; Gössmann, *Glaube und Gotteserkenntnis*, 10–14.

36. On Abelard see Hippolyte Ligeard, "Le Rationalisme de Pierre Abélard," *Revue des sciences religieuses* 2 (1911): 383–95; Lief Grane, *Peter Abelard* (New York: Harcourt, Brace & World, 1970); Gössmann, *Glaube und Gotteserkenntnis*, 14–19; Dulles, *History of Apologetics*, 82–84.

37. On Bernard of Clairvaux see Etienne Gilson, *The Mystical Theology of Bernard of Clairvaux* (New York: Sheed Ward, 1940); Erich Kleineidam, "Wissen, Wissenschaft, Theologie bei Bernhard von Clairvaux" in *Bernhard von Clairvaux, Mönch und Mystiker*, ed. Joseph Lortz (Wiesbaden: F. Steiner, 1955), 128–67; Elizabeth Gössmann, "Zur Auseinandersetzung zwischen Abaelard und Bernhard von Clairvaux um die Gotteserkenntnis im Glauben," in *Petrus Abaelardus (1079–1142)*, Trierer theologische Studien, Bd. 38, ed. Rudolf Thomas (Trier: Paulinus-Verlag, 1980), 233–42. On the characteristics of monastic theology see Jean Leclerq, *The Love of Learning and the Desire for God: A Study of Monastic Culture*, 2d ed., rev. (New York: Fordham University Press, 1974), 233–86.

38. On William of Saint Thierry see Georg Englhardt, *Die Entwicklung der dogmatischen Glaubenspsychologie in der mittelalterichen Scholastik vom Abaelardstreit (um 1140) bis zu Philipp dem Kanzler (gest. 1236)*, Beiträge zur Geschichte der Philosophie und Theologie des Mittelalters, Bd. 30, Heft 4–6 (Münster: Aschendorff, 1933), 10–17; Gössmann, *Glaube und Gotteserkenntnis*, 23–27.

39. *De sacramentis christianae fidei*, Bk. I, Pt. 10; PL 176:327–31; ET, Roy J. Deferrari, *On the Sacraments of the Christian Faith* (Cambridge, Mass.: Mediaeval Academy of Amer-

ica, 1951). On Hugh of St. Victor see Englhardt, *Entwicklung*, 17–22; Gössmann, *Glaube und Gotteserkenntnis*, 28–35.

40. *Sententiarum Libri Quattuor*, Lib. III, Dist. 23–25; PL 192:805–811. On Peter Lombard see Gössmann, *Glaube und Gotteserkenntnis*, 38–42.

41. On the three theologians mentioned in this paragraph see the very full exposition of Englhardt, *Die Entwicklung*, 161–398; more briefly, Gössmann, *Glaube und Gotteserkenntnis*, 55–64.

42. Bonaventure's theology of faith is well treated in George H. Tavard, *Transiency and Permanence: The Nature of Theology According to St. Bonaventure* (St. Bonaventure, N.Y.: Franciscan Institute, 1954). See also von Balthasar, *The Glory of the Lord*, 2:260–363, especially 279–82.

43. *Breviloquium*, V, chap. 7, no. 4; trans. José de Vinck, *The Works of St. Bonaventure*, vol. 2 (Paterson, N.J.: St. Anthony Guild Press, 1963), 208.

44. *The Journey of the Mind to God (Itinerarium mentis in Deum)*, chap. 7, no. 3; in *Works of St. Bonaventure*, 1:55–58.

45. See Carl Feckes, "Wissen, Glauben und Glaubenswissenschaft nach Albert der Grossen," *Zeitschrift für katholische Theologie* (1930): 1–39; Gössmann, *Glaube und Gotteserkenntnis*, 88–95.

46. Albertus Magnus, *Opera omnia*, 38 vols. (Paris: Vivès, 1890–99), 28:407.

47. On this topic see Albert Lang, *Die Entfaltung des apologetischen Problems in der Scholastik des Mittelalters* (Freiburg: Herder, 1962), especially 76–114, and literature therein referred to.

48. The treatise on faith in the *Summa theologiae* is available in many editions. Valuable for the notes and appendices is the Latin-English text in the Blackfriars edition (London: Eyre & Spottiswoode), vol. 31, *Faith*, 2–2ae, qq. 1–7 (edited by T. C. O'Brien, 1974) and vol. 32, *Consequences of Faith*, 2a2ae, qq. 8–16 (edited by Thomas Gilby, 1974). Another translation is *On Faith: Summa theologiae 2-2. qq 1–16*, trans. Mark D. Jordan (Notre Dame, Ind.: University of Notre Dame, 1990). A German edition exists with a commentary by Heinrich M. Christmann: *Summa theologica*, vol. 15, *Glaube als Tugend*, 2a2ae, 1–16 (Graz: Pustet, 1950). A French translation with a commentary by Rogatien Bernard is available in the Éditions de la Revue des Jeunes, *La Foi*, 2 vols. (Paris: Desclée, 1950). An important text, Questions 1–4 of Thomas's *Commentary on the "De Trinitate" of Boethius*, is translated with the introduction and notes by Armand Maurer under the title, *Faith, Reason and Theology* (Toronto: Institute of Medieval Studies, 1987). St. Thomas's most thorough treatment of faith, Question 14 of his *De veritate*, exists in an English translation by James V. McGlynn, *Truth*, vol. 2 (Chicago: Regnery, 1953), 207–66.

Among the most important secondary literature the following may be singled out: Juan Alfaro, "Supernaturalitas fidei iuxta S. Thomam," *Gregorianum* 44 (1963): 501–42, 731–88; Benoit Duroux, *La psychologie de la foi chez S. Thomas d'Aquin* (Tournai: Desclée, 1963); Marie-Dominique Chenu, *La parole de Dieu*, vol. 1 (Paris: Cerf, 1964), especially 13–68, 77–111; Otto H. Pesch, *Theologie der Rechtfertigung bei Martin Luther und Thomas von Aquin* (Mainz: Matthias-Grünewald, 1967); James A. Mohler, *The Beginning of Eternal Life: The Dynamic Faith of Thomas Aquinas, Origins and Interpretation* (New York: Philosophical Library, 1968); Aubert, *Problème de l'acte de foi*, 43–71.

49. Thomas Aquinas, *In Evangelium secundum Joannem*, cap. 4, lect. 5 (Turin: Marietti, 1925), 137–38.

50. On John Duns Scotus see Josef Finkenzeller, *Offenbarung und Theologie nach der Lehre des Johannes Duns Skotus* (Münster: Aschendorffschen Verlagsbuchhandlung, 1960); Ludwig Walter, *Das Glaubensverständnis bei Johannes Duns Scotus* (Munich: Schöningh, 1968); also Gössmann, *Glaube und Gotteserkenntnis*, 109–18.

51. On Ockham see M. de Gandillac, "Ockham et la 'via moderna' " in *Histoire de l'Église*, vol. 13, ed. Augustin Fliche and V. Martin (Paris: Bloud & Gay, 1955), 417–73; Paul Vignaux, "Nominalisme," *DTC* 11:717–84; Paul Vignaux et al., "Occam," *DTC* 11:864–904; Gordon Leff, *William of Ockham: The Metamorphoses of Scholastic Discourse* (Manchester, Eng.: Manchester University Press, 1975); Marilyn McCord Adams, *William Ockham*, 2 vols. (Notre Dame, Ind.: University of Notre Dame, 1987), esp. chap. 20, "Faith and Reason" (2:961–1010); Gössmann, *Glaube und Gotteserkenntnis*, 119–23.

52. For a presentation of Ockham's arguments to this effect, see Leff, *Ockham*, 339–46.

53. See Heiko Oberman, *The Harvest of Medieval Theology* (1963; reprint, Durham, N. C.: Labyrinth Press, 1983), 57–89.

54. On Capreolus and Cajetan see Elios Giuseppe Mori, *Il Motivo della Fede da Gaetano a Suarez*, Analecta Gregoriana, vol. 60, Series Theologica, Sec. B, no. 25 (Rome: Gregorian University, 1953). On Cajetan's dealings with Luther see Jared Wicks, *Cajetan Responds: A Reader in Reformation Controversy* (Washington, D.C.: Catholic University of America, 1978).

55. Leclerq, *Desire of Learning*, 264.

# 3

# Sixteenth to Eighteenth Centuries

### Reformation

Martin Luther (1483–1546), as a young member of the Hermits of St. Augustine, studied theology under Nominalists in the tradition of William of Ockham and Gabriel Biel.[1] Although he accepted some of their positions, in many respects he reacted vehemently against his masters. He particularly criticized what he took to be a Pelagian tendency in Scholasticism to attach too much importance to human reason and human works as approaches to faith and justification. On the basis of his biblical studies, in combination with his Augustinian spirituality, he recaptured a more theocentric theology of faith. Justification, he contended, is God's act in us. By passively accepting what God is doing for us and in us, we allow Christ's righteousness to be imputed to us and receive what Luther liked to call "alien righteousness."

Faith, for Luther, has its source not in the believer but in the word of God. God creates faith in us through his word, and more especially through the word of the gospel, which promises the free gift of salvation to sinners who believe. The word must be proclaimed orally through preaching and visibly through the ministry of the sacraments. In opposition to the radical wing of the Reformation (represented by Andreas Carlstadt and Thomas Müntzer) Luther conceded a measure of causal efficacy to the sacraments. Unlike the Catholics, however, he considered that the sacraments had salutary value only or primarily insofar as they arouse or strengthen faith. In his dispute with Cajetan about the sacrament of penance, Luther contended that the penitent could not benefit from absolution without believing, as a matter of faith, that God was then and there forgiving his or her sins.

Like his Catholic contemporaries, Luther was convinced that the Bible was the word of God, and that its teaching must be fully accepted as a matter of faith. Going beyond the explicit teaching of the Bible, Luther accepted the creeds and the dogmatic decisions of the early councils concerning the Trinity and the Incarnation. They were, in his view, binding interpretations of God's word in Scripture. "Here one must be silent and say: God has spoken and I hear that there is one God and three persons. How that is possible I do not know."[2]

In comparison with the medieval theologians we have examined, Luther had a much keener sense of the tension between faith and reason. Faith and reason, for him, stand in perpetual conflict. Since it endures constant contradiction from reason and experience, faith stands in a necessary relationship to doubt. The only practical solution to this conflict is to submit reason totally to faith. In some of his writings, Luther extols faith as a sacrifice by which believers perform a most pleasing act of worship, "for by this sacrifice they slay reason, which is the greatest and most invincible enemy of God."[3] Yet this and other negative statements about reason do not represent Luther's full position. He made extensive use of reason as the handmaid of faith in interpreting the Scriptures and defending his positions.

Luther distinguished between two kinds of faith. The first is simply an acceptance of what God says as true. Such faith is necessary but not sufficient. It belongs more to the category of knowledge than to that of faith. Faith in the second sense is fiducial; that is to say, it is an act of trust or confidence. "The other way is to believe in God, as I do when I not only believe that what is said about Him is true, but put my trust in Him, surrender myself to Him, and make bold to deal with Him, believing without doubt that he will be to me and do to me just what is said of Him. . . . That faith, which in life or death, dares to believe that God is what He is said to be, is the only faith that makes a man a Christian and obtains from God whatever it will."[4]

Luther frequently asserted that justification was effected by faith alone.[5] By such statements he meant that, placing no hope in ourselves, we accept Christ as our righteousness. In faith I am certain that Christ's work has been done all for me, for my sins.[6] By a "cheerful exchange" (*fröhlicher Wechsel*) Christ takes our sins and weaknesses upon himself and communicates to us his own innocence and righteousness. Faith is the wedding ring that secures the marriage between Christ and the soul.[7]

Although some of Luther's statements might seem to imply that faith leaves us as sinful as we were before, he frequently dwells on the beneficial effects of faith. In his Preface to the New Testament (1522) he writes: "Truly, if faith is there, he [the believer] cannot hold back; he proves himself, breaks out into good works, confesses and teaches this gospel before the people, and stakes his life on it."[8] When he talks of "faith alone" Luther does not mean the "unformed faith" or "dead faith" discussed in medieval theology. On the contrary, he means a living, active faith, one that is inseparable from love and good works. "Where works and love do not break forth, there faith is not right, the gospel does not yet take hold, and Christ is not rightly known."[9]

The same line of thinking is eloquently developed in Luther's 1522 Preface to Paul's Letter to the Romans, where he declares:

Faith is a living, daring confidence in God's grace, so sure and certain that the believer would stake his life on it a thousand times. This knowledge of and confidence in God's grace makes men glad and bold and happy in dealing with God and with all creatures. And this is the work which the Holy Spirit performs in faith. Because of it, without compulsion, a person is ready and glad to do good to everyone, and to serve everyone, to suffer everything, out of love and praise to God who has shown him this grace. Thus it is impossible to separate works from faith, quite as impossible as to separate heat and light from fire.[10]

Luther's doctrinal positions were authoritatively synthesized for his contemporaries and successors by his disciple, Philipp Melanchthon (1497–1560), who composed the Augsburg Confession (1530) and the Apology of the Augsburg Confession (1531). On the basis of Hebrews 11:1 and some of Augustine's homilies, the Augsburg Confession asserts that faith should be understood as meaning "confidence in God, assurance that God is gracious to us, and not merely such a knowledge of historical events as the devil also possesses" (AC 20:26). The content of justifying faith is "that Christ suffered for us and that for his sake our sin is forgiven and righteousness and eternal life are given to us" (AC 4:2). Love and good works are treated as necessary consequences of faith. "Good works are meritorious—not for the forgiveness of sins, grace, or justification (for we obtain these only by faith) but for other physical and spiritual rewards in this life and in that which is to come."[11]

With John Calvin (1509–1564) a second major stream of Reformation theology took its rise.[12] Calvin's doctrine of faith, which at many points resembles that of Luther, is distributed in numerous sermons and biblical commentaries, but it is stated most systematically in his principal work, *Institutes of the Christian Religion* (last edition, 1559).[13] Faith is treated principally in Book III, chapter 2. Here Calvin consciously keeps in balance the intellectual and affective elements, assent to truth and trust in God's promises, as appears from the following definition: "We shall possess a right definition of faith if we call it a firm and certain knowledge of God's benevolence toward us, founded upon the truth of the freely given promise in Christ, both revealed to our minds and sealed upon our hearts through the Holy Spirit" (III.2.7). This definition, modeled on Hebrews 11:1, is the focal point of the entire chapter, and is explained and elaborated in all that precedes and follows.

The object of faith, here described as God's benevolence toward us, and alternatively as the truth of God's promises to us, is authoritatively set forth, Calvin maintains, in Holy Scripture. We are bound to believe the whole of Scripture as the word of God, but that which truly engages the assent of faith is God's message of benevolence toward us or, in other words, the gospel. God's promise of mercy is therefore "the proper goal of faith" (2.29). More specifically, the object of faith is Jesus Christ, in whom alone we are reconciled with God (2.30).

The divine benevolence, as Calvin understands it, includes not only what God has objectively done for the human race in Jesus Christ, but the salvation or eternal life for which each individual hopes. The assurance of faith, he states, rests on the expectation of the life to come (2.28). God would not be truly benevolent toward us, Calvin reasons, unless he predestined us to eternal glory. Thus faith necessarily includes the assurance of the believer's own salvation. In the context of Calvin's doctrine of predestination, this means a conviction that we ourselves are among the elect and will therefore persevere to the end (2.40). Paul, according to Calvin, attributes faith exclusively to the elect (2.12). Calvin devotes considerable space to the contention that the reprobate, although they may seem to have faith, do not really have faith at all (ibid.).

The certainty of faith is a crucial element in Calvin's definition. He calls faith a "firm and certain knowledge," but by knowledge he does not mean a merely theoretical grasp. Faith is knowledge in the "existential" sense, as we might say today. The believer is united to Christ, and cleaves to him with an unbreakable bond of fellowship (2.24). The certainty of faith does not come from rational proof, for human reason, since the Fall, is utterly incapable of rising to the things of God. Our minds must be illuminated by the Holy Spirit in order for us to apprehend God's benevolence to us in Christ. But this illumination of the mind, Calvin adds, would be insufficient unless the Holy Spirit were also poured into our hearts (2.33). In describing the work of the Spirit, Calvin frequently borrows the Pauline metaphor of the seal, interpreting it through the analogy of a mark authenticating a royal decree. "The Spirit accordingly serves as a seal, to seal up in our hearts those very promises the certainty of which it has previously impressed upon our minds" (2.36).

Calvin is aware, of course, that some Christians are assailed by doubts. They are tempted and, as Calvin puts it, "in perpetual conflict with their own unbelief" (2.17). In the end, however, true faith always triumphs over the difficulties that besiege and seem to imperil it (2.18).

On the ground that God's promises are the central content of faith, Calvin, like Luther, gives strong emphasis to the fiducial component in faith. In a sense he goes beyond Luther, for he understands trust systematically in relation to a highly developed doctrine of predestination. For Calvin and his disciples, true faith, since it assures the believer not only of the present grace of God but also of election to salvation, can never be lost.

A further difference between Luther and Calvin concerns the connection between faith and the Holy Spirit. Luther, arguing from Galatians 3:2, held that the gift of the Holy Spirit presupposes that the recipient already has faith.[14] Calvin, on the contrary, holds that we could not come to faith unless the Spirit of God were already given to us (2.33).

Calvin argues at some length against what he regards as weaknesses in the Roman, or Scholastic, doctrine of faith. He denies that there is any such thing as "dead faith" or "unformed faith," that is to say, faith unaccompanied by love (2.8). Even as an assent, he holds, faith proceeds from a devout inclination of the heart (ibid.). Though the Scriptures occasionally speak as if faith could exist without love, these texts must refer, in Calvin's opinion, to a mere illusion of faith, not to faith in the proper sense of the word (2.9–10). Calvin seems not to recognize any difference between the devout inclination to believe and what the Scholastic theologians understood by charity.

Like Bonaventure and Thomas Aquinas, Calvin admits that the faith of the ancient Israelites was directed in an obscure way to Christ the Redeemer. In this sense Calvin admits the idea of "implicit faith." Naaman, he conjectures, must have been instructed by Elisha in principles that would give him "some taste, however small, of Christ" (2.32). Even Christians, when they believe, have "implicit faith" in the sense that they are not distinctly aware of all the contents of faith. Nevertheless Calvin objects on two grounds to the Scholastic doctrine of implicit faith. His first objection is that it concentrates the believer's attention too much on the

Church as the source and criterion of saving doctrine. Second, Calvin thinks that the Scholastic teaching encourages a certain indifference to the contents of faith. Catholics, he remarks, tend to brag about their ignorance, comfortable in the thought that they submit in all things to the judgment of the Church (2.3).

## The Catholic Reaction; The Council of Trent

Prior to the Council of Trent (1546–1563) a number of Catholic controversialists responded to Luther and Melanchthon. They did not, however, pinpoint the issue of faith as central. At the Diet of Regensburg (1541) a group of six collocutors, including on the Protestant side Melanchthon and Martin Bucer, and on the Catholic side John Eck and John Gropper, met to try to work out the differences. John Calvin was present en route from Strasbourg to Geneva, and Cardinal Gasparo Contarini was present as papal legate to the Diet of Regensburg. Contrary to expectations, the collocutors came to a consensus on the doctrine of justification by faith. They proposed a doctrine known as "double justification." Justification, according to this theory, involves an inner regeneration that shows itself in good works. But the inherent righteousness of human beings is not sufficient for salvation without faith, which allows the perfect righteousness of Christ to be imputed. This compromise formula, though accepted by all parties to the Regensburg Colloquium, was rejected by Luther and failed to win the support of Rome.[15]

The Council of Trent was the first official response of the Catholic Church to the questions about faith raised by the Reformation.[16] The nature of faith was intensely discussed in connection with the Decree on Justification, drawn up in the second half of 1546. The discussion proved difficult because there was no ready-made Catholic set of answers to the questions raised by the Reformers. The Catholics themselves were divided into three major groups, usually designated as Augustinian, Scotist, and Thomist. The Augustinians, prominently represented by Cardinal Girolamo Seripando, Superior General of the Augustinian order, affirmed on the basis of texts from Paul and Augustine that faith has the power to effect justification. The Thomists held that justification is effected by the gift of habitual grace, which inseparably brings with it the three theological virtues of faith, hope, and charity. The Scotists, attending more to the act of faith than to the infused virtue, looked on faith as one of a series of acts that necessarily precedes the justification of an adult.

The Council wished to present a coherent Catholic doctrine that would exclude the errors of the Reformers without condemning the positions of any of the recognized Catholic schools. In spite of the strong differences of opinion, the Council succeeded in drawing up an impressive statement that won unanimous approval in January 1547. Although it named no adversaries, the Decree on Justification was primarily directed against Luther and the Augsburg Confession. The doctrines of other Reformers, such as Calvin and Zwingli, were only lightly touched on in the debate.

Chapters 5 and 6 of the Decree on Justification treat the role of faith in the process by which the sinner comes to righteousness. Chapter 5 reaffirms the Augustinian position that for even the beginning of faith the human heart must be touched by the illumination of the Holy Spirit (DS 1525; cf. can. 3, DS 1553). Thus no scope is given for Semi-Pelagianism. On the other hand, the Council insists that the human subject, instead of being passive in the process of justification, freely cooperates with the grace of God (DS 1525; cf. canons 4–6, DS 1554–56).

Chapter 6, which supports the teaching of Scotus and of Luther's opponent, John Gropper, details the psychological and ethical aspects of the approach to justification. Faith, as the first of six preparatory acts, is described primarily as an assent to the truth of the proclaimed message: "They [adults] are disposed for that righteousness when, aroused and assisted by the grace of God, they conceive faith from hearing, and are freely led toward God, believing to be true that which has been divinely revealed and promised, especially that the sinner is justified by God's grace" (DS 1526). Specifically repudiated is the "fiducial" position that justifying faith is nothing except trust in God's mercy (canon 12, DS 1562).

Chapter 7 takes up the essence and causes of justification itself. Here the imprint of Thomism is most evident. The instrumental cause of faith, without which no one can be justified (cf. Heb 11:6), is baptism, the sacrament of faith. In speaking of the formal cause of justification the Council seems to repudiate, at least by implication, the doctrine of double justification. The sole formal cause of justification, according to the Council, is the gift by which God's righteousness inheres in us—that is to say, created grace (DS 1529). In this rebirth our sins are remitted and we receive simultaneously the three infused gifts of faith, hope, and charity (DS 1530). Faith, unless accompanied by hope and charity, is held to be dead and insufficient to insert one vitally into Christ or to dispose one for eternal life (DS 1531).

In chapter 8 the Council accepts in a qualified way the Augustinian formula that the ungodly are "justified by faith and freely" (DS 1532). When Paul speaks of being justified by faith without works of the law (e.g., Rom 3:28 and Gal 2:16), he means, according to the Council, that faith is "the beginning, foundation, and root of all justification." Although this might seem to suggest that faith is a mere point of departure, these expressions may better be interpreted as signifying that faith accompanies and sustains the whole process by which the sinner turns toward God and advances in the way of salvation. Justification, according to the Council, is "gratis" in the sense nothing that precedes justification strictly merits grace (*pro-meretur,* DS 1532).[17] Here again the Council clearly distances itself from Semi-Pelagianism.

Chapters 9 through 15 of the Decree on Justification give Catholic responses to a variety of other Protestant theses regarding faith. Chapter 9 contests the view commonly attributed to Luther that faith brings with it an infallible certitude of one's own justification. In this connection the Council rejects the thesis that no one can be validly absolved without certainly believing that he or she has been absolved and that absolution and justification are effected by faith alone (DS 1534). These points are further emphasized in canons 13 and 14 (DS 1563–64).

Chapter 11 deals with the necessity of observing the commandments. Faith alone, it is asserted, does not justify unless one obeys the other commandments (DS 1538; canons 19 and 27, DS 1569, 1577). Chapter 12 repudiates the presumptuous view that one may and must be certain, without special divine revelation, of being among the elect (DS 1540; canons 15 and 16, DS 1565–66).

A final point regarding faith, treated in chapter 15, concerns the possibility of losing grace and charity while retaining the habit of faith. Against the Protestant view that true faith is never "unformed" or "dead" (cf. Jas 2:26), canon 28 declares: "If anyone says that together with the loss of grace through sin faith is always lost, or that the faith that remains is not true faith, granted that it is not living faith; or that anyone who has faith without charity is not a Christian, let him be anathema" (DS 1578).

The theology of faith is treated not only in the Decree on Justification but also to some extent in the canons on the sacraments in general. Here the Council of Trent asserts that faith is not to be exalted in a way that makes the sacraments superfluous or unnecessary for salvation (can. 4), nor may it be held that the sacraments were instituted simply to arouse faith (can. 5), or that they are merely external signs of grace received through faith (can. 6), or that grace is truly given only through faith in the divine promises, rather than by the sacraments themselves (can. 8; cf. DS 1604–8).

In its teaching on faith, and especially in its magnificent Decree on Justification, the Council of Trent corrected certain Pelagian tendencies in late Nominalism. It accommodated the distinctive positions of Paul and Augustine within a broadly Scholastic framework that owes much to Thomas Aquinas and something, it would seem, to Duns Scotus. In so doing the Council met certain concerns of the Protestant Reformers, while at the same time preserving the Catholic emphasis on human cooperation and the objective efficacy of the sacraments. The judgment of the Protestant historian of dogma, Adolf Harnack, has often been quoted: "The Decree on Justification, although a product of art, is in many respects remarkably well constructed; indeed, it may be doubted whether the Reformation would have developed itself if this Decree had been issued at the Lateran Council at the beginning of the century, and had really passed into the flesh and blood of the Church."[18]

## Post-Tridentine Controversial Literature

In the fifty years after Trent the lines of division between Protestants and Catholics became more rigid. From the Protestant side the teaching of the Council on faith was attacked by John Calvin in a highly polemical work of 1547, *Acta synodi tridentinae. Cum Antidoto*.[19] Calvin accused the Council of teaching that justification is ascribed only partly to God because it is attributed in part also to human freedom. He objected that the true biblical concept of faith was mutilated by the Scholastic distinction between *fides informis* and *fides formata*. He also found it insufficient in the light of Scripture to speak of faith as the beginning or foundation of justification.

A fullblown refutation of Trent from the Lutheran side, entitled *Examen concilii tridentini*, was published in 1565 to 1583 by the conservative dogmatician, Martin Chemnitz (1522–1586).[20] First, in answer to certain Scholastic interpretations of Trent, he polemicized at length against the doctrine that justification might be "congruously," even though not "condignly" (i.e., strictly), merited—a doctrine that he evidently considered to be favored by Trent. Second, Chemnitz held that although love and good works necessarily flow from living faith, faith alone (not love or good works) is the ground of justification, for it reaches out to the righteousness of Christ, which is imputed to the sinner. In a third section of his discussion of faith Chemnitz maintained that genuine faith involves confident trust in one's own justification and in the forgiveness of one's own sins.

Chemnitz was one of the principal authors of the *Formula of Concord*, a theological consensus statement designed to overcome the controversies that had been raging among Lutherans, especially since the death of Luther. Published in 1577 and adopted by many of the German princes of Lutheran territories, the *Formula* was a precise and vigorous statement of Lutheran orthodoxy, in some ways corresponding to the Council of Trent on the Catholic side. In its statements of faith it opposed what were considered to be Roman errors. For example, it declared: "Faith's sole office and property is to serve as the only and exclusive means and instrument with and through which we receive, grasp, accept, apply to ourselves, and appropriate the grace and the merit of Christ in the promise of the Gospel. From this office and property of application and appropriation we must exclude love and every other virtue or work" ("Solid Declaration," 3:38; Tappert ed., *Book of Concord*, 546). In subsequent paragraphs the *Formula* condemns the errors of those who hold that faith cannot justify without works or who hold that faith justifies only insofar as it is associated with love (SD 3:43; BC 547).

Catholic polemicists in the second half of the sixteenth century defended the decrees of Trent and replied to the Protestant attacks. Domingo de Soto, Ruard Tapper, and Thomas Stapleton insisted even more strongly than Trent itself on the strictly intellectual character of faith as an assent to revealed truth. They gave arguments from Holy Scripture and the fathers of the Church to prove that "dead faith," although deficient, is a gift of God, uniting one in some measure to Christ and keeping one on the path that can lead to salvation. They denied that faith necessarily involves trustful confidence of being justified or predestined to eternal glory.

The most thorough and instructive Catholic response to the Protestant positions on faith is probably the monumental work, *Disputationes de controversiis christianae fidei adversus hujus temporis haereticos* (published in Ingolstadt, 1586, 1588, and 1593) by Robert Bellarmine (1542–1621). In comparison with other controversialists of his age, Bellarmine is remarkably fair, clear, and systematic in presenting the teachings of the various Reformers, including, on the subject of faith, Calvin, Melanchthon, and Chemnitz. He points out how the Protestants distinguish three major kinds of faith: historical faith, miracle-faith, and faith in God's promises. Within the third category, he observes, they distinguish between "general" and "special" faith in the promises and mercy of God. Only "special" faith in the divine promises as availing to oneself is for these Protestants conducive to salvation.

For Bellarmine, as for other Catholics, the object of faith is the truth of God's word. Faith, he asserts, does not consist essentially in knowledge or apprehension, as Calvin held, but in assent. It is an obedient submission of the intellect prompted by the inclination of the will, drawn by grace. The Protestant conception of fiducial faith, in Bellarmine's estimation, is faulty because faith could not be certain and infallible if it rested on anything but God's word. Nowhere in the word of God is it stated that I myself am saved or that my sins are forgiven. Bellarmine also rejects the idea of salvation by faith alone. The act of faith, he holds, is only one of the disposing causes of justification. There are others such as fear of punishment, repentance and, most of all, love. The true cause of justification is, as Trent taught, God's righteousness inhering in us, a righteousness infused together with charity.[21]

Controversial exchanges between Lutherans and Catholics on the subject of faith continued vigorously throughout the seventeenth century. The Lutheran orthodox theologian Johann Gerhard (1582–1637), an opponent of Bellarmine, adhered to the standard Lutheran position on faith and justification. "In justification, we say, faith reigns alone without our love; indeed, it is the task of faith alone to lay hold of Christ and, in him, of God's grace, the forgiveness of sins, and eternal life."[22]

Lutheran orthodoxy gave rise to a new Scholasticism in which the Scriptures were read through the prism of the Book of Concord. In this system faith was seen as consisting of three elements: knowledge, assent, and trust *(notitia, assensus, fiducia)*. In his *Theologia didactico-polemica* Johannes Andreas Quenstedt (1617–1688) observed that this threefold division was equivalent to the medieval Scholastic distinction between *credere Deum, credere Deo,* and *credere in Deum* (IV, 282). The first two elements of faith, he noted, pertain to the intellect, the third to the will. Trust, or confidence, was regarded as the principal part of faith, correlative with God's promise of mercy in Christ. But these orthodox writers were anxious not to give any occasion for minimizing the importance and certainty of sound doctrine.[23]

A parallel development took place within the Calvinist tradition. A series of Reformed confessions of faith were drawn up, canonizing the principal theses of Calvin's theology. One of the most influential was the Second Helvetic Confession, composed by Heinrich Bullinger in 1566. In chapter 16, on Faith and Good Works, it offers the following definition:

> *What is Faith?* Christian faith is not an opinion or human conviction, but a most firm trust and a clear and steadfast assent of the mind, and then a most certain apprehension of the truth of God presented in the Scriptures and in the Apostles' Creed, and thus also of God himself, the greatest good, and especially of God's promise and of Christ who is the fulfilment of all promises.[24]

The same confession declares that we are justified by faith alone, that we receive Christ by faith, that faith is a pure gift of God, and that faith is efficacious and active through love.

The Heidelberg Catechism, composed for German-speaking Calvinists in 1563, is notable for the warm and personal tone of its evangelical testimony. To Question 21, "What Is True Faith?" it responds:

> It is not only a certain knowledge by which I accept as true all that God has revealed to us in his Word, but also a wholehearted trust which the Holy Spirit creates in me through the gospel, that, not only to others, but to me also God has given the forgiveness of sins, everlasting righteousness and salvation, out of sheer grace solely for the sake of Christ's saving work.[25]

Confessions and catechisms such as these (including the Westminster Confession, which we shall consider later) soon became the basis of a Calvinist orthodoxy that would be stoutly defended in the seventeenth century by Scholastic theologians such as Gisbert Voet (1589–1676) of Utrecht, François Turretin (1623–1687) of Geneva, and Johann Heinrich Heidegger (1633–1698) of Zürich.

The Reformed Scholastic theologians held that faith was a supernatural habit, infused into the soul by God. Like their Lutheran counterparts, they analyzed faith in terms of its three components: *notitia, assensus*, and *fiducia*.[26] The element of *notitia* (knowledge), they believed, excluded the Roman Catholic doctrine of "implicit faith," which they understood as a blind surrender of one's soul to the pope. With regard to *assensus*, the Reformed dogmaticians, like the Thomists, held that faith is a firm assent, essentially distinct from mere opinion. The third element, *fiducia* (personal trust), pertained to the will. It included an immovable conviction that the believer is really taken up by God into the covenant of grace and is assured of salvation. These theologians, while agreeing that faith was deficient unless accompanied by this element of trust, debated among themselves as to whether there could be genuine faith that was not yet *fiducia*.

The efficient cause of faith, according to Reformed dogmatics, was God acting through the Holy Spirit. In the normal case, God used his word as instrumental cause. In opposition to both Catholics and Lutherans, these theologians denied that baptism and the prayers of the Church could be instrumental causes of faith. Against the Lutherans, Reformed theologians denied that elect children were capable of acts of faith, but, against the Anabaptists, they affirmed that such children receive the "seed of faith" from God. Baptism, they held, is a sign and seal of election.

## The English Reformation

The Thirty-Nine Articles of 1563, a revision of the Forty-Two Articles of 1553, provided a minimal basis for a national church that sought to preserve both the Catholic and the Protestant traditions. Article 11 stated: "We are accounted righteous before God only for the merit of our Lord and Saviour Jesus Christ by Faith, and not for our own works or deservings. Wherefore, that we are justified by Faith only, is a most wholesome Doctrine, and very full of comfort, as more largely is expressed in the Homily of Justification."[27]

The Twelve Homilies of 1547, issued under Edward VI for reading in local churches, set forth the Reformation teaching on justification in moderate fashion.[28] The homily "Of the Salvation of Mankind" affirms justification by faith alone, insofar as faith sends us directly to Christ, whose merits alone justify. For our faith to be justifying, it needs to be more than dead faith barren of works. Rather it must be living faith that works by charity. If works do not follow, our faith is no better than that of the devils—a point further emphasized in the succeeding homily, "Of the True, Lively, and Christian Faith."[29]

Richard Hooker (1554–1600) became the first great systematic theologian of the Church of England. Opposing the Puritan party, he sought to maintain continuity with the ancient tradition, and approvingly cited Peter Lombard and Thomas Aquinas. In his great work, *Of the Laws of Ecclesiastical Polity* (1593), he maintained that while it is faith that justifies, and while everything necessary for salvation is found in Holy Scripture, right reason is a gift of God and must be used for bringing people to the faith and for distinguishing true inspirations of the Holy Spirit from delusions.[30] Hooker's rationalistic tendency is indicated in his "A learned and Comfortable Sermon of the Certainty and Perpetuity of Faith in the Elect, especially of the Prophet Habakkuk's Faith" (1585–1586), in which he asserts: "That which we see by the light of grace, though it indeed be more certain, yet is it not to us so evidently certain, as that which sense or the light of nature will not suffer a man to doubt of."[31]

## Mysticism and Baroque Scholasticism

St. John of the Cross (1542–1591), who studied philosophy and theology as a Carmelite at Salamanca from 1564 to 1568, wrote extensively on faith, not as a systematic theologian but as a mystical theologian. Connecting the three theological virtues with the faculties of intellect, memory, and will, he looks upon faith as a means of uniting the intellect with God under the conditions of this life.[32] He describes it as "the only proximate and proportionate means to union with God" (*Ascent of Mount Carmel*, II.9.1). Inasmuch as faith is informed by grace and charity, it becomes a means of "transforming union" and participation in the very life of God (*Ascent*, II.5.3–7). "In a way, this dark, loving knowledge, which is faith, serves as a means for divine union in this life as does the light of glory for the clear vision of God in the next" (*Ascent*, II.24.4).

John recognizes that faith comes initially from the preaching of the gospel and that the faithful may never cease to rely on the doctrine of the Church that comes from hearing (*Ascent*, II.27.4; cf. II.3.3). But he gives primacy to the interior word of God, to which we must listen in silence (*Spiritual Canticle*, 14–15.15; *Maxims and Counsels*, no. 21). Christ, he insists, is the one word in which God has said all he has to say. To seek any word beyond Christ is to show a lack of faith in him (*Ascent*, II.22.5).

Commenting on a stanza of his *Spiritual Canticle*, John explains that the articles or propositions of faith, in their explicit teaching, are silver; the substance of the faith that lies hidden in them is gold (*Spiritual Canticle*, Stanza 12, 4–5). Like the soldiers of Gideon, he says elsewhere, we must hold the light of the divinity in the earthenware jars of faith so that, when the clay of this earthly existence is shattered, the content of faith may be revealed in splendor (*Ascent*, II.9.3–4; cf. Jg 7:16–19).

John of the Cross teaches that faith, as it progresses, must learn to dispense with the supports of sensory and intellectual evidence. The light of faith, being too bright for the intellect, produces a kind of blindness (*Ascent*, II.3.1). "Faith nullifies the light of the intellect" but its darkness, like the cloud that surrounded the children of Israel (Ex 14:20), is luminous (*Ascent*, II.3.4). The dark night of faith is the medium in which the soul advances toward God. Even the touches of the divinity that are occasionally given to contemplatives are profoundly mysterious, and do not make God's presence evident to the senses or the intellect (*Ascent*, II.26.5). Nevertheless, God does impart true wisdom to the soul in faith. "The purer and more refined a soul is in faith, the more infused charity it possesses, and the more charity it has the more the Holy Spirit illumines it and communicates his gifts, because charity is the means by which they are communicated" (*Ascent*, II.29.6).

The sixteenth-century Spanish Dominicans developed their doctrine of faith principally through commentaries on Thomas Aquinas in the tradition of Cajetan. Francisco da Vitoria (c. 1486–1546), who held the prime chair of theology at Salamanca from 1524 to 1546, taught from the *Summa theologiae* as his text. He was succeeded at Salamanca by a series of eminent Dominican Thomists, including Melchior Cano (1509–1560), Domingo de Soto (1495–1560), and Domingo Bañez (1528–1604). These theologians concurred in holding that faith is primarily caused by interior grace, which takes the form of an illumination. The light of faith exhibits the contents of faith in a way that makes it apt to be believed by a supernatural act of faith.

A number of sixteenth-century Jesuit theologians of faith, including Francisco de Toledo (1533–1596), Juan de Maldonato (1533?–1583), Gregory of Valencia (1549–1603), Gabriel Vasquez (1549–1604), and Francisco Suarez (1548–1617), studied at Salamanca. They agreed with the Spanish Dominicans that the natural evidence for the Christian religion is sufficient to establish the credibility of revelation. The judgment of credibility thus pertains to the preambles of faith. Infused faith, having a supernatural motive, differs specifically from natural faith. The motive of faith is believed by a supernatural act.[33]

Luis Molina, S.J., (1536–1600) differed from the Salamanca theologians because he held that acquired faith is essentially the same as supernatural faith, and that both have the same formal object, i.e., God who reveals. Grace, he maintained, does not provide a new formal object but only gives new efficacy or facility in performing acts of faith.

Francisco Suarez was the first to produce a major independent treatise on faith, not in the form of a commentary on the *Sentences* or on St. Thomas.[34] By faith Suarez means intellectual assent founded on the testimony of a speaker. Divine faith, he holds, is a supremely firm assent founded on the authority of God obscurely revealing. Suarez agrees with the Salamanca school that infused faith is specifically distinct from acquired faith, that it is essentially supernatural, and that it has a supernatural formal object. The formal object is God as first truth both in knowing and in speaking *(prima veritas in cognoscendo et dicendo)*. Both God's knowledge and his wisdom are constitutive of his authority.[35]

Regarding the approach to faith, Suarez taught, as did the Dominicans, that the motives of credibility are conditions, not causes, of faith. Credibility does not make the fact of revelation evident, but only worthy of belief. Contrary to Cajetan and many Thomists, however, he denied that the evidence of credibility arises from the light of faith, although that light can, he concedes, better dispose a person to discern the objective signs. Between the natural judgment of credibility and the act of faith, Suarez posited an essentially natural judgment of credentity (i.e., recognition of the obligation to believe), and added that this judgment must be supernaturally elevated in order to motivate the will to command the unconditional assent of faith.

The primary material object of faith, for Suarez, is God himself, but the human mind does not know God except by putting together mental concepts, as occurs when we assert that God is triune. The immediate object of faith, therefore, is not the infinitely simple divine essence but created truths, such as those contained in the creed and others defined by popes and councils. The proposal of the revealed object by the Church is the rule of faith for Catholics, but it is not an absolutely necessary condition of faith, since there can be faith in something not taught by the Church, e.g., a private revelation. Proposal by the Church leads to faith only in the case of those who already accept the Church as an organ of revelation. Thus faith in the Church depends upon faith in God who reveals.

The supernatural light of faith, for Suarez, is a condition *sine qua non* of faith, but it does not pertain to the motive of faith, nor is a particular individual's possession of such a light attested by revelation. Suarez was concerned that an excessive reliance on the light of faith, as propounded by some of the Dominicans, could lead to subjectivism and to a heretical tendency to accept only what the individual felt interiorly inclined to believe.

The sole motive of faith, according to Suarez, is the uncreated authority of God. This motive could not have the requisite firmness unless it were itself revealed. By faith we accept, in one and the same act, both the content of revelation and the authority of God who reveals that content. Suarez was aware that his position on this point seemed to involve an infinite regress, in which each act of faith would depend on a prior act of faith. How could I believe something on the authority of the revealing God when the ground for accepting God's authority was itself ascertained by faith? To this Suarez replied somewhat weakly: "We must admit in the first place that this is a great mystery of faith . . . and that an act of this kind is entirely supernatural and would be impossible without the special help of grace."[36] He went on to say that it is no more absurd for God to attest that he is truthful and that he is speaking than for us to know that we are knowing. Whenever I give testimony I implicitly say that I am speaking and that I am truthful. Faith, Suarez added, is not an inference drawn from previously known premises, but an essentially simple act which, on analysis, may be seen to include knowledge of its own formal object as virtually contained within it. Faith, he maintained, is not formally but virtually discursive.[37]

The position of Suarez on the grounding of faith (or "analysis of faith") would subsequently be accepted, with modifications, by Jesuits such as Rodrigo de Arriaga, Camillus Mazzella, and Santo Schiffini, as well as by Dominicans such as Charles René Billuart and Réginald Garrigou-Lagrange. Many, however, judged that Suarez had recourse to mystery rather too early in the game, and that a better explanation could be devised.

The Jesuit Juan de Lugo (1583–1660), who succeeded Suarez as professor at the Roman College, wrote an exhaustive treatise on the virtue of faith in which he devoted considerable attention to the question of the "analysis of faith," that is to say, the explanation of the ultimate grounding of the certitude of faith. Faith, he held, is the conclusion of a syllogism, either formal or virtual, to the following effect:

Divine revelation cannot deceive;
But God has revealed that the Word became man;
Therefore the Word did become man.[38]

The first premise, according to de Lugo, is immediately evident from the terms themselves, for anyone who understands what is meant by the term *God* must know that God is all-perfect and that whatever God reveals must be true. This natural assent, however, must be elevated by grace in order to enter into the supernatural assent of faith.[39]

More difficult is the task of explaining how the fact of revelation can be established. According to de Lugo, rational arguments can establish the credibility of revelation, but they cannot give more than probable knowledge of the fact of revelation. That fact can, however, be attested by God through the word of the Church, which proposes the word of God. The miracles, the testimony of the martyrs, the teaching of prophets and that of the Church itself, while they function, under one aspect, as rationally convincing signs of credibility, may also be seen from another point of view as "mediate revelation." They are vehicles by which God makes his authority concretely present to the believer. When the mind considers the signs of credibility, divine grace is at work enabling the believer to perceive in the signs the voice of God himself. By an immediate apprehension, obscure yet fully certain, the believer becomes aware that God himself certifies as his own the meaning disclosed by the created signs or witnesses.[40]

Although de Lugo, like Suarez, rejects the idea that acquired faith is a presupposition of infused faith, he differs from Suarez because he holds that faith rests on a kind of rational discourse which, elevated by the light of faith, enters into the motive of faith itself, for it is through this rational insight that God makes his authority present and known. He is at one with Suarez in denying that the habit or light of faith pertains to the motive. That light, he asserts, is a subjective help, but it is not experienced and is in no sense an object.[41]

De Lugo's position on the analysis of faith continued to have great influence for several centuries. It was accepted by the seventeenth-century Jesuits Juan Martinez de Ripalda and Caspar Hurtado, and would appeal to the nineteenth-century Jesuits Johann Baptist Franzelin and Joseph Kleutgen. Many theologians continue to hold that faith does depend on some kind of supernatural illumination of the mind, logically prior to faith itself. A weakness in de Lugo's theory, according to many critics, is that he apparently looked on faith as a deduction depending on premises that are themselves objects of a prior act of assent. In this respect he seems to have over-rationalized the genesis of faith.

Suarez and de Lugo both regarded themselves as followers of Thomas Aquinas, seeking to clarify certain points that he had not treated explicitly. But they made several significant shifts. For one, they distinguished more sharply between the natural and supernatural phases of the approach to faith, and tended to see grace as intervening relatively late in the process. Second, they regarded the act of faith as terminating immediately in propositions about God, rather than terminating in God by means of propositions. Third, these theologians were driven by a concern to ground the act of faith in speculatively certain knowledge that would infallibly guarantee the truth of the assent, whereas St. Thomas seems not to have felt that concern. Fourth, the Jesuits of the baroque period insisted that the light of faith was unconscious and that it in no way affected the intentionality of the act. For this reason they looked upon the light of faith as having no bearing on the formal object.

The Carmelites of Salamanca, in their voluminous course on Thomistic theology (1679), defended a generally Thomistic position on the analysis of faith but combined this with a strong insistence on the role of reason in the approach to faith. In their treatise of grace these Carmelites asserted that faith, since it rests on the testimony of God as author of the supernatural order, requires a motive of the same supernatural order, the *lumen fidei*. This supernatural light, they acknowledged, need not be distinctly experienced, but it is implicitly present in consciousness as something coexperienced; for this reason it constitutes the light under which the assent of faith attains its object. Unless this light were operative, the assent of faith would not be an exercise of the supernatural virtue.[42]

In their treatise on faith, the Salamanca Carmelites asserted that the act of faith presupposes, as a prior condition on which it depends, perception of the evident credibility of revelation. This credibility can be known by a natural exercise of reason, independently of grace.[43]

## The Salvation of the Unevangelized

As a result of the great voyages of discovery, theologians in the sixteenth century became increasingly concerned with the question of the salvation of the vast populations of other continents who had never had an opportunity to hear the proclamation of either the Israelite or the Christian faith.[44] Must it be held that they and their ancestors were all condemned for a lack of faith for which they were not personally responsible? Medieval theologians, regarding the unevangelized populations as relatively small, were content to propose exceptional remedies, such as evangelization by an angel specially sent from God. In the sixteenth century, however, theologians began to search for solutions that would lie within the ordinary providence of God.

This problem does not seem to have vexed Luther, Calvin, and their disciples. Insisting on faith in Christ alone as the condition of salvation, they were disposed to hold that unevangelized pagans were predestined to damnation. Luther in his "Large Catechism" lays down the principle that "where Christ is not preached, there is no Holy Spirit to create, call and gather the Christian church, and outside it no one can come to the Lord Christ."[45] Calvin asserts that "by shutting off the reprobate from knowledge of his name or from the sanctification of the Spirit, he [God], as it were, reveals by these marks what sort of judgment awaits them."[46] If God leaves some seeds of true religion among barbarous peoples, this is simply to deprive them of any excuse for not worshiping him as he deserves.[47] Even Zwingli, who assured King Francis of the salvation of ancient heroes such as Hercules, Theseus, Socrates, and the Catos,[48] wrote to the Emperor Charles V: "Wherever prophets and preachers of the word are sent, it is a sign of the grace of God, who wills to give knowledge of himself to his elect; and for those to whom this is denied, it is a sign of his impending wrath."[49]

The Portuguese Jesuit Jacobus Payva d'Andrada in his *Explanations of the Controverted Points of Religion* maintained that "There can be no more shocking harshness and cruelty than to deliver up human beings to everlasting torments on account of lack of that faith which they could in no way obtain."[50] He held that contemporary pagans were in a state like that of the ancient Greeks who, according to Justin and Clement of Alexandria, could be saved by a philosophical knowledge of God under the law of nature. Chemnitz, in his *Examination of the Council of Trent*, accused Andrada of Pelagianism and stated that the fathers cited by Andrada "most manifestly conflict with the Scripture."[51]

Andrada was only one of many sixteenth-century theologians who questioned the classic doctrine, stemming from Augustine, that under the dispensation of the new law no one can be saved without explicit belief in fundamental doctrines such as the Trinity and the Incarnation. Domingo de Soto, in his *De natura et gratia* (1547), proposed that belief in the existence of God as known by the light of natural reason could suffice for the faith necessary for salvation. The Franciscan Andrea Vega, in his *De Justificatione* (1548), went so far as to deny that any act of faith was necessary on the part of a person invincibly ignorant of the existence of God. On the other hand, many Dominicans such as Cano and Bañez, and some Jesuits such as Gregory of Valencia, continued to hold that since the promulgation of the gospel explicit faith in Christ is necessary for salvation.

Suarez, in a minute and exhaustive study of the problem,[52] proposed a mediating view to the effect that explicit faith in Christ was "a necessary means, although not always [present] in actual fact, [always present] either in fact or in desire."[53] Explicit faith in Christ, he held, was a necessary means for salvation as a matter of divine positive law. If it so happened that a person could not obtain the necessary means, God would accept the desire or wish to use such means. Thus a non-Christian who believed in God and sincerely desired to please God in all things might be understood as having implicit faith in Christ and an implicit desire for baptism. While verbally Suarez supported the necessity of explicit faith, his position in the end favored the more liberal view.

Juan Martinez de Ripalda, in his celebrated *De ente supernaturali* (1634), proposed a very ingenious position—namely that whenever an infidel posits an act of natural virtue God has already raised the act with a supernatural help so that it is extrinsically supernatural.[54] The pagans who come to believe in God with the stirrings of supernatural grace can perform salutary acts. They do not have faith in the strict sense, since they do not accept any revealed truth on the authority of God as witness, but they have faith in the broad sense *(fides late dicta)* insofar as their belief in naturally knowable truths is supernaturally motivated and illuminated by grace. Later, in his *De fide divina* (posthumously published in 1662), Ripalda concedes that according to the received opinion, which he does not reject, faith in the strict sense is necessary for justification, but he adds that if this is true it is not because of the very nature of justification but because of an extrinsic law imposed by the divine will.

Juan de Lugo discussed at some length the question whether a Muslim, a Jew, or a heretic could have sufficient faith to be justified and saved. He agreed in essence with Suarez and in part also with Ripalda.[55] He held that those who, with the assistance of grace, do what is in their power will receive the enlightenment they need to seek the true way of salvation, thus disposing themselves for justification. But he added that they would have to make an act of faith in the strict sense. Since some revealed truths are accessible in non-Catholic Christianity, in Judaism, and in Islam, adherents of these religions could, with the help of grace, make supernatural acts of faith and have the virtue of divine, infused faith. Regarding the content of such an act of justifying faith, de Lugo denied that explicit belief in the Incarnation would in all cases be essential. Implicit belief in Christ, contained in faith in God as savior, might suffice in the case of believers to whom the Christian faith had not been credibly proposed.

With respect to the sufficiency of faith that was explicitly Christian, therefore, a number of Franciscan, Dominican, and Jesuit theologians of the early modern period took positions more optimistic than those of Augustine and his medieval followers. Their liberal views led to bitter opposition on the part of other theologians who exalted the authority of Augustine, notably the followers of Baius (Michel de Bay, 1513–1585) and Jansenius (Cornelius Jansen, 1585–1638), both of whom taught at Louvain. Although the pessimism and "rigorism" of these two theologians was condemned by the Holy See in 1567 and 1642, respectively (and many times thereafter), the movements did not die out.

A leader in the French Jansenist party, Antoine Arnauld (1612–1694), wrote a tract *On the Necessity of Faith in Jesus Christ for Salvation*, in which he argued that anyone to whom the Christian faith had not been preached would inevitably be damned. "Only within the Pelagian heresy," he maintained, "could one question the damnation of all these Americans before they were illuminated by the light of the gospel."[56]

## The Controversy about Probabilism

The disciples of Baius and Jansenius in France and the Low Countries labored to get opinions contrary to their own condemned as "laxist." In 1677 three professors from the University of Louvain, where rigid Augustinianism continued to thrive, went to Rome with several lists of allegedly laxist propositions. Pope Innocent XI gave the delegation a hearing and had the propositions examined by papal commissions. Sixty-five of the propositions were rejected by a Decree of the Holy Office dated March 2, 1679. They were not, however, condemned as necessarily heretical or even erroneous. The censure reads: "All these propositions are condemned and prohibited as they stand, as being at least scandalous and pernicious in practice" (DS 2166). The propositions touching specifically on faith are 4 and 19 through 23.[57]

Proposition 4 states: "An unbeliever who does not come to faith when following a less probable opinion is excused from the sin of infidelity." Commentators commonly attribute the thesis to the Spanish Jesuit Juan Sanchez. It is unclear why it is condemned, but possibly it could be interpreted as permitting a person to make use of imprudent doubts and tenuously probable arguments in order to avoid conversion.

Proposition 19 is important for the theology of faith. It reads: "The will cannot make the assent of faith in itself firmer than the weight of the reasons impelling one to assent deserves." The statement is found in the writings of Gilles Estrix, S.J., who was disliked in Louvain both for his espousal of probabilism and for his defense of the Immaculate Conception. While he indeed held that the firmness of faith, precisely as an intellectual assent, depends solely on the evidence, he added that faith, considered as a practical submission to God, has a firmness depending on the will moved by grace. The position was rejected, one may suppose, because it seemed to neglect the power of grace to illuminate the intellect.

Proposition 20 deals with loss of faith. Estrix held that it is possible for a Catholic living in a heretical or non-Christian region to fall away from Catholic faith inculpably, and even prudently. The condemned proposition states: "Hence one may prudently repudiate one's own previous supernatural assent." Possibly Estrix's thesis seemed to give excuses for apostasies that could, with the help of grace, be avoided.

Proposition 21 reads: "A salutary and supernatural assent of faith can coexist with a merely probable knowledge of revelation and even with the fear that God may not have spoken." This is closely connected with Proposition 19 and is condemned for the same reason. Estrix believed that the intellectual component in the act of faith need not always be firm.

Propositions 22 and 23 deal with the content of faith absolutely necessary for salvation. Proposition 22 censures the opinion that "The faith necessary as a means *(necessaria . . . necessitate medii)* of salvation would seem to be only faith in the one God, not explicit faith in the Rewarder *(Remuneratoris)*." This view, which commentators attribute to Estrix, seems to have been held also by Rodrigo de Arriaga and might be ascribed to several of the authors summarized above. Significantly, the Holy Office does not say that explicit faith in the Trinity or the Incarnation is always essential for salvation. Holders of the more liberal opinion could satisfy the requirements of this proposition by pointing out that the act of faith, as they conceive it, must bear not only on the existence of God but on God as rewarder, in accordance with Hebrews 11:6.

Proposition 23 rejects the proposition, "Faith in the broad sense, based on the testimony of creatures or the like, suffices for salvation." This position, commonly attributed to Estrix, resembles that of Ripalda, at least in his *De ente supernaturali*, if that work is read without attention to the further qualifications introduced in his *De fide divina*.

The condemnations of 1679 are obviously conditioned by the controversies about moral theology occurring at the time, and are open to reconsideration in the more serene light of posterity. Theologians such as Sanchez and Estrix, Ripalda and Arriaga, were loyally trying to adapt Catholic theology to the changed religious situation occasioned by the breakdown of Christian unity in Western Europe and by the discovery of vast continents where biblical faith had never been known. They were also sensitive to the criticism of traditional theological positions by early champions of Enlightenment. Some of these theologians no doubt opened themselves to criticism for ambiguities or excesses, but the hostility against them was chiefly due to the bitterness of the Jansenists, whose narrow views were far from Catholic orthodoxy.

## Seventeenth-Century Rationalism and Sentimentalism

Rationalism in its modern form began on the European continent in the seventeenth century as an effort to overcome the wave of skepticism represented by thinkers such as Michel de Montaigne (1533–1592) and Pierre Charron (1541–1603). René Descartes (1596–1650) strove to build an impregnable system of knowledge based on sure and indubitable principles. As a first step in this construction he began by doubting all that he was capable of doubting. In his philosophical enterprise he rejected the use of authority, which he regarded as incapable of delivering anything more than probability. He also sought to exclude all concepts that were vague or indistinct. As a believing Catholic, he exempted religious doctrines from his program of universal doubt. Some of his followers, however, extended his method so that religious beliefs could be subjected to methodic doubt with the idea of later reasserting them on the basis of self-evident principles.

The leading theologians of the sixteenth century, as we have seen, regarded the truths of the Christian faith as incapable of being strictly demonstrated, but only as capable of being seen as credible by the light of unaided reason. In the rationalistic climate generated by Cartesianism, some apologists were impelled to establish faith on a firmer rational basis. Miguel de Elizalde, S.J. (1616–1698), and his disciple Thyrsus Gonzalez de Santalla, S.J. (1624–1705), maintained that pure reason can demonstrate the fact of revelation and the truth of the Christian faith. In continuity with the tradition, however, they held that this demonstration is not a premise upon which the act of faith depends, but a mere preamble or presupposition of faith. Faith itself has as its intrinsic motive the authority of God who reveals, an authority perceived in faith.[58]

The negative influence of rationalism on faith may be studied in the philosophy of Benedict Spinoza (1632–1677), an excommunicated Dutch Jew. He looked upon faith as a rough approximation of true knowledge suited to uneducated people who were incapable of rising to the level of clear and distinct ideas. The value of faith, for him, lay in its capacity to move people to live virtuously and to treat their fellow human beings kindly. Accordingly he defined faith as "a knowledge of God, without which obedience to him would be impossible, and which the mere fact of obedience to him implies."[59] As a corollary he asserted that "faith does not demand [so much] that dogmas should be true as that they should be pious—that is, such as will stir up the heart to obey."[60]

In the course of the seventeenth century it became increasingly common to grant that faith was not a matter of strict rational demonstration but rather a matter of the heart. But this position did not authorize doubts about faith. On the contrary, committed believers tended to hold that the "reasons of the heart" are a surer avenue to religious truth than the deductions of the head.

Blaise Pascal (1623–1662), a genius in science and mathematics, underwent an intense personal conversion, following which he left the world and retired to the Jansenist monastery of Port-Royal near Paris in 1655. He sewed into his clothes a memorial of this experience, containing the words:

> Fire
> "God of Abraham, God of Isaac, God of Jacob,"
> not of the philosophers and scientists.
> Certitude. Certitude. Feeling. Joy. Peace.
> God of Jesus Christ
> "My God and your God"

In the memorial he went on to elaborate on the joy, certitude, and spiritual peace he had found in total submission to Jesus Christ. Reflecting on his conversion, he became convinced that the geometrical method popularized by Descartes was inapplicable to the spheres of metaphysics and faith, which deal with mysteries beyond the reach of human reason. Theological knowledge, for Pascal, rests not on reason and experiment, but rather on authority.[61]

As an apologist Pascal did not hesitate to marshal evidence for the fact of Christian revelation from biblical miracles and prophecies and from the course of human history. But he called attention to the need of the right moral and spiritual dispositions in anyone seeking to interpret these signs. In his *Pensées* he writes: "The heart has reasons, which the reason knows not, as we see in a thousand instances" (626). "It is the heart that is conscious of God, and not the reason. This, then, is faith: God sensible in the heart, not in the reason" (627). And again: "Faith is a gift of God: do not believe that we could ever call it the result of a reasoning process" (629). A little later he concludes: "Do not wonder, then, that certain simple people believe without reasoning. God brings them to love him and to hate themselves. He inclines their hearts to believe. Belief is never strong nor faith unquestioning, except where God Himself has touched the heart" (631).[62]

About the same time a parallel revolt against the formalism of religious life and the aridity of theological teaching occurred in German Protestantism. Philipp Jakob Spener (1635–1705), the founder of Pietism, exemplifies this trend. Together with his disciple August Francke, Spener revitalized some segments of Lutheran Christianity by a renewed emphasis on experiential faith in the living Christ. Although he professed the doctrines of Lutheran Christianity, he placed the emphasis not so much on the content of faith *(fides quae creditur)* as on the act by which we believe *(fides qua creditur)*. As a Lutheran, Spener affirmed that justification is given by faith alone and that good works contribute nothing toward it; he held likewise that faith comes through hearing the word of God, which is the means by which God presents grace to those who believe. But Spener was convinced that many Protestants of his day were deluded by the devil into imagining that they could be saved by faith while living a sinful life. He addressed them as follows:

> You hear the Word of God. This is good. But it is not enough that your ear hears it. Do you let it penetrate inwardly into your heart and allow the heavenly food to be digested there, so that you get the benefit of its vitality and power, or does it go

in one ear and out the other? If the former, then the words of the Lord in Luke 11:28 apply to you: "Blessed are those who hear the Word of God and keep it."[63]

In seventeenth-century England various tendencies may be distinguished: high-church traditionalism, rational religion, enthusiasm, and biblicism.[64] A number of the "Caroline divines," such as Lancelot Andrewes, William Laud, and Jeremy Taylor, held a sacramental form of Christianity nourished by the fathers of the Church. Jeremy Taylor (1613–1667) emphasized the inseparability of Christian faith from obedience and love. "Faith," he wrote, "is not a single star, but a constellation, a chain of graces, called by St. Paul 'the power of God unto salvation of every believer.' " We must move, he says, "from faith believing, to faith obeying, from imperfect faith, to faith made perfect by the animation of charity," thus proceeding "from remission of sins to become the sons of God, and at last to an actual possession of those glories to which we were here consigned by the fruits of the holy Ghost."[65]

The second tendency is exemplified by those Anglicans who were more influenced by the prevailing rationalism of the day. While seeking, as Hooker had done, to maintain both reason and revelation, they showed greater confidence in the powers of reason to establish the essentials of true religion. Archbishop John Tillotson (1630–1694) and Bishop Edward Stillingfleet (1635–1699), while responding to the Deists, conceded that the principal elements of true religion could be established by natural reason and that faith itself was based on rational evidence for the fact of revelation.

The Cambridge Platonists, who were known as Latitudinarians because of their lack of commitment to the specific positions of any one denomination, resembled the theologians just mentioned in their high esteem for reason in religion. Their concept of reason, however, was more Platonic and contemplative. For them it was a power of directly apprehending spiritual reality. John Smith (1616–1652) composed *A Discourse Concerning the True Way or Method of Attaining Divine Knowledge.*[66] He maintained that divine truth is discernible by its "inward beauty" (81) and "inward sweetness and deliciousness" (82), which may be perceived by the senses of the souls of those who are pure of heart and free from sensuality. In his esteem for the heart as an organ of religious knowledge surpassing discursive reason, Smith is reminiscent of Pascal.

The third tendency, enthusiasm, characterized religion as a response to the indwelling light. Some sects, such as the Ranters, discarded all external standards and attended only to the Spirit within themselves. A moderate form of the religion of inner light was advocated by George Fox (1624–1691), the founder of the Society of Friends, popularly known as the Quakers. He looked on the divine light as transcendent, not immanent in the human soul, and as a gift to be implored from God. But the divine testimony was for him a vivid experience and was not necessarily dependent on familiarity with any Scriptures.

The fourth tendency, characteristic of the Puritans, may be called "biblicism." The Westminster Confession (1646) in its first chapter, gave peremptory authority to the canonical Scripture as the word of God. While maintaining that the divine authority of Scripture can be proved by many arguments (essentially the same ones mentioned by Calvin), the Confession went on to say that "our full persuasion of the infallible truth, and divine authority thereof, is from the inward work of the Holy Spirit, bearing witness by and with the Word in our hearts" (chapter I, art. 5). In a later chapter faith is described as "the alone instrument of justification," with the added observation that justifying faith "is no dead faith, but worketh by love" (chapter XI, art. 2).

The Puritan John Owen (1616–1683) gave theological backing to the Westminster Confession in his *The Reason of Faith; or, An Answer Unto That Inquiry, "Wherefore We Believe the Scripture to Be the Word of God"* (1677).[67] He argued that faith could not depend ultimately on arguments, which were necessarily human and fallible, and that an assent based on natural evidence "overthrows the nature of faith" (*Works*, 4:54). Faith in the divine origin of Scripture therefore depends on the Holy Spirit. By its spiritual light, which it derives from its author alone, Scripture infallibly shows itself to be the word of God.[68] Owen maintained that this illumination gives us a spiritual sense of the divine origin and authority of Scripture and evokes assent to the truth contained in it (*Works*, 4:57). Unlike the enthusiasts, Owen held that faith is an assent based on testimony, not an immediate intuition of the truth. The inward testimony of the Holy Spirit inclines us to accept the external testimony of God contained in the Scripture, which is self-authenticating.

John Locke (1632–1704) is notable for his hostility to "enthusiasm," which he described as an attribution of ideas to divine inspiration simply on the basis of feeling. Indirectly, while criticizing enthusiasm, he rejected the positions of intuitionists such as John Smith and biblicists such as John Owen. In his *Essay Concerning Human Understanding* (1690) he ridiculed those who maintain that a proposition "is a revelation because they firmly believe it" and "believe it because it is a revelation" (Book IV, chap. 19, no. 10). Locke held that even though God can reveal truths that are beyond the grasp of reason, we ought not to accept them by faith until it has been shown by reason that they have been revealed. Otherwise it would be impossible to distinguish between the inspirations of the Holy Spirit and the delusions of Satan (IV.19.13).

Locke defined faith in purely intellectual, and indeed propositional, terms as "the assent to any proposition, not thus made out by the deductions of reason, but upon the credit of the proposer, as coming from God, in some extraordinary way of communication," that is to say, by revelation (IV.18.2). Looking on faith as a form of knowledge inferior to reason, Locke recommended great caution in the acceptance of purported revelations. No proposition, he contended, should be entertained "with greater assurance than the proofs it is built upon will warrant" (IV.19.1). Reason, he asserted, "must be our last judge and guide in everything" (IV.19.14).

Occasionally Locke speaks as though the certitude of faith could be absolute, for the testimony of God "is of such an one as cannot deceive or be deceived." The assent of faith based on revelation "absolutely determines our minds, and as perfectly excludes all wavering as our knowledge itself; and we may as well doubt of our own being as we can whether any revelation from God be true. So that faith is a settled and sure principle of assent and assurance, and leaves no manner of room for doubt or hesitation" (IV.16.14).

But Locke then goes on to say that before we assent to any proposition as revealed we must first employ our own reasoning powers to identify it as revealed and to interpret the words in which it is conveyed. The human assertions in which God's word comes to us will have only the relative credibility of human testimony.

In *The Reasonableness of Christianity as Delivered by the Scriptures* (1695) Locke relied principally on biblical prophecies and miracles to accredit Christ as God's messenger. Later, in his *Discourse of Miracles* (1703), he concluded that "The number, variety, and greatness of the miracles wrought for the confirmation of the doctrine delivered by Jesus Christ, carry with them such strong marks of an extraordinary divine power, that the truth of his mission will stand firm and unquestionable, till any one rising up in opposition to him shall do greater miracles than he and his apostles did."[69]


## Eighteenth Century: Philosophers and Evangelicals

The discussion of faith in the eighteenth century continued along the lines set by seventeenth-century Pietists and rationalists. Some of Locke's disciples, such as John Toland, in his *Christianity not Mysterious* (1696), and Matthew Tindal, in his *Christianity as Old as Creation* (1730), reduced biblical revelation to a republication or clarification of the religion of nature. For them, therefore, the realm of faith did not surpass that of reason.

A number of Anglican apologists, such as Samuel Clarke (1675–1729), while opposing Deism, defended Christian revelation chiefly on the ground of its conformity to reason. Joseph Butler (1692–1752), the leading British apologist of his century, argued in *The Analogy of Religion, Natural and Revealed, to the Constitution and Course of Nature* (1736) that Christianity has sufficient probability for it to be reasonably believed. He was typical of his age in avoiding any theological discussion of faith. William Law (1686–1761), an admirer of the German mystic Jakob Böhme, stood against the general tide. In response to Tindal he bluntly asserted that reason is incompetent in the spheres of morality and religion.

On the European continent the debate between rationalists and fideists continued to rage. The French philosopher Pierre Bayle (1647–1706) may be understood either as a rationalist or as a fideist. He asserted paradoxically that faith is contrary to reason, but that it should be followed even in the face of irrefutable objections. Gottfried Wilhelm Leibniz (1646–1716) replied to Bayle in the "Discourse on the Conformity of Faith with Reason" prefixed to his *Theodicy* (1710). Leibniz admitted that some Christian tenets clashed with the lessons of experience and common sense, but he denied that it was possible to prove by strict demonstration that these tenets were false. Although the Christian mysteries may appear improbable when regarded only from the standpoint of reason, they are not absurd and are supported by the authority of Holy Scripture, which is justified by strong motives of credibility. Leibniz added:

> Divine faith itself, when it is kindled in the soul, is something more than an opinion, and depends not upon the occasions or the motives that have given it birth; it advances beyond the intellect, and takes possession of the will and of the heart, to make us act with zeal and joyfully as the law of God commands. Then we have no further need to think of reasons or to pause over the difficulties of argument which the mind may anticipate.[70]

A little later, after citing Luther's response to Erasmus, Leibniz concludes: "One may therefore say that the triumph of true reason illumined by divine grace is at the same time the triumph of faith and love" (no. 45, p. 22).

The German dramatist and critic, Gotthold Ephraim Lessing (1729–1781), distinguished sharply between the necessary truths of reason and the "accidental" truths of history. On the ground that it was impossible to pass from the probable arguments of history to the spiritual truths of faith, Lessing rejected the historical proofs of Christianity based on biblical miracles and prophecies. Christianity, he maintained, must be accepted on the basis of its inner truth, insofar as it speaks with certainty to the heart.[71]

One of the few eighteenth-century theologians who addressed the question of faith in depth was the New England Calvinist Jonathan Edwards (1703–1758). In an unpublished theological memorandum he discussed faith under the aspects of belief, trust, and obedience, but ended by describing it primarily in terms of union: "Faith is the proper active union of the soul with Christ as our Saviour, as revealed to us in the gospel."[72] Justifying faith, he comments, is the soul's "entirely embracing the revelation of Jesus Christ as our Saviour." As approximate synonyms for "embracing" he proposes "adhering," "acquiescing," and "entire yielding of the mind and heart" (495). The certainty of faith, according to Edwards, cannot be achieved by logical arguments but only by an immediate apprehension of the beauty and excellence of the divine message.

Edwards frequently describes the light of faith in language borrowed from sense experience. For example, in a sermon of 1731, "God Glorified in Man's Dependence," he describes faith as "a sensibleness of what is real in the work of redemption."[73] In 1734, taking as his text the words of Jesus to Peter, "Flesh and blood have not revealed it unto thee," he preached on the necessity of "a spiritual and divine light" immediately imparted to the soul by God. Unlike inspiration, he explained, this spiritual light does not reveal new truths but "gives a due apprehension of those things that are taught in the word of God." It instills "a real sense and apprehension of the divine excellency of things revealed in the word of God" and "a saving conviction of the truth and reality of these things"[74] He then moves into the language of conversion and transformation. The divine illumination, he explains, "conforms the heart to the gospel" and "changes the soul into an image of the same glory that is beheld," so that the heart is able to embrace the joyful tidings "and entirely to adhere to, and acquiesce in, the revelation of Christ as our Saviour." The whole soul, thus disposed to "symphonize" with the revelation, cleaves to it with full inclination and affection, and gives itself up entirely to Christ (19).

In a series of sermons preached in 1741–1742, subsequently collected as *A Treatise Concerning Religious Affections*, Edwards applies these principles to the problem of discerning the authenticity of the phenomena surrounding the Great Awakening then in progress. Against those who would insist that believers should walk in darkness, blindly trusting in Christ, Edwards maintains that genuine faith is always accompanied by spiritual enlightenment and holy experience. "Men not only can't exercise faith without some spiritual light, but they can exercise faith only just in such proportion as they have spiritual light."[75] Salvific conviction of the truth of revelation depends upon the mind being enlightened by the Spirit of God (296). The Spirit gives a sense and taste of the divine and holy excellence of the things exhibited in the gospel (297). In judging whether persons have saving faith, we may look for various signs or marks of the Holy Spirit. Among the twelve that he lists, Edwards attaches chief importance to the last, practice. Whenever people are truly close to Christ by faith, they will manifest that closeness by their actual conduct. Edwards therefore favors "experimental religion," which brings religious affections to the test of fact (452). In his final pages Edwards shows that his position is consistent with the doctrine of justification by faith alone (455–61).

No individual in the eighteenth century contributed more to the resurgence of religion than the English founder of Methodism, John Wesley (1703–1791). His own conversion was inspired by Luther's teaching on faith in his Preface to the *Epistle to the Romans*. In a famous entry in his *Journal*, dated May 24, 1738, he describes how he was affected by hearing a reading from this Preface by one of the Moravian Brethren in London. "About a quarter before nine [in the evening], while he was describing the change which God works in the heart through faith in Christ, I felt my heart strangely warmed. I felt I did trust in Christ; Christ, alone for salvation; and an assurance was given me that he had taken away *my* sins, even *mine*, and saved *me* from the law of sin and death."[76]

From then on faith became one of the favorite themes of Wesley's preaching. The first sermon in his collected works, preached at St. Mary's in Oxford on June 11, 1738, is on the text "By grace ye are saved through faith" (Eph 2:8). Here and elsewhere he proposes a doctrine of faith that synthesizes the early Reformation concern for justification by faith alone with an insistence on the experience of conversion and on personal holiness that is reminiscent of the Pietism of Spener.

Wesley derives his basic, or generic, conception of faith from the Epistle to the Hebrews. For him "Faith in general is a divine, supernatural ʼἔλεγχος, evidence or conviction 'of things not seen,' not discoverable by our bodily senses, as being either past, future or spiritual."[77] Since nothing is in the intellect that was not previously in the senses, natural human understanding cannot attain to the world of the spirit. Faith, however, supplies for this defect and gives conviction about matters that concern the human soul, angelic beings, the triune God, the final judgment, heaven, and hell (Sermon 117, *Works*, 4:29–34).

Wesley allows for a great variety in the kinds and degrees of faith. The lowest, which does not really deserve to be called faith at all, is that of the materialist, who denies the being of God. Slightly higher in the scale is the faith of the Deist, who accepts the existence of God, but denies biblical revelation. Still higher is the faith of good pagans, from whom little will be required since they have received but little. They may learn the essentials of true religion if they hearken to God's inward voice. The Mohammedans, Wesley believes, are in a condition similar to the heathen. Above them are the Jews, at least the ancient Jews, who lived according to God's law and looked forward to the coming of Christ. Within the highest degree of faith, that of Christians, Wesley prefers that of Protestants, who accept the written word as the sole rule of faith, to that of Roman Catholics, who have made additions, notably at the Council of Trent. But the additions, Wesley concedes, do not so contradict the faith once delivered to the saints as to render it of no effect (Sermon 106, *Works*, 2:493–496).

Following the Reformers, Wesley is ready to say that faith is the condition, and indeed the only condition, of justification (Sermon 5, *Works*, 1:195). "Grace is the source, faith the condition of salvation" (Sermon 1, *Works*, 1:118). He sees the effect of faith not simply as forensic justification but as salvation from sin, from guilt for past sin, from servile fear, and from the power of sin. Although it is impossible to be justified or saved by good works, justifying faith is "necessarily productive of all good works and holiness" (Sermon 1, *Works*, 1:125). "If good works do not follow our faith," he writes, "even all inward and outward holiness, it is plain that our faith is nothing worth; we are yet in our sins" (Sermon 35, *Works*, 2:28).

For Wesley, then, faith in the sense of mere conviction that certain things are true cannot be salvific (Sermon 106, *Works*, 2:496). Justifying faith "is not barely a speculative, rational thing, a cold lifeless assent, a train of ideas in the head; but also a disposition of the heart" (Sermon 1, *Works*, 1:121). When John writes that whoever believes that Jesus is the Christ is born of God (1 Jn 5:1), he cannot be speaking of a barely notional or speculative faith, or bare assent to the proposition. This would be the faith of devils, dead faith. True faith, by contrast, is more than an act of understanding; it is "a disposition which God hath wrought in his heart" (Sermon 18; *Works*, 1:418).

To describe the two kinds of faith, Wesley often distinguishes between the faith of a servant and that of a son, or child, of God. The former kind of faith "has evidence of the spiritual world so far as it can exist without living experience" (Sermon 117, *Works*, 4:35). If they are faithful to the light given them, servants of God will in time receive the adoption of sons, and will be able to confess, "The life that I now live, I live by faith in the Son of God, who loved me and gave himself for me" (Gal 2:20; Sermon 106; *Works*, 2:498). Every Christian should covet the best gifts and seek to follow the more excellent way (ibid.). This latter kind of faith involves a fuller assurance of faith, given by the Holy Spirit witnessing to our spirits that we are children of God (Sermon 117, *Works*, 4:36). In describing this full assurance, Wesley likes to quote in Greek the New Testament term, πληροφορίαπίστεως (Heb 10:22; see Sermon 18, *Works*, 1:423; Sermon 117, *Works*, 4:36).

In speaking of the living experience of conversion, Wesley sometimes uses the language of illumination in a manner reminiscent of Edwards. This is notably the case in Sermon 119, preached in 1788, on "Walking by Sight and Walking by Faith" (*Works*, 4:49–59). God, he says, commands his light to shine in the hearts of those to whom he reveals. Those who walk by faith, although they do not live by sight, have the eyes of their understanding opened (Eph 1:18). They continually see "the light of the glorious love of God in the face of Jesus Christ" (2 Cor 4:6 as quoted in *Works*, 4:56).

Wesley's attitude toward "enthusiasm" differs sharply from that of Locke and Butler. In dismissing the true spirit of religion as enthusiasm, he says, the modern world imitates Festus, who regarded Paul as driven to madness by his faith (cf. Acts 26:24). Those who have acquired the art of forgetting God suppose "that the experience of the invisible, eternal world is nothing but the waking dreams of a heated imagination" (Sermon 119, *Works*, 4:58).

Like Edwards, Wesley sees the need of criteria for evaluating true Christian faith-experience. In a sermon, "The Marks of the New Birth," he attends to the fruits of faith, which he enumerates as four: power over sin, peace, lively hope, and love. The greatest of these marks, he holds, is love of God, which is inseparable from love of neighbor and from obedience to God's commands.

The evidence for revealed religion was critically assessed by the Scottish empiricist philosopher David Hume (1711–1776). The conclusions of Hume, the skeptic, resemble, in a curious way, those of William Law, the fideist. Both agree that faith cannot be grounded in reason, as Locke and others had maintained. Hume's *Essay of Miracles* ranks as a classic.[78] Defining a miracle as a violation of the laws of nature, and assuming that "firm and unalterable experience has established these laws," Hume reasons that the nonoccurrence of miracles is always more likely than the truth of the human testimony supporting them. The falsehood of the biblical accounts, accordingly, is more probable than the reality of the miracles recounted in Scripture. Divine revelation consequently cannot be established from reason, as Locke and others attempted to do. Hume ends his critique with a curious assertion:

> Our most holy religion is founded on faith, not on reason. . . . Mere reason is insufficient to convince us of its veracity. And whoever is moved by faith to assent to it is conscious of a continued miracle in his own person which subverts all the principles of his understanding and gives him a determination to believe what is most contrary to custom and experience.[79]

Johann Georg Hamann and Søren Kierkegaard would subsequently espouse the very fideism that Hume here proposes with evident irony. They would argue that faith, not being founded on reason, needs no rational supports and is incapable of being rationally refuted.

Toward the end of the century Immanuel Kant (1724–1804) enthusiastically heralded the advent of Enlightenment. The main point of Enlightenment, he maintained, was "man's release from his self-caused immaturity, primarily *in matters of religion*."[80] By immaturity he meant "the incapacity to use one's intelligence without the guidance of another" (132). The motto of the Enlightenment for Kant was "*Sapere aude!* Have the courage to use your own intelligence!" (ibid.).

In such a framework it might seem that faith would be excluded. Kant, however, made room for faith by redefining it, no longer as belief accepted on external authority, but rather as belief resting on motives that are subjectively sufficient and objectively insufficient. In his *Critique of Pure Reason* (1781) he distinguished three kinds of belief.[81] The first, pragmatic belief, was a conclusion reached on the basis of limited evidence, in which a risk or gamble is taken, as happens when a physician, on the basis of a few symptoms, prescribes a treatment for phthisis, knowing full well that others might make a different diagnosis. Belief in a stronger sense is realized when, in matters that defy cogent proof, we make a speculative judgment on grounds that we judge to be persuasive. Kant regarded the teleological argument for the existence of God, for example, as capable of sustaining a faith of this kind. The assent in these cases was, according to Kant, somewhat lacking in stability because of the unresolved speculative difficulties.

Belief or faith in the strongest sense, for Kant, meant moral belief. This occurs when it becomes evident, on the basis of moral experience, that a given end is absolutely necessary and that something further is implied as the only possible condition under which the end can be attainable in practice. As an example, Kant submitted that we perceive through moral experience that we are unconditionally obliged to keep the moral law and that this obligation could have no practical force unless there were a God and a future life. Such practical reasoning can lead, not indeed to knowledge in the strict sense, but to moral certitude based on one's own moral sentiments. The grounds for affirming the existence of God and of the future life are subjectively certain but objectively insufficient.

In his *Critique of Practical Reason* (1788) and his *Critique of Judgment* (1790) Kant explored in greater depth the transcendental ideas of freedom, immortality, and God as postulates of moral reason or practical faith. On the basis of moral experience, he concluded, we are driven to postulate human freedom, personal immortality, and the existence of God as conditions of possibility for the categorical imperatives of the moral law. Faith, he argued, has its proper ground in the voice of conscience and in the sense of moral obligation.

A somewhat broader concept of faith emerges in Kant's *Religion within the Bounds of Reason Alone* (1793). Only a rational faith, grounded on the postulates of pure practical reason, can serve as the basis of a universal religion. Positive or statutory religion, therefore, should not be proposed as essential. But Kant does not reject the possibility that God, as educator of the human race, may have used the symbols of historical religion to bring certain peoples to a closer approximation of pure rational religion than they could otherwise have attained. Kant speaks of "parerga," by which he means aspects of religious life or doctrine that rational religion can neither integrate into itself nor reasonably ignore. In this category he places special revelation, grace, miracles, and mysteries. In his final thought, therefore, Kant does not exclude faith in a gracious providence, though as a philosopher he does not clearly affirm it. Pure rational faith remains for him the norm and goal of all religion, whether natural or statutory.[82]

## Catholic Orthodoxy

In the Catholic clerical world of the eighteenth century, textbooks of dogmatic theology intended principally for the instruction of seminarians continued to be produced in much the same style as in previous centuries. Among the Dominicans the Belgian Charles René Billuart (1685–1757) is eminent for clarity and learning.[83] He stands very much in the tradition of his Dominican predecessors, including John of St. Thomas (1589–1644) and Cardinal Vincenzo Ludovico Gotti (1664–1742). Like them, he defends the necessity of a supernatural formal object for infused faith. Faith, he holds, is ultimately motivated by the authority of God who reveals, and the motive is coaffirmed in belief in the contents of revelation. On the question of credibility, Billuart follows St. Thomas, as interpreted by other Dominicans. As a man of his own day, Billuart argues against the "pestilential errors" of the Deists that the credibility of the Christian faith can be established from biblical miracles and prophecies, as well as from the wonderful propagation of the faith.

The Jesuits, for their part, issued at Würzburg in 1766–1771 a fourteen-volume summa of dogmatic theology commonly known as the *Theologia Wirceburgensis*. The treatise on faith is by Heinrich Kilber (1710–1783), the most prominent of the four authors of this collective work.[84] Like Billuart, Kilber takes up the standard questions debated in the treatises of the seventeenth century, and does not claim originality. As a Jesuit, he insists strongly against the Jansenists on God's universal salvific will and on the possibility for salvation even of the unevangelized, while taking care all the while not to defend any of the propositions condemned by Innocent XI. He asserts the probability that explicit faith in Christ is not a necessary means of salvation, even under the new law (no. 127, p. 109). He follows Suarez in holding that the motives of credibility are merely a disposing cause for the act of faith, which is formally motivated by the authority of God who reveals (nos. 160–62, p. 140). Grace is necessary to give infallible firmness to the assent of faith (no. 198, p. 170), but grace does not add a new motive of credibility, since it is not a known object and does not provide any new content (nos. 178–79, pp. 150–51). Following de Lugo, he maintains that there can be no irresistible evidence of the fact of revelation (no. 210, pp. 180–82).

As these theses indicate, Kilber is not a creative speculative theologian. He writes a textbook designed for seminary students. The burning questions of the age, which he sought to address, were not dogmatic but rather, apologetic. Kilber's colleague, Ignaz Neubauer (1726–1795) provided a full reply to the Deists and other adversaries in another part of the Würzburg course. About the same time, another Jesuit, a Bavarian, Benedict Stattler (1728–1797), produced apologetical treatises influenced by the rationalism of Christian Wolff. To this extent he rejoined seventeenth-century apologists such as Elizalde, mentioned earlier.

## Conclusion

The period surveyed in this chapter may be said to span the transition from medieval to modern times. It is marked by greater tensions and conflicts among Christians regarding the nature and functions of faith than any previous era.

The sixteenth century is dominated by the controversies between Protestants and Catholics on the question of faith and justification. The Protestant position, leaning toward justification by "faith alone," conceived in a fiducial manner, is set forth with different nuances by Luther, Melanchthon, and Calvin. The Catholic response, which regards faith as an assent and as merely preparatory for justification, and which speaks of charity and good works as necessary for salvation, receives offical expression in the Council of Trent. In the post-Tridentine period Chemnitz and the Formula of Concord solidify the Lutheran position. The issues continue to be debated by theologians such as Bellarmine, representing the Catholic view, and Gerhard, representing the Lutheran view.

In Spain mystics such as John of the Cross develop a profound spirituality of faith that builds on medieval Scholastic psychology and is in some ways reminiscent of the mysticism of Greek patristic thought.

Suarez and de Lugo, at the dawn of the seventeenth century, engage in thorough and subtle discussions about technical issues concerning the formal object of faith. They make a sharp distinction between the judgment of credibility, which is in principle purely natural, and the assent of faith, which is necessarily supernatural. They also break new ground in exploring the problems raised by the new voyages of discovery concerning the salvation of the unevangelized. Their relative optimism, severely contested at the time by the Jansenists and other conservative Augustinians, was to prevail in official Catholic teaching in the nineteenth and twentieth centuries.

The new climate of rationalism introduced by Descartes and Spinoza had serious implications for the theology of faith, as recognized by Locke, Hume, and Bayle. Some theologians, such as Samuel Clarke, submit faith to purely rational criteria, and move toward Deism. Others, like Pascal, Spener, and Law, abandon the search for rational supports and rely instead on "reasons of the heart." A mediating school, represented by John Smith, George Fox, John Owen, and especially Jonathan Edwards, maintains that faith can be securely based on spiritual experience and the inward assurances given by the Holy Spirit. John Wesley combines a typically Reformation insistence on faith alone and Scripture alone with a Pietist appeal to the inner experience of conversion.

Dominicans and Jesuits of the eighteenth century continue to produce voluminous textbooks heavily dependent on the post-Tridentine Scholastics for their theology of faith. In this framework they seek to refute the attacks of contemporary unbelievers. They especially seek to defend the historicity of the biblical miracles.

Toward the end of the eighteenth century Kant approached the theology of faith from a new direction, on the basis of his distinction between speculative and practical reason. His reformulation of the issues was to have enormous repercussions in the theology of the nineteenth century.

## Notes

1. On Luther see Brian A. Gerrish, *Grace and Reason: A Study in the Theology of Luther* (Oxford: Clarendon, 1962); Gerhard Ebeling, *Luther: An Introduction to His Thought* (Philadelphia: Fortress, 1964); Paul Althaus, *The Theology of Martin Luther* (Philadelphia: Fortress, 1966); Otto H. Pesch, *Theologie der Rechtfertigung bei Martin Luther und Thomas von Aquin* (Mainz: Matthias-Grünewald, 1967); Daniel Olivier, *Luther's Faith: The Cause of the Gospel in the Church* (St. Louis: Concordia, 1982).

2. Martin Luther, "Die Promotionsdisputation von Petrus Hegemon" WA 39[II], 364–65; cf. Althaus, *Theology of Martin Luther*, 52–53, especially note 29.

3. Idem, Commentary on Galatians, 1535; LW 26:229.

4. Idem, "A Brief Explanation of the Ten Commandments, the Creed, and the Lord's Prayer" (1520) WA 7:215; *Works of Martin Luther*, vol. 2 (Philadelphia: Muhlenburg Press, 1943), 368.

5. E.g., in Luther's German translation of the Bible, Rom 3:28 (WA DB 7:38); also in his Smalcald Articles 2.1.4–5; *The Book of Concord* ed. and trans. Theodore G. Tappert (Philadelphia: Fortress, 1959), 292.

6. Luther, "Theses Concerning Faith and Law," On Faith, Thesis 18; LW 34:111.

7. Idem, "Freedom of a Christian," LW 31:352 (WA 7 Lat. 42–49).

8. Idem, "Preface to the New Testament," LW 35:361.

9. Ibid.

10. Idem, "Preface to the Romans," LW 35:370–71.

11. Philipp Melanchthon, "Apology for the Augsburg Confession," 4:194, with reference to 1 Cor 3:8; *The Book of Concord*, 133.

12. On Calvin see Edward A. Dowey, *The Knowledge of God in Calvin's Theology* (New York: Columbia University Press, 1952); Wilhelm Niesel, *The Theology of Calvin* (Philadelphia: Westminster, 1956); Walter E. Steuermann, *A Critical Study of Calvin's Concept of Faith* (Doctoral Dissertation, Tulsa, Okla.; Ann Arbor, Mich.: Edward Brothers, 1952); Victor A. Shepherd, *The Nature and Function of Faith in the Theology of John Calvin* (NABPR Dissertation series, vol. 2. Macon, Ga.: Mercer University Press, 1983).

13. The *Institutes* are here cited according to the Library of Living Classics edition, vols. 20–21, ed. John T. McNeill (Philadelphia: Westminster, 1960).

14. "It is faith that gains the giving of the Spirit." Luther, *Lectures on Galatians* (1519) 4:6; LW 27:291.

15. On the Regensburg Colloquy, see Jill Raitt, "From Augsburg to Trent," in *Justification by Faith: Lutherans and Catholics in Dialogue 7*, ed. H. George Anderson et al. (Minneapolis: Augsburg, 1985), 200–17.

16. Regarding the handling of faith in the Decree on Justification, see Hubert Jedin, *A History of the Council of Trent*, vol. 2 (St. Louis: B. Herder, 1961), 166–316.

17. The term *promeretur* certainly excludes strict, or condign, merit. It probably leaves open the question whether justification can be congruously merited. See *Justification by Faith*, 324, note 96.

18. Adolf Harnack, *History of Dogma*, vol. 7 (New York: Dover Publications, 1968), 57.

19. Calvin, *Acta synodi tridentinae. Cum Antidoto,* CR 35:442–506.

20. Martin Chemnitz, *Examination of the Council of Trent*, vol. 1 (St. Louis: Concordia, 1971), Ninth Topic "Concerning Faith," 545–611.

21. Robert Bellarmine, *Disputationes . . .* in *Opera Omnia* (Naples: Giuliano, 1856–62), vol. 4, Part 1, *De justificatione*, Bk. 1, *De fide justificante*, 461–503.

22. Johann Gerhard, *Loci theologici* 16:120; quoted by Robert P. Scharlemann, *Thomas Aquinas and John Gerhard* (New Haven, Conn.: Yale University Press, 1964), 227.

23. A concise summary of Lutheran orthodox positions on faith may be found in Heinrich Schmid, *The Doctrinal Theology of the Evangelical Lutheran Church* 3d ed., rev. and trans. from the German (Minneapolis: Augsburg, 1961; reprint of 1899 ed.). For further information about the theologians and the theological trends, see Robert D. Preus, *The Theology of Post-Reformation Lutheranism* (St. Louis: Concordia, 1970).

24 Quoted from *Reformed Confessions of the 16th Century*, ed. Arthur C. Cochrane (Philadelphia: Westminster, 1966), 257.

25. Ibid., 308.

26. The following brief summary is based on quotations in Heinrich Heppe, *Reformed*

*Dogmatics*, ed. Ernst Bizer (London: George, Allen & Unwin, 1950; reprinted, Grand Rapids, Mich.: Baker, 1978), 526–42.

27. Text and commentary in E. J. Bicknell, *A Theological Introduction to the Thirty-Nine Articles of the Church of England*, 3d ed., rev. by H. J. Carpenter (London: Longmans, Green and Co., 1955), 199.

28. *Certain Sermons or Homilies, Appointed to be read in churches in the time of the late Queen Elizabeth* (Oxford: Oxford University Press, 1832). These homilies are usually printed in the works of Thomas Cranmer, their reputed author.

29. See *Miscellaneous Writings and Letters of Thomas Cranmer* (Cambridge, Eng.: Cambridge University Press, 1846), 128–34 and 135–41. On Cranmer's theology of faith see G. W. Bromiley, *Thomas Cranmer the Theologian* (New York: Oxford University Press, 1956), 28–41.

30. Richard Hooker, *Of the Laws of Ecclesiastical Polity*, 3 vols. (Cambridge, Mass.: Belknap, 1977). See especially Bks. 2–3 in first volume.

31. Idem, "A Learned and Comfortable Sermon," included in Everyman's Library edition of the *Laws of Ecclesiastical Polity* (London: J. M. Dent, 1907, reprinted 1925), 2.

32. *The Ascent of Mount Carmel*, in *The Collected Works of St. John of the Cross*, ed. Kieran Kavanaugh (Washington, D.C.: Institute of Carmelite Studies, 1973), Book II, chapter 6, no. 2. On John of the Cross see M.-Michel Labourdette, "La Foi théologale et la connaissance mystique d'après S. Jean de la Croix," *Revue thomiste* 41 (1936): 593–624; 42 (1937): 16–57, 189–229; Kieran Kavanaugh, "St. John of the Cross on Faith," *Spiritual Life* 5 (1959): 277–87, and Karol Wojtyla, *Faith According to St. John of the Cross* (San Francisco: Ignatius, 1981).

33. On the Dominicans and Jesuits of the sixteenth century Salamanca school, see Elios Giuseppe Mori, *Il Motivo della Fede da Gaetano a Suarez* (Rome: Gregorian University, 1953).

34. Francisco Suarez, *De fide*, posthumously published, 1619, in his *Opera omnia*, vol. 12 (Paris: Vivès, 1858), 7–596. On Suarez's theology of faith see Mori, *Il Motivo*, 167–81; Heinrich Petri, *Glaube und Gotteserkenntnis von der Reformation bis zur Gegenwart,* Handbuch der Dogmengeschichte I/2c (Freiburg: Herder, 1985), 86–91.

35. Suarez, *De fide*, disp. 3, sec. 4, no. 7; 12:54.

36. Ibid., disp. 3, sec. 6, no. 8; 12:66.

37. Ibid., disp. 6, sec. 4, no. 4; 12:176.

38. Juan de Lugo, *Tractatus de virtute fidei divinae* in his *Disputationes scholasticae et morales*, vol. 1 (Paris: Vivès, 1868), disp. 1, sec. 6, no. 77, p. 29. On de Lugo, see Petri, *Glaube und Gotteserkenntnis*, 91–98.

39. de Lugo, *De virtute fidei*, disp. 1, sec. 6, nos. 99–105; 1:37–39.

40. Ibid., sec. 7, nos. 114–31; 1:42–49.

41. Ibid., sec. 10, nos. 194–95; 1:70.

42. Salmanticenses, *Cursus theologicus*, vol. 9 (Paris: Palme, 1878), *Tractatus XIV, De gratia Dei*, disp. 3, *De necessitate gratiae ad ea quae sunt ordinis supernaturalis*, especially *Dubium* 3, nos. 25–55.

43. Ibid., vol. 11 (Paris: Palme, 1879), *Tractatus XVII, De Fide, Disputatio I, De Objecto Fidei, dubium 5, Utrum assensus fidei resolvatur ultimo in primam veritatem*. The interpretation of these texts has given rise to some disagreement. Stéphane Harent in his article "Foi" for the *Dictionnaire de théologie catholique*, cols. 472 and 492, attributed to the Salamanca Carmelites the view that faith is a conclusion from two prior premises and that a purely natural knowledge of the formal motive suffices for the supernatural act of faith. Dulau seems to be correct in arguing that on both points Harent misinterpreted the texts. See Pierre Dulau, "Notes et Discussions. La Pensée de Suarez et celle des Salmanticenses dans la ques-

tion, 'De ultima fidei resolutione.' L'Opinion de Harent," *Revue thomiste* 31 (1926): 517–22.

44. On this theme, see Louis Capéran, *Le problème du salut des infidèles*, vol. 1, *Essai historique*, rev. ed. (Paris: Beauchesne, 1934); Stéphane Harent, "Infidèles (Salut des)," *DTC* 7:1726–1930; Francis A. Sullivan, *Salvation Outside the Church?: Tracing the History of the Catholic Response* (New York: Paulist, 1992).

45. Luther, "Large Catechism" 2:45; in *Book of Concord*, 416.

46. Calvin, *Institutes*, Bk. III, chap. 21, no. 7; cf. chap. 24, no. 16.

47. Ibid., Bk. I, chap. 3, no. 1.

48. Cited by Capéran, *Salut des infidèles*, 1:242–43.

49. Ibid., 1:231.

50. Jacobus Payva d'Andrada, *Orthodoxarum explicationum . . . libri decem* (Venice, 1564), quoted by Chemnitz in his *Examination of the Council of Trent*, Sixth Topic, sec. 1, no. 7; 1:393.

51. Chemnitz, ibid., no. 4; 1:391.

52. Suarez, *De fide*, disp. 12 (*Opera*, 12:334–60). Some quotations are given in English in Sullivan, *Salvation Outside the Church?*, 91–94.

53. "Unde etiam dici potest medium necessarium, quamvis non semper in re, sed vel in re vel in voto," *De fide*, disp. 12, sec. 4, no. 10 (*Opera* 12:353).

54. Juan Martinez de Ripalda, *De ente supernaturali*, Bk. I, disp. 20, sec. 3, nos. 11–15; vol. 1 (Paris: Palmé, 1870), 154–56. On Ripalda's views on the salvation of the "infidels" see Capéran, *Salut des Infidèles*, 1:332–43, 348–50; also Harent, "Infidèles (Salut des)," cols. 1764–70.

55. De Lugo, *Tractatus de virtute fidei divinae*, disp. 12, sec. 1–4, pp. 385–426; cf. Capéran, *Salut des Infidèles*, 1:343–51; Sullivan, *Salvation Outside the Church?*, 94–98.

56. Antoine Arnauld, *De la nécessité de la foi en Jésus Christ pour être sauvé . . .*, Part IV, chap. 5; cf. Capéran, *Salut des infidèles*, 1:326–27. This book of Arnault, posthumously published in 1701, is reprinted in *Oeuvres d'Arnauld* (Paris, 1777), 10:39–377. See also Sullivan, *Salvation Outside the Church?*, 101.

57. For commentary see Roger Aubert, *Le problème de l'acte de foi*, 2d ed. (Louvain, E. Warny, 1950), 87–102.

58. See Gerhard Heinz, *Divinam christianae religionis originem probare* (Mainz: Grünewald, 1984), 63–79. Heinz finds in Elizalde and Gonzalez the beginnings of the "apologetical rationalism" that would arise in the eighteenth century, stemming more directly from Christian Wolff (79, notes 281 and 282).

59. Benedict Spinoza, *Theologico-Political Treatise* (New York: Dover Publications, 1951), 184.

60. Ibid., 185. On Spinoza see Leo Strauss, *Spinoza's Critique of Religion* (New York: Schocken, 1965).

61. Blaise Pascal, "Préface sur le traité du vide," in *Opuscules et lettres (choix)*, ed. L. Lafuma (Paris: Aubier, 1955), 50.

62. The *Pensées* are here cited from *The Essential Pascal*, ed. Robert W. Gleason (New York: Mentor Omega Books, 1966), 195–96.

63. Philipp Jakob Spener, *Pia Desideria*, trans. Theodore G. Tappert (Philadelphia: Fortress, 1964), 66.

64. See Basil Willey, *The Seventeenth Century Background* (London: Chatto Windus, 1949) and H. D. McDonald, *Ideas of Revelation: An Historical Study* (London: Macmillan, 1959).

65. Jeremy Taylor, "Discourse VIII of Faith," in *Selected Works*, ed. Thomas K. Carroll (New York: Paulist, 1990), 277–90, at 282 and 283.

66. Text in Gerald R. Cragg, ed., *The Cambridge Platonists* (Oxford: Oxford University Press, 1968), 76–90; also in C. A. Patrides, ed., *The Cambridge Platonists* (Cambridge, Mass.: Harvard University Press, 1970), 128–44. John Smith will here be cited according to pagination in the Cragg edition.

67. John Owen, *Works*, ed. W. Goold, vol. 4 (1850–1853; London: Banner of Truth Trust, reprint, 1968). On Owen, see Paul Helm, *The Varieties of Belief* (New York: Humanities Press, 1973), 104–14, and Jack B. Rogers and Donald K. McKim, *The Authority and Interpretation of the Bible* (San Francisco: Harper Row, 1979), 218–23.

68. Rogers and McKim, *Authority and Interpretation*, 220.

69. John Locke, *Works*, rev. ed., 10 vols. (London, 1823; reprinted Aalen, Germany: Scientia Verlag, 1963)), 9:256–65, quotation from 261; see Avery Dulles, *History of Apologetics* (New York: Corpus, 1971), 138–40; Helm, *The Varieties of Belief*, 85–92.

70. Gottfried Leibniz, "Preliminary Dissertation on the Conformity of Faith with Reason", no. 29, *Theodicy* (Indianapolis, Ind.: Bobbs-Merrill, Library of Liberal Arts, 1966), 16.

71. See Gotthold Lessing, "On the Proof of the Spirit and of Power" (1777) in *Lessing's Theological Writings*, ed. Henry Chadwick, (Stanford, Cal.: Stanford University Press, 1957), 51–57.

72. "Concerning Faith," *Miscellaneous Remarks on Important Doctrines*, in Jonathan Edwards, *Works*, 10 vols. (New York: Burt Franklin, 1968), 8:507.

73. "Sermon: God Glorified in Man's Dependence," Ibid., 6:448.

74. Sermon I, "A Divine and Supernatural Light" (1734), Ibid., 8:7–8.

75. Idem, *A Treatise Concerning Religious Affections*, in *Works* (New Haven, Conn.: Yale University Press, 1959), 2:176.

76. Extracts from John Wesley's *Journal*, in *John and Charles Wesley: Selected Writings and Hymns* (New York: Paulist, 1981), 99–107, at 107.

77. John Wesley, *Works*, ed. Albert C. Outler (Nashville, Tenn.: Abingdon) vol. 1 (1984), 194; cf. vol. 2 (1985), 492; vol. 4 (1987), 30, 52. Subsequent references in the text will be according to this edition.

78. See A. E. Taylor, *David Hume and the Miraculous*, (Cambridge, Eng.: Cambridge University Press, 1927). A lucid explanation of Hume's philosophy of religion may be found in James Collins, *The Emergence of Philosophy of Religion* (New Haven, Conn.: Yale University Press, 1967), 3–88.

79. Hume, "Of Miracles," Chapter 10 in *An Inquiry concerning Human Understanding*, ed. Charles W. Hendel (Library of Liberal Arts. Indianapolis, Ind.: Bobbs-Merrill, 1955), at 140–41.

80. "What Is Enlightenment?" (1784) in *Immanuel Kant's Moral and Political Writings*, ed. Carl J. Friedrich (New York: Modern Library, 1949), 138–39; emphasis Kant's.

81. Kant, *Critique of Pure Reason* (Garden City, N.Y.: Doubleday Anchor Books, 1966), 523–29.

82. On this work of Kant see Michel Despland, *Kant on History and Religion* (Montreal: McGill University, 1973).

83. *Summa Sancti Thomae hodiernis academiarum moribus accommodata, sive Cursus theologiae juxta mentem divi Thomae*, vol. 9, *Tractatus de Fide et regulis fidei* (Paris: Méquignon, 1820).

84. RR. Patrum Societatis Jesu, *Theologia Dogmatica*, editio altera (Paris: Julien, Lanier, 1852), 4:45–198.

# 4

# Nineteenth Century

## Protestant Philosophical Theologians

The early nineteenth century, in Germany as elsewhere, was marked by a lively romantic revival typified by literary figures such as Johann Gottfried Herder (1744–1803), Friedrich Schlegel (1772–1829), and Friedrich Hölderlin (1770–1843). The philosopher Friedrich Heinrich Jacobi (1743–1819), while while sharing Kant's views on the limited range of knowledge, *(Verstand),* exalted the faculty of the higher reason *(Vernunft),* which he regarded as capable of attaining the divine in an intuitive manner. Faith for him was the inner illumination of the higher reason, an achievement of the heart *(Gemüt)* rather than of the speculative reason.[1]

Friedrich D. E. Schleiermacher (1768–1834), after being educated in the Pietism of the Moravian Brotherhood, went to Berlin, where he became associated with Schlegel and others in the romantic movement. Schleiermacher agreed with Kant's critique of the speculative reason, but did not follow his moralism. Like Jacobi, he gave a more existential and affective meaning to the term "faith." The concepts of piety, religion, and faith in his usage blend into one another.

Schleiermacher's youthful discourses *On Religion* (1799) eloquently speak of faith as a sense of the presence of the divine Spirit that is the source of unity and beauty in the world. He dismisses as servile the notion of faith as a mere acceptance of what other persons have said. This base view of faith, he warns, must be rejected by all who would enter into the sanctuary of religion.[2]

In his magnum opus, *The Christian Faith,*[3] Schleiermacher begins with the concept of piety, which he defines as the consciousness of being absolutely dependent (#4, p. 12). This feeling of absolute dependence is a consciousness of God, who is the condition of possibility of any such feeling. By faith in God, Schleiermacher means the certainty that the feeling of dependence expresses a relationship to a transcendent reality. Every religious community, he continues, has a distinct form of piety, depending on the particular origin of that community. The originality of the fact that lies at the source of a religious community is what Schleiermacher understands by revelation (#10, p. 50). Hence every religion is revealed. Each religion, moreover, has a faith corresponding to the certainty that accompanies its specific form of self-consciousness.

Jesus Christ, according to Schleiermacher, had a uniquely powerful consciousness of God and makes it possible for us to share in this through the Church. Faith in Christ, as the certainty of having been redeemed by him and having entered into his God-consciousness, is the prerequisite of participation in the Christian community (#14, p. 68). Faith consists not primarily of knowledge but of an experience whereby we appropriate the perfection and blessedness of Christ (#108, p. 481). "The original language of Scripture," Schleiermacher maintains, defines faith as "the inward condition of one who feels content and strong in fellowship with Christ" (#108, p. 483). Since faith alone gives a share in the blessedness of Christ, Schleiermacher is able to accept the Reformation principle that faith alone saves (#109, p. 504). The believer is passive in faith, which arises through the sole agency of Christ (ibid.).

Christian proclamation, according to Schleiermacher, is "testimony as to one's own experience, which shall arouse in others the desire to have the same experience" (#14, p. 69). Faith springs from testimony, not from proof (#14, p. 70). Miracles are not sources of faith, but a person who already believes in Christ will be prepared to accept testimonies that he performed miracles (#14, p. 72).

Schleiermacher goes beyond Kant in his esteem for history and his recognition of religion as a distinct and necessary aspect of human existence. But he upholds faith only on the basis of personal experience. He sets aside dogma, miracle, prophecy, and inspired Scripture as being at least unnecessary. He rejects the idea of faith as knowledge based on the authority of another, even that of God the revealer. Commenting on Schleiermacher's interpretation of "faith alone," Karl Barth remarks: "One could hardly imagine a stranger travesty of this Reformation principle."[4] At least it must be said that Protestantism, in Schleiermacher, has moved a long way from Luther's sense of being unconditionally bound by the word of God.

Georg F. W. Hegel (1770–1831), having studied theology at Tübingen as a young man, brought many religious concerns to his philosophical work. He agreed with Jacobi and Schleiermacher that faith arises from an immediate experience of the divine Spirit, but he was dissatisfied with Schleiermacher's insistence on the passivity of the human subject and on the feeling of absolute dependence.[5] In Hegel's system, faith is the concurrent activity of the Spirit of truth and of the believing subject. Although faith can exist in inauthentic forms as a turning away from the world and a reaching out toward the Beyond, faith in authentic form is able to grasp the unity of the finite and the infinite, of the human and the divine. This it does preeminently by accepting Christ as the synthesis of both.

Faith, according to Hegel, does not rest on sensible signs or external authorities but on the immediate presence of the self-revealing Spirit. Faith enters into its own when the appearances vanish, as they did for the disciples after the resurrection and ascension of Christ. In faith the content is both true and certain, but the mode in which it is grasped is merely figurative. What faith apprehends vaguely under the veils of myth and symbol, philosophy comprehends in a clear and rational manner.

For Hegel, then, faith is not opposed to reason; the two have the same content; philosophy is truly theological. Somewhat like the eschatological vision of God in traditional theology, philosophy in Hegel's system gives clear intelligibility and cogent evidence for what faith perceives only in an obscure manner. Hegel is a rationalist insofar as he believes that human reason, even in this present life, can rigorously establish the truth of revealed religion, supplanting faith.

In his *Phenomenology of Spirit* and his *Lectures on the Philosophy of Religion* Hegel brilliantly retrieved many of the central doctrines of his own Lutheran Christianity, but he in some measure reshaped the dogmas of faith to suit the demands of his highly rational system. Some of his disciples, such as Philipp Marheineke (1780–1846), adhered closely to traditional orthodoxy, but others, such as David Friedrich Strauss (1808–1874) and Ludwig Feuerbach (1804–1872), collapsed the divine into the worldly and propounded a kind of humanistic pantheism. Thus the Hegelian synthesis must be regarded as ambiguous and unstable.

In England the poet Samuel Taylor Coleridge, operating in the Anglican tradition, felt the influence of German philosophy, especially in the persons of Lessing and Schleiermacher.[6] Unlike some of the Germans, he was clearly committed to historical Christian faith, in which he shared by moral experience, prayer, and worship. Eager to transcend the dichotomy between faith and reason, he attacked the narrowly rationalistic concept of reason purveyed by the Anglican apologist, William Paley (1743–1805). In his *Aids to Reflection* (1825) Coleridge maintained that faith cannot exist apart from reason, and that reason, in its highest form, is a faculty of apprehending spiritual truth. It involves the imagination, the will, and conscience. Faithful reason ventures forth to commit itself freely to the truth intimated by conscience and moral experience.

The Danish philosopher Søren Kierkegaard (1813–1855) developed his thought in conscious opposition to Hegel, whom he accused of blurring the infinite qualitative distinction between God and creature and of denaturing the Christian dogmas by accommodating them to his immanent logic of becoming.[7] For Kierkegaard it was an illusion to hold that there could be a higher standpoint than that of faith, by which he understood religious and supernatural assent to the doctrine of the God-man.

In his *Philosophical Fragments* (1844) Kierkegaard asserted that the objective unity between God and man in Christ is an absolute paradox offensive to human reason. But the offense of the "unhappy encounter" can be overcome by faith, which is a happy encounter between reason and the paradox. In his *Concluding Unscientific Postscript* (1846) Kierkegaard returned to the same themes. "The absurd," he asserted, is "that God has come into being, has been born, has grown up, and so forth . . . and this absurdity, held fast in the passion of inwardness, is faith."[8] Faith, then, seeks no objective assurance; it regards proof as its enemy. Denying that the paradox of the presence of the eternal in time can be established by historical research, especially in such a way that one can stake one's life upon it, Kierkegaard ridicules the standard apologetical arguments for Christianity.[9]

Faith, for Kierkegaard, is the infinite subjective passion that impels the believer to embrace as subjectively certain what is offensive, even absurd, to human speculation. The Christian paradox evokes the highest exercise of inwardness. Faith is a risk, a venture, a matter of subjectivity. Only by this route can the believer attain the objective reality of faith's object. Inwardness at its maximum, therefore, proves to be objectivity once again.[10]

Accompanied though it must be by fear and trembling, faith must not be confused with anxiety or despair. Melancholy and distress are products of sin and unbelief, whereas faith stands the test of uncertainty and overcomes it.[11] Abraham as a unique individual was able to triumph over the universal law that would have denied him his progeny for, in fear and trembling, he never ceased to believe.[12]

Kierkegaard has sometimes been misunderstood as a fideist scorning human reason and substituting an arbitrary act of will. But he can be interpreted, more soundly, as protesting against the rationalistic concept of reason that had for several centuries been dominant in Western Europe. Unlike the idealists of his day, he refused to make logic the norm for history or to reshape logic, as Hegel did, to match the facts of history. He stands at the beginning of a new effort to explore the inner dynamism of human subjectivity as the means of access to faith's real object. Although he was not by profession a theologian, Kierkegaard's philosophical musings on his Lutheran heritage were to have a major formative influence on twentieth-century existential theologians, both Protestant and Catholic.

## Catholicism before Vatican I

About the beginning of the nineteenth century several Catholic theologians attempted to integrate into their theologies of faith certain elements in the new philosophies of Kant and Fichte. The Benedictine Marianus Dobmayer (1753–1805), in his posthumously published *Systema theologiae catholicae* (1808), defined faith as holding something true on subjective but sufficient grounds.[13] He distinguished between two types of faith. If the principles of the assent come from the cognitive powers of the subject who believes, it is called rational faith *(Vernunftglaube);* if from trust in another subject, it is called positive faith or faith on authority *(Autoritätsglaube).* Christian faith, he holds, rests on the divine authority of Christ, and Catholic faith accepts the Christian belief system as authoritatively mediated by the Catholic Church. Belief on divine authority, for Dobmayer, always presupposes rational faith and makes use of the principles of natural religion to guard against fraud or illusion.

A little later the German priest-professor Georg Hermes (1775–1831) developed a Christian apologetic that took over certain ideas from Kant and Fichte.[14] Crucial to his system was the dichotomy between speculative and practical reason. Unlike Kant, he held that speculative reason (or, more technically, the intuitive intelligence he called *Vernunft*) has the capacity to establish the existence of God as the immutable First Cause. But he conceded that speculative reason could not prove certain divine attributes, such as the justice of God, nor could it establish with certitude the historical facts upon which the Christian religion is based. These tenets, however, do not lie beyond the scope of practical reason. Sensing within ourselves a categorical imperative to promote human dignity, we are able to ascertain the need of believing the Christian message in order to motivate ourselves to live up to the demands of the moral law or, in other words, to observe the categorical imperative.

In order to justify one's faith before the bar of reason one must, Hermes believed, call it into doubt and then let the arguments in its favor bring one back to a state of assent. The doubt that Hermes recommended was—or at least has usually been interpreted as—real rather than methodical in the sense of fictitious. Since there were stringent reasons, both speculative and practical, for accepting Christianity, grace, according to Hermes, was not needed for the assent of faith. In deference to the traditional doctrine regarding the necessity of grace for faith, Hermes introduced a distinction between two kinds of faith: rational faith *(Vernunftglaube)* and faith of the heart *(Herzensglaube).* While the first could be an achievement of unaided reason, the second did require grace. Only God could move one to submit one's whole life to the revelation accepted by "rational faith."

After Hermes's death his writings were submitted to a commission of theologians in Rome. In 1835 several of his works were condemned and in 1836 placed on the Index of Forbidden Books. The main objections were to his doctrine on doubt and his contention that the assent of faith could be preferred without the assistance of grace.[15]

After the atrocities of the French Revolution there was in France a strong reaction against the rationalism of the Enlightenment, in favor of authority and tradition. One manifestation of this was the philosophical system known as traditionalism. The most extreme representative of this system, Félicité de Lamennais (1772–1854), expounded his views on society and the Church in his four-volume *Essai sur l'indifférence en matière de religion* (1817–1823).[16] Every human being, he maintained, is confronted with a choice between two alternatives: individual reason, leading to absolute skepticism, or faith, leading to certitude. The first principles of religion and morality, including the existence of God, are not accessible to individual human reason but must be accepted on faith, which ultimately depends on divine revelation mediated through tradition. According to Lamennais the claims of the one true religion were proved by the universal consent of the human race. The teaching of the Catholic magisterium was for him the voice of humanity as a whole. The political and epistemological views of Lamennais were condemned by Pope Gregory XVI in the encyclical *Singulari nos* (1834).

Another French philosopher, Louis Eugène Bautain (1796–1867),[17] without being a strict traditionalist, maintained that tradition mediated by society was indispensable for the education of individual reason so that it could receive the supernatural self-manifestation of God. Influenced by the intuitionism of Jacobi, he attempted to revive the Augustinian view of "faith seeking understanding" as an alternative to the scholastic Aristotelianism. In order to arrive at divine faith, he held, we must accept with human faith the teaching of Scripture and Tradition, thereby allowing our minds to be inundated with the divine truth that radiates from these sources, illumining the heart. Thanks to this supernatural light, we can attain a vague but powerful sense of the divine, sufficient for a faith that can subsequently be confirmed by reflective knowledge and study. In the final analysis, for Bautain, faith is justified not by miracles or other external arguments of credibility but by an inner spiritual experience.

Bautain was never condemned, but he fell into some difficulty with the bishop of Strasbourg, and was several times required, both by this bishop and by Roman authorities, to subscribe to lists of propositions affirming the power of reason, apart from faith, to establish certain religious truths, including the existence of God and the credibility of the Christian religion.[18] His difficulties were partly due to the fact that he was operating with a concept of faith different from that of the Scholasticism current in the clerical circles of his day. For him, faith was not an assent to propositions attested by God as witness but rather a taste or feeling for supernatural truth.

Among the deviant developments of the mid-nineteenth century it is common to list the system of the Austrian priest, Anton Günther (1783–1863), who has been characterized as a "semi-rationalist."[19] An admirer of Descartes and Hegel, he held that, although there were certain supernatural truths attainable by faith alone, reason, working in the light of faith, had the capacity to understand and demonstrate these doctrines once they had been revealed. In his system, as in Hegel's, faith seemed to be a merely provisional form of knowledge, capable of being supplanted, in this life, by rational demonstration. When a Roman commission, in 1857, judged Günther's system to be tainted with rationalism, he humbly submitted.[20]

The influence of new philosophical currents made itself felt in the Catholic Tübingen school. The founder of the school, Johann Sebastian von Drey (1777–1853), centered his theology on revelation as God's action in history for the education of the human race. While avoiding the semi-rationalism of Günther, Drey emphasized the value of believing as the path to a higher form of understanding achieved by philosophical reflection on the contents of faith. Faith, he held, gives rise to a type of knowledge *(Wissen),* but the knowledge of revelation never simply replaces the faith on which it is built.[21]

Johann Adam Möhler (1796–1838), the most creative theologian of the Catholic Tübingen school, was in close contact with contemporary thinkers such as Schleiermacher and Schelling.[22] In his early work on unity in the Church, *Die Einheit in der Kirche* (1825), he drew heavily on the Greek fathers, including Clement of Alexandria. He depicted faith not as a merely intellectual acceptance of another's word but as an inner transformation effected by the Holy Spirit. Faith, as an interior grace-given consciousness of the divine, is the root of doctrine, which Möhler describes as "the conceptual expression of the Christian spirit."[23] In his work on Athanasius,[24] Möhler moved somewhat away from subjective idealism; he emphasized both the interiority of faith as a spiritual outlook and the correspondence between faith and doctrine.

In his last major work, *Symbolik,*[25] Möhler defended the Tridentine doctrine of faith. He observed, however, that the Council of Trent gave no official definition of faith. As the nearest thing to an official Catholic definition, he quoted the Roman Catechism: "The word 'faith' does not mean to think, estimate, or have an opinion but, as Holy Scripture teaches, means the very certain assent by which the mind firmly and constantly assents to God as he discloses his mysteries."[26] Möhler interpreted this to mean that faith is a free act of submission to God the revealer out of a sense of reverence and obligation. He then added:

> Catholics consider faith as the reunion with God in Christ, especially by means of the faculties of knowledge, illuminated and confirmed by grace, with which the excitement of various feelings is more or less connected. It is, in their estimation, a divine light, whereby man discerns, as well as recognizes, the decrees of God, and comprehends not only what God is to man, but also what man should be to God.[27]

Finally, in a defense of his *Symbolik* against Ferdinand Christian Baur, Möhler decisively rejected any suggestion that faith could result from an immanent development of human religious faculties. According to the New Testament concept, he asserted, faith is an adherence to truth that cannot be known except on the word of another.[28]

In his final works, therefore, Möhler came full circle. From having originally insisted on the inner transforming activity of grace, he came eventually to emphasize the external word that comes by hearing. Without contradicting his earlier work, or falling into a propositional theory of faith, he manifestly shifted the accent from the pneumatological to the Christological.

The theology of faith of the Catholic Tübingen school was further perfected by Johann Evangelist von Kuhn (1806–1887), who sought to respond to Hegel and Strauss while profiting, as did Bautain, from the "philosophy of feeling" of Friedrich Jacobi.[29] Supernatural faith, Kuhn held, presupposes a kind of natural or rational faith *(Vernunftglaube)*, which delivers an immediate but vague and unvalidated awareness of God. Christian faith goes beyond this, and is essentially an acceptance of God's historical revelation in Christ, as transmitted by the Church. The corporate consciousness of the Church confirms the faith of the individual and enables the assent to be firm and unwavering. The infallibility of the Church's teaching office protects the faith of the Catholic against subjective delusions.

In the second edition of his *Einleitung in die katholische Dogmatik* (1859) Kuhn further enriched this account of faith, emphasizing how faith claims the entire person of the believer, arising not simply from the intellect but from the spirit *(Geist)*, the original unity of intellect and will. Faith enkindles divine life in the believer and effects a profound union with God.

Faith, according to Kuhn, is oriented toward knowledge, which can be obtained by reflecting on the immediate objects of consciousness and establishing that the Church, which is our immediate teacher in matters of faith, has a divine origin and enjoys the assistance of the Holy Spirit. Reason can demonstrate that the doctrines of faith do not contradict naturally known truths, but it cannot positively establish the contents of revelation, since these are above the reach of reason.

The contributions of Möhler and the Tübingen school were in some ways paralleled by those of John Henry Newman (1801–1890). Raised as an Anglican evangelical, Newman then studied Aristotle and became keenly interested in logic and epistemology. Touched by the romantic revival, he sought to overcome the dessicated rationalism of eighteenth-century Anglicanism and to combat the rising liberalism of his day. In his years as an Anglican divine at Oxford University, he immersed himself deeply in the Greek fathers.[30] Like Möhler, he became particularly attached to the Alexandrian school, including Athanasius. In the Christian intellectualism of the fathers he found a corrective to two current aberrations—an evangelicalism that tended to eliminate the dogmatic component, making faith a mere matter of feeling and taste, and a rationalism that depicted faith either as a demonstrated truth or as a probable conclusion reached through philosophical investigation. For Newman, faith had a definite intellectual content given in the word of God, but it could not be achieved without a sincere longing for enlightenment from above. In his own words, "By faith then is meant the mind's perception or apprehension of heavenly things, arising from an instinctive trust in the divinity or truth of the external word, informing it concerning them."[31]

The gradual evolution of Newman's doctrine on faith under its cognitive aspect may be studied in his *Fifteen Sermons Preached at Oxford University* between 1826 and 1843. His position reaches relative maturity in the twelfth sermon, "Love the Safeguard of Faith against Superstition," preached in 1839. Here Newman seeks to answer the objection that faith, if it is not subject to the control of reason, lies open to every kind of credulity and superstition. He replies that, since faith does not arise out of reasoning, it need not be fortified or regulated by reason. Love, not reason, is the discriminating principle that keeps faith from degenerating into enthusiasm or superstition. He continues:

> Right Faith is the faith of a right mind. Faith is an intellectual act; right faith is an intellectual act, done in a certain moral disposition. Faith is an act of Reason, viz., a reasoning upon presumptions. Faith ventures and hazards; right Faith ventures and hazards deliberately, seriously, soberly, and humbly, counting the cost and delighting in the sacrifice. As far as, and whenever, Love is wanting, so far, and there, Faith runs into excess and is perverted.[32]

Adducing many biblical citations, Newman reinforces his contention that faith depends on a devout state of mind, which he identifies with the *pia affectio* or *pius credulitatis affectus* spoken of by the church fathers and the early councils. "The divinely enlightened mind sees in Christ the very Object whom it desires to love and worship—the Object correlative to its own affections."[33]

Newman was unwilling to surrender either the dogmatic or the personal dimension of faith. The latitudinarian view that Christian faith does not involve the profession of a definite creed, Newman contended, conflicts with the clear intent of Scripture to proclaim an imperative message and with the tenaciously dogmatic character of primitive Christianity.[34] But the dogmas, for Newman, are not the essence of revelation. Serving only to articulate aspects of an idea or impression that is prior to them, they can never exhaust the fullness of that idea. The idea is mediated by the words of Scripture and of the creeds—words that are addressed not simply to the intellect but also to the imagination and the affections. In his *Grammar of Assent* (1870) Newman explores the nonconceptual aspect of the assent to revelation with a view to explaining how faith, notwithstanding its necessary intellectual content, can be a real personal assent, involving conviction and commitment. The Christian idea, he maintains, is presented concretely in a manner that appeals to the imagination and kindles the affections of minds already attuned to revelation through the intimations that God gives of himself in nature, in history, and in the inner voice of conscience.

After his conversion to Roman Catholicism in 1845 Newman became concerned with harmonizing his own views of faith, which had taken shape during his Anglican period, with the Scholasticism current in Roman ecclesiastical circles. At Rome in 1847 he composed twelve theses on faith. These theses, not published until

1937, are based on Counter-Reformation Scholastic theologians such as Suarez and de Lugo.[35] They so stress the objective signs of credibility as to make it appear that faith must be preceded by a purely natural judgment of credibility. Thus they do not do justice to Newman's personal insights, especially with regard to the role of grace-given desires and presentiments of the heart in assuring the prudence of the act of faith.

In his *Lectures on Justification* Newman explored the salvific dimensions of faith.[36] Writing as an Anglican, Newman attempted to salvage the formula "justification by faith alone," while insisting, against the extreme Protestant position, that righteousness is an inherent transformation of the sinner thanks to the indwelling of Christ. "Salvation by faith," he explains, "is but another way of saying salvation by *grace* only" (283). Faith, for Newman, never exists by itself alone apart from other virtues such as humility, fear, zeal, and obedience (265–66), but faith has a special role insofar as it points to Christ as the sole justifier. "To look to Christ is to be justified by faith" (339). In a compact formula Newman summarizes his doctrine of justification: "Justification comes *through* the Sacraments; is received *by* faith; *consists* in God's inward presence; and *lives* in obedience" (278).

In the eight volumes of his *Parochial and Plain Sermons,* preached at the Anglican parish of St. Mary the Virgin at Oxford between 1825 and 1843, Newman speaks eloquently of the relationships between faith and sight, faith and obedience, faith and love. In these sermons he makes it clear that no single quality, taken in isolation, can be the guarantee of holiness. In Christ, he says, the blessings of peace, hope, love, faith, and purity are all given, "the will and the power, the heart and the knowledge, the light of faith, and the obedience of faith."[37] Treating faith not as an isolated grace, but as it concretely exists in those who live by the gospel, Newman proposes a comprehensive spirituality of faith.

The Jesuit theologians of the Roman College made an important contribution to the theology of faith in the nineteenth century, not because of their originality but rather because of their learning, their prudence, and their influence with the Holy See. They were able apologists and watchdogs of orthodoxy. Giovanni Perrone (1794–1876) taught at the Roman College from 1824 to 1848 and again from 1851 until shortly before his death. While keeping abreast of new developments all over Europe, and accepting certain contributions of the Catholic Tübingen school, he faithfully followed the teaching of the Council of Trent, Robert Bellarmine, and the post-Tridentine Scholastics. His treatment of faith in his *Praelectiones theologicae* (1835) and in his work on the theological virtues, *De virtutibus fidei, spei et caritatis* (1865) are models of orderly exposition.

Perrone wrote against Hermes and was a member of the commission that condemned him. When Bautain visited Rome, Perrone persuaded him to moderate his fideism. In 1847 he exchanged memoranda with Newman on the development of dogma. In the course of his long career he wrote voluminously, especially in the apologetical field, and by his teaching and personal influence formed a whole generation of Jesuit scholars.

Johann Baptist Franzelin (1816–1876), a pupil and then a colleague of Perrone, was heavily involved in the preparations for the First Vatican Council. After composing the first draft of the conciliar text on faith, he played a major role in the discussions themselves. We shall see more of his work below.

## Vatican Council I

Of the two dogmatic constitutions produced by Vatican Council I only the first, that on Catholic Faith, is of central interest for the present study. The historical context for this constitution was set by a whole series of papal pronouncements against fideism, traditionalism, and rationalism issued between 1832 and 1864. A synthetic presentation of the Catholic position on the relations between faith and reason was desired. At the request of the Preparatory Commission, Franzelin wrote the first schema *De doctrina christiana,* consisting of eighteen chapters. When the Council met, the Commission on Faith approved of the positions taken in Franzelin's schema but asked for a briefer and less technical document. A commission of three bishops, headed by Konrad Martin of Paderborn, was appointed to rework the text with the advice of the German Jesuit, Josef Kleutgen. In February 1870 the commission presented a revised schema of nine chapters. The first four of these, dealing with faith and reason in general terms, were debated in March and April and, with some amendments, solemnly approved on April 24, 1870. Because the Council was interrupted by war, it never got around to considering the remaining chapters dealing with specific beliefs such as the Trinity, the creation of the human race, the Fall, and the redemption.

Chapter I, dealing with the nature of God, the freedom of the act of creation, and the universality of divine providence, is directed against pantheism and other current errors. The second chapter, on revelation, affirms the possibility of a natural knowledge of God by human reason and the necessity of revelation, especially because of humanity's call to a supernatural destiny. The same chapter teaches the inspiration of the canonical Scriptures and the competence of the Church to interpret the Scriptures authoritatively.

Chapter III, on faith, is of particular concern for purposes of this study, and calls for closer analysis.[38] It consists of seven paragraphs (DS 3008–3014) and six canons (DS 3031–3036).

Paragraph 1 (DS 3008) takes up the nature of faith and the obligation to believe. Faith is first defined in somewhat "existential" terms as the full submission of the intellect and will to God who reveals. The obligation to submit is derived from humanity's total dependence on God as Creator and Lord and on the subjection of created reason to uncreated Truth. In the second sentence, faith is described as "the supernatural virtue whereby, inspired and assisted by the grace of God, we believe that what he has revealed is true, not because we perceive its intrinsic truth by the natural light of reason but because of the authority of God the revealer, who can neither be deceived nor deceive." The Council here begins not with the act but with the virtue of faith, which, however, is defined in terms of the act to which it leads. Unlike the Council of Trent, Vatican I makes no reference to the promises of God as the object of faith. Its concern is less with justification and more with faith as an assent to truth. The accent, in response to rationalism, falls heavily on authority.

Paragraph 2 (DS 3009) takes up the question whether faith is in accord with reason. It replies in the affirmative and makes reference to the biblical miracles and prophecies, which are described as certain signs suited to the intelligence of all. The Council does not, however, state that every Christian is obliged to accept miracles and prophecies as the rational grounds for his or her own faith. Nor does the Council deny that grace may be needed for one to see the force of the signs of credibility. By declaring that God conjoins the external evidence with the interior aids of the Holy Spirit, Vatican I seems to suggest that de facto grace is always at work in the approach to faith. In canon 3 (DS 3033) the Council denies that believers are obliged to rely only on interior experience or private inspiration. Presumably the intention of this canon was to exclude the position of Schleiermacher, who held that miracles were signs only for those who already believed.

In paragraph 3 (DS 3010) the Council turns to the role of grace and freedom in faith. In continuity with Orange II and Trent, Vatican I affirms that faith can never be an achievement of pure reason and that no one can believe as needed for salvation without the illumination and inspiration of the Holy Spirit. The corresponding canon (can. 5, DS 3055) makes it clear that the doctrine of Hermes is here envisaged. According to the canon the arguments of credibility never constrain the mind to assent. Grace, moreover, is needed not only for a living faith (presumably corresponding to Hermes's "faith of the heart") but also for "unformed faith," which is to be regarded as a gift of God (DS 3010).

Paragraph 4 (DS 3011) is concerned with the object of faith—namely revealed truth contained in Scripture and tradition and proposed by the Church as requiring to be believed. The Church proposes such truth either by means of a solemn definition or by the universal preaching of the magisterium. The text is carefully composed so as not to take a position on papal infallibility, which had not yet been discussed at the Council.

Paragraph 5 (DS 3012) deals with the necessity of faith. As Scripture attests, no one can be justified or saved without faith. In order that we may be in a position to embrace the true faith and persevere in it, God has accredited the Church as the guardian and teacher of his revealed word. In his report on behalf of the Commission on Faith, Bishop Martin referred to the Church as "a kind of concrete divine revelation."[39]

In paragraph 6 (DS 3013) the Council speaks of the way in which the signs of credibility converge upon the Catholic Church as the authorized witness to revelation. The Church itself, by its wonderful properties, is described as a self-authenticating witness. The Council here alludes to a type of apologetical argumentation that had recently been popularized by Cardinal Victor Dechamps, C.SS.R., a member of the Commission on Faith.[40]

In the closing paragraph (DS 3014) the text discusses the questions of change and perseverance in one's religious affiliation. Because the signs of credibility and the grace of the Holy Spirit always impel one toward the true faith and the true Church, people are warranted in being converted to Catholic Christianity but not in departing from it. In this connection, Vatican I repudiates the doctrine of Georg

Hermes, already alluded to, and that attributed to the Munich theologian Alois von Schmid (1825–1910), to the effect that Catholics, like others, have sufficient reason for calling their faith into question.[41] Canon 6 anathematizes the error pointed out in this paragraph.

It is disputed whether Vatican I here teaches that no one can fall away from the Catholic faith without subjective sin.[42] The Council speaks directly of those who, after being raised under the instruction of the Church, deliberately doubt in order to make their faith more "scientific." Nothing is here said about simple believers who, because of erroneous teaching or deceitful propaganda, lose sight of the motives of credibility. One cannot prove from the text of Vatican I that such persons have failed to correspond to the graces given to them.

The relationship between faith and reason, while it pervades the whole Constitution on Catholic Faith, is specifically treated in chapter 4.[43] The chapter in its first paragraph (DS 3015) asserts the twofold order of human knowledge, a favorite theme of Kleutgen. Unlike natural reason, which is restricted in its scope, faith gives access to mysteries hidden in God, in the measure that God is pleased to reveal them. Divine mysteries, according to paragraph 2 (DS 3016) so exceed the capacity of the human intellect that, even after being revealed, they remain wrapped in obscurity and cannot be comprehended this side of heaven. This assertion is made against the "semi-rationalists," including Günther and Jakob Frohschammer.

The remaining paragraphs (DS 3017–3020) teach that faith and reason, being derived from one and the same God, can never contradict each other. Indeed, they mutually assist one another, for "right reason demonstrates the foundations of faith" (DS 3019) and can achieve a measure of theological understanding, whereas faith can enrich reason with the data of revelation and can free reason from errors into which it would fall unless assisted. The Church has a responsibility to promote science and culture (DS 3019) and to proscribe philosophical and scientific opinions that are contrary to true faith (DS 3018). The deposit of faith, delivered to the Church as guardian, must not be treated as a philosophical theory to be perfected by human speculation (an error sometimes ascribed to Günther). Dogma develops, but only in a homogeneous way, consistent with its own origins and with the previous utterances of the Church (DS 3020). By implication, the Council here rejects the application of Hegelian dialectics to the history of dogma.

Concerned as it was with the faith-reason relationship, Vatican I approached the question of faith from an intellectualist perspective. While presenting faith as a form of knowledge based on divine authority, it did not deny that faith could be treated from other perspectives, for example, in opposition to disobedience (Paul), worldliness (John), pride (Augustine), or despair (Luther).

In its discussion of the dynamics of faith, Vatican I traced a narrow path between the errors of fideism and rationalism. It particularly emphasized the reasonableness of the decision to submit to the authority of God as witness. In assessing the arguments of credibility the Council was concerned with their de jure value rather than with the de facto question of what moves a given individual to believe. Rejecting any retreat into blind decisionism or emotion, the Council vindicated the public character of revelation and faith. Its statements on the powers of reason prior to faith are framed within the intellectual world of post-Tridentine Scholasticism, in which the relative claims of nature and grace were passionately debated. Within the limitations of its own cultural perspective, Vatican I produced a remarkably rich, concise, balanced, and coherent document, vindicating the rights of reason and authority against the excesses of authoritarianism and rationalism.

## Catholicism after Vatican I

After the Council, the participating theologians continued to debate the thorny question of the "analysis of faith," which Kleutgen called the "cross of theologians" *(crux theologorum)*.[44] The appendix on faith in Franzelin's postconciliar work on Tradition[45] is in some respects an authoritative commentary on Vatican I, though it also embodies the author's personal positions. Aligning himself with de Lugo against Suarez, Franzelin holds that the act of faith rests on a virtual syllogism, in which the major premise is the authority of God who reveals. The formal object or motive of faith, he maintains, must be accepted with a supernatural assent through the power of grace. Although the mediation of the Church is not absolutely required for each and every act of divine faith, the authority of the Church, for Catholics, normally enters into the motive of faith itself. The Church is accepted as an infallible instrument of the Holy Spirit.

Matthias Joseph Scheeben (1835–1888), who had studied at Rome under Perrone, Franzelin, and Kleutgen before taking up his professorship at Cologne, tried to base his theology of faith more directly on Thomas Aquinas, bypassing the baroque commentaries.[46] He branded as "abstract and mechanical" de Lugo's effort to account for faith as the conclusion of an implicit syllogism having as its premises the truthfulness of God and the fact of revelation. According to Scheeben, there is in the human heart a natural instinct, fortified by grace, to believe in God as Creator and Lord. The key to the act of faith is a *pius affectus credulitatis,* leading on to a voluntary self-commitment *(willige Hingabe).* The "authority" of God consists not primarily in his veracity but in his being "author" of our natural and supernatural existence. The closest created analogy to divine faith is the implicit trust that a child puts in the word of its parent. In faith we reverently submit to the word that God addresses to us, because, as stated in Vatican I, we are bound to offer the full submission of intellect and will to God, on whom we depend totally as our Creator and Lord.

Although Scheeben held that the *obsequium* of faith is fully reasonable in view of the signs of credibility mentioned by Vatican I, he denied that the evidence of credibility enters to any degree into the motive of faith itself. The authority of God is the sole formal object of faith. Nothing falls under the act or the virtue of faith except insofar as it is contained in God's word. The Church is not an additional authority, nor is its role restricted to offering the material object of faith. It is a living instrument through which God speaks.[47] Faith, therefore, is divine both in its source and in its object.

In his *Handbuch der katholischen Dogmatik,* Scheeben vigorously attacked the "rationalism" of Kleutgen. Kleutgen in a postscript to the volume on faith in the second edition of his *Die Theologie der Vorzeit*[48] protested against Scheeben's polemic against him. He added that Scheeben's eccentric theory ("höchst sonder-liche Theorie") fell far short of his goal of vindicating the insights of Suarez and the earlier Thomists, and in fact fell into conflict with uncontestable theological prin-ciples. Kleutgen, who like Franzelin preferred the positions of de Lugo, elsewhere accused Scheeben of excessive voluntarism in substituting God's dominion for his veracity as the formal object. Responding in the journal *Katholik,* Scheeben argued that de Lugo and Kleutgen wanted to keep faith too much under the control of human reason. In his article "Glaube" in the *Kirchenlexikon* (especially col. 634) Scheeben concedes, in response to Kleutgen's criticism, that the intellectual motive of faith includes acknowledgement of God's infallible knowledge and truthfulness.

In its essentials Scheeben's approach to faith resembles Möhler's final position. Both of them were opposed to systems that base faith on inner experience or ratio-nal self-assertion, thus making it, in effect, a conquest of the human spirit. Instead, they called for a radical shift whereby anthropocentrism is abandoned. Faith, they affirmed, is a reverent submission to a word that comes from above, a personal word of address from a gracious God. Only those who are willing to become like little children, trusting in the word of another, can enter into the household of faith.

## Liberal Protestantism

In the closing decades of the nineteenth century Protestant theology reacted against against romanticism and idealism. Liberal Protestantism was in many respects a return to Kant in an atmosphere of increasing scientific and historical conscious-ness. The leading architect of this movement was Albrecht Ritschl (1822–1889). A church historian indebted to Ferdinand Christian Baur and the Protestant Tübingen school, he repudiated both the romantic mysticism of Schleiermacher and the speculative idealism of Hegel. Rejecting all metaphysical arguments for the existence of God, he preferred Kant's reliance on practical reason. God, for Ritschl, was to be discovered through value judgments, in which the religious consciousness reached out toward its own highest good.

Ritschl's analysis of faith is found primarily in his three-volume work, *The Christian Doctrine of Justification and Reconciliation* (1870–1874).[49] Faith, he explains, is a subjective response whereby we appropriate the benefits God confers upon us in Christ. Eschewing objectivism, Ritschl uses by preference the category of trust, which suggests a loving movement of the will toward God. "For faith, regarded as trust, is no other than the direction of the will turned toward God as the highest end and the highest good" (*Justification and Reconciliation,* 3:103). Faith, then, is not a purely intellectual assent. To believe in Christ is not to adhere to objec-tive dogmas but to accept the value of the divine love manifest in Christ's life and work (3:591–93). In these assertions Ritschl was confident of following in the foot-steps of Luther and Melanchthon.

For all his emphasis on trust, Ritschl shied away from the view that faith always brings with it an infallible assurance of one's own justification or salvation. He interpreted Melanchthon and Calvin as holding that true faith can be accompanied by some anxiety about one's own spiritual condition. On this point his teaching agrees with that of many Catholics and with the Council of Trent. Faith, however, excludes despair. It must keep steadily turned toward the God of grace, taking encouragement from the sacraments and one's own good works as signs of election (3:142–52).

Central to Ritschl's system is the relationship between religion and ethics, or between faith and love. For Ritschl Christianity was a distinctively ethical religion. Luther and the Reformers, he believed, failed to recognize the organic connection between justification and regeneration, or the power to perform good works (1:168–81). Kant was the first to perceive the religious importance of the idea of the Kingdom of God as an association of virtue (3:11). As an invisible reality, the Kingdom is perceived only by faith. Faith cannot be dissociated from love and good works. Ritschl was willing to accept the medieval formula that charity is the form of faith, in the sense that faith lacks something essential unless it turns lovingly toward God (3:103–6). The ethical impulse to love one's fellow human beings, he held, is a further consequence, depending on an appropriation of the idea of the Kingdom.

Ritschl maintained that faith in Christ can arise only within the Church, but the Church, he insisted, is not autonomous. It depends historically on Christ and perpetuates his memory. Reacting against pietistic mysticism, Ritschl sought to root faith in historical fact. He was confident that objective historical investigation could recover the real traits and intentions of Jesus and the impact that Jesus had made on his first disciples. The historical Jesus, for Ritschl, was normative for the Christian community of any age (3:406, 590).

## Conclusion

The nineteenth century is an exceptionally complex, rich, and interesting period in the theology of faith. Protestant and Catholic thinkers alike entered into vigorous dialogue with new philosophical movements such as British empiricism, Kantianism, Hegelianism, and Neo-Kantianism.

The romanticism of the early part of the century, harking back to the Pietism and sentimentalism of the previous two centuries, rebelled against rationalism and Scholasticism. Authors such as Schleiermacher and Coleridge, Lamennais and Drey, sought to ground faith in life and history, taking account of sentiment, community, and tradition. Möhler and Newman, still under the influence of romanticism, fruitfully mined the great masters of the patristic era and were thereby enabled to appreciate the transformative and unitive aspects of faith. Newman drew on Aristotle's ethical theory and the Platonism of the fathers in constructing his personal response to the British empiricists.

A second major current of theology made use of Kant and his idealist successors to defend or revise Christian theology. From different perspectives, the Protestants Marheineke, Baur, and Strauss achieved a new synthesis of faith and reason with the help of Hegelian dialectics. In Catholic circles Bautain, Hermes, Günther, and Kuhn, among others, borrowing philosophical insights from Kant, Jacobi, and Hegel, sought to fortify and update the Catholic theology of faith. These efforts at modernization, both Protestant and Catholic, met with strong opposition. Kierkegaard, reacting against the Hegelianism prevalent in Lutheran circles, laid the foundations for modern theological existentialism. The Catholic opposition to critical idealism took the form of a return to Scholastic realism and supernaturalism.

The Roman school of Catholic theology, represented at its best by Perrone and Franzelin, showed the capacity of Bellarmine, Suarez, and de Lugo to speak effectively to the issues of a later age. The First Vatican Council achieved an impressive restatement of Tridentine orthodoxy in opposition to German rationalism. Scheeben, educated in the Roman school, felicitously combined the best features of Scholasticism with ideas drawn from the Greek fathers, thus avoiding the excessive concern with abstract conceptual analysis that had become characteristic of Catholic academic theology. Kleutgen, while heavily indebted to de Lugo, professed a marked predilection for Thomas Aquinas, whose theology he regarded as normative for the whole Church.

Toward the end of the century, Ritschl's retrieval of Luther in the context of neo-Kantian positivism opened up a fresh current that would flow vigorously, as we shall see, until the first World War. In many sectors of Protestantism the new science of history would virtually displace dogma, metaphysics, and mysticism as a source of theological knowledge. Faith would be relegated to the sphere of value judgments.

# Notes

1. See the brief sketch of Jacobi's religious epistemology in Frederick Copleston, *A History of Philosophy,* vol. 6, pt. 1 (Garden City, N.Y.: Doubleday Image Books, 1964), 169–70.

2. Friedrich Schleiermacher, *On Religion: Speeches to Its Cultured Despisers* (New York: Harper Torchbooks, 1958), 88–89.

3. Idem, first German edition, *Der christliche Glaube nach den Grundsätzen der evangelischen Kirche im Zusammenhange dargestellt,* 2 vols. (Berlin: G. Reimer, 1821–22; 2d ed., 1830–31); ET of 2d German edition, *The Christian Faith* (Edinburgh: T. and T. Clark, 1928; reprinted, New York: Harper & Row, 1963). Page references in parentheses will be to ET.

4. Karl Barth, *The Theology of Schleiermacher* (Grand Rapids, Mich.: Eerdmans, 1982), 243.

5. On Hegel see Raymond Keith Williamson, *Introduction to Hegel's Philosophy of Religion* (Albany, N.Y.: State University of New York Press, 1984).

6. See Claude Welch, *Protestant Thought in the Nineteenth Century,* vol. 1 (New Haven, Conn.: Yale University Press, 1972), 113–20.

7. On Kierkegaard see Louis Dupré, *Kierkegaard the Theologian* (New York: Sheed Ward, 1963), especially 142–46; Cornelio Fabro, "Faith and Reason in Kierkegaard's Dialectic," in *A Kierkegaard Critique,* ed. Howard A. Johnson and Niels Thulstrup (New York: Harper, 1962), 156–206; H. V. Martin, *The Wings of Faith* (London: Lutterworth, 1950); Welch, *Protestant Thought in the Nineteenth Century,* 1:292–304.

8. Søren Kierkegaard, *Concluding Unscientific Postscript* (Princeton, N.J.: Princeton University Press edition, 1941), 188.

9. Ibid., 25–47.

10. Idem, *Journals,* 1849, no. 1021, ed. Alexandre Dru (London: Oxford University Press, 1938), 355.

11. Ibid., *Journals,* 1850, no. 1064, pp. 377–78.

12. Idem, *Fear and Trembling* (Princeton, N.J.: Princeton University Press, 1983), 76–81.

13. On Dobmayer see Petri, *Glaube und Gotteserkenntnis,* 111–15.

14. On Hermes see Karl Werner, *Geschichte der apologetischen und polemischen Literatur,* vol. 5 (Regensburg: Georg Manz, 1867), 193–96; Karl Eschweiler, *Die zwei Wege der neueren Theologie: Georg Hermes—Matth. Jos. Scheeben* (Augsburg: Benno Filser, 1926), 81–130; Edgar Hocedez, *Histoire de la Théologie au XIXe siècle,* vol. 1 (Paris: Desclée De Brouwer, 1949), 177–95; Gerald A. McCool, *Catholic Theology in the Nineteenth Century* (New York: Seabury/Crossroad, 1977), 59–67.

15. See the papal brief *Dum acerbissimas* of September 26, 1835 (DS 2738–2740).

16. On Lamennais, see Louis Foucher, *La philosophie catholique en France au XIXe siècle* (Paris: Vrin, 1955), especially 31–50.

17. On Bautain, see Walter M. Horton, *The Philosophy of the Abbé Bautain* (New York: New York University Press, 1926); Paul Poupard, *L'Abbé Louis Bautain* (Paris: Desclée, 1961); McCool, *Catholic Theology in the Nineteenth Century,* 46–56.

18. See the sets of propositions proposed respectively by the bishop of Strasbourg in 1835 and 1840 (DS 2751–2756) and by the Roman Congregation of Bishops and Regulars in 1844 (DS 2765–2769).

19. See Joseph Pritz, *Glauben und Wissen bei Anton Günther* (Vienna: Herder, 1963), an introduction to Günther's thought with a selection of texts; also Karl Beck, *Offenbarung und Glaube bei Anton Günther* (Vienna: Herder, 1967).

20. Brief of Congregation of the Index to the Archbishop of Cologne, *Eximiam tuam,* June 15, 1857 (DS 2828–2831).

21. See Wayne L. Fehr, *The Birth of the Catholic Tübingen School: The Dogmatics of Johann Sebastian Drey* (Chico, Cal.: Scholars Press, 1981), 62–69.

22. On Möhler's theology of faith see Josef R. Geiselmann, *Die katholische Tübinger Schule* (Freiburg: Herder, 1964), 146–53.

23. Johann Adam Möhler, *Die Einheit in der Kirche* (Cologne: Hegner, 1957), 23.

24. Idem, *Athanasius der Grosse,* 2 vols. (Mainz: Kupferberg, 1827).

25. Idem, *Symbolik, oder Darstellung der dogmatischen Gegensätze der Katholiken und Protestanten nach ihren Bekenntnisschriften* (Mainz: Kupferberg, 1832), reprinted 2 vols., ed. J. R. Geiselmann (Cologne: Hegner, 1958). ET, *Symbolism: or, Exposition of the Doctrinal Differences between Catholics and Protestants, as Evidenced by Their Symbolical Writings* (New York: Benziger Bros., 1906).

26. *Catechismus ex Decreto Concilii Tridentini* (Regensburg: Georg Manz, 1866), Pars I, cap. 2, no. 2, p. 15; quoted by Möhler, *Symbolism,* no. 15, pp. 120–21.

27. Möhler, *Symbolism,* no. 15, p. 121. Cf. *Symbolik,* Geiselmann ed., 1:190.

28. Idem, *Neue Untersuchungen,* 2d ed., corrected (Mainz: Kupferberg, 1835), n. 46, p. 270.

29. See Kuhn's *Einleitung in die katholische Dogmatik,* vol. 1 of his *Katholische Dogmatik,* (Tübingen: Laupp, 1846; 2d ed., 1859). On Kuhn see F. Wolfinger, *Der Glaube nach Johann Evangelist von Kuhn* (Göttingen: Vandenhoeck & Ruprecht, 1972; also Petri, *Glaube und Gotteserkenntnis,* 127–37.

30. On Newman's theology of faith, see Sylvester P. Juergens, *Newman on the Psychology of Faith in the Individual* (New York: Macmillan, 1928); Philip Flanagan, *Newman: Faith and the Believer* (Westminster, Md.: Newman, 1946); William R. Fey, *Faith and Doubt: The Unfolding of Newman's Thought on Certainty* (Shepherdstown, W. Va.: Patmos, 1976).

31. John Henry Newman, *Lectures on the Doctrine of Justification* (1838, 3d ed., 1874; reprinted Westminster, Md.: Christian Classics, 1966), 253. Newman cites Theodoret as authority for this description.

32. Newman's *University Sermons. Fifteen Sermons Preached before the University of Oxford, 1826–1843* (London: SPCK, 1970), Sermon XII, p. 239.

33. Ibid., 236.

34. Idem, *The Arians of the Fourth Century,* new ed. (London: Longmans, Green, 1871), 146. Cf. Avery Dulles, "From Images to Truth: Newman on Revelation and Faith," *Theological Studies* 51 (1990): 252–67, at 256.

35. Henry Tristram, ed., "Cardinal Newman's Theses *de Fide* and His Proposed Introduction to the French Translation of the University Sermons," *Gregorianum* 18 (1937): 219–60.

36. Cited above, note 31. For a more complete presentation see Thomas L. Sheridan, *Newman on Justification* (Staten Island, N.Y.: Alba House, 1967).

37. Newman, "The State of Salvation," in *Parochial and Plain Sermons* 5:13 (San Francisco: Ignatius, 1987), 1063.

38. On Vatican I's teaching on faith see Jean-Michel-Alfred Vacant, *Etudes théologiques sur les Constitutions du Concile du Vatican: La Constitution Dei Filius,* 2 vols. (Paris: Delhomme et Briguet, 1895); Roger Aubert, *Le problème de l'acte de foi,* 2d ed. (Louvain, E. Warny, 1950), 132–222; Hermann J. Pottmeyer, *Der Glaube vor dem Anspruch der Wissenschaft* (Freiburg: Herder, 1968).

39. "Relatio generalis," in J. D. Mansi, ed., *Sacrorum Conciliorum nova collectio,* 51:314B.

40. Regarding the influence of Dechamps on the text, see Pottmeyer, *Der Glaube,* 319–20, 323–24. Maurice Becqué, *L'Apologétique du Cardinal Dechamps* (Paris: Desclée De Brouwer, 1949), does not treat this question expressly; cf. 103 (with references).

41. On the interpretation of Hermes and Schmidt at Vatican I, see Pottmeyer, *Der Glaube,* 305–13.

42. Aubert, *Problème de l'acte de foi,* 218–19, and Pottmeyer, *Der Glaube,* 341–47 treat this question well.

43. Pottmeyer, *Der Glaube,* 348–459.

44. Josef Kleutgen, *Die Theologie der Vorzeit,* vol. 4 (Münster: Theissing, 1873–74), 134.

45. Johann Baptist Franzelin, *De divina traditione* (Rome: S.C. de Propaganda Fide, 1870; 2d ed., 1875).

46. Matthias Joseph Scheeben's views on faith are most fully expounded in his *Handbuch der katholischen Dogmatik,* vol. 1 (Freiburg: Herder, 1873), 269–419, and in his article "Glaube" in *Kirchenlexikon,* ed. Heinrich Joseph Wetzer and Benedict Welte, 2d ed., vol. 5 (Freiburg: Herder, 1888), cols. 616–74. In English, one may consult Joseph Wilhelm and Thomas B. Scannell, *A Manual of Catholic Theology Based on Scheeben's "Dogmatik,"* vol. 1 (London: Kegan Paul, Trench and Trübner, 1890), Bk. I, pt. 2, pp. 112–53. For discussions of Scheeben, see Karl Eschweiler, *Die zwei Wege der neueren Theologie,* chap. 3, pp. 131–5; John Courtney Murray, "The Root of Faith: The Doctrine of M. J. Scheeben," *Theological Studies* 9 (1948): 20–46; D. Thomas Hughson, *Matthias Scheeben on Faith: The Doctoral Dissertation of John Courtney Murray* (Queenstown, Ont.: Edwin Mellen Press, 1987).

47. Scheeben, "Glaube", col. 651.

48. Cited above, note 44.

49. Albrecht Ritschl, *Die christliche Lehre von der Rechtfertigung und Versöhnung,* 3 vols. (Bonn: A. Marcus and E. Weber, 3d ed. rev., 1888–1889); ET, *The Doctrine of Justification,* vol. 1 (Edinburgh: Edmonston and Douglas, 1872); vol. 3 (New York: Scribner, 1900, reprinted Clifton, N.J.: Reference Book Publishers, 1966).

# 5

# Early Twentieth Century

## Continuation of Liberal Protestantism

In the European universities, dominated by post-Kantian philosophy, the Protestant theology faculties continued to pursue the liberal agenda at least until World War I. They combined a positivist approach to history with a voluntarist approach to faith. The church historian Adolf von Harnack (1851–1930) popularized the system of Ritschl, notably in his lectures *Das Wesen des Christentums.*[1] Looking back to the historical Jesus as the norm, Harnack extolled the utter simplicity of Jesus' message of love, while vehemently denying that the gospel is a theoretical system of doctrine. Jesus, he asserted, never spoke of any kind of creed except "to do the will of God, in the certainty that He [God] is the Father and the one who will recompense" (147). After a long period of degeneration, culminating in modern Roman Catholicism, Luther recovered the pure essence of the gospel as comprising two essential elements, the word of God and faith. By the word of God Luther meant, according to Harnack, "the message of the free grace of God in Christ" rather than the Bible or Church doctrine. Harnack understood Luther as teaching that faith is the inward experience that corresponds to God's word, an experience of the certainty of grace (270).

Another liberal theologian deeply concerned with the question of faith was Wilhelm Herrmann (1846–1922). More conscious than Ritschl and Harnack of the difficulties of reconstructing the historical Jesus from the scientific study of the New Testament, he distinguished sharply between historical science and religious inquiry. In his major work, *The Communion of the Christian with God,*[2] he concentrates on the picture of Jesus conveyed by the Gospels, and reserves the name *faith* "exclusively for the trust which the picture of Jesus awakens in us and the new purpose and courage which are born of that trust" (241). The experience of communion with God, he maintains, comes into our life as a sheer gift when we submit to the power of the Gospels. "The one thing which the gospels will give us as an overpowering reality which allows no doubt is the most tender part of all: it is the inner life of Jesus himself" (75). In the experience of the revelation of God we encounter Jesus as the ground of our salvation (82). Without any reliance on historical criticism of the Gospels and without prior inquiry into their credibility, the believer encounters the real and historical *(geschichtlich)* Christ as the one through whom God enters into communion with us (143). Faith, then, takes the form of joyful consciousness of the blessing by which God lifts us into communion with Himself (213).

While building on Luther's doctrine of faith, Herrmann found certain unfortunate remnants of Catholic dogmatism in Luther himself and in sixteenth-century confessional writings such as the Formula of Concord. Within his own Lutheran tradition, Herrmann sought to combat the "orthodox" view that some kind of assent to doctrine might be a necessary preamble to trustful self-surrender (223). Such dogmatic faith, according to Herrmann, would inevitably become a work which the believer would regard as his own.

Like Ritschl, Herrmann criticized Luther for having failed to clarify the relationship between faith and ethical conduct. For his part, Herrmann accepted the Pauline formula of "faith working through charity" in the sense that the impulse that controls faith presses on to activity that itself belongs to the communion of the Christian with God (319–20).

Liberal Protestantism took a more subjectivist and sentimental turn in France with Auguste Sabatier (1839–1901), the dean of the faculty of Protestant Theology at Paris. Sabatier proudly professed himself a son of the Reformation—a movement that for him involved two basic principles. The first, justification by faith—which he understood as referring to "trust of the heart"—freed the Christian from the tutelage of the priesthood and the bondage of creeds and dogmas. The second principle, operative in the field of dogmatics, "substituted the internal principle of Christian experience for the external principle of authority; it made of Christianity a moral life and no longer a metaphysic."[3]

The object of faith, for Sabatier, "is always a moral and religious reality immediately manifest to consciousness, without any other demonstration than the inward demonstration of the Holy Spirit."[4] Truths of the moral and religious order, founded in "the feeling of subjective life, or moral evidence" are known by "a subjective act of what Pascal calls *the heart*."[5]

For Sabatier it was essential to distinguish between faith, as an act of the heart and will, and belief, as an "intellectual act by which the mind gives its consent to a historic fact and to a doctrine." That which saves the soul, he added, is faith, not belief.[6]

Sabatier's close colleague at the Protestant Faculty of Paris, Eugène Ménégoz, coined in 1884 the term "symbolo-fideism" to designate the positions shared by himself and Sabatier. *Symbolism,* he held, was necessary because the essence of things escapes us; we know God and the objects of religion only through sensory appearances. *Fideism* for him signified that "we are saved by faith independently of beliefs." Faith is a movement of the heart whereby we forsake sin, repent, and give ourselves to God. By this movement we are saved regardless of what we believe. Faith, as an activity of the whole person, does have an influence on what we think, and hence tends to be accompanied by certain kinds of beliefs. Doctrines have pedagogical value, but they should not be taken as though they gave us direct and accurate access to religious realities themselves.[7]

## Orthodox Reactions in Protestantism

The liberal movement in Protestant theology did not go unchallenged. In the Dutch Reformed churches and in North American Presbyterianism there was a vigorous revival of an older theology of faith. This revival, inspired by Calvin and by the Calvinist confessional documents, adhered staunchly to the Bible as the divine instrument of saving knowledge. It stressed both the cognitive and the fiducial aspects of faith.

As a Dutch representative of this tendency Abraham Kuyper (1837–1920) may be considered. His theology of faith is accessible in two volumes that have been translated into English: *The Work of the Holy Spirit*[8] and *Principles of Sacred Theology*.[9]

In opposition to the Kantians, who separated faith from knowledge, Kuyper insists that faith is a necessary means of gaining cognitive certainty, whether about material realities or about those that are spiritual. "By faith," he writes, "you are sure of all those things of which you have a firm conviction, but which conviction is *not* the outcome of observation or demonstration" (P 131). All human knowledge, even that based on observation, ultimately rests on faith, for there is no way of demonstrating the existence of one's own ego, the reliability of one's senses, or the reality of the external world (W 385, P 129–40). In religion, faith obtains absolute significance, for religious knowledge rests totally on the self-revelation of God as the higher Power on whom we are utterly dependent (P 148). In the spiritual order, faith is all-important because it guarantees not only the formal principles (as it does also in mundane matters) but the very content, for which observation offers no support (P 149).

God, although he is naturally knowable to human beings in the state of original innocence, is knowable to sinners only with the help of grace. Sin turns the mind away from God and causes the affections to cling to creatures (P 276–77). The Holy Spirit illuminates the mind to see the glory of God reflected in the Christ who manifests himself in the Scriptures (W 401). The Spirit also rectifies the will so that it may serve the changed consciousness (W 404). The grace of the Spirit is irresistible; it carries all before it (P 366).

In saving faith there are three phases, designated by the classical authors as *notitia, assensus,* and *fiducia* (W 400). The first phase, perception or knowledge of the testimony, is a precondition of faith. In the second phase we assent by faith to the things revealed. Then follows, thirdly, the persuasion that the revelation concerns us personally and brings salvation *(fiducia)*.

The sole object of saving faith, for Kuyper, is "Christ in the garments of Sacred Scripture" (W 397). Faith not only accepts the Scripture as the testimony to Christ; more importantly, it submits to Christ as the one of whom the Scripture speaks (W 399). Faith, as a gift of the Holy Spirit, is a disposition "planted by the Holy Spirit in the consciousness and will of the regenerate person whereby he is enabled to accept Christ" (W 415).

Kuyper gives various arguments for holding that revelation must be given by writing (and eventually by the printed word), but in the end he relies not on a priori reasoning but on what he takes to be the fact that saving faith in the testimony of God is not found except where the Scriptures have been the divine instrument in God's hand (P 368). The true ground for believing in Scripture is the testimony that goes out from the Holy Spirit as its author to our own personal ego (P 556–57). Elsewhere Kuyper writes: "Faith and Scripture go together; the Holy Spirit intended the one for the other" (P 419).

Although Kuyper differs from the liberals by reason of his confessional orthodoxy, his biblicism, and his cognitive view of faith, he resembles Schleiermacher, Ritschl, Herrmann, and Sabatier in his emphasis on the affections of the heart and the feeling of dependence. Like them, he rejects any approach to God through natural theology or apologetics. Faith for him is an absolute new beginning, an irresistible gift of the Holy Spirit. "What God Himself does not bear witness to in your soul personally (not mystic-absolutely, but through the Scriptures) can never be known and confessed by you as Divine. Finite reasoning can never obtain the infinite as its result. If God then withdraws Himself, if in the soul of men He bear no more witness to the truth of His Word, men *can* no longer believe, and no apologetics, however brilliant, will ever be able to restore the blessing of faith in the Scripture" (P 366).

Kuyper's younger colleague at Amsterdam, Herman Bavinck (1854–1921), likewise held that the inner testimony of the Holy Spirit is the real ground of faith and that the object of faith is Christ as attested by the Scripture.[10] In another work, *De Zekerheid des Geloofs,* he stated that "Apologetics is the fruit, not the root, of faith."[11]

Very different from the Reformed theology represented by Kuyper and Bavinck was the Presbyterian theology typified by Charles Hodge (1797–1878) and his disciple, Benjamin B. Warfield (1851–1921), at Princeton Theological Seminary. The Princeton theologians developed the rational and evidential aspects of Calvinism with the help of Scholastic Aristotelianism and Scottish "common sense" realism. Although they approved of the orthodoxy of Jonathan Edwards, they were suspicious of the latter's emphasis on religious experience.

Warfield, while greatly admiring Kuyper and Bavinck, criticizes their views on faith and reason. The Amsterdam theologians, he objects, indulge a mystical tendency that substitutes the internal testimony of the Holy Spirit for the objective grounds perceptible to reason.[12] As a result, both these authors "minify" apologetics, which has a part to play in conversion and in evangelization. The Holy Spirit does not produce faith without grounds but enables us to grasp the objective validity of the grounds.

Warfield's own views on faith are impressively set forth in his 1905 article "Faith" for Hastings's *Dictionary of the Bible,* and especially in his article "On Faith in Its Psychological Aspects."[13] In common speech the terms "belief" and "faith" are sometimes used to mean persuasion on grounds that are less than cogent, but this cannot be the essential meaning of the term (381). In biblical usage and theology "faith" refers to a firm conviction, which would be impossible unless the grounds were perceived as adequate. In faith we do not affirm what we wish were true, but we yield to what we perceive ourselves as bound to accept. Faith differs from knowledge not because it is less well grounded but because the grounds are not theoretically grasped. Positively, faith is an assent that rests on authority perceived to be trustworthy (389). Religious faith rests with adoring trust on a person on whom we depend (393). In such a case the engagement of the whole person is more observable, but the determination of the response by the evidence is no less stringent (394). Thus the confidence of faith is neither arbitrary not ungrounded.

As a conservative Calvinist, Warfield recognizes the three standard elements of faith. While trust, or commitment *(fiducia),* is essential for salvation, the fiducial element should not be stressed at the expense of *notitia* and *assensus. Fiducia* is a product of *assensus,* which in turn presupposes *notitia,* by which we perceive the object to be believed (402–3).

Warfield, like Kuyper, asserts that fallen human nature is incapable of faith unless it is regenerated by grace. Grace removes the rebelliousness by which people seek to make themselves independent of God; it illumines their minds to respond to the evidence and softens their hearts so that they can commit themselves to God as their Savior (398). But grace does not take the place of evidence. On the contrary, it makes the evidence perceptible as having compelling force, so that, in the end, faith is a "forced consent."

## Catholic Modernism

The French exegete Alfred Loisy (1857–1940), taking on the role of an apologist, produced a Catholic response to Harnack and Sabatier. He faulted them for an individualism that overlooked the social and historical character of religion. Harnack, he believed, was also mistaken in seeking the permanent essence of Christianity in the teaching of the historical Jesus, who stands only at the beginning of a religion that has developed far beyond him. Loisy's response to Harnack and Sabatier was first expressed in a series of articles published under the pseudonym of A. Firmin in the *Revue du clergé français* (1898–1900). A little later he composed *The Gospel and the Church,*[14] a book-length reply to Harnack's *What is Christianity?* In two other small books he defended his responses to Harnack against his Catholic critics.[15]

According to Loisy, God makes faith available to all human beings, even those unacquainted with biblical revelation, for all have a rudimentary sense of God's presence behind the phenomenal world (*Autour d'un petit livre,* 196). Faith takes its rise from a sense of God and of the conformity of religion with human needs and aspirations ("Les preuves de l'économie de la révélation," 140–42.)[16] Faith is not the result of metaphysical or historical proofs, but the signs of credibility, taken cumulatively, provide a very high probability or moral certitude, and thereby help to establish conditions favorable to Christian faith (*Simples réflexions,* 65). The higher light of faith illumines the historical facts and apologetical arguments ("Les preuves . . . ," 132). "The perception of religious truths is not the fruit of reason alone; it is a work of intelligence carried out, so to speak, under the pressure of the heart, of the religious and moral feeling, and of a genuine aspiration for the good" (*Autour*, 197). What is called revelation is simply man's acquired consciousness of his relation to God. The faith-consciousness of the Christian is a communication of Christ's consciousness of his own intimate relationship with God (*Autour*, 195–96).

Faith lives in the simple truths contained in vague assertions of faith before it becomes elaborated in precise doctrinal formulas (*Simples réflexions*, 159–60). Dogmatic concepts and formulas are symbols and metaphors of the ineffable as perceived at a certain stage of humanity's intellectual evolution. The dogmas must constantly be recast to keep pace with the actual state of human knowledge. If the magisterium fails to keep its official formulations abreast of the scientific development of humanity, conflicts arise between faith and reason, resulting in crises of faith.[17]

Harnack and Sabatier, Loisy charges, were wide of the mark in imagining that the Catholic Church confuses revelation with immutable doctrines. Revelation is mutable in the sense that its symbols are subject to transformation, but it always remains for faith substantially identical with itself. It preserves its spirit and its continuity in the course of its development.

Loisy differs from Harnack and Sabatier in his acute consciousness of historical change and relativity, and in his reliance on the magisterium of the Church to adapt the formulations of faith to the existing state of human culture. But in his sharp distinction between faith and doctrine, and in his insistence on the role of the heart and religious feeling in the act of faith, Loisy adopts positions closer to his liberal Protestant adversaries than to his Catholic coreligionists.

The English Jesuit George Tyrrell (1861–1909), after teaching ethics for a time at a Jesuit scholasticate, became a popular spiritual director and counselor, especially for intellectuals who were experiencing problems of faith. Many university-educated Catholics at the time felt that their faith was threatened by recent developments in science and historical criticism that were hard to reconcile with the Bible and official Church teaching. Tyrrell's remedy was to make a sharp distinction between faith and theory and to admit that the theoretical understanding of faith must be adapted to the progress of secular knowledge.

For Tyrrell, everything turns on a correct conception of faith. Faith in its true and evangelical sense is an acceptance of what Matthew Arnold called "the Power that makes for Righteousness"—a Force whereby we feel impelled upward and onward toward the Ideal, the Better and the Best (*A Much-Abused Letter*, 71).[18] The faculty of faith is a power of religious perception that relates us to a world beyond the grasp of clear consciousness. Faith is rightly called divine and supernatural, for the vision of this higher world is not at our command; it is given to us at "moments when we seem to be most filled with God, when we are truest to all that is best in our spiritual nature" (ibid., 69–70).

Faith, for Tyrrell, is not a matter of believing on hearsay (ibid., 69). Still, the words of inspired teachers can play an important part in evoking an inner recognition of what God is saying to us personally. "The faculty of faith, or religious intuition, . . . strives, by assimilation and sympathetic self-adaptation, to re-experience in itself that religious experience of which the Bible is a written record" (*The Programme of Modernism,* 149).[19] I can believe on the strength of God's word to another if, and only if, God illumines it for me and brings it home to me by suprarational intuitive certitude (*Through Scylla and Charybdis,* 305).[20] Without personal revelation, then, there can be no faith.[21] The light of faith and the *pius affectus credulitatis,* as understood by Tyrrell, are personal, incommunicable experiences (*Scylla,* 316).

Tyrrell holds that the New Testament and the creed, as inspired expressions of the apostolic faith, continue to have normative force. The beliefs embodied in these sources transmit values corresponding to the highest human possibilities. The creed appeals to the imagination and to the implicit reason of the heart rather than the explicit reason of the understanding (*Lex credendi,* viii).[22] The affirmations in the creed are in some sense sacramental. They signify and convey abiding spiritual values under culturally conditioned forms (*Lex orandi,* 205).[23] Life, not logic, is the ultimate criterion for judging which beliefs and forms of belief are fit to survive (ibid., 211). Right beliefs are validated by their fruits in practical life (ibid., 113). Tyrrell interprets Thomas Aquinas as holding that the habit of faith gives an instinctive power of discernment whereby even the unlettered can scent out heresy through a kind of connaturality or "sympathy of spirit with spirit" (*Lex credendi,* 18).

In opposition to the neo-scholasticism of his day, Tyrrell denies that the theoretical content of dogmatic declarations can be binding on members of the Church. Popes, bishops, and councils, he asserts, are guardians of the deposit of the faith. They may condemn whatever corrupts the faith of the Church, but they cannot require acceptance of their own positive understanding of the faith. The protective significance of dogma, not its theological significance, is binding.

In line with the logic of this position, Tyrrell in his later works denies that there can be any legitimate development of dogma. If the faith had grown as a seed grows into an oak tree, we would be in a position superior to the apostles; revelation would have increased since the time of the apostles rather than being, as Catholics hold, closed (*Scylla,* 323).

Although Tyrrell is bitterly critical of liberal Protestantism, he stands close to Schleiermacher and Sabatier in his high esteem for personal religious experience as providing the real content and norm for the assent of faith. Although he strives to distance himself from sentimentalism, he gives minimal content to the assertions of faith. While attributing some doctrinal authority to the ecclesiastical magisterium, he severely limits that authority insofar as he deprives the positive intellectual content of dogmatic pronouncements of obligatory force. Church authorities, for him, are not capable of authoritatively clarifying or spelling out what was obscure or implicit in the original deposit of faith. In this respect Tyrrell diverges from Loisy's uninhibited developmentalism.

Church authorities found fault with many of the positions of Loisy and Tyrrell. As early as 1903 Cardinal François M. B. Richard of Paris and other prelates began compiling lists of errors in the writings of Loisy and his school which they forwarded to the Holy See for condemnation. On July 3, 1907, the Holy Office issued a Decree, *Lamentabili sane exitu,* proscribing sixty-five propositions taken in substance from the writings of various Modernists (DS 3401–3474). Although no authors or books were named, a number of the propositions are evidently taken from Loisy, and others seem to be drawn from authors such as Tyrrell, Le Roy, and Houtin.

Proposition 21 condemns the view that "the revelation that constitutes the object of Catholic faith, was not complete with the apostles." This may have been the view of Loisy, but certainly is not that of Tyrrell in his later works.

Proposition 25 rejects the view that "the assent of faith ultimately relies on an accumulation of probabilities." This does not represent the real thinking of either Loisy or Tyrrell, but Loisy apparently agreed with Newman that the rational judgment of credibility is a moral certainty arising from what Newman called a "convergence of probabilities." Presumably the Holy office had no intention of condemning Newman's apologetical approach.

On September 8, 1907, Pope Pius X published *Pascendi dominici gregis,* an encyclical in which he affixed the term "Modernism" to a general movement which he described as a "synthesis of all heresies."[24] The body of the encyclical systematically expounds the alleged Modernist positions on a variety of problems in the fields of philosophy, faith, theology, history, biblical criticism, apologetics, and ecclesiology. Once again, no names are mentioned, nor is any attempt made to specify which of the errors are in themselves heretical. As portrayed in this document, the Modernists explain faith as resulting from an inner sense that arises from the heart because of a need for the divine. This religious sense puts the soul in immediate contact with the divine, which is perceptible only in faith. Since reason is unable to prove the reality of God, the purpose of apologetics is not to give rational demonstrations but to induce an experience of religion, which is the only source of faith. History, the Modernists maintain, is incapable of discerning God's interventions in the world, which are perceptible only to faith. Faith, therefore, is separated from history, as it is from philosophy.

Faith initially expresses itself in primitive formulas that are accepted and sanctioned by the heart. Some of these formulas are found in Scripture and the creeds. Subsequently faith, again under the guidance of the heart, issues in secondary formulations of a more technical character. Dogmas are those secondary formulations which the magisterium sanctions as responding to the common consciousness of the faithful. Dogmas are not propositional statements of revealed truth, but as symbols they stimulate the religious sense to apprehend the divine. Dogmas must be changed to correspond to the state of evolution of human consciousness.

The entire system of the Modernists, according to Pius X, is vitiated by the philosophical errors of agnosticism and immanentism. It leads to pantheism and eventually to atheism.

On September 1, 1910, the pope issued a *motu proprio* containing the Oath against Modernism. The first five articles in this oath are pertinent here. First, it is declared that God can be known with certainty by the natural light of human reason from the visible works of creation. Second, the proofs of the divine origin of the Christian religion from miracles and prophecies are still valid. Third, the Church was instituted by the real and historical Christ. Fourth, dogmas do not evolve and change from one meaning to another differing from what the Church previously held. Fifth,

> I hold with certainty and sincerely confess that faith is not a blind sentiment of religion welling up from the depths of the subconscious under the impulse of the heart and the pressure of a morally informed will, but is a genuinely intellectual assent to truth received from outside by hearing, whereby we accept as true, on the authority of God who is supremely truthful, that which has been said, attested, and revealed by the personal God, our Creator and Lord. (DS 2145)

By accentuating the truthfulness of God in its treatment of the motive of faith this formulation seems to favor the positions of de Lugo and Franzelin that the veracity of God constitutes a true cause, rather than a mere condition, of the act of faith, and that it is the veracity of God, rather than his sovereign lordship, that engenders faith. But it would be unwarranted to conclude that the Oath intends to condemn other positions such as those held by the Carmelites of Salamanca and Scheeben.

## Neo-Scholasticism

In the years following the Modernist crisis the Catholic theology of faith divided into two streams. One stream, dominant in Scholastic circles, reacted against Modernism by minimizing the experiential component and concentrating on the authority and transcendence of God the revealer. The other stream sought to accommodate the legitimate concerns of Modernism by emphasizing the immanence of the divine and the value of the religious experience.

Louis Billot (1846–1931), a French Jesuit professor at the Gregorian University, may be taken as representative of the first tendency.[25] His position was not unique to himself since it coincides in great part with that of the German Jesuit, Christian Pesch.[26] Billot's views were popularized by the French Jesuit Jean Vincent Bainvel, some of whose terminology will be borrowed in the present exposition of Billot's system.[27]

By the assent of faith Billot means believing not because of intrinsic reasons (those directly establishing the truth of the proposition assented to) but because of the testimony of another. Faith in God, or divine faith, has for Billot, as it had for de Lugo, the same structure as human faith and may accordingly be elucidated by reference to the latter. Unlike de Lugo, Billot distinguishes between two species of faith. In the one case, recognized by de Lugo, the assent rests upon evidence that the witness could not be departing from the truth. Thus a historian or a detective might be able to show from the multitude of independent and concordant testimonies that the facts must be as reported. Under these circumstances one could have what Bainvel calls "scientific faith"—that is to say, faith based on evidently true testimony. But this assent hardly deserves the name of faith because it does not involve personal trust in the witness. Faith is more properly verified when one assents out of reverence for the dignity of the witness, as does a child who trustingly adheres to the word of an esteemed parent. This faith of homage or, as Bainvel calls it, "faith of simple authority," is the best analogy for divine, salutary faith.

Billot does not deny that a scholar might be able to prove the truth of the Christian religion indirectly by demonstrating philosophically that God is truthful and by establishing through historical research the fact of revelation. In such a case de Lugo's analysis of faith as an implied syllogism would hold. But "scientific" faith of this kind, for Billot, would lack the qualities of salutary Christian faith. To be a believer in the theological sense, one must adhere trustingly to the word of God out of reverence for the Revealer. Such faith is necessarily free, because the mind cannot assent out of reverence except under the influence of the will. Faith of this kind can, moreover, be absolutely certain because the firmness of the assent is proportionate to the dignity of the witness, which is the motive.

Does faith of "simple authority" meet the requirement of reasonableness, laid down by Vatican I? Contrary to the school of de Lugo, Billot answers that it does, provided that the believer has prior certainty of the truthfulness of God and of the fact of divine revelation. In the case of educated believers, explicit argument will be required to validate these preambles. The conclusion of the argument will not be the truth of the proposition attested to, but the credibility of the witness. Thus room is left for a free assent to the revelation out of reverence for God the Revealer. The judgment of credibility is not the motive of faith but a mere prerequisite; it is a condition, not a cause. The act of faith does not follow automatically from the judgment of credibility.

Can uneducated persons obtain sufficient rational evidence to exclude the probability of error? Billot and his school reply that such persons cannot be held to a type of certitude exceeding their capabilities. To accept the fact of revelation on the word of parents or teachers may be prudent for them, although not for more educated Christians. Their rational certitude of the fact of revelation can be "relative" or "respective," in the sense of being adequate for themselves.

Turning to the traditional problem of the analysis of faith, Billot puts the questions: What is the motive? Must the motive be known, and if so, how? For Billot, as for Vatican I, the motive or formal cause of divine or salutary faith can only be the authority of God who reveals. That authority must be known, or it could not motivate the act of assent. It can be known in two alternative ways. Before the act of faith, God's authority is known through the evidence of credibility, which indicates that he has indeed spoken. In the act of faith, it is known simply as the motive of the assent. De Lugo, according to Billot, erred in holding that faith rests on an implied syllogism. If we had to make a prior judgment to the effect that whatever God reveals is true, God's authority would be an additional material object, not the formal object of the assent. For Billot the authority of the Revealer is known not as the content of an assent but only as the motive; not as a "what" but as a "why."

Must faith have a *supernatural* formal object? In other words, does the believer have to perceive God in some supernatural way, as graciously drawing the believer to himself? For Billot, no such perception is necessary. Since faith is a theological act, its formal object must be uncreated. The formal object, therefore, is God himself, not the believer's awareness of God. Hence it suffices that the believer submit reverently to God, precisely as God, the sovereign witness whose word is known to be absolutely worthy of credence. The dispute between the schools of de Lugo and Suarez about whether the formal object is known naturally or supernaturally is based, according to Billot, on a misunderstanding of the nature of the formal object.

Like all other Catholic theologians Billot holds that grace is at work in any salutary act of faith. Grace elevates the human powers "entitatively," i.e., in their physical reality, but not "intentionally," i.e., in their mode of knowing and willing. When we make an act of supernatural faith, we do not consciously perceive the action of grace within us. Supernatural faith differs from natural faith by reason of the eliciting principle—a faculty elevated by grace—but not by reason of the formal object.[28]

To many of Billot's contemporaries it seemed that at length the difficult question of the analysis of faith had been solved. His theory was taken up in many of the leading manuals, such as those of Lennerz, Van Noort, Hervé, and Cathrein. It seemed to do justice to Vatican I by preserving both the freedom of faith and its certitude; both its supernaturality and its rational grounding.

Others, however, wondered whether Billot's success was anything more than verbal. If the fact of revelation could be, and in some sense had to be, demonstrated by unaided reason, what room was left for the freedom of faith? Would it be psychologically possible to be certain that God had spoken and still to withhold assent to what God had said? And if assent based on a merely natural knowledge of the motive could be absolute, what need would there be of grace? Billot asserted the influence of grace but failed to assign it any clear function. In dealing with the faith of the simple and uneducated, Billot seemed to demand too little by way of evidence, for he admitted that the motives on which these believers relied were fallible. Even the learned, in Billot's system, had only a moral certitude of the fact of revelation before the act of faith. What, then, prevents faith from being an overcommitment? In stating that the authority of God is known in faith simply as faith's own motive, Billot could be accused of falling back into the fideism ascribed to Suarez. Faith seemed to be grounded, in the last analysis, on one of its own ingredients.

An alternative version of the neo-scholastic approach to faith, based more directly on a study of St. Thomas himself, was offered by the French Dominican Ambroise Gardeil (1859–1931). In a series of articles later reworked into a volume, *La crédibilité et l'apologétique,*[29] he set forth an elaborate account, involving no fewer than twelve steps (pp. 31–35). He regarded the first half of the approach to faith (steps 1–6) as substantially natural, although he did not exclude the de facto working of grace. The mind, motivated by a naturally upright intention of finding God's will, disposes itself to adhere to whatever God may have revealed. By examining the signs in history, it then arrives at a naturally certain judgment of credibility, involving "scientific faith" in the fact of revelation. Then the second, supernatural part of the process (steps 7–12) unfolds. It begins with a supernatural judgment of credentity whereby the individual judges that he or she has a personal obligation to assent to the content of revelation. This judgment is elicited by the mind under the supernatural attraction to believe, traditionally known as the *pius credulitatis affectus.* In the light of this judgment the intellect chooses to believe and, under the command of the will, makes the act of faith.

Like Billot and Bainvel, Gardeil wrestled with the problem of accounting for the faith of those who, owing to ignorance or simplicity of mind, cannot reach a critically tested certainty about the fact of revelation. Gardeil held that for such believers a merely probable judgment of credibility would suffice, if accompanied by supernatural moral inclinations to which he gave the name "subjective supplements" *(suppléances subjectives).*

In summary, Gardeil admitted two alternative routes to faith, the one through a natural process of reasoning terminating in *fides scientifica,* the other through merely probable indications reinforced by impulses of grace. Bainvel and the followers of Billot were pleased with the first route, but found the second too subjectivistic. They wanted every believer to have objectively sufficient grounds for a firm judgment of the truth of revelation. A second school of theologians, including Maurice Blondel and Pierre Rousselot, rejected the whole concept of scientific faith and applauded at least the intention of Gardeil's second route. But they faulted Gardeil for having failed to integrate the inclinations of the will into the process by which the credibility of the Christian religion is discerned.

Stimulated by the criticisms made of his work, Gardeil published a revised edition in 1912,[30] in which he explained that his previous exposition had been abstract and doctrinaire. While continuing to insist on the possibility of purely natural scientific faith, Gardeil now conceded that, in the real order, grace is at work throughout the whole approach to faith. In this new approach he could pass directly from the judgment of credibility to that of credentity without positing a step in which grace elevated the intellect to the supernatural plane. The "subjective supplements" in this edition were described not as exceptional but as normal, since the soul is from the beginning in tension toward its supernatural end. But Gardeil did not wholly satisfy his critics since he held on to the concept of scientific faith and continued to speak of the affective impulse as pertaining to the appetibility rather than the rational credibility of faith. To Blondel and Rousselot he seemed to overlook the illuminative power of the grace of faith.

## From Blondel to Rousselot

A more philosophical approach to faith emerges in the work of Maurice Blondel (1861–1949), a pious Catholic layman whose objective in life was to combat the anti-Catholic prejudices in the secular academic world of his day. During the period of his studies at the École Normale in Paris (1881–1886) the reigning atmoshere was neo-Kantian. Rebelling against the grandiose systems of the idealists and the dogmatism of the materialists, a number of the leading thinkers held that reason could establish very little in the metaphysical field and that good moral dispositions were necessary to permit one to recognize religious truth. From masters such as Léon Ollé-Laprune, Blondel acquired an interest in the will and in belief as a voluntary act.

Standing at the outer fringes of the Modernist movement, Blondel aimed to conciliate the legitimate demands of modern thought while maintaining Catholic orthodoxy. In his dissertation, *L'Action* (1893),[31] he sought to prove that the most reliable path to truth lies in the analysis of the irrepressible needs and aspirations that underlie human action. The will seeks ever to surpass what human powers can achieve; it aspires to enter into communion with the infinite. This very effort degenerates into superstition unless God freely gives himself. The profound inclination of the will to mystical communion with the divine is therefore the point of insertion for the supernatural and for faith. The gift of faith, when received, becomes a principle of action. Right action recoils upon the agent; it renders one capable of thinking better and perceiving what would otherwise escape notice. By acting in accord with faith the believer can attain a certitude not available through merely rational arguments.

In several pseudonymous articles published between 1906 and 1908 Blondel applied his philosophy of action to the theological problem of faith.[32] Starting with a typology, he constructs a square of opposition in which intellectualism is contrasted with voluntarism, autonomy with heteronomy. In the intellectualist-autonomous corner of the square he situates the adherents of "scientific faith." The intellectualist-heteronomous position is that of the champions of "faith of simple authority." Voluntarist autonomism is represented by Kant. The voluntarist-heteronomous option is attributed to the traditionalists.

Most fundamentally, these disagreements raise the question whether faith is an intellectual judgment depending on the testimony of someone else or a practical judgment rooted in the dynamism of the individual will. Refusing the dichotomy, Blondel finds it necessary to say with Augustine and Newman that in faith, as a movement of the whole person toward the divine, knowledge and love are inextricably interwoven. As against the linear logic of rationalism, Blondel proposes a logic of circumincession, in which the priorities of will and intellect, and those of individual and society, are reciprocal.

For the purposes of analysis, Blondel distinguishes three stages in the approach to faith (the same three recognized by Scholastic theologians such as Gardeil and Bainvel): credibility, credentity, and faith itself. At the first stage the intellect considers the external signs of credibility. Miraculous events are meaningful and credible insofar as they are visible analogues of God's gracious condescension and refer the mind to God's saving intentions. Miracles can be seen as religious signs because they announce the good news for which our hearts are restless. By making us aware of the gift of God, these signs give valid rational motives for accepting the solicitations of grace.

The crucial stage for Blondel is the second, the personal judgment that God is requiring me to believe. For this judgment to be made, I must see that the religion in question is good for me, that it is attractive to me and meets my real needs. Otherwise I could not find it credible that God demands that I should assent to his decrees. The attraction of the will for the uncreated Good unleashes what theologians have called the *pius affectus credulitatis.* The will proposes the good to the intellect, which grasps "the good under the aspect of the true." In so doing the will renders the intellect more perceptive to the truth. Love—at least the beginning of love, if not the full love of charity—lets reason be captivated, so that it freely renounces its private judgment without having to be violently compelled by an alien power. This stage of the approach to faith is characterized by a happy encounter between the interior and the exterior, well described by Cardinal Victor Dechamps in his "Method of Providence."[33]

After these two preliminary steps, Blondel turns to the nature of faith itself. It is an infused virtue, a free gift of God. The testimony of God within us takes the form of an enlightenment, the *lumen fidei*. Without that illumination the assent of faith, Blondel argues, would be impossible. The ability to say, "I believe this because God says so," depends upon a supernatural gift, inwardly received. Since faith is the dawn of the interior light by which we hope to see God for all eternity, there can be no such thing as natural faith. Without the illumination and inspiration of grace we would be incapable of the full self-surrender that faith requires. Against Bainvel and his school, Blondel insists that simple folk and scholars are in essentially the same position before the demands of faith, for each must rely not primarily on historical evidence but on the inner call of God.

Blondel insists, moreover, that faith must be supernatural by reason of its formal object. The external signs could not be seen as warranting the full surrender of faith unless reinforced by an inner inclination that comes from grace and enters into the experience of faith itself. The Church's doctrine of grace accounts for the psychological phenomena felt by the believer. In systems like Billot's, as Blondel understands them, grace performs no real function; the whole process could be explained without it.

Against Billot and his school, therefore, Blondel asserts that the inclination of the will, arising under the influence of grace, contributes to the intellectual certitude. The will does not simply command adherence to a teaching that was previously seen by the intellect as certain. The desirability of the revelation enters into the constitution of its credibility. It sheds light on the real needs of the believer and on the divine origin of miraculous phenomena.

In comparison with the Scholastics, Blondel develops a richer concept of faith. He finds the current definitions too narrowly intellectualist and objectivist. In a brief note on faith for a philosophical dictionary Blondel admirably summarizes his concept:

> If faith increases our knowledge this is not first and foremost because it teaches us, through authoritative testimony, certain objective truths, but because it unites us to the life of a subject, because it introduces us, by loving thought, into another thought and another love. Belief (which already belongs to a more cognitive or logical order) is generally a derivative and partial form of faith. . . . Love, grounded in reason, though not on reasonings, is alone capable of knowing and loving. And that is why faith terminates in the most realistic of the forms of knowing.[34]

As frequently happens to those who seek to mediate between extreme positions, Blondel found himself attacked from both sides. For some admirers of Modernism, such as Lucien Laberthonnière, he was still too much under the shadow of Aristotelian objectivism, dualism, and intellectualism.[35] The Scholastics, on the contrary, accused Blondel of subjectivism, voluntarism, naturalism, and immanentism. More specifically, Eugène Portalié and Christian Pesch complained that Blondel failed to distinguish between the objective grounds for affirming the truth of Christianity and the practical motives that engage the will to embrace it.[36] Hippolyte Gayraud protested that Blondel compromised the gratuity of the supernatural by making it a gift demanded by the exigencies of nature.[37] Marie-Benoît Schwalm found Blondel guilty of a fideism that destroyed the rational grounding of faith.[38] Joseph de Tonquédec held that Blondel's apologetical method of recourse to religious experience was condemned in the encyclical *Pascendi*.[39] After surveying some of the criticisms, Roger Aubert faults Blondel for having left in the shadow the crucial truth that faith is "a knowledge by testimony *propter auctoritatem Dei revelantis*."[40] Many of the criticisms seem to be based on assumptions contested by Blondel, but one must concede that Blondel's conception of a gift that is both gratuitous and necessary raises some difficult questions that he himself did not fully resolve.

The French Jesuit Pierre Rousselot (1878–1915) came to the problem of faith after having written two dissertations, the one on the problem of love in the Middle Ages, the other on the intellectualism of Thomas Aquinas.[41] His importance for the theology of faith rests primarily on a single article, "Les Yeux de la Foi,"[42] in which he summarized the main findings of a course he had given the previous year as a professor at the Institut Catholique in Paris. Maurice Nédoncelle calls this article "beyond dispute the most stimulating work of the first half of the twentieth century."[43]

As compared with Blondel, Billot, Gardeil, and other contemporaries, Rousselot takes an independent approach which he regards as being in full accord with Thomas Aquinas. He rejects both the voluntarist position that faith precedes the recognition of its rational grounds and the rationalist position that would begin with a rational judgment of credibility and then proceed to the act of faith. The first position, which he attributes to Bautain and perhaps by implication to Blondel, fails to respect the demands of intellectual probity and the psychological impossibility of believing without rational grounds. The second position, which Rousselot finds in Hermes and the school of Billot, seems to him to imperil the freedom of the act of faith.

To avoid the dilemma, Rousselot proposes a theory in which will and intellect, love and understanding, are mutually prior to each other. According to Thomas Aquinas, he maintains, the practical judgment that one may and ought to believe both produces and is produced by the election of the will that commands the assent of faith. Love enables one to perceive the credibility of the revelation; conversely, the perception of its credibility enables one to believe. Far from hampering the intellect—as a selfish or inordinate desire would do—the love of the First Truth perfects reason in its very intellectuality, so that the mind sees more clearly the reasons for believing.

Against Billot, Bainvel, and Gardeil, Rousselot holds that natural or scientific faith is impossible. To refute them he relies partly on the condemnation of Georg Hermes. He ridicules the idea of a natural faith that would have to be reduplicated by a supernatural faith having no distinctive content or discernible existence. Yet, like these authors, Rousselot holds that reason can, at least with the help of grace, demonstrate the fact of revelation.

To explain the necessity of grace, Rousselot contends that the ability to discern the signs given in history depends on an active power of synthesis. Grace gives the needed sympathy with the supernatural reality; it bestows what Newman called the "illative sense." The force of the arguments of credibility is perceived not by syllogistic logic, which moves step by step, but by a logic of convergence in which all the elements reciprocally support one another.

Against Billot, Rousselot asserts that faith has a supernatural formal object. In other words, grace gives a different perspective or point of view. The believer sees reality from the standpoint of God who reveals. The created light of faith (the *habitus fidei*) is a participation in God's uncreated truth. The light of faith is an anticipation of the light of glory by which the blessed in heaven contemplate God. It therefore belongs to the same supernatural order.

In opposition to certain seventeenth-century Catholic theologians (Antonio Perez and Sforza Pallavicino), Rousselot denies that we can normally perceive the presence of grace within us. To that extent he agrees with Billot. He also distances himself from Victor Dechamps and Maurice Blondel, who referred to the inclination of grace as an "internal fact" from which one could make certain inferences. For Rousselot the light of faith is something by which we see, not something seen. It is, in Scholastic terminology, an *obiectum quo,* not an *obiectum quod.* It gives us the "eyes of faith."

Rousselot sees no reason for positing real distinctions between the judgment of credibility, the judgment of credentity, and the act of faith. For him the ultimate judgment of credibility and the judgment of credentity are achieved under the influence of the habit of faith, of which they are, so to speak, the disposing causes. The ultimate disposition is effected by the actual advent of faith, the formal cause.

The merits of Rousselot's theory are many. By his forthright attack on the concept of "scientific faith" he called attention to the Scotistic and Nominalistic elements that had denatured the Thomistic theology of faith in baroque and modern Scholasticism. He made it clear that faith, as an entrance into a new sphere of life, depends more vitally on the spiritual dispositions of the believer than on the materials presented for consideration. He deserves credit for reviving the doctrine of Thomas Aquinas that the grace of faith is a light—an active power of discernment—given to the mind by God, and that it instills in the soul a vital connaturality with the things of God. Rousselot's theory, better than most others, gives intelligibility to the strong affirmations of Orange II regarding the impossibility of advancing toward faith without the help of grace. It also brings into Scholastic theology the insights of Newman regarding the logic of convergence. It shows that the factual occurrence of miracles cannot be established without reference to their religious significance, and that the two dimensions of the miracle—the exceptional fact and the religious sign—are interdependent. For all these reasons, Rousselot continued to have great influence for at least fifty years after his death.

Because Rousselot strongly challenged many of the dominant positions, he excited sharp opposition. The opposition came from two sides. One group considered him too fideistic, since he made the gift of faith indispensable for the perception of rational credibility. The other group considered him too rationalistic, since he equated faith with the perception of rational credibility. Both groups contested Rousselot's refusal to make a real distinction between faith and its rational grounds.

The first line of criticism, typified in Stéphane Harent's article on Faith in the

*Dictionnaire de théologie catholique,*[44] contests Rousselot's tenet that the credibility of the Christian revelation can be seen only from within the circle of faith. This position is held to be contrary to a long tradition stretching from Augustine through Pius IX, to the effect that a responsible act of faith presupposes that one has already recognized rational grounds for believing. Rousselot's theory, by limiting the efficacy of arguments of credibility to persons who already had the *habitus* of faith, undermined the value of apologetics. In his system, moreover, no room was left for the sin of formal infidelity, which consists in failing to believe what one sees as worthy of belief.

The second line of criticism was urged especially by some Dominicans such as Réginald Garrigou-Lagrange[45] and Yves Congar.[46] Rousselot, it was objected, being obsessed with the question of credibility, wrongly introduced the perception of credibility into the very heart of faith itself. The arguments of credibility, according to these critics, do not enter causally into the act of faith, but merely dispose the subject to make a free act of faith motivated solely by the uncreated testimony of God. By doing away with the distinction between the judgment of credibility and the act of faith, Rousselot seemed to make faith itself an exercise of rational knowledge.

Thomistic scholars confirmed both lines of criticism.[46] They pointed out that according to the Angelic Doctor it was possible for demons and heretics, who lacked the gift of infused faith, to accept certain revealed doctrines on purely rational grounds. Rousselot's theory of connaturality, therefore, differed from that of Aquinas. Although Thomas Aquinas spoke of connaturality in connection with faith, he never said that the light of faith illuminated the signs of credibility or gave them probative value. Rather, he looked on the external signs and the inner instinct as two distinct motives, the former being merely dispositive and preparatory for the act of faith.

## Conclusion

During the first decades of the twentieth century the discussion of the theology of faith revolved around the validity of Kant's subjectivism and the acceptability of the historical-critical method in biblical studies. The liberal Protestants accepted both with a confidence, sometimes naive, that historical research would yield a picture of Jesus as a teacher of Kantian morality. The liberals adopted a moralistic concept of faith, which was modified, in the case of Herrmann and Sabatier, by a strong emphasis on religious feeling.

Conservative Protestantism sought to preserve the commitment of the Reformers to the Bible as interpreted in the creeds and dogmas of the early Church. In Holland, Kuyper and Bavinck gave a rather Kantian twist to the Calvinist insistence on the inner testimony of the Holy Spirit. In the United States, Benjamin Warfield hued more closely to the Calvinist Scholasticism of theologians like François Turretin. Although Warfield's biblicism is characteristically Protestant, his high confidence in the powers of reason linked him in some ways to medieval Scholasticism.

The Catholic Modernists recognized the futility of seeking to validate a Kantian style of faith by historical-critical scrutiny of the Gospels. Loisy and Tyrrell shared Kant's agnosticism toward metaphysics and dogma and Schleiermacher's tendency to found faith on the inclinations of the heart. Their efforts to integrate these perspectives within Catholic orthodoxy were repudiated by the Roman magisterium.

Jesuits such as Billot and Dominicans such as Gardeil continued to deal with the problems about faith and reason, nature and grace that had preoccupied earlier scholastic theologians, especially since the sixteenth century. They came up with rather complex solutions that, as we have seen, did not fully meet the objections of their critics.

With Blondel and Rousselot, Catholic theology began to incorporate certain insights from Kant into a sincere and integral acceptance of the Catholic tradition. They were able to make use, likewise, of Newman's inductive logic. Blondel's approach was more voluntarist; that of Rousselot, more intellectualist. Both gave new applications to the Thomistic idea of the *lumen fidei*, applying it to the approach to faith and the study of credibility. Billot, Gardeil, and their followers strongly attacked this new synthesis, partly because they regarded it as a departure from authentic Thomism. Nevertheless this new line of thinking, as we shall see, was destined to gain the allegiance of the most creative Catholic theologians of the next generation.

## Notes

1. Adolf von Harnack, *Das Wesen des Christentums* (1900); ET, *What is Christianity?* (New York: Putnam, 1901).

2. Wilhelm Herrmann, *Verkehr des Christen mit Gott* (Stuttgart: Cotta, 1886); ET of fourth German edition of 1903, *The Communion of the Christian with God* (New York: Putnam, 1906, reprinted 1971).

3. Auguste Sabatier, *Outlines of a Philosophy of Religion based on Psychology and History,* 3d ed. (London: Hodder and Stoughton, 1906), 254.

4. Idem, *Religions of Authority and the Religion of the Spirit* (New York: McClure Phillips and Co., 1904), 336.

5. Idem, *Outlines,* 311–12.

6. Idem, *Religions of Authority,* 335.

7. See Eugène Ménégoz, "Symbolo-fideism," in *Encyclopaedia of Religion and Ethics,* vol. 12, ed. James Hastings (New York: Scribner, 1925), 151–52.

8. Abraham Kuyper, *Het Werk van den Heiligen Geest,* 3 vols. (Amsterdam: J. A. Wormser, 1888–1889); ET, *The Work of the Holy Spirit* (New York: Funk and Wagnalls, 1900); hereafter referred to in parentheses as W.

9. Idem, *Encyclopaedie der heilige Godgeleerdheid,* 3 vols. (Amsterdam: J. A. Wormser, 1894); ET, *Principles of Sacred Theology* (1898, reprinted Grand Rapids, Mich.: Baker Books, 1980); hereafter referred to in parentheses as P.

10. Herman Bavinck, *Gereformeerde Dogmatiek* (1895), 564–65, as cited in Jack P. Rogers and Donald K. McKim, *The Authority and Interpretation of the Bible* (San Francisco: Harper & Row, 1979), 389–90.

11. Quoted by Rogers and McKim, *Authority and Interpretation,* 330.

12. See Benjamin B. Warfield's Introduction to Francis R. Beattie, *Apologetics, or the Rational Vindication of Christianity* (1903), in Warfield's *Selected Shorter Writings,* vol. 2 (Nutley, N.J.: Presbyterian and Reformed Publishing, 1973), 93–105, and Warfield's 1903 review of Bavinck's *De Zekerheid des Geloofs, SSW* 2:106–23.

13. Idem, *Princeton Theological Review* 9 (1911): 537–66, here cited as reprinted in Warfield's *Biblical and Theological Studies* (Philadelphia: Presbyterian and Reformed Publishing Co., 1952), 375–403.

14. Alfred Loisy, *L'Évangile et l'Église,* (Paris: Picard, 1902), ET, *The Gospel and the Church* (New York: Scribner, 1904).

15. Idem, *Autour d'un petit livre* (Paris: Picard, 1903); *Simples réflexions sur le Décret du Saint-Office "Lamentabili sane exitu" et sur l'Encyclique "Pascendi dominici gregis"* (Ceffonds: Chez l'auteur, 1908).

16. Idem, *Revue du clergé français* 22 (March 15, 1900): 126–53.

17. Idem, "L'Idée de la révélation," *Revue du clergé français* 21 (January 1, 1900): 250–71.

18. London, 1904 (anonymous); reprinted London, 1906, under George Tyrrell's name. Tyrrell does not give his source more precisely, but the idea is pervasive in Matthew Arnold's *Literature and Dogma: An Essay Towards a Better Apprehension of the Bible* (New York: Macmillan, 1903). In the Conclusion Arnold declares: "We make God, as Israel made him, to be simply and solely 'the Eternal Power, not of ourselves, that makes for *righteousness'*" (348).

19. *The Programme of Modernism: A Reply to the Encyclical of Pius X, "Pascendi Dominici Gregis"*; translation from the Italian by George Tyrrell, with an Introduction by A. Leslie Lilley (London: Longmans, 1906). Lilley's Introduction is based on a text supplied by Tyrrell; cf. David G. Schultenover, *George Tyrrell: In Search of Catholicism* (Shepherdstown, W.Va.: Patmos, 1981), 339.

20. Idem, *Through Scylla and Charybdis; or The Old Theology and the New* (London: Longmans, 1907).

21. Ibid., 306; see also idem, "Revelation as Experience," *Heythrop Journal* 12 (1971): 117–49, especially 134–39.

22. Idem, *Lex Credendi: A Sequel to Lex Orandi* (London: Longmans, 1906).

23. Idem, *Lex Orandi: or Prayer and the Creed* (London: Longmans, 1903).

24. Text in ASS 40 (1907): 596–650; ET in *The Papal Encyclicals* 3 (1903–1930), ed. Claudia Carlen (Wilmington, N.C.: McGrath Publishing Company, 1981), 71–98; quotation from no. 39, p. 89.

25. Louis Billot, *Tractatus de Ecclesia Christi* (1st ed., 1898; 5th ed., Rome: Gregorian University, 1927), Introductio *De Assensu Fidei,* 32–42; *De virtutibus infusis* (Rome: Gregorian University, 1901).

26. Christian Pesch, *Praelectiones theologicae,* vol. 8, 3rd ed. (Freiburg i. Br.: Herder, 1910), Tractatus II, *De Fide theologica,* 50–219.

27. Jean Vincent Bainvel, *La foi et l'acte de foi* (Paris: Lethielleux, 1898, 2d ed., 1908); ET, *Faith and the Act of Faith* (St. Louis: B. Herder, 1926).

28. Cf. Bainvel, *Faith and the Act of Faith,* 119.

29. Ambroise Gardeil, *La crédibilité et l'apologétique* (Paris: Gabalda, 1908). For a similar treatment see his article "Crédibilité" in *DTC* 3:2201–2309, published in 1907.

30. Idem, *La crédibilité et l'apologétique,* 2d ed. (Paris: Gabalda, 1912, reprinted 1928).

31. Maurice Blondel, *L'Action* (1893); ET, *Action (1893)* (Notre Dame, Ind.: University of Notre Dame, 1984).

32. F. Mallet (pseud.), *Qu'est-ce que la foi?* (Paris: Bloud & Gay, 1908), reprinting articles from *Revue du clergé français* 47 (1906): 449–73, 591–605. See also F. Mallet, "L'unité complexe du problème de la foi," *Revue du clergé français* 53 (1908): 257–85. A partial translation of the 1906 article appears in *Communio* (U.S. edition) 14 (1987): 162–92.

33. In *Entretiens sur la démonstration catholique de la religion* (1857) Victor Dechamps, C.SS.R., had maintained that God in his providence makes the Catholic Church, with its unity, perpetuity, and other attributes, a sign marvelously corresponding to the human need for divine revelation. On Dechamps see above, chap. IV, at note 40.

34. Maurice Blondel, Article "Foi," in A. Lalande, ed., *Vocabulaire technique et critique de la philosophie,* 10th ed. (Paris: Presses universitaires de France, 1968), 360.

35. See Maurice Blondel and Lucien Laberthonnière, *Correspondance philosophique* (Paris: Seuil, 1961), 268–70, 273.

36. See Roger Aubert, *Problème de l'acte de foi,* 2d ed. (Louvain, E. Warny, 1950), 215 and 331.

37. Joseph de Tonquédec, "Une nouvelle apologétique chrétienne," *Annales de philosophie chrétienne* 133 (1896–97): 257–73, 400–408; cf. Aubert, *Problème de l'acte de foi,* 297.

38. Aubert, *Problème de l'acte de foi,* 297.

39. de Tonquédec, *Immanence,* 4th ed. (Paris: Beauchesne, 1930), Appendix III, "L'Encyclical *Pascendi* et les doctrines de M. Blondel," 292–96.

40. Aubert, *Problème de l'acte de foi,* 293.

41. On Rousselot see Erhard Kunz, *Glaube-Gnade-Geschichte: Die Glaubenstheologie des P. Rousselot, S.J.* (Frankfort: Knecht, 1969); John M. McDermott, *Love and Understanding: The Relation of the Will and Intellect in Pierre Rousselot's Christological Vision* (Rome: Gregorian University, 1983) Aubert, *Problème de l'acte de foi,* 451–511.

42. Pierre Rousselot, *Recherches de science religieuse* 1 (1910): 241–59, 441–75; ET, *The Eyes of Faith* (New York: Fordham University Press, 1990).

43. Maurice Nédoncelle, Introduction to Newman, *Sermons universitaires* in *Textes Newmaniens,* vol. 1 (Bruges: Desclée De Brouwer, 1955), 35.

44. Stéphane Harent, article "Foi," *DTC* 6:55–514, especially cols. 260–75.

45. Cf. Réginald Garrigou-Lagrange, "Les vertus théologales et la nuit de l'esprit," *La vie spirituelle* 117 (1927–28): 269–90. This article makes no explicit mention of Rousselot but is in line with the author's criticisms of Rousselot in his review of "Les Yeux de la Foi," *Revue thomiste* 21 (1913): 485–89.

46. M.-J. Congar, book review of H. Lang, *Die Lehre des hl. Thomas von Aquin von der Gewissheit des übernaturlichen Glaubens, Bulletin thomiste* 7 (1930): 40–46, esp. 46.

47. Hippolyte Ligeard, "La crédibilité de la révélation d'après S. Thomas," *Recherches de science religieuse* 5 (1914): 40–59; Anselm Stolz, *Glaubensgnade und Glaubenslicht nach Thomas von Aquin* (Rome: Herder, 1933); José de Wolf, *La justification de la foi chez S. Thomas d'Aquin et le Père Rousselot* (Paris: Desclée De Brouwer, 1946).

# 6

# Mid-Twentieth Century

## Dialectical Theology

During the decades following World War I Protestantism developed a very rich theology of faith springing out of contrasting elements in the Protestant tradition. This new phase is often called "dialectical theology" because of its reliance on antitheses and paradoxes in speaking about the divine. In different ways Karl Barth, Rudolf Bultmann, and Paul Tillich exemplify the dialectical movement.

The most eminent leader in this renewal was the Swiss Reformed theologian Karl Barth (1886–1968). In the second edition of his commentary on Romans[1] he launched a theological revolution against liberalism. He had been a student, first of Adolf von Harnack in Berlin, then of Wilhelm Herrmann in Marburg. The latter persuaded him, against Harnack, that faith does not arise out of historical scholarship but is self-attesting. Influenced by Kierkegaard and others, Barth then became convinced that there is an impassable abyss between faith and humanly acquired knowledge. Faith does not rest on any preliminaries; it is its own initiation, its own presupposition (*Romans,* 99). God is intelligible only from within the position of faith (112). Faith, therefore, is a leap into the dark, into the void (98–99).

Since faith is an impossibility for all, the learned and the unlearned are equally remote from it (99). No finite subject can lay hold of the infinite: *Finitum non capax infiniti* (212). Piety and asceticism cannot prepare the way to faith for, as human works, they stand under God's universal condemnation (366). The religion of reason is a positive obstacle, for it puts unacceptable limits on the freedom and sovereignty of God (386). Nor is historical criticism of the Bible capable of validating the contents of faith. By its very failure to produce results that concern us, such criticism may indirectly open up the road to faith, which relies on a believing, nonhistorical interpretation (148; cf. 2–15).

Because it is inaccessible to human nature, faith is a radical miracle (116, 121). The believer, like Abraham, must cling to the impossibility from which all possibility emerges (123). Faith accepts the paradox that we are forgiven only when God

116

condemns us (*Credo quia absurdum,* 112). Faith, then, is possible only when all human possibilities have been exhausted. It tells us that Christ has died in our place and that we now stand with the "new man" on the far side of the cross. Understood in this way, faith "lies completely beyond the range of psychological analysis, for faith is the actual and positive impossibility which is unable to reckon with the possibility of sin having any existence on the plane of grace" (202).

Faith is a decision we make, not by our own power but in the power of God's word. It involves putting one's trust in God and determining to base one's life on God alone (39). Faith is the irrevocable step over the frontier between the old and the new, a conversion from which there is no looking back, no return (201).

The *Epistle to the Romans* is a work of great rhetorical power but it does not present, in the ordinary sense, a theology of faith. Barth here writes in paradoxes and metaphors, as though he felt that normal theological language could only deform and dilute the tremendous reality that is his theme.

In a 1931 book, *Anselm: Fides Quaerens Intellectum,*[2] Barth takes a further step. While insisting that faith is an absolute beginning to which there are no bridges, he maintains that the submission of faith provides an objective light and contains within itself "an embryonic *intelligere*" (40).[3] Theology, grounded in faith, can be a truly rational discipline. After his Anselm book Barth was in a position to begin his *Church Dogmatics,* a multi-volume treatise left incomplete at his death.

In the *Church Dogmatics* Barth initially discusses faith under the *Doctrine of the Word of God.*[4] Here he insists, as before, that fallen human nature has no capacity for the Word of God (236). Miraculously, God creates in man the point of contact whereby the Word of God can be received (238–40). Faith is the event in which the knowledge of God becomes real (228). It continually lives off its object, seeking it ever afresh (231). Faith trusts that God will continue to bestow both his Word and the capacity to receive it. Relying as it does on God's fidelity, faith has a fiducial character (234). In faith the mind acquires a certain conformity to the Word of God and hence the capacity to accept and confess it with final human seriousness (243).

The *Church Dogmatics* takes up the question of faith most thematically in a volume devoted to *The Doctrine of Reconciliation.*[5] Building on the work of Luther and Calvin, Barth is concerned to avoid giving the impression that believers save themselves by making acts of faith. This would be to reduce faith to a "work" in the pejorative sense of the term. The Reformation slogan *sola fide* can only mean for Barth that faith clings to Christ alone as Savior (*solus Christus,* 612). Faith stands or falls with its object, Jesus Christ. To make an act of faith is to find the center of one's existence in him (742–44). Faith is the basis of Christian existence for the individual (740). It is an act of the individual, but it occurs only in relation to the community, which is bound and committed to Christ as Savior and Head (753). The Holy Spirit is the power by which Christ makes people free for the decision of faith (748).

Against all anti-intellectuals Barth insists that faith is a form of knowledge *(Erkennen);* it has a definite intelligible content (764). But he sees this cognitive element as secondary. Primarily faith is an obedient act of compliance and acknowledgment (*Anerkennen,* 758). It is self-involving and in that sense existential (765). As a believer I know that Jesus Christ is my Lord, the One who is for me *(pro me).*

In the third place, faith is confession *(Bekennen)*. Like Thomas Aquinas, though without referring to him, Barth holds that the confession of faith is integral to faith itself. Ignited by the Word of God, the believer becomes a lighted candle radiating the splendor of Christ (776–79).

In opposition to the Bultmann school, which we shall presently consider, Barth attaches little importance to the act of faith as an event (767). The saving event for Barth is what took place in Christ, nothing else. Bultmann, he says, falls into the same basic error as Catholics, who attribute redemptive value to the Mass and the saints (767–68).

In its negative aspect, Barth explains, faith means radical humility and distaste for vainglory (619). Positively, it is adherence to Jesus Christ as the one who has taken on our sins and become the source of our justification (629). Faith trusts totally in Christ and thus reaches out like an empty hand to a righteousness not its own *(iustitia aliena,* 631). Yet it is not sterile. Despite its appearance of emptiness and passivity, justifying faith is supremely full and active (636). It takes the believer up into the pattern set by Christ, who was humble and obedient even to the point of death on the cross, and was exalted on that account (635). The Christian is conscious of being one with Christ in suffering and in confidence, both in *mortificatio* and in *vivificatio* (772–75).

Barth made an immeasurable contribution to the theology of faith in the present century. He showed eloquently and persuasively that faith must be seen as an obedient acknowledgment, a cognitive event, and an accomplishment of the Holy Spirit. He made it abundantly clear that faith can never be a merely human achievement, but is always an unmerited gift of God. In so doing he effectively countered certain Pelagian tendencies that he detected in modern theology, especially in liberal Protestantism.

Barth's theology of faith, however, encountered certain persistent criticisms that have not faded away with the years. In his zeal to prevent all human boasting, his critics complain, he looked too exclusively to God's saving decree in Jesus Christ, and failed to give sufficient salutary importance to the choice that must be made between belief and unbelief. For him, eternal salvation did not seem to depend on the personal faith of the believer, even as a condition. God's justifying act in Christ, as he understood it, is an event embracing all human beings so that "unbelief has become an objective, real and ontological impossibility and faith an objective, real and ontological necessity for all men and for every man" (IV/1, 747).

Barth, then, has to reinterpret salvation by faith alone to mean salvation by Christ alone. Can he do this and still speak, as Paul and the Reformers did, of being justified by faith? Can he still speak, as the New Testament repeatedly does, of the faith that saves? Can he hold that the good news does *not* benefit those who fail to receive it (cf. Heb 4:2)? The Dutch Reformed theologian Gerrit C. Berkouwer, after calling attention to texts such as these, remarks that Barth, in his zeal to prevent faith from being a "creative component" of salvation, or a source of merit, tends to overlook the urgent call of Scripture for faith as necessary for salvation.[6] From a Roman Catholic point of view, Hans Urs von Balthasar observes that "Barth had great difficulty in treating how it is possible for men not to have faith."[7] Another

Catholic, Henri Bouillard, comments that in denying that personal faith is even a condition for justification, Barth is unfaithful to Paul.[8]

Barth is not an irrationalist. At least in his later work he holds that the act of faith is posited in the full light of reason, which is enhanced, not diminished, by the Word of God. But he does not admit that, in the approach to faith, reason can rely on evidence perceived apart from faith itself. His position on this point is subject to many of the objections previously urged against Bautain. Barth makes much of the inner miracle of faith itself, but neglects the authentication of the Word of God by external signs. Here again he fails to do justice to the teaching of Jesus and the New Testament (Mt 11:3–5, 20–24, etc.).

Rudolf Bultmann (1884–1976) was, like Barth, a student of Harnack in Berlin and of Herrmann in Marburg. He also learned the principles of critical exegesis under masters such as Hermann Gunkel and Johannes Weiss. Influenced by Kierkegaard, he joined Barth and several others in the "dialectical theology" movement after World War I. But the principal philosophical influence on his work has been that of the existentialist Martin Heidegger, who came to Marburg as a professor in 1922. Bultmann resembles the early Barth in his admiration for Luther and his Kierkegaardian existentialism. But he differs from Barth in his commitment to critical biblical studies and in holding that theology depends on philosophical presuppositions. Although primarily an exegete, Bultmann is a highly systematic thinker, and he tends to find his own version of Christianity in the biblical authors, especially Paul and John.[9]

With heavy reliance on Paul, Bultmann describes human life without faith (*Kerygma and Myth,* 17–19).[10] It is a life weighed down by anxiety, which is born of the struggle to achieve security by worldly means. In this effort people become slaves of the very realities they hoped to master, and become dominated by the tools whereby they seek to control their destiny. In the quest for domination people run into conflict with one another, and fall prey to envy, anger, jealousy, and violence.

In contrast to this, Bultmann describes the life of faith as an abandonment of all self-contrived security. By giving up every attempt to save ourselves by means of creatures, we can open ourselves freely to the future as it comes to us from God, putting our trust in him alone (*Jesus Christ and Mythology,* 40–41).[11] Paradoxically, faith means security where no security can be seen. It is also freedom, for freedom is lost in the pursuit of security in the world (*Kerygma and Myth,* 211).

Faith, then, is a venture. For human nature it appears as a leap into the dark, but for those caught up in the Christian message it is a knowing venture, a real encounter with God, not a game of chance.[12]

Among the attributes of faith, Bultmann stresses freedom, detachment from worldly concerns, peace, and joy. Expecting all things from God, faith is closely related to trust and hope. As a decision it involves commitment and radical obedience. And it cannot but express itself in confession (*Theology of the New Testament,* 1:317).

Faith is not a work that people perform by their own powers. It is not self-assertion but self-renunciation. "Faith is God-wrought to the extent that prevenient grace first makes the decision possible, with the result that he who has made the decision can only understand it as God's gift" (*Theology of the New Testament,* 1:330). It never loses its character as a gift; it never becomes a stable possession that can be taken for granted. On the contrary, the decision of faith has to be made again and again as a reception of God's new gift (*Theology of the New Testament,* 1:322; *Kerygma and Myth,* 204).

In the footsteps of Luther, Bultmann confidently asserts that faith alone justifies. For Bultmann, in contrast to Barth, faith is a necessary condition for receiving salvation. It delivers one from the compulsion to sin that affects those who live without faith (*Theology of the New Testament,* 1:316).

Faith, according to Bultmann, does not rest on any grounds outside itself. There is no rational foundation for faith that can be established prior to the act of faith. Miracles, as God's acts, cannot be perceived except by the light of faith (*Kerygma and Myth,* 197). Bultmann gives credit to Herrmann for having taught him that faith would be insecure if it depended on proofs from verifiable phenomena (*Kerygma and Myth,* 201; cf. *Jesus Christ and Mythology,* 72). Faith does have grounds in the facts of saving history, but these grounds, Bultmann insists, are visible only to believers. "Only in faith," he writes, "is the witness recognized as legitimate. In other words, the object of faith makes itself accessible to nothing but faith" (*Theology of the New Testament,* 2:68–69).

The true content of faith is God's saving act in Christ, more specifically, in the death and resurrection of Jesus. To believe in Jesus Christ is to believe in the saving efficacy that makes the cross the cross of Christ. In other words, faith in the resurrection is an aspect of faith in the cross. "Faith in the resurrection is the same thing as faith in the saving efficacy of the cross, faith in the cross as the cross of Christ" (*Kerygma and Myth,* 41). Bultmann rejects the idea that the resurrection is a miracle adduced to prove the saving power of the cross. To imagine it as the resuscitation of a corpse would be in his judgment mythological.

The cross and resurrection constitute a saving mystery only because they are taken up in the faith of the Christian community and proclaimed as saving deeds. "Christ meets us in the word of preaching and nowhere else" (*Kerygma and Myth,* 41). Faith is a response to the proclamation of God's grace in Jesus Christ (*Kerygma and Myth,* 201).

The event of salvation is never a mere happening of past history. It is a source of faith and justification only because it continually happens in the word of proclamation. In this context it retains its character as event. Like the gift of revelation, the response of faith must be new every morning (*Jesus Christ and Mythology,* 76).

For Bultmann faith is not the acquisition of some theoretical knowledge about God that can subsequently be applied to the human situation. Rather, faith is essentially transformative and for that very reason salvific. Faith does have a cognitive dimension, which Bultmann describes as a new self-understanding. By this, however, he does not mean a new theory about the self, but rather a new orientation in which human existence is interpreted in the light of the Christian kerygma. This interpretation includes a knowledge that liberates the believer for loving service toward others. The new self-understanding is inextricably bound up with a new attitude and a resolve to act in accordance with what is grasped in faith.

Faith brings with it a new way of thinking and speaking about God. God is understood as acting so as to confront, address, judge, and bless those who believe. In faith I speak about God not in a neutral, theoretical way, but in a way that expresses the existential relationship I have toward God (*Jesus Christ and Mythology,* 68–69).

Faith for Bultmann is in some ways dogmatic, in other ways undogmatic (*Theology of the New Testament,* 1:318). It is dogmatic insofar as the Christian proclamation and commitment include acceptance of a word that comes by hearing. But it is undogmatic in the sense that it involves no objectivizing statements of a metaphysical or cosmological character. The dogmatic theology of the ancient Church, which formulated the doctrine of the two natures of Christ, is in Bultmann's view alien to the New Testament and "impossible for our thought."[13] In his suspicion of Greek metaphysical thinking Bultmann remains the true heir of nineteenth-century liberal Protestantism.

By his penetrating and thoroughly consistent analysis of the existential component of faith, Bultmann made a major advance. Speaking primarily to a generation disillusioned by the promises of technology and empirical science, he set forth a biblically inspired theology of conversion with rich implications for the theology of proclamation and for spirituality. Other theologians criticized him not so much for what he affirmed as for what he seemed to exclude. Barth accused him of confining the biblical message within the limits of existentialist philosophy and thus seeking to dominate the word of God. Bultmann's anthropocentrism, he objected, fell back into the errors of liberal Protestantism from which dialectical theology had sought to escape.[14]

Many other critics, Lutheran, Reformed, Anglican, and Catholic—accused Bultmann of posing artificial dilemmas between nature and person, essence and existence, fact and meaning, proclamation and doctrine. Granted that God addresses me here and now through his word, can faith say nothing except that I am addressed? Can it say nothing about God as he is in himself and about God as Creator and universal Lord? If God comes through his word, why can he not come through historical events, sacraments, and other means? By eliminating large areas of traditional theology, Bultmann presented a narrowly existential view of faith. These criticisms obviously raise questions of a broadly systematic character that go far beyond the theology of faith as a specific discipline.[15]

Paul Tillich (1886–1965) was a philosophical theologian standing fundamentally in the Lutheran tradition. Trained in Berlin and Halle, he wrote philosophical and theological dissertations on Friedrich Schelling, who continued to be the dominant philosophical influence on his mature work, most of which was published after his emigration to the United States in 1933. Tillich's theology of faith may conveniently be studied in his little volume, *Dynamics of Faith,*[16] but many of the elements are treated more extensively in the three volumes of his *Systematic Theology.*[17]

Although he insisted on the ultimacy of God's revelation in Christ and, with Luther, on the absolute primacy of grace, Tillich was concerned to build bridges with faiths other than Christianity and with modern secular disciplines such as sociology and psychology. He is generally grouped with Barth and Bultmann under the vague rubric of "dialectical theology," but his approach to faith was very different from theirs. He severely criticized Barth's word-theology as excessively authoritarian and heteronomous.

In a sense, says Tillich, everybody has faith, for it is impossible to stifle completely the relationship to the unconditional that lies at the heart of human existence. In this generic sense, faith is the state of being grasped by an ultimate concern. Faith is distorted if it invests preliminary realities with the dignity that belongs only to the infinite and the unconditional (*Systematic Theology,* 3:130; *Dynamics,* 1–3).

In a more specific sense, faith is the state of being grasped by the Spiritual Presence, the presence of the ultimate, manifest in Jesus as the Christ. This definition, as formulated, is Christological, but in Tillich's opinion it is universally valid, for as a Christian he is convinced "that it expresses the fulfillment toward which all forms of faith are driven" (*Systematic Theology,* 3:131).

As a total and centered act of the whole person, faith transcends the different faculties and functions characterizing human life. Yet it has ramifications in the realms of cognition, volition, and affectivity. First, it includes an assent to the truth of our relation to what concerns us ultimately and to the symbols expressing that relation. Second, it involves obedience to the Spiritual Presence that has grasped us. Third, it involves an ecstatic feeling that overcomes anxiety by taking into itself the power of transcendent unity (*Systematic Theology,* 3:132–33; *Dynamics,* 4–8).

If any one of these three elements is emphasized to the detriment of the others, the notion of faith is distorted. Thus there are three kinds of distortion. The intellectualist distortion looks upon faith either as knowledge with a low degree of evidence (Tillich may be thinking of Locke's epistemology) or as knowledge based on submission to authority that takes the place of evidence. The voluntarist distortion, found in Thomas Aquinas, regards faith as the fruit of a grace-given will to believe or, in some Protestant theologians, as a dutiful act of obedience. The emotionalist distortion exaggerates the element of feeling. As examples of this third aberration, Tillich cites Schleiermacher and his disciples (*Dynamics,* 30–38).

For faith to be anything more than a generic state of ultimate concern it must come to concrete expression. "The language of faith is the language of symbols" (*Dynamics,* 45). Revelatory symbols are powerful because they participate in the power of the reality to which they point, and thus have a transforming impact on persons who accept them. The awareness of the divine presence in particular symbols arouses the experience of the holy. Symbols of the holy enable us to submit to the demands of what concerns us ultimately and to entrust ourselves totally to it (*Dynamics,* 12–16, 41–44).

"God is the fundamental symbol of what concerns us ultimately" (*Dynamics,* 46). Jesus as the Christ symbolizes for Christians the victory of the creative ground of life over the forces of destruction and estrangement—a victory establishing what Tillich calls the "New Being," and bringing salvation to those who participate in its symbolic power. Christian faith, therefore, is predicated on the conviction that Jesus as the Christ is the most adequate symbol of our ultimate concern. The symbol of the cross of Christ communicates the transcendence of its meaning because, through the element of self-negation, it expresses its own lack of ultimacy (*Systematic Theology,* 1:136, 2:158–59).

Tillich was fascinated by the paradoxical relationship between faith and doubt. Faith embraces certain symbols as mediations of the ultimate. Inasmuch as it experiences the holy and participates in its own object, faith contains an element of certainty, but inasmuch as faith is a finite act that falls short of the object in which it participates, faith is a risk requiring courage. Faith takes into itself, and in that sense overcomes, the element of doubt. Existential doubt, although it is not a permanent experience, is always part of the structure of faith and is capable of asserting itself in the form of anxiety. Serious doubt, according to Tillich, is not the negation of faith; rather, it indicates the seriousness of faith's concern (*Dynamics,* 16–22).

The lack of perfect identity between the symbols of faith and their infinite object gives rise to what Tillich calls "the Protestant principle." As a Protestant, Tillich asserts that the Church and all its symbols are subject to critical probing and stand under divine judgment. To deny this, he holds, is to absolutize the finite and thus to fall into idolatry and fanaticism (*Dynamics,* 28–29; *Systematic Theology,* 3:175–77).

In extreme cases a believer may be overwhelmed by the anxiety of doubt, to the point where the symbols cease to mediate any real meaning. In such cases, Tillich holds forth the prospect of what he calls "absolute faith." Faith of this type, clinging to "the God who appears when God has disappeared in the anxiety of doubt," can sustain the courage to affirm oneself in spite of nonbeing.[18]

Tillich sought to overcome the traditional opposition between faith and reason, an opposition that he attributed to the exaltation of "technical reason," operating though precise concepts and logical rules. Superior to technical reason is ontological reason, the structure of the mind enabling it to grasp and shape reality (*Systematic Theology,* 1:72). Under the conditions of actual existence, Tillich believed, reason is estranged from the ultimate reality that is its ground. Having lost contact with its true ground, it becomes superficial and distorted. Revelation is needed to reunite reason with its own depth. Faith is the act by which reason, healed by revelation, "ecstatically" reaches beyond itself, overcoming its estrangement. Reason, then, is the presupposition of faith, and faith is the fulfillment of reason. Faith, as the state of ultimate concern, is reason in ecstasy. Reason and faith stand within each other (*Dynamics,* 76–77).

Tillich maintained that because scientific reason and revelation operate in different spheres they can never fall into real conflict (*Dynamics,* 80–85; *Systematic Theology,* 1:130). He also sought to insulate the contents of Christian faith from the results of scientific history. "Knowledge of revelation, although it is mediated primarily through historical events, does not imply factual assertions, and it is therefore not exposed to critical analysis by historical research" (*Systematic Theology,* 1:130; cf. *Dynamics,* 85–89). In his Christology Tillich attempted to apply these principles to the question of the Jesus of history (*Systematic Theology,* 2:97–118).

As a highly creative systematic thinker, Tillich introduced into the theology of faith a whole new set of methods, terms, and categories. Boldly addressing the questions of the day, he broke out of the narrow molds of traditional orthodoxy. In so doing he spoke to the experience of many who found themselves wrestling with the problem of unbelief. By the same token, Christians who were firmly committed to biblical revelation and church tradition found Tillich's system too ambiguous.

Deriving faith from the universal human experience of participation in the unconditioned, and submitting the Christian symbols to criticism and doubt, Tillich seemed to relativize what was specifically Christian. In denying the necessary connection between Christian faith and the facts of history, Tillich opened himself to the charge of espousing a new kind of Gnosticism. In his system the gospel is accepted not because it testifies to actual events but because it provides symbols that mediate a transforming awareness of the power of being-itself.[19]

## Further Developments in Protestantism

In addition to Barth, Bultmann, and Tillich, several other Protestants made significant contributions to the theology of faith toward the middle of the twentieth century. They worked partly under the shadow of the three great theologians just named.

The Swiss Reformed theologian Emil Brunner (1889–1966) developed a system indebted to the existentialism of Kierkegaard and the personalism of Ferdinand Ebner and Martin Buber. Rereading the Bible and the sixteenth-century Reformers in the light of this system, he rejected mysticism, rationalism, and dogmatic orthodoxy. Christian faith, he held, depended on the once-for-all act by which God gave himself to sinful humanity in redemptive love through the incarnation, death, and resurrection of his Son.[20]

Faith, in Brunner's theology, is the act by which the revelation or self-communication of God in Christ is received. It is first of all an act of knowledge, an awareness of revelation. It is also self-surrender, obedience, and trust in the God to whom one fully commits oneself. Faith is a wholly personal relation having as its sole object the self-revelation of God in Jesus Christ. It is an I–Thou, not an I–It relationship.

Faith, Brunner concedes, cannot exist without sound doctrine. But he denies that faith is itself an understanding or acceptance of doctrines—a view that he regards as the Catholic distortion. In the doctrinal understanding, which affected much Protestant post-Reformation theology too, the subject-subject relation becomes an object-subject relation. This deformation, in Brunner's judgment, "is the ultimate reason for the perversion and weakness of Christianity and the Church, from the second century down to the present day" (*Revelation and Reason,* 39).

Rightly understood, faith means being gripped in the very center of one's being by the Word of God. Faith therefore is not just an understanding but a decision. It arises only when we are reduced to despair and reach out for the only help available. God's word comes to us paradoxically as a judgment of condemnation and acquittal.

While accepting the Reformation doctrine of justification by faith alone, Brunner rejects the "orthodox" doctrine of merely forensic justification. God, he maintains, not only declares us righteous but also makes us new. "In faith the old man really dies and in faith the new man actually lives" (*Truth as Encounter,* 127). Faith, then, is rebirth and personal transformation. It is wholly the work of grace but it enables nature to become that for which it was created. Genuine faith issues in love and works of love.

Brunner devoted considerable attention to the problem of faith and history. Christianity, he maintained, is a historical religion in which God encounters us through his action in history, and specifically in the event of Jesus Christ. The bare fact that God entered our history and showed himself in the form of a servant would not, as Søren Kierkegaard imagined, suffice for Christian faith. For faith as a living encounter it is necessary that Jesus should have been the kind of person the Gospels describe him to be. Modern historical scholarship has called into question many details, but even in radical scholarship, as represented by Bultmann, the basic picture of Jesus remains intact. In similar fashion, detailed studies have shown that the biblical authors differ on some points of doctrinal teaching. But neither these doctrinal differences nor the inconsistencies of historical detail destroy the fundamental unity of the apostolic witness to Jesus—a unity that can be grasped in faith, which reaches beyond the narratives and doctrines to encounter the living God.

Brunner's system, while it brilliantly exhibits the existential and personal dimensions of faith, is at times too polemically stated. He frequently seems to drive the personal against the objective, the communal against the institutional, kerygmatic testimony against factual occurrence, and confession of faith against doctrine. But in developing his positions, Brunner often nuances them and bridges the apparent dichotomies.

Dietrich Bonhoeffer (1906–1945) produced no full theology of faith in his rather short career, but his many profound remarks on the subject have engaged the attention of later theologians. In a 1932 essay "Concerning the Christian Idea of God" he wrote in a Barthian vein: "The basis of all theology is the fact of faith. Only in the act of faith as a direct act is God recognized as the reality which is beyond and outside of our thinking, of our whole existence. Theology, then, is the attempt to set forth what is already possessed in the act of faith."[21] By the "direct act" Bonhoeffer meant the act of belief that Christ creates within us by giving the Holy Spirit and proving himself to be the free Lord of our existence.[22] The reflex act, by which faith turns back consciously on itself, in Bonhoeffer's view, necessarily falls short of its object. Recollection and analysis of faith can be a service to the Christian community, but they do not achieve any rational justification of faith, which eludes our cognitive grasp.[23]

Bonhoeffer accepted the Reformation thesis that faith alone justifies. In his *Ethics* (1940–1943) he explains why justification is effected not only by grace alone, but by faith alone: "That is the teaching of the Bible and of the Reformation. A life is not justified by love or by hope, but only by faith. For indeed faith alone sets life upon a new foundation, and it is this new foundation alone that justifies my being able to live before God. This foundation is the life, the death, and the resurrection of the Lord Jesus Christ. Without this foundation a life is unjustified before God."[24] He goes on to say that although faith alone justifies, faith is never alone. It would be a false faith unless it were accompanied by hope and love (122).

Throughout his writings Bonhoeffer emphasized the close links between faith and obedience. In *Christ the Center* (1933) he wrote: "There is only faith where a man so surrenders himself to the humiliated God-man as to stake his life on him, even when this seems against all sense."[25] He develops this theme eloquently in *The Cost of Discipleship* (1937), protesting against the misuse of the formula "justification by faith alone."[26] "The word of cheap grace," he declares, "has been the ruin of more Christians than any commandment of works" (59). "The road of faith," he goes on to say, "passes through obedience to the call of Jesus. . . . *Only he who believes is obedient, and only he who is obedient believes*" (68–69). Faith and obedience are mutually prior to each other; each is both a presupposition and a consequence of the other.

In several of his works Bonhoeffer treated the communal and ecclesial aspects of faith. In his earliest book, *Sanctorum Communio* (1927), he argued that the one holy Church in which we profess to believe in the creed is beyond all human possibility; it is possible only out of faith in Christ and the working of the Holy Spirit. In believing that Christ is Lord we also believe in the community over which Christ reigns.[27] Similar themes are set forth in his *Life Together* (1938), a series of reflections on Christian life in community. "It is not the experience of Christian brotherhood, but solid and certain faith in brotherhood that holds us together. . . . We are bound together by faith, not by experience.[28]

In his last, posthumous work, *Letters and Papers from Prison,* Bonhoeffer concerned himself with the "worldly" character of Christian faith. He did not mean to question the reality of God or the need of prayer and worship but, under the influence of Feuerbach, Nietzsche, and Barth, he disparaged "religion" in the sense of a narrow preoccupation with the sacred, a flight from the world, and a posture of weakness and immature dependence. Thus he felt authorized to set up an antithesis between faith and religion. "The 'religious act,'" he wrote, "is always something partial; 'faith' is something whole, involving the whole of one's life. Jesus calls men, not to a new religion, but to life."[29] Faith, therefore, calls for "worldliness," for involvement in life's duties, experiences, and perplexities (370). Because Jesus is "the man for others" faith makes the believer solicitous for others. "Faith is a participation in the being of Jesus (incarnation, cross, and resurrection)" (381).

In his *Prison Letters* Bonhoeffer made sharp criticisms of Barth, Bultmann, and Tillich. Barth, he said, fell into a "positivism of revelation," failing to give concrete guidance for the nonreligious interpretation of theological concepts. Bultmann, with his demythologizing program, lapsed into the typical liberal process of reduction. Tillich attempted to give a "religious" interpretation of the evolution of the world, "but the world unseated him and went on by itself" (327). All three of them, Bonhoeffer suggested, engaged in the apologetical maneuver of trying to drive the world into "existential despair," convincing mankind that it was really unhappy and desperate. Bonhoeffer objected to this attack on the adulthood of the world as pointless, ignoble, and unchristian.He proposed, on the contrary, to give a positive interpretation to the world's coming of age on the basis of the gospel and in the light of Christ (329). But these criticisms and proposals, contained in personal letters from prison, remain fragmentary and enigmatic.

Bonhoeffer's emphasis on obedience and on responsible action in the world as requirements of faith constituted a helpful corrective to some Lutheran "fiducial" theologies. The "religionless Christianity" in his late writings was open to the most various interpretations, and it lent itself to exploitation by some theologians of the "God is Dead" movement in the 1960s.[30]

Another Protestant word-centered theology of faith, very popular in mid-century, was proposed by the so-called "post-Bultmannians," a school of former Bultmann pupils who criticized their master on some points. For our purposes, Gerhard Ebeling (1912–     ) may be taken as representative. After studying under Bultmann at Marburg, he studied under Emil Brunner in Zurich and attended a seminary directed by Bonhoeffer at Finkenwalde in 1937 before beginning his academic career at the end of World War II. He then entered a long teaching career in church history and theology at Tübingen and Zurich.[31]

The word of God, for Ebeling, is an event of proclamation and communication. God's revealing word is a summons to faith, and faith, correspondingly, is the appropriate response to that word. Faith is, so to speak, the arrival of the word of God at its goal.

Ebeling repudiates the idea that faith is a purely formal concept—an empty sack that can be filled with any number of different objects. He also denies that its object is a plurality of "revealed truths." Its one and only object, he asserts, is the true God as the source of salvation. Faith existed in embryonic form among the Israelites of the Old Testament period, but from the standpoint of the New Testament, Christian faith is *the* faith. It is the fulfillment of the faith of Abraham.

Jesus is the awakener of faith. He confronts his hearers with the decision of faith, which is grounded in his own witness. As the "author and finisher" of faith, Jesus identifies himself with faith to such a degree that he never speaks of himself as having faith. Jesus' witness to faith discloses his own faith. To have faith is to accept Jesus as the event of the word of God par excellence.

The word of God is not static. It occurred in Christ and continues to occur today wherever authentic proclamation takes place. The Bible has unique authority as a witness to the word of God as it comes to us in Jesus. Its authority is not the prescriptive authority of a legal text but the originating power of a "document of preaching" whereby faith can continue to be kindled and nourished. As a limited human response to the word of God, the Bible is subject to theological criticism. It is a link in the chain of tradition. The Church is the event of proclamation continuing through history.

The word of God summons people to ground their existence in that which gives existence its true foundation, namely in God, who is manifested and made present in Christ. For Ebeling, as for Bultmann, to have faith is to abandon every effort to secure one's own existence; it is to surrender one's life to him who alone can assure it. The assurance of faith is opposed to self-assurance. Its hallmark, nevertheless, is certainty. The certainty of the word of God, radically opposed to self-certainty, can hold up in the most adverse situations. Grounded in God, faith participates in the omnipotence of him who raised Jesus from the dead. By liberating us from guilt and anxiety, the power of the cross enables us to live unselfishly and to exist authentically as persons.

The certainty of faith, accompanied by peace, freedom, and joy, is continually threatened by the power of sin and unbelief. Some vainly seek to certify faith by proofs from reason and experience, but such proofs do not diminish the risk of faith. The only valid proof of faith is faith itself.

A study of Ebeling proposes this succinct summary:

> Faith for Ebeling is thus man existing as fulfilled word event, grounded in the God Who comes only in word, made certain by the Word of God in which God Himself is present, liberated from the radical questionableness of his existence-in-the-world, participating in God's unlimited power through his encounter with the Word of God, existing as an answer which can be answered-for before his fellowmen.[32]

As an existential word theology, Ebeling's doctrine of faith has many of the same strengths and weaknesses that have been noted above in connection with Bultmann. Ebeling's quasi-sacramental understanding of the proclaimed word has unquestionable elements of value, especially since he does not limit proclamation to oral discourse, but includes sacraments among the events of proclamation. Extending Bultmann's theology of the word in the light of the philosophy of the later Heidegger and the hermeneutics of Hans-Georg Gadamer, Ebeling makes room for a positive evaluation of tradition and of the Church as the bearer of tradition. But Ebeling's concentration on proclamation as the catalyst of faith may be too narrow to do full justice to faith in all its dimensions. In his focus on event and encounter he neglects the importance of reflection and doctrine in the communication and assimilation of faith. In his individualism he does not seem to recognize the value of the Church as an institution of faith, still less as an indefectible teacher. In his emphasis on Christian proclamation, finally, he fails to provide any clue to the possibility of salvation for the unevangelized, if he does not entirely exclude this possibility.

The American H. Richard Niebuhr (1894–1962) formulated a theology of faith strongly influenced by Martin Buber's personalism, but in other respects quite different from Brunner's work. His mature reflections on the subject are most fully set forth in his posthumous work, *Faith on Earth*.[33]

Like Barth and Brunner, Niebuhr writes from a "confessional" perspective, as a member of a particular faith-community. But he rejects Barth's proposal to begin with the word of God, considered as an objective reality. Even Barth, he protests, cannot speak of the word of God except from the standpoint of his own perspective as a believer. Thus Niebuhr sides with Schleiermacher and the liberals by preferring to begin with an analysis of the human religious consciousness, investigating the structure of faith from within (23–30).

Like the liberals, again, Niebuhr contemplates faith as a universal human phenomenon. Influenced by Josiah Royce and George Herbert Mead, he holds that every human community is grounded on relationships of mutual trust and loyalty and thus has a fiduciary structure. This structure is in fact triadic: it involves the individual, the companions, and the cause or ideal by which they are united. The "cause" evokes the trust and loyalty that cement the community (46–62).

In his *Radical Monotheism and Western Culture*[34] Niebuhr describes different types of faith in relation to their respective centers of loyalty. In a "polytheistic" culture, he says, there are many unrelated centers of loyalty, but no organizing framework is provided. In "henotheism" some one finite center of loyalty is exalted to a position of dominance, as though it were infinite and universal. In "radical monotheism" the unconditioned absolute, the transcendent, is taken as the focus, with the result that a worthy center of ultimate loyalty is provided. With such a center the community is capable of becoming universally inclusive, and of overcoming the fanaticism and idolatry of henotheism.

Although he disavows the role of apologist, Niebuhr comes close to giving what he calls a "pistological" argument for the existence of God. In *Faith on Earth* he claims to be speaking simply as a believer, already committed to the reality of God. His concern is not to persuade the unbeliever or to argue to the existence of God as if it were not already known. Nevertheless he does contend, against those who would deny it, that faith in God is implied in "the familiar ground of ordinary personal loyalties" (64). Since we are, as human beings, bound to each other and to a third reality that gives meaning to our relationship, it is impossible for God, as the universal focus of loyalty and commitment, not to exist. "The reality of human faith implies the existence of the God of faith" (ibid.).

Human history, in its general outlines, exhibits the pattern neither of faithfulness nor of faithlessness but rather of broken faith. Niebuhr devotes an important chapter ("Broken Faith," 63–82) to the distortions of faith: distrust, suspicion, unkept promises, and treason. Humanity, he concludes, has no power to extricate itself from its fallen situation, but God provides a remedy. Jesus Christ suffers the ultimate consequences of human distrust and betrayal, but by his unwavering trust in God and fidelity to his divine commission he rebuilds faith on earth. In the resurrection of Jesus, God keeps his promises, and thus authentic faith becomes once more a human possibility.

The risen Jesus is found today, Niebuhr maintains, not primarily in the biblical stories of the empty tomb and of appearances to the witnesses of antiquity but rather in the present community of faith. As participants in the living community we take inspiration from the memories of those who have believed before us, ever since the origins as described in the early chapters of Genesis. We also look forward in hope, confident "that treason can never be the last word, that faith is always the victory which overcomes the world" (112). The Church is "catholic" in the sense that everyone who trusts in God and keeps faith with him participates in the life of this universal interpersonal community, which is not identical with any of the visible societies that go by the name of churches (116).

Niebuhr placed theologians in his debt by introducing into theology valuable insights derived from the social philosophies of Josiah Royce and George Herbert Mead. By situating the theology of faith in the context of Mead's "interactional" social anthropology, and in presenting faith as the ground of all human community and human selfhood, Niebuhr gave added credibility and relevance to the Christian claims. He showed how the Christian vision of the Church as universal community serves to purify and intensify the trust and fidelity that undergird all meaningful human relationships.

In the incomplete manuscript of his book on faith Niebuhr contents himself with analyzing the phenomenon of faith as it appears in contemporary human experience. As an ethician he is more interested in the practical implications of faith than in its doctrinal content. It is not surprising, therefore, that he does not draw as a richly as did Barth and others on the biblical witness to Jesus Christ and on the Christian dogmatic tradition. Jesus in Niebuhr's book appears as the prototypical faithful man but less clearly as the incarnate Word of God. The Holy Spirit appears as a principle of unity in the community of faith but scarcely as a divine person. Niebuhr does not deny these great Christian dogmas; in fact he affirms them. He confesses, however, that his method of reflection on the structures of faith as an experienced activity does not lend itself to a full recovery of the doctrine of the Trinity. The systematic theologian, while gratefully accepting many of Niebuhr's positive contributions, will regret that this able and modest thinker omitted to address many of the important questions arising out of the Christian sources and the ecclesial tradition.

## Catholic Phenomenology

While the reigning neo-scholasticism continued to grapple with the standard questions revolving about the recognition and certitude of revealed truths, new currents of thought were affecting the more creative Catholic theologians. Two heralds of change were, in Germany, Karl Adam and Romano Guardini, both strongly influenced by the phenomenology of religion of Rudolf Otto and Max Scheler. Thanks to all four of these thinkers, faith began to be conceived less as an intellectual assent to revealed truths than as a total self-commitment to God as he turns to his creatures in love.

Karl Adam (1876–1966), a priest who taught at the University of Tübingen, stood in conscious continuity with earlier Tübingen theologians such as Johann Adam Möhler and Johann Evangelist Kuhn.[35] Like them, he wished to accent the role of the Holy Spirit and of the Church in the genesis of faith. The phenomenological school, he maintained, rightly pointed out that every cognitional act requires an inner relatedness to the object apprehended (*Son of God,* 22).[36] Judgments of fact are posterior to, and dependent on, judgments of value, which proceed from feeling and the will. The supreme value, the divine, is apprehended by a specifically religious faculty, well described by Rudolf Otto under the category of the "numinous." The religious sense is an irreducibly distinct element of the human spirit, expressing itself in vital forms that go far beyond the conceptual content (*Spirit of Catholicism,* 61).[37]

Where there is a question of God disclosing himself, the inquirer must abandon the objective, impersonal, scientific approach and must be reverently attentive to a message that may be expected to involve the hearer's total existence. In terms of Thomistic faculty psychology, Adam can translate this to mean: the appearance of the divine attracts the will and enables it to overcome the hesitations of the intellect. The *habitus fidei,* reinforced in the justified believer by the gifts of knowledge and wisdom, makes one akin to the divine, and hence able to assent with a firmness surpassing the force of the arguments of credibility, which have a merely preparatory or confirmatory value (*Son of God,* 39–40).

Like Thomas Aquinas, Adam asserts that the principal cause of faith is God himself, who through interior graces inclines the will to embrace the highest good. "The intellect, illumined by the light of Grace, eager for what is divine and holy, discovers all those traces, indications, and testimonies in the historical appearance of Christ that make his heavenly nature and divine calling credible" (*Christ of Faith,* 15).[38] More importantly, the assent of faith is determined by the will "because in the image of Christ it encounters that *summum bonum* to which its nature is directed, and which completes, fulfils and commits it. . . . From the psychological point of view, then, the belief in Christ is *an experience of good,* wrought by God, and not an *experience of certainty.* In its depths it is irrational, incomprehensible, or rather, beyond all conceiving; but nevertheless it is also rational to the extent that the intellect can at least make the good it has experienced credible" (ibid., 16).

Adam was sometimes accused of falling into irrationalism, but he replied that the First Vatican Council, while asserting that faith is under one aspect rational, insisted that it is achieved by the inspiration and assistance of God's grace (DS 3008). When charged with having accepted the Protestant theory of private inspiration, he replied, quite correctly, that he had always emphasized the ecclesial community as the necessary context in which the grace of faith is accessible. The Church, he maintained, knows Christ through its living self-awareness. "Whoever seeks Christ without the Church, putting his trust in his own insight and what goes by the name of criticism, deprives himself of all possibility of finding the living Christ" (*Christ of Faith,* 5). Christ is not a mere set of concepts but a living person who communicates himself through the vitality of the Church, his Mystical Body (*Spirit of Catholicism,* 60–64).

Romano Guardini (1885–1968) was a priest and professor at Munich.[39] For him, as for Adam, faith is neither an act of thought nor a product of feeling but a personal encounter with God. Influenced by Scheler's phenomenology and Ebner's personalism, Guardini holds that the person is essentially dialogic and achieves integration though a living encounter with God. Faith is not the simple result of any logical or psychological antecedents. Just as we awaken in the morning to find ourselves in a bright, sunlit world, so in faith we find ourselves in a new realm of spiritual light. Faith is a fresh beginning, having its origin in itself (*The Life of Faith,* 31–32).[40]

Even though we do not experience a sudden or dramatic transformation, our faith is a Christian existence arising through the creative power of the Holy Spirit. "Faith in itself is a mystery and must be believed by an act of faith. There is no such thing as a natural theory of faith by which it can be deduced from the existence of the world or of man, for it springs from God's creative grace" (ibid., 8–9).

Faith in the New Testament sense of the word means "the complete revolution of the heart, revaluation of values, reconstruction of the entire intellectual process that Paul so often preaches" (*The Lord,* 436).[41] "To believe means to be so rooted in Christ that he becomes the foundation of one's own existence, the beginning and end of the movement known as life, its measure, and source of strength" (ibid., 445). Faith is in a continual state of becoming (*Life of Faith,* 51). The believer does well to say not that he is a Christian but that he is trying to become one (*The Lord,* 446).

Like Karl Adam, Guardini emphasizes the ecclesial dimension of faith. Normally speaking, faith is awakened through contact with the believing community. It is like a candle lit from the flame of another candle already burning. Our personal faith draws its life from the believing environment and from our communion with those who have believed before us. The church itself believes; it is the "we" of faith (*Life of Faith,* 105).

Guardini addressed with great pastoral sensitivity the struggles of contemporary believers. In works such as *The Faith and Modern Man*[42] he traced the different forms of faith characteristic of different epochs in history, different stages of life, and different types of personality. He analyzed the crises of faith and showed how they could serve as moments on the way to a new and higher stage of faith.

## The "Nouvelle Théologie"

In France the renewal of theology took place not so much through dialogue with modern philosophy as through a return to the sources *(ressourcement).* The Dominicans led the way to a recovery of the teaching of Thomas Aquinas and the early Scholastics, as distinct from the baroque and neo-scholastic theology that had gone by the name of Thomism. Marie-Dominique Chenu (1895–1990),[43] in a series of articles dealing with medieval Scholasticism and in a short book on the history of the Dominican theologate, Le Saulchoir,[44] deplored the overemphasis on dogma and orthodoxy that, in his opinion, had resulted from reactions to the Protestant Reformation, impoverishing modern Catholic theology (*Faith and Theology,* 9–11).[45] Chenu proposed to return to an earlier theology of faith, which placed the emphasis not on obedient acceptance of propositions taught by the magisterium but rather on a direct relationship to God the Revealer. For Thomas Aquinas, according to Chenu, faith consisted primarily of a divinely infused light, a quasi-mystical grace, putting the believer in immediate communion with God, the very source of our eternal blessedness. God, in this view, bears witness to himself within the human spirit. "Whoever believes in the Son of God has the testimony in himself" (1 Jn 5:10). Faith, then, is substantially, and not only modally, supernatural; it belongs to the same order as the beatific vision (*Une École,* 1985 ed., 135–38).

Chenu did not deny the necessity of propositions to mediate the contact between the human mind and God, but he held that the propositions were a mere means or medium through which faith passes in attaining its real object. Faith, for St. Thomas, was an intellectual assent, but that assent was brought about by an affective choice, under the impetus of the will attracted by grace. The intellect, continually dissatisfied by the lack of cogent evidence, strives to attain some understanding, yet the understanding, in this life, can never be complete (*Faith and Theology,* 18).

Although Chenu resembled Rousselot in the importance he attributed to the inner light of faith, he did not share Rousselot's confidence in the evidential force of the signs of credibility. For Chenu the signs were extrinsic and preparatory, rather than truly constitutive of faith itself.

Chenu's positions were in some circles considered dangerous and threatening.

In 1938, a year after the publication of his book on Le Saulchoir, he was required by Roman authorities to sign ten propositions, the first of which read: "Dogmatic formulas enunciate absolute and immutable truth."[46] In 1942 Chenu's book, together with a book on theological method by a Belgian Dominican, Louis Charlier, was placed on the Index of Forbidden Books. According to Monsignor Pietro Parente, *definitor* of the Holy Office, the two theologians were guilty of discrediting Scholasticism, of preferring experience to reason, and of holding that dogmatic formulas have a merely analogical value in relation to the revealed datum.[47]

The French Jesuits of Lyon-Fourvière were likewise concerned with revitalizing Catholic theology by a return to the sources. Several of them, including Henri de Lubac (1896–1991), were specialists in the Greek and Latin fathers.[48] From this perspective, together with his broad acquaintance with modern trends, de Lubac developed a very rich theology of faith in books and articles published over many decades.

In Christianity, de Lubac holds, the term "faith" has a meaning not paralleled in any other religion, still less in secular speech. Christian faith is a total self-gift in response to God's gift of himself in Christ. The Christian lives a new life "by faith in the Son of God who loved me and gave himself for me" (Gal 2:20). Faith, then, is a movement by which we adhere to God as our total good. Without being a merely intellectual act, faith includes belief: it accepts God's testimony, which resounds in the heart of the individual as well as in the confession of the Church. "Of all modes of being it is in itself, paradoxically, the firmest and most assured, even though it always remains free and threatened."[49]

De Lubac insists strongly on the unity of faith. All believers are one in their faith, and faith is directed to a single object. The whole of Christian dogma is compressed in the redemptive act of God giving himself in his Son. To separate redemption from the *revelation* of redemption is already to perform an abstraction. To separate out particular truths such as Trinity, Incarnation, grace, and the rest is a further abstraction, legitimate but dangerous, since it runs the risk of obscuring the unity of the living whole.[50]

The concrete All is not proposed simply to our intelligence, as though it were a matter of supplementing what we already know by reason. Rather, the revelation in which the Spirit of Christ enters history is a call to the Kingdom of God, into which no one can enter except by conversion. Conversion is a new creation, a reconstitution of our very being; it gives us new eyes with which to gaze on a new world.[51]

In faith we have to do with mystery, not with a fact like other facts. We cannot measure mystery with our minds, but we must let ourselves by measured by it. It surpasses and therefore disconcerts us. Every insight we gain about it enhances the darkness. Mystery, far from being contained in human concepts, breaks all our concepts open, requiring us continually to revise them.[52]

Believers, then, do not have to burden themselves with theories, and if they have theories they must not be attached to them. Faith does not seek to take possession of its object; it immerses itself in the object. Raising us above all theories, faith establishes us in God.[53]

Faith cannot be reduced to doctrinal conformity. Those who seek to enclose

revealed truth in precise formulas seek too human a security.[54] They show insufficient respect for the suppleness of God's ways and for the surprising initiatives of
the Holy Spirit. All impositions of literal conformity with official statements are
insufficient to safeguard the purity of faith.[55]

The truth of revelation is not alien to the human spirit, which has a double
character, historical and interior, each aspect qualifying the other. History is meaningful because there is present in each person the seal of the Eternal, who stamps
his image upon every human being and thereby gives inviolable worth to each individual. A true humanism orients us beyond history to the eternal.[56] Inasmuch as
God always draws us to himself, "the Christian knows that the only way to a real
encounter with God is the Living Way which is called Jesus Christ."[57]

For de Lubac, faith is a night, but paradoxically a luminous night. From John
of the Cross he quotes the stanza of the Prologue to *The Ascent of Mount Carmel*
asserting that the night "guided me more surely than the light of noon." The darkness of faith, adds de Lubac, protects us from all the false lights that could mis-
lead us.[58]

A close colleague of de Lubac in the revival of patristic theology was Jean Daniélou (1905–1975).[59] Like de Lubac, Daniélou was a Jesuit of broad culture, keenly
sensitive to contemporary cultural and philosophical trends. In his *God and the
Ways of Knowing*[60] he expounds a theology of faith grounded on the new biblical
theology of salvation history, skillfully interwoven with the theology of the mystics
and with contemporary religious phenomenology. Daniélou refers frequently to
Max Scheler and Rudolf Otto, and builds consciously on the work of Guardini.

Fundamental to Daniélou's theology is the idea that God is essentially personal; he is sovereign subjectivity. Persons as such, he holds, can be known only if
they reveal themselves, and this they do especially by a word of testimony calling
for a response of trust. God gives a first revelation of himself by his work of creation
and a further, more personal, self-disclosure through his mighty acts in salvation
history; but these divine interventions cannot be securely interpreted except by
God's word, to which the prophets are the inspired witnesses. Faith, then, is the act
by which we affirm the reality of God's saving acts as interpreted by God's own
word.

The truth of revelation, for Daniélou, does not rest on evidence. It is not trans-
parent to the intellect. In contrast to the Greek concept of truth as unveiling *(aleth-
eia),* the Bible proposes a concept of truth as reliability *('emet).* God's testimony,
warranted by his own fidelity, gives a higher mode of certainty and is the means of
access to realities of a higher order—namely the inner mystery of God and his saving plan, both of which are inaccessible apart from revelation. Rudolf Otto's
description of the phenomenon of the Holy corresponds to the experience of revelation set forth in biblical texts such as the sixth chapter of Isaiah, and can be verified likewise from the experience of the mystics, including Gregory of Nyssa,
Augustine, and John of the Cross. The faith that responds to God's word is a unique
type of knowledge corresponding to the paradox of God's presence as mystery at
the heart of the profane world. This presence evokes awe and fear, but at the same
time it attracts us by its sublime goodness. Faith is a trusting self-commitment in

which we hand ourselves over to the all-holy God and seek to conform our lives to his will for us.

A third French Jesuit who flourished in the years before and after World War II was Pierre Teilhard de Chardin (1881–1955).[61] Although not a professional theologian, he was deeply interested in the question of faith, and his name is often associated with the *nouvelle théologie*. His principal achievement was to insert the theology of Christian faith in a larger framework that included the biological theory of evolution, the great world religions, and humanist ideologies such as Marxist Communism. He justified his Christian adherence on the ground that it was, of all faiths, the most in harmony with his most fundamental intuitions about the world and the meaningfulness of human activity. He perceived all the religions of the world as converging upon what he called "the universal Christ," the Christ who makes himself one with the world by incarnation.[62]

In his effort to achieve an intellectual synthesis, Teilhard distinguished three levels of understanding.[63] The first was a phenomenological synthesis of scientific data concerning the evolutionary process. The pattern of the past seemed to suggest the possibility that progress would continue. It opened up the hypothesis of final success but gave no assurance that the evolutionary process would escape ultimate failure. At the second level Teilhard placed what he called a "psychological act of faith" in a personal force of love that is leading the universe toward its own plenitude of being. This force he called the "Omega," the "prime Mover ahead." Psychological faith of this type was an extrapolation, necessarily fragile, but recommended because it was in harmony with the scientific data and because it made human effort seem worth while. Full assurance, however, required something more. At the third level came supernatural faith in the Incarnate Word as the reality in whom all things hold together. This supernatural faith, which alone could give historical concreteness to the Omega, was a response to Christian revelation.

Many of our contemporaries, according to Teilhard, felt torn between two types of faith—a cosmic faith in the immanent perfectibility of the world in evolution, and a Christic faith in the redemptive plan of God. For Teilhard it should not be necessary to choose between the two. Although science and revelation did not fully coincide, they were on a path of convergence. The Christian's faith in the Upward can harmonize with the humanist's faith in the Forward if it were understood that the parousia of Christ would come only at the point when the world had been matured through human activity. Salvation, therefore, would be the joint outcome of a movement that led both Upward and Forward.[64]

Teilhard never questioned the traditional concept of Christian faith as an intellectual adherence to revealed truth, but he looked on faith as including a practical conviction that God's beneficent strength continues to shape the universe according to its inherent possibilities. Faith, in this sense, was a power of action.

If we believe, then everything is illuminated and takes shape around us: chance is seen to be order, success assumes an incorruptible plenitude, suffering becomes a visit and a caress of God. But if we hesitate, the rock remains dry, the sky dark, the waters treacherous and shifting. And we may hear the voice of the Master, faced with our bungled lives: "O men of little faith, why have you doubted?"[65]

In 1941, another French Jesuit, Henri Bouillard (1908–1981), completed at Lyon-Fourvière a doctoral dissertation on the doctrine of justification in Thomas Aquinas.[66] He published this dissertation in 1944, acknowledging his indebtedness to de Lubac among many others. St. Thomas, Bouillard noted, had no doctrine of actual grace. He explained conversion in terms of the Aristotelian physics of generation. The acts of the theological virtues (faith, hope, and charity), for Thomas, depended upon the infusion of a supernatural *habitus,* a stable principle of action. Post-Tridentine theology, in abandoning Aristotelian physics, found it necessary to introduce the doctrine of actual grace.

In his conclusion Bouillard drew some general lessons about the relationship between faith and theology.[67] Christian truth, he asserted, never exists in a pure state. It is always imbedded in contingent schematizations that determine its rational structures. Such is the law of incarnation. Historical study, however, does not lead to relativism. It permits one to see how the immutable truths of faith can be expressed with the help of contingent, variable representations. Even councils are not exempt from this law. The Council of Trent, for example, made use of the concept of formal causality in its teaching on the nature of justification (DS 1529) but it did not require Catholics to accept that concept. It simply borrowed notions common in the theology of the day. Theology, as a living, active, and personal reflection on the divine mystery, can never absolve itself from recourse to history.

A number of more conservative neo-scholastic theologians, including some very prominent French-speaking Dominicans, became alarmed at the tendencies they discerned in Teilhard de Chardin and the Jesuits of Lyon-Fourvière. M.-Michel Labourdette maintained that the so-called return to the sources involved in some cases "an open disparagement of Scholastic theology" and even a surrender to the relativism and subjectivism of modern thought.[68] Thomas Deman accused the new theologians of a personalist view of faith that failed to respect the propositions in which the object of faith is attained.[69] M. L. Guérard des Lauriers insisted against Bouillard that the representations in dogmatic formulations are not contingent but absolute, because an assent cannot transcend the concepts in which is its formulated.[70] The venerable Réginald Garrigou-Lagrange, who taught at the Angelicum in Rome, wrote a general denunciation of the *nouvelle théologie* in which he saw the very nature of truth as being the heart of the problem. For the classical and Thomistic notion of truth as conformity to the real *(adaequatio rei et intellectus)* the new theologians were substituting adequacy to the demands of life *(adaequatio mentis et vitae).* In other words, a Blondelian philosophy of action was being substituted for an orthodox philosophy of being.[71]

The apprehensions of the conservative neo-scholastics received some official support in the encyclical *Humani generis* issued in August 1950 by Pius XII.[72] With regard to the judgment of credibility the pope seemed to reject the position of Rousselot and his disciples; he spoke of the many and wonderful signs that God has given as being "sufficient to prove with certitude by the natural light of reason alone the divine origin of the Christian religion" (DS 3876). The pope went on to deplore the fictitious tenets of evolutionism "which repudiate everything that is absolute, firm, and immutable," and to reject existentialism for neglecting all consideration of immutable essences (DS 3878). After pointing out the dangers of historicism, which overthrows the foundation of Christian dogmas (ibid.), the pope specifically rebuked those who seek to free dogma from terminology long established in the Church and from philosophical concepts held by Catholic teachers (DS 3881). In positive terms, Pius XII then affirmed that the mysteries of faith can be expressed in truly adequate concepts and not simply by approximate and ever changeable notions in which the truth is to some extent distorted (DS 3882). The latter position, according to the pope, not only leads to, but actually contains, dogmatic relativism (DS 3883).

The encyclical listed a multitude of errors in contemporary Catholic theology, many of which seemed to resemble positions held by Teilhard de Chardin or by the Jesuits of Lyon-Fourvière. Some suspected that the Dominicans of Le Saulchoir (M.-D. Chenu and Yves Congar) were also envisaged. But the encyclical mentioned no theologians by name. It allowed all theologians to say that they did not hold the positions condemned by the pope. Yet the fact remains that some progressive theologians, especially in France, were under suspicion throughout the decade of the 1950s. At that point in history, it was far from certain that the innovations that had been introduced by Adam and Guardini, Chenu and de Lubac would survive and bear fruit.

## Catholic Personalism

The personalism to which we have adverted in the work of Martin Buber and Emil Brunner had its counterparts in European Catholicism. The French philosopher and dramatist Gabriel Marcel (1889–1973), after his conversion in 1929, made the concept of faith fundamental to his existential phenomenology. Without claiming or wishing to speak as a theologian, Marcel returned frequently to the theme of faith insofar as it entered into his own life experience. He used the term "faith" in a very broad sense to mean an interpersonal relationship in which one freely puts trust in, and places oneself at the disposal of, another, in response to an invitation that is capable of being refused. The fidelity of the person in whom one believes is, as it were, invoked.[73] Whenever by faith I commit myself to another person, I implicitly invoke God, who alone is unconditionally faithful. A faith grounded in God manifests itself in creative fidelity and flowers in works of love.[74]

Faith, for Marcel, cannot be understood except from within. It pertains to the realm of being, rather than that of having. When I live my belief, I become identified with it, and it is in no way an opinion, but if I detach myself from it and try to describe it to myself or others, it becomes external to me and degenerates into a mere opinion.[75]

In his phenomenology of testimony Marcel traced the process by which the witness is transformed by faith and radiates it to others. To be a witness is to guarantee one's word; it is to speak in the presence of transcendence; it is to bind oneself, at least implicitly, by an oath. The testimony of a consecrated life is a powerful catalyst of faith.[76]

More theological than Marcel is his contemporary, Canon Jean Mouroux (1902–73), whose work reflects the influence of Rousselot and Maréchal and a keen interest in renewal of Catholic biblical studies. In a highly influential little book, significantly titled in French *Je crois en toi: Structure "personnelle" de la foi*,[77] he presented a personalist interpretation of Thomas Aquinas's theology of faith. Faith, he insisted, involves a personal relationship to God himself as its material object *(credere Deum)*, as its formal motive *(credere Deo)*, and as the goal toward whom it tends *(credere in Deum)*. The principal element in faith is always the person in whom one believes (cf. *S. th.*, 2–2.11.1).

God bears witness to himself, Mouroux asserts, not only through the external word of the gospel but more intimately in the depths of the spirit where grace effects an inner transformation, calling the person into a beatifying union with the divine. In a particularly interesting section of his book Mouroux explains how the affirmations of faith, borne by the dynamism of grace, go beyond the representational elements. "The concepts and formulas which express this commitment can often be extraordinarily inaccurate" (p. 71). The essential element in the assent of faith, for Mouroux, is not the representation but the personal orientation of the believer to the reality of the saving God. From this insight Mouroux goes on to appreciate what John of the Cross has to say about the painful purifications of faith as it outgrows the inadequate human ideas in which it had been clothed in order to draw closer to the divine mystery itself. Mouroux is likewise able to throw light on situations in which erroneous doctrinal assertions, and even certain professions of atheism, coexist with an affirmation of God and of religious truth that is implicit in the real movement of the mind.

In a concluding section of his book, reminiscent of Marcel, Mouroux speaks of the transmission of faith through personal testimony and especially through the corporate testimony of the Church.

Mouroux's work, typical of the progressive theology of the day, constituted an implied criticism of the reigning neo-scholasticism, which appeared to identify faith simply as an intellectual assent to a body of correct teaching on the basis of the authority of the witness. In many ways Mouroux anticipated what was to become the doctrine of Vatican II. But he was careful to avoid polemics and to veil the novelty of his positions by covering them, as far as possible, with the authority of St. Thomas.

An Alsatian Jesuit, August Brunner (1894–1985), developed a personalist philosophy of religion in dialogue with the phenomenology of Edmund Husserl. He maintained that the fundamental datum of consciousness is the concrete reality of other persons. Persons manifest what is most intimate to themselves through word and gesture. Faith, as a free acceptance of the self-revelation of another person, is the only means by which we can enter into the personal center of the other and view the world through the other's eyes. Faith in this sense is not only the basis of religion but is fundamental to the constitution of any society.[78]

During the 1950s a Brazilian Jesuit, Carlos Cirne-Lima, working under the guidance of Karl Rahner at Innsbruck, applied Brunner's personalist phenomenology to the theological problem of faith. Beginning with an analysis of human faith, he maintained that faith is grounded in a concrete intuition of other persons in their historical concreteness. In faith, taking a personal attitude, I freely decide to say Yes to the other's self-communication.

Divine faith, for Cirne-Lima, is the cognitive moment of a free option by which one commits one's personal center to God as he concretely draws near through Christ and the Church. In the very act of faith itself the mind passes from a superficial external knowledge to an intimate personal knowledge, and in light of this further insight a higher measure of certitude is attained. Divine faith, therefore, is "a personal 'yes' spoken to Christ, who is present—who speaks and acts."[79]

Like the other personalists, Cirne-Lima shifted the core of faith from the assent to revealed truth to loving personal acceptance of the revealer. But he insisted that in saying Yes to the person, the believer becomes committed to assent to what the person says. We may doubt the testimony of a mere acquaintance, says Cirne-Lima, but then he adds, with some exaggeration: "A person whom we love however can be believed, or rather must be believed, in everything he says" (p. 41).

The personalist phenomenology of faith gave added force to what many theologians since Newman had been saying about the radical difference between faith and scientific demonstration. If faith was a grace-filled assent to the loving self-gift of God, it should be approached by some other route than rational apologetics. The prospective believer must be prepared to welcome the good news with interior joy and gratitude and to dwell within the Church as the community of faith. By displacing the center of faith from purely intellectual assent to a total personal relationship, these theologians called into question the then-dominant Scholastic view that the formal object of faith could be adequately described as the truthfulness of God. Although they did not question the official teaching of the Church, the personalists made room for the supposition that someone might have authentic faith without being able to assent sincerely to every dogma. The new spirit of this theology would find its legitimation at the council announced by Pope John XXIII in 1959.

## Vatican Council II

The Second Vatican Council (1962–1965) marks a new turning point in the official Catholic teaching about faith.[80] It did not directly follow in the line of development that stretches from the Council of Trent, through Vatican I and the Anti-Modernist documents, to *Humani generis.* Without contradicting this recent tradition, Vatican II pursued a more personalist, vitalist approach nourished by a combination of biblical theology with twentieth-century personalist phenomenology. The novelty of the approach was, however, cloaked by the use of traditional language.

The only thematic treatment of faith in the documents of Vatican II occurs in the Constitution on Divine Revelation, *Dei Verbum,* article 5. In an extremely dense sentence the Council asserts: "'The obedience of faith' (Rom 16:26; cf. 1:5; 2 Cor 10:5–6) must be given to God who reveals, an obedience by which one commits one's whole self freely to God, offering 'the full submission of intellect and will to God who reveals,' and freely assenting to the truth revealed by him" (*DV* 5). With a direct quotation from Vatican I, the Council here calls attention to three dimensions of faith. First, faith is described in Pauline terms as obedience; then it is depicted as a free and trusting self-commitment to God the Revealer, and finally as a willing and free assent to the divinely revealed truth. In the next sentence Vatican II asserts, as had Orange II and Vatican I, that for such faith to arise, the grace of the Holy Spirit must precede and assist by moving the heart and opening the eyes of the mind. Then the Council affirms that for the achievement of a deeper understanding of revelation, faith must be perfected by the gifts of the Holy Spirit—a theme dear to Thomas Aquinas that had been absent from previous conciliar teaching.

Whereas Vatican I and *Humani generis* had insisted on a judgment of credibility attained by the natural light of human reason as a preamble to the act of faith, this theme is not found in Vatican II. From *Dei Verbum,* articles 1–4, one gets the impression that faith is induced by the confident proclamation of the mighty acts of God in salvation history rather than by human inquiry and reasoning. This impression is reinforced by other documents of Vatican II. The Constitution on the Liturgy quotes Paul in Romans to the effect that the preaching of the gospel must precede faith and conversion (*SC* 9; cf. Rom 10:14–15).

Vatican II, however, does not reject the standard distinction between the two orders of faith and reason. Indeed, it explicitly affirms that distinction in the Pastoral Constitution on the Church in the Modern World (*GS* 59). In the Constitution on Revelation it approvingly quotes Vatican I on the possibility of gaining sure knowledge of God from created things by the natural light of human reason (*DV* 6). But it does not say that such natural knowledge must precede faith. Rather, it intimates the opposite by discussing natural knowledge of God after revealed knowledge, reversing the order of Vatican I. Vatican II, moreover, does not speak of a purely natural judgment of the credibility of revelation. It does not repeat, but at most alludes in passing to, the traditional arguments from prophecy and miracles. Although signs of revelation are referred to in *Dei Verbum,* they are presented not as extrinsic signs of credibility but rather, it would seem, as integral parts of revelation itself (*DV* 2 and 4). If the resurrection is at one point described as a confirmatory sign, it is not held to be discernible without grace (*DV* 4).

It would be a mistake to imagine that Vatican II intended to deny all that it did not assert. On the contrary, the assumption should be that it took for granted, and intended to build on, the teaching of previous popes and councils. Yet it is significant that this council approached faith from a different perspective, in which certain traditional theses lost their previous importance.

Vatican II reasserted the traditional doctrine of the necessity of faith, but it did so with a difference. The Decree on Priestly Ministry states simply that no one can be saved without first believing (*PO* 4). The Constitution on the Church, after citing several biblical texts on the necessity of faith, affirms that no one who knows that God has made the Church necessary for salvation can be saved without entering the Church (*LG* 14). The implication is that some who do not have this knowledge can be saved without entering the Church. Other texts from Vatican II point in the same direction. Non-Catholic Christians are described as lovingly believing in God and in Christ (*LG* 15). The Decree on Ecumenism asserts that "faith, hope, and charity can exist outside the visible boundaries of the Catholic Church" (*UR* 3); it also praises the living faith displayed by Protestants (*UR* 23). Going yet further, the Decree on the Church's Missionary Activity asserts that "God in ways known to himself can lead those inculpably ignorant of the gospel to that faith without which it is impossible to please him (Heb 11:6)" (*AG* 7)—a statement that seems to imply that saving faith lies within reach of the unevangelized.

As may be seen from what has already been said, Vatican II reflects the tension found throughout the Bible and Christian tradition between the idea that faith comes through hearing the proclamation of the gospel (*LG* 17; *SC* 9) and the doctrine that salutary faith can exist before the gospel is heard (*AG* 7). The Council speaks almost as though there are two kinds of faith, both dependent on the grace of the Holy Spirit, who is invisibly at work in the hearts of all persons of good will (*GS* 22), impelling them to follow their conscience and disposing them to accept the truth of the gospel when they hear it (*LG* 16). The Decree on the Church's Missionary Activity takes account of both the universal and the specifically Christian phases of faith: "The Holy Spirit, who calls everyone to Christ by the seeds of the word and the preaching of the gospel, stirs up in their hearts the obedience of faith" (*AG* 15).

From the sixteenth century on, many official documents had insisted on the freedom of the act of faith. The sociopolitical implications of this theme were brought out by Vatican II, especially in its Declaration on Religious Freedom, *Dignitatis humanae,* which repudiated anything savoring of coercion in matters of religion (*DH* 4). Because Christian faith is by its very nature a free act, said the Council, no one is to be forced to profess the faith involuntarily (*DH* 9–10). The example of Christ in bearing witness to the truth and patiently accepting its rejection is normative for Christians and for the Church (*DH* 11).

Although the treatment on faith in *Dei Verbum* 5 might appear rather individualistic, other documents of Vatican II bring out its social and ecclesial character. The Preface to *Dei Verbum* links adherence to the gospel with fellowship in the believing community (*DV* 1). The Constitution on the Church speaks of a "supernatural sense of the faith" abiding in the People of God as a whole thanks to the Holy Spirit, who dwells in it (*LG* 12). This supernatural sense enables the members of the Church to cling without fail to the word of God, to penetrate its meaning more deeply, and to apply it more fully in their lives (ibid.). The faith of the people of God is to be stirred up and nourished by the preaching of bishops (Decree on the Pastoral Ministry of Bishops, *CD* 12; cf. *GS* 43) and presbyters (*PO* 22). Liturgical worship (*SC* 33) and especially participation in the sacraments (*SC* 59) nourish, strengthen, and confirm faith.

In conclusion, it must be asked whether Vatican II altered the previous Catholic positions regarding the formal and material objects of faith. With its preference for skirting technical questions disputed among Scholastic theologians, the Council avoided directly answering these two questions. In answer to two requests to amend *Dei Verbum* 5 by mentioning "the authority of the revealing God" as the formal object of faith, the Theological Commission replied, in November 1964, that this amendment was unnecessary, since faith was already held to be a submission to God who reveals.[81] This answer appears to me to be true, but incomplete. In the perspectives of Vatican II, faith insofar as it is an assent does indeed rest on the authority of God who reveals, but faith is described also, and more fundamentally, as obedience and trusting commitment. The formal object of faith in its totality would seem to include not simply the knowledge and truthfulness of God (the traditional meaning of "authority") but also his goodness and his trustworthiness.[82]

So too with the material object of faith.[83] For Vatican I the content of faith is a body of supernatural knowledge: the revealed truths or mysteries passed down in Scripture and Tradition. For Vatican II, faith grasps not only revealed truths, in the sense of doctrines, but more fundamentally the reality and life of God insofar as he offers himself to be shared by human subjects. The intellectual component, far from being denied, is explicitly asserted; but the assent is taken up into the broader framework of a relationship of the entire created world to God. In order to live out its faith, the Church is obliged to "listen to the various voices of our day, discerning, interpreting, and judging them in the light of the divine word" (GS 44). Faith is not complete in its own order unless it passes into life. With its doctrine that faith is perfected, precisely as faith, by hope, by love, and by the gifts of the Holy Spirit, Vatican II stands within a tradition that antedates Scholasticism by many centuries. This broader tradition is at once more biblical and more ecumenical.

## Conclusion

The mid-twentieth century was an extremely fertile period for the theology of faith, both in Protestantism and in Catholicism. In both branches of Western Christianity the polemical oppositions of the sixteenth century were in great measure overcome. Renewal was achieved by a return to the biblical sources and by exposure to new philosophical currents, including existentialism and personalist phenomenology.

In Protestantism these developments resulted in a theology of the word as a self-expression of God, who brings his chosen hearers to place their ultimate trust in him alone. This type of theology, depicting faith as an obedient response to God's sovereign word, was represented in different ways by Barth, Bultmann, Emil Brunner, and Ebeling. Tillich, reserved toward word-theology, stands closer to Schelling and Hegel, but he too was influenced by Kierkegaard and the existentialists. He regarded faith as an act of ecstatic reason, bringing the believer into a vital communion with the ground of being.

H. R. Niebuhr, perhaps the most important American theologian of faith, drew on European and American predecessors. Like Royce and Mead, he was convinced that faith involves interpersonal loyalty and thus constitutes a building block not only for the Church but for every society. His "radical monotheism" sets him apart from the Christocentrism of most word-theologians, especially Barth.

Catholic authors of this period, writing under the vigilance of the Roman magisterium, were more cautious in their innovations. But personalist phenomenology had a profound effect on Adam, Guardini, Marcel, Mouroux, August Brunner, and Cirne-Lima, among others. Many of the Catholics of these decades, emphasizing the personal relationship between the believer and God, as well as the ecclesial bonds among believers, tended to relativize the importance of exact dogmatic formulations.

These years were, for Catholics, a time of return to the sources. Authors such as Chenu and Mouroux went back to Thomas Aquinas and the medieval Scholastics, seeking to read them with fresh eyes, rather than through the Counter-Reformation tradition. They depicted faith as a response to the inner testimony of God, who speaks directly within the human spirit, and who invites believers to enter into communion with himself.

De Lubac, Daniélou, and others explored the patristic sources, rereading the fathers in the light of contemporary phenomenology. They saw faith as an opening of oneself to the utterly transcendent God, who lovingly makes himself present in his Son, inviting believers to enter into a mysterious subject-subject relationship. Bouillard and others, in the spirit of the *nouvelle théologie,* emphasized the historically conditioned character of propositions, including dogmatic formulations.

Several authors of this period sought to connect faith more closely with secular existence. On the Protestant side Bonhoeffer, especially in his later writings, held that faith calls for a "worldly" involvement in life's duties as a mode of participation in Christ's being for others. On the Catholic side Teilhard de Chardin understood faith as a force that guides the believer into the future, where Christ stands as the ultimate goal, the Omega, in whom the history of the universe finds its final point of convergence. These themes of Bonhoeffer and Teilhard de Chardin were to make a great impact in the 1960s.

Until the early 1960s the Roman magisterium was worried that the new theological trends might signal a revival of the Modernist heresy. Vatican II, however, was cordial to new developments. It consciously sought to avoid Scholastic disputes and to get beyond the apologetical and polemical concerns of the preceding four centuries. With ecumenical sensitivity the Council favored a biblically grounded concept of faith as trust in God's saving action in Christ. It portrayed faith as a unitive force that could draw all Christians, and indeed all peoples, into unity. While promoting dialogue with all communions, religions, and ideologies, the Council did not disguise its conviction that all things find their unity in Christ, and that faith necessarily involves the believer in a relationship, either overt or hidden, to him. Vatican II, choosing not to settle technical questions that could be legitimately debated among Catholics, left many theological problems unsolved. It gave a new starting point and a new agenda for the theology of faith, at least among Catholics, for the remainder of the century.

## Notes

1. Karl Barth, *The Epistle to the Romans,* ET of sixth German edition (London: Oxford University Press, 1933; paperback, 1968).

2. Idem, *Anselm: Fides Quaerens Intellectum,* 2d ed. (Richmond, Va.: John Knox, 1958).

3. Barth's interpretation of Anselm is difficult to square with some of Anselm's own statements, and has frequently been criticized as slanted. See, for example, M. J. Charlesworth, *St. Anselm's Proslogion* (Oxford: Clarendon, 1965), 40–46.

4. Karl Barth, *Doctrine of the Word of God,* vol. I, pt. 1 of *Church Dogmatics* (German original, 1932; ET, Edinburgh: T. & T. Clark, new translation, 1975).

5. Idem, *The Doctrine of Reconciliation,* vol. IV, pt. 1 of *Church Dogmatics* (German original, 1953; ET, Edinburgh: T. & T. Clark, 1956).

6. Gerrit C. Berkouwer, *The Triumph of Grace in the Theology of Karl Barth* (Grand Rapids, Mich.: Eerdmans, 1956), 263–74.

7. Hans Urs von Balthasar, (New transl.) *The Theology of Karl Barth* (New York: Holt, Rinehart and Winston, 1971), 202; more fully in German original, *Karl Barth: Darstellung und Deutung seiner Theologie,* 2d ed. (Cologne: Hegner, 1962), 257–58.

8. Henri Bouillard, *Karl Barth,* vol. 3 (Paris: Aubier, 1957), 39–40; compare the criticisms of Hans Küng in his *Justification: The Doctrine of Karl Barth and a Catholic Reflection* (New York: Nelson, 1964), 279.

9. See Rudolf Bultmann's *Theology of the New Testament,* 2 vols. (New York: Scribner, 1951).

10. Rudolf Bultmann, "New Testament and Mythology," in *Kerygma and Myth,* ed. Hans Werner Bartsch (New York: Harper Torchbooks, 1961), 1–44. This volume includes also Bultmann's important "Reply to His Critics," 191–211.

11. Idem, *Jesus Christ and Mythology* (London: SCM, 1960).

12. Idem, *Existence and Faith: Shorter Writings of Rudolf Bultmann* (New York: Meridian Books, 1960), 57.

13. Idem, *Essays Philosophical and Theological* (New York: Macmillan, 1955), 286.

14. Karl Barth, "Rudolf Bultmann—An Attempt to Understand Him," in *Kerygma and Myth* 2 (London: SPCK, 1962), 83–132.

15. For a clear exposition of Bultmann's doctrine of faith see Walter Schmithals, *An Introduction to the Theology of Rudolf Bultmann* (Minneapolis: Augsburg, 1967). The two volumes edited by Hans Werner Bartsch, *Kerygma and Myth* and *Kerygma and Myth* 2 (a partial translation of the larger German series), contain a variety of Protestant responses. Among Catholic critiques one may recommend Léopold Malevez, *The Christian Message and Myth* (Westminster, Md.: Newman, 1958) and René Marlé, *Bultmann and Christian Faith* (Westminster, Md.: Newman, 1967).

16. Paul Tillich, *Dynamics of Faith* (New York: Harper and Brothers, 1957).

17. Idem, *Systematic Theology,* 3 vols. (Chicago: University of Chicago Press, 1951, 1957, and 1963).

18. Idem, *The Courage to Be* (New Haven, Conn.: Yale University Press, 1952), 180.

19. For criticisms of the kind summarized in this paragraph see, from a Roman Catholic perspective, George Tavard, *Paul Tillich and the Christian Message* (New York: Scribner's Sons, 1962), 8–55 and, from a Protestant perspective, Kenneth Hamilton, *The System and the Gospel* (London: SCM, 1963), 96–115, 218–26.

20. Emil Brunner's position on faith may conveniently be found in his *Revelation and Reason: The Christian Doctrine of Faith and Knowledge* (Philadelphia: Westminster, 1946). See also his *The Christian Doctrine of God.* Dogmatics, vol. 3 (Philadelphia: Westminster 1962), chapters 10–18, and his *Truth as Encounter* (Philadelphia: Westminster, 1964).

21. Dietrich Bonhoeffer, "Concerning the Christian idea of God," *Journal of Religion* 12 (1932): 177–85, at 179.

22. Idem, *Act and Being* (German original, 1932; ET, New York: Harper & Row, 1956), 141.

23. Ibid., 148–51.

24. Idem, *Ethics* (New York: Macmillan, 1965), 121.

25. Idem, *Christ the Center* (New York: Harper & Row, 1966), 114.

26. Idem, *The Cost of Discipleship* (New York: Macmillan, 1963), 55.

27. Idem, *Communion of Saints* (New York: Harper & Row, 1963), 119.

28. Idem, *Life Together* (San Francisco: Harper & Row, 1954), 39.

29. Idem, *Letters and Papers from Prison,* enlarged edition (New York: Macmillan, 1972), 362.

30. A helpful study of Bonhoeffer's theology of faith is Geffrey B. Kelly, *Liberating Faith: Bonhoeffer's Message for Today* (Minneapolis: Augsburg, 1984).

31. Ebeling's theology of faith is expounded in many of his books, notably the following

three: *Word and Faith* (Philadelphia: Fortress, 1963); *The Nature of Faith* (Philadelphia: Muhlenberg, 1961; reprint, Fortress, 1967) and *Dogmatik des christlichen Glaubens,* 3 vols. (Tübingen: Mohr, 1979). Ebeling's pamphlet, *Was Heisst Glauben?* (Tübingen: Mohr, 1958), reprinted in his *Wort und Glaube* 3 (Tübingen: Mohr, 1975), 225–35, contains a concise summary of his basic positions on faith.

32. Patrick J. Burns, *The Word of God in Human History: A Hermeneutic Analysis of Gerhard Ebeling's Doctrine of the Word of God in Human History* (unpublished S.T.D. dissertation, Woodstock College, 1968), 55. Another study is that of Peter Knauer, *Verantwortung des Glaubens: Ein Gespräch mit Gerhard Ebeling* (Frankfurt: Knecht, 1969).

33. H. Richard Niebuhr, *Faith on Earth* (New Haven, Conn.: Yale University Press, 1989). An excellent commentary, drawing on Niebuhr's unpublished manuscripts, is James W. Fowler, *To See the Kingdom: The Theological Vision of H. Richard Niebuhr* (Nashville, Tenn.: Abingdon, 1974).

34. H. Richard Niebuhr, *Radical Monotheism and Western Culture* (New York: Harper & Row, 1960).

35. On Adam's theology of faith see Roger Aubert, *Le problème de l'acte de foi,* 2d ed. (Louvain: E. Warny, 1950), 522–47; Uwe Gerber, *Katholischer Glaubensbegriff: Die Frage nach dem Glaubensbegriff in der katholischen Theologie vom. I Vatikanum bis zur Gegenwart* (Gütersloh: Gerd Mohn, 1966), 152–55. To situate the author in his time and place see Robert Anthony Krieg, *Karl Adam: Catholicism in German Culture* (Notre Dame: University of Notre Dame, 1992).

36. Karl Adam, *The Son of God* (New York: Sheed and Ward, 1934).

37. Idem, *The Spirit of Catholicism* (Garden City, N.Y.: Doubleday Image Books, 1954).

38. Idem, *The Christ of Faith* (New York: Pantheon Books, 1957).

39. On Guardini see Aubert, *Problème de l'acte de foi,* 626–30; Gerber, *Katholischer Glaubensbegriff,* 159–67.

40. Romano Guardini, *The Life of Faith* (New York: Paulist Deus Books, 1961).

41. Idem, *The Lord* (Chicago: H. Regnery, 1954).

42. Idem, *The Faith of Modern Man* (New York: Pantheon Books, 1952).

43. On Chenu's theology of faith see Aubert, *Problème de l'acte de foi,* 588–94.

44. Marie-Dominique Chenu, *Une École de Théologie: le Saulchoir* (1937; reprinted Paris: Éditions du Cerf, 1985). The reprint edition contains new articles by Giuseppe Alberigo and others, putting Chenu's theology in the context of the time.

45. Idem, *Faith and Theology* (New York: Macmillan, 1968).

46. For the wording of the ten propositions see Chenu, *Une École,* 35.

47. See ibid., 23–24; also Gustave Thils, *Orientations de la théologie* (Louvain: Ed. Ceuterick, 1958), 57.

48. On de Lubac, see Gerber, *Katholischer Glaubensbegriff,* 209–26.

49. Henri de Lubac, *The Christian Faith* (San Francisco: Ignatius, 1986), 145.

50. Idem, "Le problème du développement du dogme," *Recherches de science religieuse* 35 (1946): 130–60, especially 156–67.

51. Ibid., 157.

52. Ibid., 147.

53. Idem, *Paradoxes* (Paris: Éd. du Seuil, 1959), 9–11.

54. Idem, "Développement . . . ," 160.

55. Idem, *Paradoxes,* 11.

56. Idem, "The New Man: The Marxist and the Christian View," *Cross Currents* 1 (1950): 67–88, especially 76.

57. Idem, *The Discovery of God* (Chicago: Regnery, 1967), 212.

58. Idem, *Paradoxes,* 169.

59. On Daniélou see Gerber, *Katholischer Glaubensbegriff,* 230–32.

60. Jean Daniélou, *God and the Ways of Knowing* (New York: Meridian Books, 1957). The next few paragraphs are based particularly on chapter 3, "The God of the Faith."

61. On Teilhard de Chardin's theology of faith see Gerber, *Katholischer Glaubensbegriff,* 188–208. The secondary literature on Teilhard is, of course, immense.

62. See Pierre Teilhard de Chardin, *How I Believe* (New York: Harper Row, 1969).

63. See Christopher F. Mooney, *Teilhard de Chardin and the Mystery of Christ* (New York: Harper & Row, 1966), 65–68.

64. Ibid., 163–65.

65. Teilhard de Chardin, *The Divine Milieu* (New York: Harper & Row, 1960), 117.

66. Henri Bouillard, *Conversion et Grâce chez S. Thomas d'Aquin* (Paris: Aubier, 1944). On Bouillard see Gerber, *Katholischer Glaubensbegriff,* 226–29.

67. See Thomas G. Guarino, "Henri Bouillard and the Truth-Status of Dogmatic Statements," *Science et Esprit* 39 (1987): 331–43; idem, *Revelation and Truth: Unity and Plurality in Contemporary Theology* (Scranton: University of Scranton Press, 1993), 25–33.

68. M.-Michel Labourdette, "La théologie et ses sources," *Dialogue théologique* (St.-Maximin [France]: Les Arcades, 1947), 23–71.

69. Thomas Deman, "Tentatives françaises pour une renouvellement de la théologie," *Revue de l'Université d'Ottawa* 20 (1950): 129–67.

70. M. L. Guérard des Lauriers, "La Théologie historique et le développement de la théologie,"*L'Année théologique* 7 (1946): 15–55, especially 50–52.

71. Réginald Garrigou-Lagrange, "La nouvelle théologie où va-t-elle?" *Angelicum* 23 (1946): 126–45, especially 129 and 143.

72. See Gustave Weigel, "Gleanings from the Commentaries on *Humani generis,*" *Theological Studies* 12 (1951): 208–30; John Auricchio, *The Future of Theology* (Staten Island, N.Y.: Alba House, 1970), 317–29.

73. Gabriel Marcel, *The Mystery of Being.* 2. *Faith and Reality* (Chicago: Regnery Gateway Books, 1960), 76–94, especially 89.

74. Idem, *Creative Fidelity* (New York: Farrar, Straus and Giroux, 1964), 162, 166–68.

75. Ibid., 121–22.

76. Idem, *Philosophy of Existence* (New York: Philosophical Library, 1949), 67–76.

77. Jean Mouroux, *Je crois en toi: Structure "personnelle" de la foi* (Paris: Cerf, 1939, republished 1948 and 1965; ET, *I Believe: The Personal Structure of Faith* (New York: Sheed & Ward, 1959).

78. August Brunner, *Glaube und Erkenntnis: Philosophisch-Theologisch Darlegung* (Munich: Kösel, 1951). For an overview of Brunner's epistemology see Gerald A. McCool, "Recent Trends in German Scholasticism: Brunner and Lotz," *International Philosophical Quarterly* 1 (1961): 668–82.

79. Carlos Cirne-Lima, *Personal Faith: A Metaphysical Inquiry* (New York: Herder and Herder, 1965), 198. On the basis of the German original, *Der personale Glaube* (Innsbruck: Rauch, 1959), Gerald A. McCool published a helpful study, "The Primacy of Intuition," *Thought* 37 (1962):59–72.

80. On the theme of faith at Vatican II see Henri de Lubac's commentary on *Dei Verbum,* art. 5, in *La Révélation divine,* Una Sancta 70a, ed. B.-D. Dupuy, (Paris: Cerf, 1968), 241–61; William V. Dych, *The Anthropological Structure of Faith: An Interpretation of Faith in the Second Vatican Council* (unpublished doctoral dissertation, Münster, 1971).

81. Cf. *Acta synodalia* IV/1, pp. 336–81, with Archbishop E. Florit's *relatio* of September 24, 1964.

82. Cf. Dych, *The Anthropological Structure of Faith,* 179–83.

83. Ibid., 177–79, 183.

# 7

# Recent Developments

The end of Vatican II does not mark a sharp break with the past, even in Catholic theology. Many of the theologians who had prepared the way for the Council, and participated in its work, continued to publish for decades after the Council, maintaining approximately the same positions as before. An example would be Henri de Lubac, whose work has already been examined, although his *The Christian Faith* was not published in French until 1969 and first translated into English in 1986. No mention has yet been made of the work of Karl Rahner, which belongs predominantly to the post-conciliar period, although he was active for two decades before Vatican II, and strongly influenced the Council documents. The present chapter, therefore, should not be read in isolation from the preceding. We shall here discuss the theology of the generation after the Council, both Catholic and Protestant, as represented by a few leading figures. It will not be possible in a survey of this type to include all the important literature.

## Theological Aesthetics

The Swiss Catholic Hans Urs von Balthasar (1905–1988) studied in France under de Lubac and acquired his master's admiration for Origen and Pierre Rousselot. From this perspective he criticized the neo-scholasticism of the preconciliar period, accusing it of making a cleavage between faith and experience and of excessively rationalizing the approach to faith. His theology of faith may be gleaned from the first volume of his monumental theological synthesis, *The Glory of the Lord.*[1]

Von Balthasar welcomes Rousselot's retrieval of the classical concept of the "light of faith" as helpful for overcoming neo-scholastic heteronomy by establishing a connaturality between the believer and the gospel. But Rousselot, according to von Balthasar, still remained too close to the Kantianism he sought to surpass. He and his disciples concentrated excessively on the inner dynamism of the subject. This approach, von Balthasar holds, runs the risk of making the "restless heart" of the creature the measure of revelation and the judge of dogma (149). In the framework of transcendental theology everything that does not seem to minister to the self-expansion of the human spirit can easily be set aside by a "demythologizing" reinterpretation.

In his alternative approach von Balthasar undertakes a phenomenology of faith that owes something to Max Scheler.[2] He draws also on the personalism of Martin Buber and Jean Mouroux but warns against looking upon the divine-human relationship as a dialogue among equals.[3]

For von Balthasar the basic reality with which faith concerns itself is the objective self-expression of the divine glory, which shines forth in greatest splendor on the countenance of Jesus Christ (141; cf. 2 Cor 4:5–6). In the manifestation of the divine glory von Balthasar finds the divine authority, which he, like most modern Catholic theologians, regards as the motive or formal object of faith. The revelation of God's glory has "a wholly peculiar colouring attributable to God alone" and "needs no justification but itself" (140).

Late Scholasticism, according to von Balthasar, suffers from an unhealthy tendency to emphasize formal authority at the expense of the authority of content. In his estimation the two coincide. "This God who reveals himself in Christ is not only the material total object of theology, but also the formal object and motive of faith" (154). God witnesses to himself not only in the divinity of Christ but also in Christ's humanity.

Von Balthasar is consciously in dialogue with the transcendental theology of Rahner, which we shall presently consider. A weakness in transcendental theology, he believes, is the neglect of the manifest content of faith. All that is seen by the human eye is described as a mere sign or pointer to the hidden reality in which we believe. The sign is played off against the thing signified, the form is set against the content, *fides qua* is magnified at the expense of *fides quae.* For von Balthasar, on the contrary, the glory of the divine majesty appears in the humanity of Jesus and in his wondrous deeds. Faith actually perceives God's light, reflected in divine signs and witnesses. "Visible form not only 'points' to an invisible, unfathomable mystery; form is the apparition of this mystery. . . . The content *(Gehalt)* does not lie behind the form *(Gestalt),* but within it" (151).

In its pursuit of the true and the good, theology has too often neglected the third transcendental, the beautiful, which alone can overcome the dualisms just mentioned (151). Von Balthasar appeals to aesthetic reason in order to resurrect the category of the beautiful. Beauty, for him, is the splendor of the true (152). "Theological aesthetics" has as its primary object "the perception of the divine self-manifestation" (11). Only on the basis of this perception, elaborated in the first part ("theological aesthetics") does von Balthasar in his great trilogy pass on in Part II ("theological dramatics") to a consideration of God's goodness and the truth of God's word (the object of the projected third part, the "theological logic"). The first volume of the first part (*The Glory of the Lord* or, in German, *Herrlichkeit*) is significantly entitled *Seeing the Form (Schau der Gestalt).* The point of the title is that the splendor of divine truth is not simply believed on the basis of signs (which would involve a kind of extrinsicism) but is actually perceived as inhering in the form *(Gestalt).* We do not merely believe; we see what we believe (419).

Von Balthasar faults late Scholasticism for having driven a wedge between faith and experience. For Suarez and his school we cannot know whether we have faith; we can only believe that we do (223). In opposition to this view von Balthasar adduces quotations from the fathers and medieval Scholastics, and especially from the New Testament. Paul speaks of the Corinthians as having an experience in faith of Christ living in them (2 Cor 13:5; cf. von Balthasar 224–32). According to John, the Christian message reports "that which was from the beginning, which we have heard, which we have seen with our eyes, which we have looked upon and touched with our hands, concerning the word of life" (1 Jn 1:1; cf. von Balthasar, 232–41). John's theology may be called "aesthetic" because it is permeated by the conviction that the divine form has appeared in the flesh of Christ (233). The cross marks the end of purely worldly aesthetics and the decisive emergence of a divine aesthetics in which glory appears under the form of humiliation; plenitude, under the form of emptiness (460–61).

Just as von Balthasar unites faith and experience, so he refuses to separate faith from knowledge. Even in the Old Testament, where the emphasis falls on trust and promise, the elements of perception and knowledge are not absent (592). In the New Testament Paul speaks uninhibitedly of knowledge and wisdom conferred by the Holy Spirit (134). For John faith and knowledge are inseparably intertwined. In a kind of circumincession, *pistis* and *gnosis* proceed from, and depend on, each other (135). Thus the medieval formula of "faith seeking understanding" falls somewhat short of what we find in the Scriptures. Faith is not merely searching and tentative, as this formula might seem to suggest. It is solidly grounded in its real object even though it continues to probe more deeply (136). For Clement and the ancient Alexandrians there is no *pistis* without *gnosis;* no *gnosis* without *pistis* (138). Gnosis, though it goes beyond simple faith, continues to rest on the faith in which it is grounded (137). "Faith alone . . . can guarantee the full objective ('rational') knowledge of things as they really are" (536).

Von Balthasar agrees with Rousselot that the spiritual capacity to see God's glory in the form of Christ cannot be obtained without the light of grace. Those who are not disposed by grace to accept the gospel are not in a position to perceive correctly what they are rejecting (509). Only persons attuned to the Spirit of God are able to understand and judge about the things of God (510). To be capable of finding the splendor of the divinity in the suffering Christ one must undergo the conversion that leads to faith (522–25). "The moment of faith coincides with the vision of the form" (524). Grace instills a connaturality with the divine realities (248), communicates a taste for God (249), and becomes the basis for a correct discernment of spirits (297–98).

Without denying what Rousselot and others have said about the subjective light of faith, von Balthasar seeks to supplement it from the biblical and classical doctrine that the light of faith is also, and indeed primarily, objective. The light is present first of all in God, whose radiance, as mentioned above, shines from the face of Christ (190, 217). The believer "finds his own light of faith as a reality within the light of Christ," who is faith's object (192). It is precisely in looking outward at the revealed reality that faith becomes luminous to itself (217). The light of faith is a participation in the light of God, who dwells in those to whom he reveals himself (179).

Because Christ in his humanity takes on the condition of sinners, he experiences a certain distance from God. His obedience to his Father's will is a created analogue of the eternal relation of the Son to the Father. In a sense Christ may be said to possess "archetypal faith" and the hiddenness of the relation to God that this implies (327). But his consciousness of God is the human experience of a divine person who "empties himself"; it cannot be judged by the laws of ordinary human psychology (328). Although he excelled in loving trust, humble obedience, and patient endurance, he did not have exactly what we experience as faith.[4]

In the period after Jesus' death and resurrection faith took on an ecclesial form, which was required in order for it to be complete (538). The form of the Church, however, is not autonomous. Its whole function is to point to Christ (557). Ecclesial ministry must always receive and transmit the form of Christ (597). The ecclesial office of authority is a service, a ministry (213). The magisterium is a means; the life of the Church is an end (214). Faith, which goes out to Christ as God's total glory, does not take the magisterium or doctrine as its true object. It discovers in them the radiant transparency of God's self-manifestation (213, 217). "The mystery of God proclaimed by the Church is his *doxa* become visible, and a beam of it, to be sure, falls on the ecclesial authority and proclamation, authenticating them" (141).

What, then, does von Balthasar understand faith to be? For him it is not just a subjective act *(fides qua creditur).* It includes the reality to which it is directed *(fides quae creditur,* 131). Subjectively, faith consists in openness to the objective evidence of revelation (418). More than an assent, it is that total condition in which human beings through the power of grace correspond to God's revelatory address (131). It is an encounter of the whole person with God who reveals (219). In faith the believer's very existence becomes centered in Christ (179). "Faith is nothing but the believer's whole existence as buried and as rising along with Christ, the Word made flesh" (197). It is "a loving surrender of one's whole person . . . into the hands of the divine Person" (202).

A variety of acts can be ascribed to faith. In the Old Testament the accent is placed on listening, obeying, yielding, hoping, and trusting. Yet Scripture connects faith also with the recognition and knowledge of God (131). Love enters constitutively into faith, as the Johannine writings attest. The life and death of the Son of God, as embodiments of God's love for the world, instruct us to respond with our love, so that faith may be realized in us (588–89). "Theology has always seen clearly that, in its very vitality, the self-surrender of faith is rooted in love. ('Dead faith' is a residue, the result of the dissolution of faith and, as such, inadequate as a model for faith)" (192).

Von Balthasar's aesthetic approach, like transcendental theology, is a reaction against the "two-storey" extrinsicism of late Scholasticism. Like transcendental theology, it retrieves the experiential aspect, making use of the traditional idea of the "light of faith." But von Balthasar faults transcendental theology for being too anthropocentric, too much focused on the subjective component of faith.

Linking faith as he does to God's objective self-manifestation in Christ, von Balthasar gets away from subjectivism and achieves a welcome integration between faith and understanding. He is unsympathetic with theories that seem to minimize the importance of explicit belief in Christ, such as Rahner's "anonymous Christianity."[5] Although von Balthasar admits that the unevangelized can have the theological virtue of faith, he has not thematically developed any explanation corresponding to Rahner's.

Von Balthasar prefers to use rather generic concepts of faith, in which faith is not clearly distinguished from other acts or virtues such as hope, trust, love, obedience, assent, and contemplation. While this generic usage can be supported from biblical and patristic sources, it lacks the precision of high Scholasticism, which distinguished virtues in terms of their acts, and acts in terms of their formal objects.

In many respects von Balthasar's theology of faith may be called post-critical or even acritical. Instead of seeking to defend Christianity on the basis of criteria available to nonbelievers, he makes a strong case for holding that its truth can be grasped only from within the commitment of faith, thanks to the "eyes of faith." He confidently proclaims that biblical revelation has a divine beauty, and that all who fail to see this are blinded by the effects of sin. Even the ugliness of the cross is taken up into the higher beauty of God's splendor. For von Balthasar it seems to be axiomatic that the truth of Christianity is self-evident to those who are open to its beauty. To his critics it may seem that in his concentration on the beauty perceived in faith he skirts the problem of credibility at a stage prior to Christian faith.

## Transcendental Theology

Transcendental theology, building on the "turn to the subject" effected by Rousselot and Joseph Maréchal, emphasizes the subjective dimension of faith. Under the influence of Kant, this school tends to make a sharper distinction between faith and knowledge than de Lubac or von Balthasar would do. Karl Rahner and Bernard Lonergan are the leading exponents of this trend in post-Vatican II Catholicism.

The German Jesuit Karl Rahner (1904–1984) grounds his theology of faith on a well articulated philosophical anthropology.[6] To be human, he holds, is to be a "spirit in the world." By a spirit he means a reality that can become luminously present to itself in freedom, knowledge, and love. The human spirit comes to itself as spirit by going out of itself and encountering the world through the body.

The human spirit is fundamentally ordered toward the transcendent absolute, which in religion goes by the name of God. When it knows fellow creatures, the human spirit grasps them only by transcending them, by seeing them against the horizon of the infinite. Even when God is not known in an explicit or conceptual manner, he is implicitly known in the inborn drive of human subjectivity, for particular objects are not intelligible except against the horizon of the Unlimited.

God is not only the horizon of all knowledge and love, but he is the ultimate goal toward whom the human spirit is oriented. As actually constituted, human beings are destined for the intuitive vision of God, the only goal that can fully satisfy the inner dynamism of the spirit. In ordering human beings to immediate union with himself, God, so to speak, commits himself to give them the grace that renders them capable of the beatific vision. According to Rahner grace, at least as offer, is constant and universal. God elevates and supernaturalizes the immanent dynamism of human nature and thereby makes grace available to everyone all the time.

Faith, for Rahner, consists primarily in the acceptance of God's self-communication to the human spirit as subject. In this "transcendental" aspect faith is not a communication of determinate truths but a global experience of the saving presence of God as holy mystery. The mystery is experienced as both awesome and alluring *(mysterium tremendum et fascinans)*. Faith, in this transcendental aspect, is a light: It gives a new horizon, a new "formal object," to human cognition, so that all realities are seen and experienced in a different manner. The transcendental experience is always mediated by some object in time and space (a "categorial" object), but this object need not be religious in nature. For the person whose spirit is drawn toward the God who communicates himself in grace, ordinary secular material will suffice to mediate the encounter with the holy mystery.

Rahner repeatedly asserts that it is possible for a person to have transcendental faith without knowing anything explicitly about Christ, the gospel, or biblical revelation. In fact, he asserts, such a faith is compatible with a profession of atheism on the level of one's explicit or conceptual consciousness. The acceptance on the unthematic level of the presence of holy mystery suffices for transcendental faith, even though the mystery be not thematized in terms of a doctrine of God or of redemption. Such "anonymous" faith has as its real though unrecognized object the one whom Christians have learned to call God—the God who calls us to himself through his incarnate Word. Real faith, consequently, can be anonymously theist and anonymously Christian.

Rahner, therefore, has no difficulty in admitting that the unevangelized may possess the gift of saving faith. Anonymous faith, consisting simply in an acceptance of one's own grace-given dynamism toward the Transcendent, is sufficient for salvation, provided that it be enlivened by hope and love.

Rahner does not deny that faith always has a material object as well as a formal object. Precisely because it has a new formal object (God communicating himself), faith involves a new manner of perceiving reality as a whole. When elevated by grace, the spirit sees depths and relationships that it would not otherwise see, and this added content may be called the material object of faith. From an ecclesial point of view the material object may be described in terms of the ideas and symbols through which faith is expressed and mediated in a given community.

Faith, according to Rahner, remains anonymously theist and anonymously Christian until it comes to an explicit recognition of God as its transcendent source and goal and of Christ as the unsurpassable self-mediation of God. Faith always has an intrinsic dynamism to realize itself explicitly. The grace-given interior experience of the saving mystery prepares a person to accept Christ and the articles of faith when these are made available through proclamation. Acceptance of the gospel and the creed would not be faith unless their contents were integrated into the experience of God's free self-communication in grace, which for Rahner is the central mystery of faith. To have explicit faith in Christ is to recognize him as the one in whom God turns with redemptive love toward humankind, and thus as the historical personality who makes it possible for our hope of salvation to be fulfilled. Jesus is the definitive answer to the question that human beings are to themselves. Not everyone, however, is able to recognize Jesus as that answer. Many live more easily in anonymous hope.

Rahner in various essays reflects on the situation of faith in today's climate of skepticism and relativism. He acknowledges that many find it difficult to assent unhesitatingly to all the dogmas of the Church. Inevitably, he holds, many Christians, not excluding Catholics, are "marginal"; they identify themselves only partially with the Church. Rahner is prepared to accept this partial identification provided that these persons do not proudly reject the definitive teaching of the Church.

Rahner's theology of faith is a radicalization of the trend inaugurated by Blondel and Rousselot. Whereas Rousselot looked upon the grace-given light of faith as a necessary presupposition for the judgment of credibility and for the act of faith in the Christian dogmas, Rahner regards the light of faith as being by itself a kind of subjective or transcendental revelation, and thus as permitting an act of faith even when unaccompanied by the explicit transmission of any specific revealed truths. Rahner is obviously concerned with explaining how non-Christians and doubting Christians can come to salvation. He solves this problem but only by seeming to say, in effect, that explicit acceptance of the Christian proclamation is of secondary importance. If one accepts that proclamation, one does so because it is seen as the best articulation of what one already believed in an implicit or nonthematic way.

Rahner has often defended this solution as compatible with the teaching of Vatican II—teaching that he may have had a hand in formulating. But it is not necessary to interpret the statements of Vatican II as supporting the Rahnerian doctrine of "anonymous Christianity." That doctrine is, moreover, somewhat difficult to harmonize with the teaching of earlier councils and with the New Testament view of faith. In the New Testament and in traditional Christian theology, faith generally means explicit acceptance of the gospel. This acceptance, furthermore, involves a radical conversion to beliefs that lie beyond all previous expectation.

Other objections are raised from other points of view. Some find that Rahner's theory gives insufficient importance to institutional Christianity and that it undermines the missionary imperative to preach the gospel. From a different perspective, some proponents of interreligious dialogue look upon Rahner's doctrine of "anonymous Christianity" as too Christocentric. It is imperialistic, they complain, for Christians to claim that other faiths are anonymous forms of Christianity.[7] Political and liberationist theologians, for their part, criticize Rahner for having unduly privatized faith and for overlooking the political and social dimensions. Thus Rahner's synthesis, brilliant and comprehensive as it is, has not as yet won anything like a consensus, even among Catholics.

A second expression of the transcendental theology of faith is found in the works of the Canadian Jesuit Bernard Lonergan (1904–1984). His first full discussion of faith occurs in chapter 20 of his *Insight*[8] in the context of a philosophical treatment of belief as acceptance of the word of another. Writing as a Thomist and adhering to the perspectives of Vatican I, Lonergan takes up faith as a species of belief. He contrasts belief, as assent on the word of another, with "immanently generated knowledge," and analyzes the conditions under which it is reasonable to believe.

He points out the necessity of believing in order to collaborate profitably with others, and illustrates such collaboration from the sciences.

Faith, as described in *Insight,* is "a transcendent belief operative within a new and higher collaboration of man with God"; it will be "an assent of intellect to truths transmitted through the collaboration and it will be motivated by man's reliance on the truthfulness of God" (720). Lonergan defends the reasonableness of faith on the ground that human beings must depend on the divine wisdom to escape errors and to solve problems that would otherwise be unsurmountable. Faith purifies the mind and gives answers that are "principally the work of God who illuminates our intellects to understand what we had not understood and to grasp as unconditioned what we had reputed error" (730). Faith in this perspective is heuristic: it is ordered to understanding according to the ancient precept, *crede ut intelligas.*

Quite different from this Scholastic treatment is the approach to faith in Lonergan's second major work, *Method in Theology,*[9] where he makes a sharp distinction between faith and belief. Faith, he writes, "is the knowledge born of religious love" (115). It is "the eye of religious love, an eye that can discern God's self-disclosures" (119).

In order to show how faith leads to knowledge Lonergan begins his analysis of faith with a description of falling in love with God. This experience, he maintains, "is the basic fulfilment of our conscious intentionality" (105). Flooding our hearts with his love through the Holy Spirit given to us (105; cf. Rom 5:5), God speaks a word pertaining to the world of immediate experience, a world prior to that mediated by meaning (112). Since the heart has reasons that reason does not know (Pascal), the experience of God's love gives rise to value judgments. "It places all other values in the light and the shadow of transcendent value" (116). In the light of faith, divine light and love are seen as the supreme originating value. Faith reveals the ultimate significance of human achievement, gives confidence to those who strive for great causes, and liberates human reasonableness from its ideological prisons (117).

The experience of faith, for Lonergan, "may be objectified as a clouded revelation of absolute intelligence" (116). But religious beliefs do not have the transcendental experience of grace as their sole source. They arise when faith encounters the "outer word" of a religious tradition. This outer word, at least in Christianity, is not just an objectification of God's gift of love. It is a new word from God himself (119); it is revelation (296–98).

Lonergan considers it important to distinguish between faith, as the "eye of religious love," and beliefs, which faith discerns as God's self-disclosures (119). Yet he affirms a close connection between faith and beliefs. Doctrines revealed by God, he says, are "truths of faith" (336).[10] "Assent to such doctrines is the assent of faith, and that assent is regarded by religious people as firmer than any other" (349).

Although Lonergan evidently holds that the beliefs enshrined in the Christian creed and in Catholic dogma are divinely revealed, he is convinced that his distinction between faith and belief provides a secure basis "both for ecumenical encounter and for an encounter between all religions with a basis in religious experience" (119). Even though the beliefs differ, a deeper unity of faith lies behind the divergent beliefs. In the light of their experience of God's inner word all may strive for common judgments of value and for a purification of their beliefs (ibid.).

As a methodologist Lonergan prefers to leave to theologians questions that may arise concerning revelation and inspiration, development and authority (119), but for that reason his treatment of faith, and even of theological method, leaves many unanswered questions. How does God's outer word come into history? What forms does it take other than dogma? Is Christ the outer word of God? Is Scripture the word of God? How does faith respond to Christ and Holy Scripture? How does the theologian make use of inspired sources?

Since he relates faith and conversion almost exclusively to the "inner word" of God's love poured into the heart, Lonergan can easily be understood (or misunderstood) as denying the salvific importance of God's outer word. In some passages he gives the impression of holding that all religious people have one and the same faith, and that they are divided not in faith but in beliefs. Some disciples of Lonergan have felt that they could abandon their belief in the teaching of the Church while retaining their faith. Charles Davis, for instance, wrote: "I am convinced that I myself should never have been able to leave the Roman Catholic Church, had it not been for my reading of Lonergan."[11] Lonergan, he says, made it possible for him to see that faith is separable from allegiance to the Roman Catholic Church with its infallible authority and unchanging dogmas. Lonergan himself, to be sure, continued to adhere to a hierarchically constituted church, but Davis maintains that in so doing Lonergan was clinging to elements of a classical culture that are neither necessary for faith nor viable in contemporary culture.

Lonergan, of course, would have rejected this interpretation of his views on faith, but he would have had to say more about the historical mediation of revelation in order to protect himself from this kind of accusation.

## Liberation Theology

Already in Europe in the 1960s, with theologians such as Johann Baptist Metz, Edward Schillebeeckx, and Jürgen Moltmann, efforts were made to link theology more closely to social and political action. Partly under the influence of these efforts there has arisen, in the Third World, a movement of "liberation theology" which reinterprets the doctrine of faith in relation to the commitment to social action on behalf of the poor and the oppressed. Two outstanding representatives of this tendency are the Peruvian diocesan priest Gustavo Gutiérrez (1928–   ) and the Uruguayan Jesuit Juan Luis Segundo (1925–   ).

Gutiérrez made his reputation when he published his *A Theology of Liberation*.[12] In this work he had no extensive treatment of faith, but the few remarks that he did make were indicative of a major shift. According to the biblical view, he asserted, faith is:

> an act of trust, a going out of one's self, a commitment to God and neighbor, a relationship with others. . . . According to the Bible, faith is the total human response to God, who saves through love. In this light, the understanding of faith

appears as the understanding not of the simple affirmation—almost memorization—of truths, but of a commitment, an overall attitude, a particular posture toward life. (6)

Later in the same book Gutiérrez treats of faith in relation to political action. He holds that while faith does not by itself give a concrete plan for social reorganization, it must express itself in a commitment to a more just society. This commitment can achieve concreteness through the mediation of a utopian vision, a historical projection. A faith lived at the very heart of history becomes the victory that overcomes the world (138–40; cf. 1 Jn 5:4).

In his book *The Power of the Poor in History*[13] Gutiérrez reprinted in revised form some of his more recent articles. The first chapter is an overview of the biblical sources of liberation theology. The Bible, he writes, is a book that tells of people's faith. To read it with faith is to read it from within a community that recognizes Christ as Lord both of its history and of its life (3–4).

Biblical faith, Gutiérrez maintains, is historical. It acknowledges God as revealing himself in history—as a God who acts. The efficacy of God's word is indicated by the fact that the Hebrew term *dabar,* used for revelation in the Old Testament, includes both word and happening (4–5). From the Bible, moreover, it is apparent that God orients history in a definite direction. His activity is pointed toward justice, toward a defense of the rights of the poor and the liberation of the oppressed. This activity constitutes his theophany, his revelation (7).

God establishes a covenant with those to whom he reveals himself. He is faithful to his promises and obliges his people to be faithful, "to practice the justice implied in God's liberating activity on behalf of the oppressed." Through the faithfulness of his people, God's promises are translated into concrete historical actuality (10). The faith of the community is celebrated in creeds that recall the past with a view to the future. In worship the community evokes its past, giving thanks and renewing its fidelity (12).

Jesus Christ is the key to the meaning of Scripture. He is the fulfillment of the promises and the full manifestation of the God who is love (12). He is the new covenant, the road to the Father, the advent of the new creation. In him God becomes poor and suffers in the cause of justice. By baptism we are buried with Christ and raised up with him. Having faith means believing not so much in his message as in him. "Our faith goes out through the gospel straight to Christ" (13). Communion with him involves community; it implies solidarity with the poor in history (16).

Faith does not end in personal assent. It shines forth in witness and action. Faith without works is dead (16; cf. Jas 2:14–26, which Gutiérrez here quotes in full). "Practice is the locus of verification of our faith in God who liberates by establishing justice and right in favor of the poor" (17). Faith therefore requires an option for the poor, for the exploited classes, and an engagement in the struggle for greater justice and liberation (52).

"To believe," then, "is to love God and to be in solidarity with the poor and exploited of this world in the midst of social confrontations and popular struggle for liberation. To believe is to proclaim the kingdom as Christ does—from the midst of the struggle for justice that led him to his death" (20; cf. 55).

A key point in Gutiérrez's theology of liberation is the link between theory and praxis. From Karl Marx he takes over the principle that history can be known only through the process of transforming it. The praxis that transforms history is not a mere application of a previously excogitated theory but is the locus in which people come to discover themselves and their world (58–59).

The concept of knowing through action, according to Gutiérrez, has biblical warrants. Truth in the Bible is not just theoretical knowledge. It is something lived. Truth includes fidelity, justice, and constancy of purpose. To believe, consequently, is to have confidence, to trust God, and to be faithful. To know is to love. "True orthodoxy is orthopraxis" (59–60).[14]

At a number of points Gutiérrez has discussed the relationship between faith as a living encounter and theology as reflection. Theology as a reasoning process always takes its departure from faith, but it also returns to faith as its point of arrival. There is no such thing as a permanent and universal theology. "Every theology asks the meaning of the word of God for its contemporaries, at a certain moment of history," and does so in function of the culture (56). "Hence theology in Latin America today will be a reflection in, and on, faith as liberation praxis. It will be an understanding of the faith from an option and a commitment" (60).[15]

Certain aspects of Gutiérrez's theology of faith are further developed in his work on liberation spirituality, *We Drink from Our Own Wells.*[16] Here he emphasizes that faith begins in an experience of encounter, in which the total initiative is God's (52). The life of faith is a venture, a journey in darkness, convincingly described by John of the Cross (85–86). "To believe in God is more than simply to profess God's existence; it is to enter into communion with God and—the two being inseparable—with our fellow human beings as well" (95–96). Although faith is always oriented to community, it passes through painful solitude, in which the desire for community is intensified (128, 132). "In the final analysis, to believe in God means to live our life as a gift from God and to look upon everything that happens in it as a manifestation of this gift" (110). To "find God in all things," according to the formula of Ignatius of Loyola, presupposes a contemplative dimension in one's life (111). Speaking of theology, Gutiérrez reiterates that it is "a discourse that sinks its roots into a faith lived in ecclesial communion and thus grafted into a history of the transmission and acceptance of the Christian message" (136). "Reflection on the mystery of God," he adds, "is possible only in the context of the following of Jesus" (ibid.)

Numerous criticisms have of course been brought against liberation theologians in general and against Gutiérrez in particular. For example, the movement is accused of substituting this-worldly fulfillment for eschatological hope, substituting confidence in political action for reliance on God, promoting violent revolution, neglecting personal sin, and failing to encourage personal prayer and interior holiness. Some of these charges appear as warnings in the Instruction of the Congregation for the Doctrine of the Faith on "Certain Aspects of the 'Theology of Liberation,'"[17] but this document makes no mention of Gutiérrez or any other liberation theologian by name. Other criticisms of liberation theology are conveniently summarized in a recent work by Arthur F. McGovern.[18] Many of these charges have some validity as signaling exaggerations to which partisans of the movement may easily be prone, but they should not be taken without examination as referring to errors actually committed by Gutiérrez or other individuals.

In 1985 Gutiérrez underwent a doctoral examination at the Catholic Institute of Lyons. The jury of five theologians raised many of the standard objections. In replying, Gutiérrez took rather traditional positions and tried to show that his own writings could be interpreted in line with the tradition.[19] He made it clear that the poor, in his conception, are not to be identified on simply economic or social grounds (10). He denied that historical realizations of liberation are tantamount to the arrival of God's kingdom (15–16). He insisted on the crucial importance of worship and personal prayer for the Christian life (17–18, 45–46). He protested that the temptation to Pelagianism had always been completely alien to him (35). He explained that faith does not and cannot present a concrete social plan (43).

Gutiérrez's theology of faith continues to draw various evaluations, both positive and negative. His dynamic view of faith as a power that does not simply wait on God but contributes actively to the course of events is attractive in an age when people are conscious of their responsibility for society and the world. Gutiérrez has been able to show that this operational view of faith has biblical grounding in texts such as Galatians 5:6, which speaks of "faith working through love," and perhaps also in 1 John 5:4, which calls faith "the victory that overcomes the world." If fidelity to the gospel contributes to the anticipatory realization of God's kingdom in history, faith may be said to have a liberative role. This insight helps to bridge the gaps between religion and politics, between individual and society, and between faith and daily life. The last of these dichotomies was described by Vatican II as "among the more serious misconceptions of our day"[20]

The negative reactions to this conception of faith arise chiefly from two considerations. In the first place, Gutiérrez clearly breaks with the Thomistic tradition, according to which faith is an act elicited by the speculative intelligence, having as its object God as supreme truth *(prima veritas)*. For Gutiérrez, faith must be seen as an act of the will and the practical intelligence; its object appears to include a future social order to be produced, under God, by human effort. Before this new conception of faith is admitted, its consequences will have to be rigorously thought through.

Secondly, praxis, as described by Gutiérrez, seems to involve a commitment to radical social change. If faith is praxis, then, it appears to follow that only social activists can be Christian believers. The new system gives no scope for contemplatives unless they are "contemplatives in action." It also makes no place, it would seem, for people who are content to work within the existing social framework.

Gutiérrez has been moving away from the Marxian inspiration of his early work, and for this reason it is particularly difficult to determine how he would answer these objections. If his position were reformulated in a manner that satisfies the objectors, it might no longer be recognizably that of liberation theology.[21]

Juan Luis Segundo develops a rather different approach, strongly influenced by the neo-Kantian distinction between judgments of value and judgments of fact. The former are ascribed to faith, the latter to ideology.

In *The Liberation of Theology*[22] Segundo lays down a basic concept of faith as a universal anthropological datum. "Real life for a human being presupposes a non-empirical choice of some ideal that one presumes will be satisfying" (104). People normally choose the ideals of persons close to them. In the case of Christian children, this will mean accepting the religious values of their parents. About the time of adolescence some will select Christ as an embodiment of cherished values. Others, for similar motives, may select a hero such as Ché Guevara (105).

Although faith, unlike ideology, claims to possess an objectively absolute value, it does not attain any absolute object (107). According to Segundo, the object of faith is neither God nor any specific revealed truth, two misconceptions that stand in conflict with the Bible. Faith's object is not God, he holds, because the Bible has much more to say about human experiences than about God (179). Faith does not have dogmas as its content because the Bible deals chiefly with the process by which truth is acquired. The dogmas of the Church, as understood by Segundo, are not definitive truths but guidelines for a process of learning (180).

The true content of faith, then, is the learning process, a process of "learning to learn" (118). Faith is "the total process to which man submits, a process of learning in and through ideologies how to create the ideologies needed to handle new and unforeseen situations in history" (120). The importance of faith can be understood only in relation to ideologies. By ideology Segundo means an idea or "system of goals and means" adopted in order to achieve values selected by faith (102). Ideology applies faith to the solution of particular problems (154). Faith "has sense and meaning only insofar as it serves as the foundation stone for ideologies" (109). Faith and ideology are inextricably intermingled (105). Faith without ideologies is dead (181).

In the Bible Segundo finds a paradigm for the faith-ideology relationship (113–18). The ideas of the biblical characters and authors are continually being corrected. The process of correction does not stop even with the New Testament (120). Jesus sends the Spirit of truth to provide the Church with further needed truth (120; cf. Jn 16:12–14). The language of Jesus, according to Segundo, "points not towards a better understanding of what has already been spoken but towards the learning of new things" (120). In a summary of Paul's teaching on faith, Segundo writes (122):

> Faith rather than the law must serve as the springboard for launching into a new adventure. . . . Therefore this faith does not consist in intellectual adherence to a certain body of revealed content as the definitive solution to theoretical or practical problems. Nor does it consist in having confidence in one's own salvation, thanks to the merits of Christ. Instead it entails the freedom to accept an educational process that comes to maturity and abandons its teacher to launch out into the provisional and relative depths of history (Gal. 4:1 ff.; Rom. 8:19–23; 1 Cor. 3:11–15).

In Segundo's own terminology, faith is "maturity by way of ideologies" (122).

Liberation theology begins with an option in favor of liberative change. Conscious of the oppressive situation the theologian sets out with an attitude of suspicion toward the reigning ideologies (9). Recognizing the unattainability of final truth, liberation theology denies orthodoxy as a final criterion. It holds for the priority of orthopraxis over orthodoxy (32).

Segundo's positions are spelled out in greater detail in a later book, *Faith and*

*Ideologies.*[23] Faith is initially defined, once again, as an indispensable component in any human life. On the ground that everybody needs trusted human witnesses to articulate a realm of values, Segundo holds that faith is the criterion by which certain witnesses are accepted or rejected. Faith is not, in the first instance, reliance on testimony. The favorable or unfavorable judgment on the witness depends on one's previous acceptance of certain values as higher than others (25).

Faith becomes religious when it adheres to a tradition or chain of witnesses that is seen as embodying divine revelation (64). Even though God may not be explicitly named (as he is not in Buddhism and Shintoism), the tradition is religious if it is established by symbols that do the equivalent (82). The judgment of revelation is based on a prior faith that disposes one to accept the values represented by the witnesses (64–65). Christian faith, like any other religious faith, is the acceptance of a tradition of human witnesses. Jesus stands in solidarity with the tradition, and does not represent himself "as the one solitary revelation of God, his Father" (75).

We cannot set aside the testimony of human witnesses to accept the authority of the revealing or self-revealing God (75), even though Thomas Aquinas and the First Vatican Council seem to speak in those terms (83–84). Rather, the authority of God is accepted on the word of human witnesses. Religious faith "constitutes a system of learning-apprenticeship transmitted by historical witnesses which enables people to recognize and discern genuine transcendent data; and those data, in turn, become defining factors of people's meaning-structures" (76).

Segundo in *Faith and Ideologies* repeats the critique of dogma given in his earlier book. Dogmas, he asserts, are "symbols of the world of value, of a world that is clearly in movement" (76–77). Far from being static definitions, dogmas evolve and are rectified in the course of time.

As in *The Liberation of Theology,* Segundo again uses the concept of ideology to mediate between abstract values and concrete realities. Ideologies are sets of means (54); they relate to efficiency in the realization of values (27). Paraphrasing the letter of James in his own terminology, Segundo repeats his earlier assertion: Faith without ideologies is dead (126).

In a recent work, *The Liberation of Dogma,* Segundo summarizes many of his previous positions. In his discussion of faith he particularly emphasizes the priority of faith to revelation. Revelation cannot come except to people who are already engaged in a quest for liberation and have freely committed themselves to certain options. "God addresses the divine word to an (anthropological) faith that is always there, and that in each human being is the fruit of an option (antecedent to hearing)."[24]

Segundo proclaims that in proposing, as he does, a new type of theology growing out of "real-life experience," he may be dispensed from treating "all the avatars of a doctrine laden with the accumulations of twenty centuries."[25] Yet the works we have examined contain little that is new. For the most part Segundo repeats the views of nineteenth-century European thinkers. From Marxism he takes over the philosophical thesis that the purpose of theory is to transform reality and the sociological thesis that a new society must be brought into existence by subverting the present order, which is oppressive. Together with this Marxian outlook Segundo resurrects the neo-Kantian concept of a self-authenticating order of values, independent of existing realities. Like the liberal Protestants, Segundo makes faith consist in value judgments unsupported by factual evidence. Dispensing with metaphysics, he prefers to approach the existence of God by way of symbols. Combining metaphysical agnosticism with historicism, he is unwilling to credit any assertions about the real order as permanently true. Like the Modernists, he looks on dogmas not as revealed truths but as symbols referring to values. Faith, for him, continually progresses "into the provisional and relative depths of history," leaving behind its former dogmas and even the person of Christ the teacher.

Although Segundo's theology of faith contains many questionable elements, it is not without merit. Against a too passive understanding of faith as an acceptance of ready-made truths, under the illusion that they are simply handed down from heaven, Segundo rightly brings out the importance of human questioning in order that revelation may find a welcome reception. He is likewise on good ground in holding that the doctrines of faith must be rethought in every generation, and that they must be applied in the search for fully human solutions to the problems of the day. The Holy Spirit, as Segundo says, is given to lead the people of God into the fullness of the truth, which still lies ahead.

## Theology of Hope

As may be seen from the examples here given, the Catholic theology of the past generation has tended to focus on the cognitive dimension of faith and on the inseparability of faith and works—two themes that had already surfaced by the time of the Council of Trent. Protestant theology, conversely, continues to emphasize the fiducial component of faith, as may be seen from the work of Gerhard Ebeling, already considered, and from a number of theologians who have emerged to prominence during and since Vatican II. We shall here consider two German authors, Jürgen Moltmann (1926–   ), an Evangelical Reformed theologian, and Wolfhart Pannenberg (1928–   ), a Lutheran.

Moltmann first attracted worldwide attention with his *Theology of Hope,*[26] a book emanating from the author's dialogue with the dissident Marxist philosopher, Ernst Bloch. Moltmann quotes Calvin to the effect that faith takes its stand on hope and that hope is therefore the "inseparable companion" of faith. According to Calvin, as quoted by Moltmann, "hope is nothing else than the expectation of those things which faith has believed to have been truly promised by God"[27] From this, Moltmann draws the conclusion: "To believe means to cross in hope and anticipation the bounds that have been penetrated by the raising of the crucified" (20–21). He formulates the relation between faith and hope as follows:

If it is hope that maintains and upholds faith and keeps it moving on, if it is hope that draws the believer into the life of love, then it will also be hope that is the mobilizing and driving force of faith's thinking, of its knowledge of, and reflections on, human nature, history and society. Faith hopes in order to know what it believes. Hence all its knowledge will be anticipatory, fragmentary knowledge forming a prelude to the promised future, and as such is committed to hope (33).

For the Reformers, Moltmann maintains, faith and God's promises are correlative. "Faith is called to life by promise and is therefore essentially hope, confidence, trust in the God who will not lie but will remain faithful to his promise" (44).

In Moltmann's estimation faith reaches its maturity in hope: "The believer becomes essentially one who hopes . . . for he has staked his future on the future of Christ" (91).

In an inaugural lecture given at the University of Tübingen in 1968, entitled "God and Resurrection," Moltmann argued that it is a mistake to try to ground one's resurrection faith on the Gospels considered as historical accounts, for the Easter event transcends the competence of historical science. "In the resurrection of Christ, a real anticipation of God's comprehensive future becomes tangible. . . . Resurrection faith is faith in the crucified one; and hope which overcomes the world, which can hope against hope, is born in the community of the crucified one."[28] The preaching of the gospel, Moltmann continues, includes an announcement of the future. For this reason faith likewise is concerned with the future. "Because a future event is realized in it, as faith it is hope" (45).

Moltmann's more recent work shows an increasing influence of liberation theology together with a continued emphasis on the link between faith and hope. In an interview published in 1977 he declared: "The faith that looks backward and wants to preserve only what is old is a negative aspect of the faith still living today among us. I consider as very positive in the present survival of the faith everything that is an opening of faith to hope in the promises of God." He went on to speak of the connection between faith and liberation. Faith, he said, impels us to enter into the messianic work and the messianic suffering of Christ. Freeing believers from fear, indifference, and oppression, faith gives them courage to struggle against the forces of massive evil. Whereas faith used to be understood as a participation in the religious life of the Church, it must today be understood as a personal experience of liberation brought about by Jesus Christ. Because Christ is the Liberator par excellence, every Christian is called upon to be a liberator for others.[29]

It is generally conceded that Moltmann has performed a real service by calling attention to the intimate nexus between faith and hope, but he is often accused of exaggeration, especially in the dichotomies he sets up between history and hope, between logos and promise. Carl Henry, for example, protests:

> The Bible represents God's revelation and promise in the form of logos, whereas Moltmann replaces the theology of the revealed Word of God by an eschatological dwarfing of history and truth. Moltmann sponsors a new gnosis. By an appeal to the future of God he relativizes the Word and truth of divine revelation in the historical past.[30]

Moltmann is evidently selective in his use of Scripture. Gerald O'Collins, although he has high praise for Moltmann, points out that *Theology of Hope* contains not a single reference to the Fourth Gospel.[31] With regard to the character of faith, Moltmann apparently admits no sharp distinction between the dispensations of the Old and New Testaments. In each case the orientation is essentially toward the future. The Christ event, like the Exodus, is understood as an event of promise rather than of accomplished redemption.

## Historical Reason and Anticipation

At the opposite pole from Moltmann's distrust of logic and history is Pannenberg's esteem for reason and historical research. Unlike Moltmann, Pannenberg seeks to ground faith securely in demonstrable past events, but at the same time to keep the accent, as does Moltmann, on faith's orientation to the future.

A recurrent theme in Pannenberg's writing is the denial that faith rests on authoritative testimony. He faults Clement, Augustine, and the medieval Scholastics for having depicted faith as an assent based on authority.[32] Too authoritarian likewise, in Pannenberg's estimation, is Bultmann's conception of faith as an obedient hearing of the word of God.[33] For Pannenberg, words by themselves are not authoritative. God's deeds in history, for him, "speak their own language, the language of facts. God has proved his deity in this language of facts."[34]

Since the Enlightenment and the advent of critical history, Pannenberg contends, the effort to base faith on authoritative texts, including even the Bible, has ceased to be tenable. But the danger is that, seeing the weakness of arguments from authority, some authors describe faith as a sheer subjective decision unsupported by rational grounds. This option, which Pannenberg attributes to Pascal, Kant, and Kierkegaard, would, he says, make faith indistinguishable from a neurosis.[35]

Positively, then, Pannenberg holds that faith must be grounded in knowledge. It must rest on reasons that hold up under examination.[36] "The proclamation of the gospel cannot assert that the facts are in doubt and that the leap of faith must be made in order to achieve certainty."[37] Paraphrasing Romans 6:8–8, Pannenberg attributes to Paul the thesis that knowledge precedes faith: Because we know that Christ has been raised from the dead, we believe that we shall also live with him.[38] More specifically, the knowledge of the resurrection of Jesus Christ as a historical event is the presupposition of Christian faith.

Faith, then, rests on assured knowledge, but it is not itself knowledge. Rather, it is a trusting surrender of one's existence to the God who has been manifested in Jesus Christ: "Faith has to do with the future. This is the essence of trust."[39]

The demonstrability of the contents of faith, according to Pannenberg, does not render faith superfluous.

> For faith involves the participation of the believer himself in the reality in which he believes, and this cannot be replaced by any knowledge. Moreover, faith always has to do with the future. The believer attaches his own future to what he has come to recognize. Precisely for that reason faith cannot be its own basis. Faith as pure risk would be blind credulity.[40]

In summary, then, Pannenberg subscribes to the fiducial understanding of faith found in some passages of Luther and in Melanchthon, but he is by no means anti-rational. He departs from the Augustinian and Lutheran tradition of basing faith on an authoritative word or a divinely given text. Rejecting the supernaturalism of such theology, he asserts that faith is founded, at least in principle, on rational knowledge. But this rational grounding is merely a preparation for faith as a trusting commitment of oneself into the hands of God as he has revealed himself in Christ. Pannenberg's concern with the future is not merely a matter of individual eschatology; rather, it resembles Hegel's concern for the meaning and outcome of universal history. Yet Pannenberg differs from Hegel because he insists that the meaning of universal history cannot be known apart from God's self-revelation in Christ.

Pannenberg's critics have frequently asserted that he exaggerates the force of the rational evidence for revelation and especially for the resurrection of Jesus, which for him counts as a historical event. It is more common to hold that the resurrection cannot be securely known except in faith, and that the signs given in history are not compelling to reason as such. Many would say that the force of the evidence cannot be conclusive except to persons who yield to the attractions of grace and the illumination of the Holy Spirit. Pannenberg, on the contrary, asserts that faith is not a gift of the Spirit, but is the necessary presupposition for receiving the gift of the Spirit.[41] In this assertion Pannenberg apparently sets himself against the Second Council of Orange and a whole series of subsequent conciliar statements. Having done so, he finds it hard to vindicate the certitude of faith itself.

In his recent work Pannenberg places greater emphasis on the dialectical interplay between faith and knowledge. More than previously, he concedes that the resurrection will not be affirmed as a fact except by those who are drawn in hope to the life it promises. He speaks of the certitude of faith as proleptic and as depending on "the anticipatory gift of divine truth."[42] In fact he writes: "The proleptic presence of the eschaton in Jesus' history also seems bound up with the presence of the divine Spirit in its contents, with the effect that the Spirit is communicated through the apostolic proclamation rather than supervening upon its content as an additional factor."[43] This appears to be a modification of Pannenberg's earlier position that the gift of the Spirit is given only after revelation is accepted and the act of faith is made. More importantly for the present discussion, Pannenberg seems willing to admit that an assent to the resurrection can be not simply an act of knowledge but an act of faith, dependent in part on an attraction to the gift of eternal life. If this interpretation is correct, Pannenberg now identifies faith not only with with trust but also with intellectual assent.[44]

## Conservative Evangelicalism

Although Barth, Bultmann, Tillich, Ebeling, Moltmann, and Pannenberg have a considerable following among English-speaking Protestants, their theological innovations have met with some resistance from theologians who stand in the conservative evangelical tradition. Many North American Calvinists adhere more closely to seventeenth-century orthodoxy, as perpetuated by the Hodges and Warfield. Many of them speak of faith as propositional in nature.

In the United States, conservative evangelicals commonly distinguish between two levels or stages of faith. Fundamentally, they assert, faith is an assent to conceptual truth conveyed by the Bible, which is the Word of God in written form. Beyond this, saving faith, which is a gift of the Holy Spirit, requires the personal appropriation of divinely disclosed information. It involves existential trust in the living God in whom one believes. Faith itself, however, is not defined in terms of trust but rather in terms of assent.

Carl F. H. Henry, in the first four volumes of his monumental *God, Revelation and Authority,* gives an impressive statement of this position.[45] The issue between orthodoxy and neoorthodoxy, he asserts, hinges on the question "whether God's revelation is rational and objectively true, or whether it is only cognitively life-transforming" (3:455). Against Barth and Bultmann, E. Brunner and Tillich, and against some evangelicals influenced by neoorthodoxy, he adduces numerous quotations from evangelicals such as James I. Packer, Gordon H. Clark, Edward J. Carnell, Francis A. Schaeffer, and Clark H. Pinnock to the effect that the Bible consists predominantly of propositions and conveys objective information. Knowledge of revealed truth, he maintains, is indispensable though not sufficient for salvation (3:460). He concludes, therefore:

> To disallow in Christian faith any necessary or proper role for assent to propositions therefore seriously mistakes the nature of Christian belief. . . . Strenuously as some neo-Protestant thinkers have in the recent past depicted Christian faith as unrelated to the truth of propositions, and as authenticating itself instead in a very different realm of personal confrontation and response, Christianity's very claim to truth collapses unless truth can be affirmed of certain core-propositions inherent in it and integral to it. If the logical-propositional truth of the Christian revelation is ignored, and is even to be disowned, on the pretext that the efficacy of personal faith can be preserved only in this way, we shall needlessly and disastrously sacrifice what superbly distinguishes Christianity from other religions, viz., the truth of certain specific propositions that cannot be affirmed by rival faiths. . . . Faith divorced from assent to propositions may for a season be exuberantly championed as Christian faith, but sooner or later it must become apparent that such mystical exercises are neither identifiably Christian nor akin to authentic belief. (3:486–87)

In substantial agreement with Henry, a close associate of his, Gordon H. Clark, puts the matter very concisely: "Faith, by definition, is assent to understood propositions. Not all cases of assent, even assent to Biblical propositions, are saving faith; but all saving faith is assent to one or more Biblical propositions."[46]

## Conclusion

The positions expounded in this chapter, being roughly contemporaneous with one another, do not yield any clear pattern of development. A concluding summary, however, may be in order.

Catholic theologians have been continuing to react against the limitations of the type of Scholasticism that had been taught in seminaries since the sixteenth century. Von Balthasar, like de Lubac, enriches the theology of faith by a return to the fathers, whose work he interprets in the light of modern personalist phenomenology. Taking his departure unabashedly from within the stance of Catholic faith, he invites his readers to share in the fruits of his contemplation, and many have been allured by the canvas he paints. Rahner and Lonergan, influenced by Kant, develop a transcendental theology of faith with greater appeal to critical minds. The transcendental theologians tend to subordinate, without eliminating, the historical and conceptual aspects of faith. Emphasizing the non-objective, they find a commonality in faith between Christians and non-Christians, including Buddhists, Hindus, and secular humanists. The differences are seen to be of the "categorial" order, pertaining to belief as an articulation of faith rather than to faith in its essential definition.

Liberation theology breaks out of the academic seclusion of seminary and university theology; it provides a welcome integration between faith and actual life in secular society. Latin American liberation theology has been strongly influenced by Marxist social analysis. In seeking to make faith relevant to the building of a just society, these authors are in danger of indulging in strained interpretations of Scripture and tradition, or of falling into a historical relativism that leaves the past behind. Gutiérrez seems to be more successful than other liberation theologians in maintaining contact with the biblical and traditional understandings of faith.

Protestant theology, like its Catholic counterpart, has indulged in new experiments. The influence of Hegel is notable in Moltmann's theology of hope and in Pannenberg's consistent eschatology. Although they differ from each other in their assessment of the word of God and of historical knowledge, both these authors are heirs of the Reformation insofar as they look upon knowledge as a mere presupposition of faith. They come close to identifying faith with hope or trust. These future-oriented theologies (like that of Teilhard de Chardin) resonated well with the optimism of the 1960s, but they have fared less well in the last quarter of the century. Moltmann has turned his attention from the theology of faith to other themes. Pannenberg, who originally seemed to make past events matters of knowledge rather than faith, seems more inclined in his recent work to admit the importance of personal interpretation to clarify the signs given in history. But in his devotion to rationality and freedom, Pannenberg still leaves relatively little place for authority and obedience in his theology of faith.

Conservative evangelicalism, represented by Carl Henry and Gordon Clark, is partly a reaction against modern trends such as Bultmann's existential hermeneutic and Moltmann's theology of hope. The evangelicals, with their reverence for the Bible as the written word of God, show the continued vitality of the Reformed tradition, especially as represented by the Princeton theology of the nineteenth century. But it is questionable whether this theology, with its commitment to early Protestant views of biblical inerrancy, can maintain itself against modern critical thinking. Another weakness is its tendency to reduce all knowledge to the conceptual and the propositional. Making little room for the preconceptual and existential factors in religious knowledge, these authors speak of faith as though faith in its cognitive aspect were simply an assent to verbally formulated propositions.

The theologians described in this chapter do not represent the full spectrum of positions defended in the past thirty years. They are a mere sampling from a field that is almost infinitely vast. Other theological currents remain lively. For example, many Protestants continue to move along the lines traced by Barth, Bultmann, and Tillich. Many Catholics still practice the kind of neo-Thomism popularized by Josef Pieper. Neo-scholasticism still has its advocates. Some Americans have been applying to the theology of faith ideas derived from the epistemologies of Peirce and Royce, James and Dewey, Whitehead and Polanyi, Wittgenstein, Jaspers, and Voegelin. Some of these efforts will no doubt find a place in the history of twentieth-century theology, when it comes to be written in future generations.

## Notes

1. Hans Urs von Balthasar, *The Glory of the Lord: A Theological Aesthetics,* vol. 1, *Seeing the Form* (San Francisco: Ignatius, 1982). Numbers in parentheses in the present section of the text refer to this work.

2. In his Preface to *Love Alone* (New York: Herder and Herder, 1969) von Balthasar notes the parallelism of his method with Scheler's, but he adds that Scheler's bracketing of the question of real existence is inadmissible in theology (p. 9).

3. Ibid., 39.

4. On this subject see the chapter *"Fides Christi:* An Essay on the Consciousness of Christ" in Hans Urs von Balthasar, *Explorations in Theology,* vol. 2, *Spouse of the Word* (San Francisco: Ignatius, 1991), 43–79, especially 52–64.

5. Hans Urs von Balthasar, *The Moment of Christian Witness* (Glen Rock, N.J.: Newman, 1969), 60–78.

6. The present synthesis will be constructed out of elements in many essays, notably "The Faith of the Christian and the Doctrine of the Church," *Theological Investigations,* vol. 14 (New York: Seabury/Crossroad, 1976), 24–46; "Anonymous and Explicit Faith," *Theological Investigations,* vol. 16 (New York: Seabury/Crossroad, 1979), 52–59; "Faith between Rationality and Emotion," *Theological Investigations* 16:60–78; "On the Situation of Faith," *Theological Investigations,* vol. 20 (New York: Crossroad, 1981), 13–32; and "The Act of Faith and the Content of Faith," *Theological Investigations,* vol. 21 (New York: Crossroad, 1988), 151–61.

7. See for example Paul Knitter, *No Other Name? A Critical Survey of Christian Attitudes Toward the World Religions* (Maryknoll, N.Y.: Orbis, 1985), 191–92. Earlier in the book Knitter pays tribute to Rahner as the "chief engineer" of the watershed change expressed by Vatican II (125–30).

8. Bernard Lonergan, *Insight: A Study of Human Understanding* (New York: Philosophical Library, 1957), chap. 20, "Special Transcendent Knowledge," 687–730.

9. Idem, *Method in Theology* (New York: Herder and Herder, 1972).

10. Elsewhere Lonergan writes that "in accepting the truths of faith we are believing not just man but ultimately God," because the tradition of the Church hands down the word first spoken in Palestine. See his "Belief: Today's Issue," in *A Second Collection,* ed. William F. J. Ryan and Bernard J. Tyrrell (Philadelphia: Westminster, 1974), 87–99, at 97.

11. Charles Davis, "Lonergan and the Teaching Church," in *Foundations of Theology: Papers from the International Lonergan Congress 1970,* ed. Philip McShane (Dublin: Gill Macmillan, 1971), 60–75; quotation from 62.

12. Gustavo Gutiérrez, *A Theology of Liberation* (1971; ET, Maryknoll, N.Y.: Orbis, 1973; revised ed., 1988). References will be to the pagination in the revised edition.

13. Idem, *The Power of the Poor in History* (1979; ET, Maryknoll, N.Y.: Orbis, 1983).

14. More recently, in the Introduction to the revised edition of his *A Theology of Liberation* (1988), Gutiérrez adds this caution: "The ultimate norms of judgment come from the revealed truth that we accept by faith and not from praxis itself. But the 'deposit of faith' is

not a set of indifferent, catalogued truths; on the contrary, it lives in the church, where it rouses Christians to commitments in accordance with God's will and also provides criteria for judging them in the light of God's word" (xxxiv).

15. The idea of faith as "liberating praxis" shows up in a number of Gutiérrez's articles, e.g., "Liberation, Theology, and Proclamation," in *The Mystical and Political Dimension of the Christian Faith,* ed. Claude Geffré and Gustavo Gutiérrez. Concilium 96 (New York: Herder and Herder, 1974), 57–77, at 70; "Faith as Freedom: Solidarity with the Alienated and Confidence in the Future," in *Living with Change, Experience, Faith,* ed. Francis A. Eigo (Villanova, Penn.: Villanova University Press, 1976), 15–54, at 40–41.

16. Gustavo Gutiérrez, *We Drink from Our Own Wells* (Maryknoll, N.Y.: Orbis, 1984).

17. "Instruction on Certain Aspects of the 'Theology of Liberation,'" *Origins* 14 (September 13, 1984): 193, 195–204.

18. Arthur F. McGovern, *Liberation Theology and Its Critics* (Maryknoll, N.Y.: Orbis, 1989), especially 47–61.

19. Gustavo Gutiérrez, *The Truth Shall Make You Free* (Maryknoll, N.Y.: Orbis, 1990), 1–52.

20. *Gaudium et spes,* 43.

21. The criticisms made at the end of my article, "The Meaning of Faith Considered in Relationship to Justice," in *The Faith That Does Justice,* ed. John C. Haughey (New York: Paulist, 1977), 10–46, would have to be adjusted to take account of the turn away from Marxism and toward spirituality in the more recent work of Gutiérrez.

22. Juan Luis Segundo, *The Liberation of Theology* (Maryknoll, N.Y.: Orbis, 1976).

23. Idem, *Jesus of Nazareth Yesterday and Today,* vol. 1, *Faith and Ideologies* (Maryknoll, N.Y.: Orbis, 1984).

24. Idem, *The Liberation of Dogma* (Maryknoll, N.Y.: Orbis, 1992), especially chap. 12, pp. 234–63; quotation from 243.

25. Idem, *The Community Called Church* (Maryknoll, N.Y.: Orbis, 1973), ix.

26. Jürgen Moltmann, *Theologie der Hoffnung,* 5th ed. (1965; ET, *Theology of Hope,* London: SCM, 1967).

27. John Calvin, *Institutes of the Christian Religion,* Bk. III, chap. 2, no. 42 (Library of Christian Classics ed., 20:590).

28. Jürgen Moltmann, "God and Resurrection," chap. 2 of his *Hope and Planning* (New York: Harper Row, 1971), 31–55; quotation from 44.

29. "A Conversation with Jürgen Moltmann" in *Conversations with Contemporary Theologians,* ed. Teofile Cabestrero (Maryknoll, N.Y.: Orbis, 1980), 121–38, quotation from 130.

30. Carl F. H. Henry, *God, Revelation and Authority: God Who Speaks and Shows,* 4 vols. (Waco, Tex.: Word Books, 1976–79), 3:292.

31. Gerald O'Collins, *Theology and Revelation* (Notre Dame, Ind.: Fides, 1968), 84.

32. Wolfhart Pannenberg, "Wahrheit, Gewissheit, und Glaube," *Grundfragen systematischer Theologie,* vol. 2 (Göttingen: Vandenhoeck & Ruprecht, 1980), 226–64, at 241 and 243; idem, "Faith and Reason," *Basic Questions in Theology,* vol. 2 (Philadelphia: Fortress, 1971), 48; idem, *Systematische Theologie,* vol. 3 (Göttingen: Vandenhoeck & Ruprecht, 1993), 165–67.

33. Idem, "Focal Essay: the Revelation of God in Jesus of Nazareth," in *Theology as History,* ed. James M. Robinson and John B. Cobb, Jr. (New York: Harper & Row, 1967), 101–33, at 229–30; "Response to the Discussion," ibid., 221–76, at 269–70.

34. Idem, *Revelation as History* (New York: Macmillan, 1968), 137.

35. Idem, "Faith and Reason," 53; "Wahrheit," *Grundfragen* 2:244–48.

36. Idem, "Response," *Theology as History,* 271.

37. Idem, *Revelation as History,* 138.

38. Idem, *Grundfragen,* 2:234.

39. Idem, *Revelation as History,* 138; cf. *Systematische Theologie,* 3:158–59.

40. Idem, *Faith and Reality* (Philadelphia: Westminster, 1977), 65.

41. Idem, *Revelation as History,* 136.

42. Idem, "Wahrheit," *Grundfragen* 2:263.

43. Idem, "Response to My American Friends," in *The Theology of Wolfhart Pannenberg,* ed. Carl E. Braaten and Philip Clayton (Minneapolis: Augsburg, 1988), 319. Pannenberg is here responding to my article in the same book, "Pannenberg on Revelation and Faith," 169–87.

44. In volume 3 of his *Systematische Theologie* Pannenberg strongly asserts the "ecstatic structure" of faith, thanks to the love of God poured forth into the hearts of believers (pp. 24, 226). But Pannenberg does not explore the influence of the Holy Spirit on the process of an individual's coming to faith.

45. Henry, *God, Revelation, and Authority,* vols. 1–4, esp. vol. 3, *God Who Speaks and Shows: Fifteen Theses, Part Two* (1979).

46. Gordon H. Clark, *Faith and Saving Faith* (Jefferson, Md.: Trinity Foundation, 1983), 118.

# 8

# Models and Issues

In our systematic reflection, which begins at this point, we shall be concerned with deciding what faith really is, how faith is grounded, whether it is free, certain, and supernatural, whether it is clear or obscure, how it is born, grows, declines, and dies, whether it is necessary for salvation, sufficient for salvation, and so forth. As previous chapters have shown, theologians disagree about all these questions. In some cases they operate on the basis of fundamentally different concepts of faith.

At this point a word of caution is in order. There is no one thing "out there" that demands to be called "faith." The word "faith" is a conventional sign that has been used to designate certain aspects of the religious life, especially in the biblical religions. Christians use it predominantly to designate a basic saving relationship with God into which people enter by responding to God as he reveals. Beyond this, there is little agreement. The biblical usage of terms such as the Hebrew *'emunah,* the Greek *pistis,* and their cognates (usually translated in the Vulgate by *fides* and its cognates) is sufficiently flexible to allow theologians to move in different directions.

From the preceding historical survey it becomes apparent that Christian theologians writing about faith tend to cluster into a relatively small number of identifiable groups. A schematic description of these typical positions can help to clarify the options and issues. In the following summary of approaches or types, the intention is not to confine any theologian to a given "model," but rather to illustrate that the types are not empty, abstract possibilities. Although few theologians can be neatly pigeon-holed within a single model, certain statements of certain theologians can serve to give actuality and concreteness to the types.

## Propositional Model

A large number of theologians look on faith as an assent to revealed truths on the authority of God the revealer. Since theologians of this school tend to understand the revealed truths as propositions, the theory is often called "propositionalist."

The theory does not necessarily look on revelation as coming in the form of verbal statements, but it insists that the truths, once known, can be formulated in declarative sentences, for example, "The Word was made flesh," "The Lord is risen." The propositions are not the spoken or written sentences but rather the meanings or truth-claims of such sentences.

The propositional model has a biblical foundation, especially in the Catholic and Pastoral Letters. The concept of faith is represented as a treasure handed "once and for all to the saints" (Jude 3). The bishops and official teachers are the custodians of the "deposit of faith" (1 Tim 6:20 and 2 Tim 1:14). They are to pass it on to others as they have received it, following "the pattern of sound words" that they have heard (1 Tim 1:13). This concern for full and accurate transmission is evident likewise in the work of the early fathers, such as Irenaeus and Tertullian, who, in opposition to the Gnostics, insisted on adherence to the apostolic "rule of faith." In the Middle Ages many Scholastic theologians, especially the Scotists and Nominalists, treated faith as an assent to divinely attested propositions.

The same tendency persisted in baroque Scholasticism, both Protestant and Catholic. It was also characteristic of Enlightenment rationalism. John Locke, reflecting the prevailing mentality of his age, defines faith as "the assent to any proposition not thus made out by the deductions of reason, but upon credit of the proposer, as coming from God, in some extraordinary way of communication," i.e., by revelation.[1]

The propositionalist theory of faith still survives in conservative evangelicalism and in Catholic neo-scholasticism, with the difference that the evangelicals look simply to the Bible, whereas the neo-scholastics look rather to the Church as the primary teacher. For many evangelicals, faith consists essentially in the acceptance of biblical statements, though it is not denied that "saving faith" involves more than intellectual assent. Gordon H. Clark, for instance, writes: "Faith, by definition, is assent to understood propositions."[2] Clark's colleague Carl Henry, as we have seen, maintains: "Faith divorced from assent to propositions may for a time be exuberantly championed as Christian faith, but sooner or later it must become apparent that such mystical exercises are neither identifiably Christian nor akin to authentic belief."[3]

The idea of faith as an assent to what God teaches through the Church is conveyed by many documents of the Catholic magisterium. Vatican Council I held that by "divine and Catholic faith" we are to believe "all those things which are contained in the word of God, written or handed down, and which the Church, either by solemn judgment or by its ordinary and universal magisterium, proposes for belief as having been divinely revealed" (DS 3011). In the Oath against Modernism faith is described as "a genuinely intellectual assent to truth received from outside by hearing, whereby we accept as true, on the authority of God who is supremely truthful, that which has been said, attested, and revealed by the personal God, our Creator and Lord" (DS 2145). In the papal bulls of definition the dogmas of the Immaculate Conception and the Assumption were described as divinely revealed truths.

In continuity with the neo-scholastics a number of contemporary Catholics hold likewise that assent to propositions is an essential ingredient of faith. They differ from the evangelicals, however, because they are thinking not only of biblical statements but also, and even especially, of statements of the ecclesiastical magisterium. The moral theologian Germain Grisez, asserts, in opposition to Karl Rahner, Gerald O'Collins, Richard P. McBrien, Gabriel Moran, and Edward Schillebeeckx, that faith cannot exist without assent to certain determinate truths. He objects to the view that revelation is ineffable and that no human expression can be adequate. Far from being a quasi-mystical intuition, faith is an acceptance of God's intelligible communication of himself, given in conceptual language. While faith undoubtedly includes a warm welcoming of God's deeds in salvation history, the deeds are made known through words. Faith therefore involves assent to "a definite body of truths articulated in human language and proposed by the Church."[4]

Another American Catholic, William Marshner, maintains that according to the classical definition, dogmas, in the sense of propositions obligatory for belief, are the objects of divine and Catholic faith. He then asserts: "To complete the classical definition it must be added that the propositions are immutable and that they bespeak mysteries." More specifically, "What is revealed and believed (a dogma) must be a sentence."[5]

For all theologians of this propositional school, faith consists essentially in the acceptance of revealed truths, which are identified as doctrines. Such assent is held to be necessary for salvation, at least in the sense that one who refused to accept truths that had been sufficiently attested to him as revealed, could not be saved. But these theologians generally add that faith in this sense is not sufficient for salvation. In order to be saved one must have, in addition to propositional faith, certain other gifts or virtues such as hope, charity, and obedience. One must not only believe in God's word; one must also trust in him, love him, and keep his commandments.

The propositional view of faith has many assets. It gives clear authority to Scripture and firm identity to the Church as a community of faith. It also allows faith to appear as a response to persistent and troubling questions. But propositionalists tend to forget that even when we assert propositions our assent goes out not to the propositions in themselves but to the reality attained by means of them. Thinkers of this school, moreover, neglect the latent and mystical dimensions of human knowledge. As the adage has it, "we know more than we can say." By means of symbols and metaphors the mind often attains to truth that eludes direct declarative statement. A true affirmation, consequently, may be made without clear concepts or propositions. Great thinkers such as Thomas Aquinas and John Henry Newman, while holding to the realism of faith-judgments, overcame the limits of propositionalism.

## Transcendental Model

According to theologians of a second tendency, faith is not, or not primarily, an acceptance of particular revealed truths. More importantly, it is a new cognitive horizon, a divinely given perspective, that enables one to see and assent to truths that would otherwise not be accepted. To some extent this view is rooted in the old Scholastic idea that the act of faith could not be performed except by someone who had faith as a virtue or stable disposition *(habitus fidei)*. Theologians in the Scholastic tradition distinguished between the faith whereby we believe *(fides qua creditur)* and the faith which is believed *(fides quae creditur)*. In this second type of theology, primacy is accorded to the former.

Early in the twentieth century Pierre Rousselot and his followers resurrected the almost forgotten concept of the "light of faith" *(lumen fidei)*, which was central to the teaching of Thomas Aquinas. While looking on faith as an assent to the Church's teaching, they held that whether we believe or not depends on whether we have the divinely infused light that enables us to see the credibility of revealed truths. That light attunes us to the content of faith; it imparts an existential affinity, which St. Thomas called "connaturality."

The role of subjectivity in faith is even more strongly emphasized by transcendental theologians, who seek to retrieve what was valid in the epistemology of Immanuel Kant and the idealists. For Karl Rahner and Bernard Lonergan, as we have seen in Chapter 7, faith is constituted not so much by an acceptance of specific revealed truths as by a grace-given, and freely accepted, dynamism of the human spirit toward God as the only adequate object of its desire and love. God's grace, according to these theologians, is operative even among persons who have never encountered the biblical message and have perhaps never heard the name of Jesus Christ. Such persons may have faith in the transcendental sense without any specifically Christian beliefs and even, it would seem without any knowledge derived from special (or "categorial") revelation. The transcendental component of faith casts a new light on everything and consequently leads to judgments and opinions not attainable without it. It will incline one to accept the outer word of revelation, and the gospel as the culmination of "categorial" revelation, when such revelation is credibly proclaimed.

Operating in this framework, Rahner can say that faith is an acceptance of the nearness of God as absolute mystery.[6] While the encounter with mystery must be mediated by some experience of the world, the mediation need not be "religious." Faith in this sense is available to everyone. "It can be found in people who consciously believe they are and must be atheists, as long as they are completely obedient to the absolute demands of conscience, that is, to use our terminology, they accept themselves unconditionally, without self-rejection, fulfilling that primordial capacity of freedom which involves the subject as a whole."[7]

Lonergan, for his part, defines faith as "the knowledge born of religious love."[8] He makes a sharp distinction between faith, as "the eye of religious love," and beliefs, which faith discerns as "God's self-disclosures."[9] This distinction, he maintains, provides a secure basis for an ecumenical encounter among all religions with a basis in religious experience.

The strategy of defining faith as a spiritual attitude that does not depend on acceptance of the biblical message makes it relatively easy to deal with the problem of the salvation of the unevangelized, which poses severe difficulties for propositionalist theologies of faith. But the transcendental theory stands in tension with the biblical and traditional concept of faith as a response to proclamation *(fides ex auditu)*. It raises the question whether a true and sufficient act of faith can be made in the absence of any special or historical, revelation. Furthermore, it leaves some unclarity as to whether central Christian doctrines, such as the Trinity and the Incarnation, are matters of faith or simply "beliefs." If transcendental theology regards faith as independent of special, historical revelation, and treats the latter as a mere matter of "belief," theologians of other schools will strenuously object.

## Fiducial Model

A third school of thought, characteristically Protestant, moves away from the intellectualism of the first two positions and identifies faith more closely with trust. This position has a strong basis in the Old Testament (Genesis, Psalms, Isaiah), in the Synoptic Gospels, in the letters of Paul (Romans, Galatians), and in Hebrews. In the Bible, terms such as *pistis* are often more suitably rendered into English by "trust" than by "faith." In the patristic era, faith was generally taken to be a purely cognitive matter, although Origen, among others, was attentive to the element of trust. In medieval Scholasticism, a sharp distinction was made between faith, as an intellectual virtue, and hope, as a virtue rooted in the will.

The Protestant Reformation reacted against the Aristotelian faculty-psychology underlying the Scholastic theology of faith. Martin Luther distinguished between two kinds of faith, the first being acceptance of what God says as true; the second, trust or confidence in God as able and willing to deliver what he has promised.[10] When he spoke of faith alone as sufficing for salvation, Luther meant the latter type of faith. The Augsburg Confession, with a reference to Augustine, stated that we should understand the word "faith" in the Scriptures to mean "confidence in God, assurance that God is gracious to us, and not merely such a knowledge of historical events as the devil also possesses."[11] "Faith," according to Philipp Melanchthon, "is not merely knowledge but rather a desire to accept and grasp what is offered in the promise of Christ."[12] To the "quibble" that he was confusing faith and hope Melanchthon replied that Holy Scripture defined faith "as the substance of things hoped for" and that "feelings cannot be divided in fact the way they are in idle scholastic speculations."[13]

John Calvin tried to keep a balance between the intellectual and affective elements in faith, between the truth of God's word and the reliability of God's promises. He therefore spoke of faith as "a firm and certain knowledge of God's benevolence toward us, founded upon the truth of the freely given promise in Christ, both revealed to our minds and sealed upon our hearts through the Holy Spirit."[14]

The fiducial understanding of faith permeated much of the liberal theology of the nineteenth and early twentieth centuries. For Albrecht Ritschl, faith, considered as trust, was a practical judgment and a loving movement of the will toward God as the highest good.[15] Wilhelm Herrmann reserved the term faith for the "trustful surrender" that is awakened in us by the picture of Jesus in the Gospels, and for the new purpose and courage that are born of such trust.[16]

Although liberal theology lost much of its popularity by the mid-twentieth century, the fiducial concept of faith has survived in much Lutheran and Reformed theology. For Wolfhart Pannenberg, faith is grounded in a sure knowledge of God's action in history, but that knowledge is not yet faith. After I have satisfied myself by rational investigation of the evidence that God has revealed himself in Christ, I must take the further step of surrendering myself into the hands of the God who has thus revealed himself. "The certainty of faith consists in the completeness of trust, which in turn is grounded in the eschatological meaning of the history of Jesus."[17] Faith as a trusting surrender always has to do with the future.[18]

Jürgen Moltmann, though he differs from Pannenberg about the rational basis of faith, agrees that faith is ordered toward the future. "Faith," he writes, "is called to life by promise and is therefore essentially hope, confidence, trust in the God who will not lie but will remain faithful to his promise."[19]

Understood according to this third approach, faith is not a purely intellectual act or virtue. It arises from the heart and the will. Nor does it have truth, in the speculative sense, as its formal object. As an essentially fiducial act, faith goes out to God under the aspect of his saving power rather than primarily his veracity. It is a lively confidence in the God who has revealed himself by his great deeds in history as recounted in the Bible. As a profoundly existential matter, I (the believer) trust in this God to rescue me from the punishment my sins deserve, to cancel out my guilt, to give me perseverance in hope, and to bring me to eternal happiness.

On biblical and traditional grounds, this group of theologians seems to have a sufficient basis for including the element of trust or hope in the definition of faith. A more contestable feature of this position is its tendency to deny that a firm assent to revealed truth is an act of faith. In some cases these theologians speak of *fides historica,* but this kind of assent, they hold, can arise from merely historical study and hence falls short of saving faith. Their adversaries deny that the mysteries of faith can be affirmed by human reason without recourse to the word of God, accepted in faith. Thus the fiducial type of theology can run into conflict with the cognitive positions, as represented by our first and second types.

## Affective-Experiental Model

A good number of theologians, constituting a fourth category, emphasize the affective component in faith and the close connection between faith and experience. For some of them the believer encounters the living Christ in his word. Others, possibly relying on certain texts from Paul (Rom 8:16; Gal 4:6) and John (1 Jn 5:10), refer to the inner testimony of the Holy Spirit as something immediately perceived. In the patristic period Pseudo-Dionysius and Maximus the Confessor connected faith with a mystical union with God. In the Middle Ages some of the monastic theologians (and others belonging to the school of St. Victor and the Franciscan order) accorded primacy to the affective dimension of faith. Some Thomists of the baroque period, including Domingo Bañez and the Salamanca Carmelites, spoke as though the supernatural attractive power of the light of faith were somehow experienced. Blaise Pascal, the German Pietists, the Cambridge Platonists, and Jonathan Edwards made much of the "reasons of the heart" and of the religious affections as constituents of faith. For John Wesley the full assurance of faith required a perception of the inward witness of the Holy Spirit.

During the romantic revival Friedrich Schleiermacher characterized faith as a state of feeling or pious affections whereby we participate in the perfection and blessedness of Christ. Christian proclamation, he asserted, must be a testimony to one's own experience with a view to eliciting similar experience in others. Schleiermacher's experiential theology found echoes in liberal Protestants such as Adolf von Harnack and Auguste Sabatier.

The Catholic Modernist George Tyrrell looked upon faith as a faculty of religious perception that relates us to a higher world. By virtue of this faculty, he declared, the believer can intuitively re-experience the revelatory events attested in Scripture.

Among contemporary theologians Edward Schillebeeckx is notable for his insistence on the linkage between faith and experience. Believers, according to him, experience the world in a new and different way because they belong to a tradition of faith. "Christianity," he writes, "is not a message which has to be believed, but an experience of faith which becomes a message, and as an explicit message seeks to offer a new possibility of life-experience to others who hear it from within their own experience of life."[20] Schillebeeckx's paradoxical manner of describing faith-experience is suggested by the following sentence: "In our human experiences we can experience something that transcends our experience and proclaims itself in that experience as unexpected grace."[21] Christian faith, for Schillebeeckx, has a "theologal" or mystical dimension insofar as it involves a loving union with God, which is intensified in mysticism properly so called.[22]

These affective and experientialist positions, insofar as they do not involve a reduction of the divine to the level of everyday empirical reality, are compatible with what is asserted in certain cognitivist and fiducial positions. Conflict can arise, however, when the immediacy is understood as a substitute for the authoritative mediation of the content of faith through historical revelation, prophetic and apostolic testimony, Scripture, Tradition, and the living Church. Some experientialists fall into an individualistic empiricism that undermines the social and ecclesial character of faith. Occasionally they propose questionable theories of a "religious faculty" that would be capable of grasping the divine almost as though it were a particular object directly encountered in a rarefied mystical experience.

## Obediential Model

Another perspective on faith, our fifth, emphasizes obedience. In a sense this view may be called Pauline, since Paul several times mentions the "obedience of faith" (Rom 1:5; 16:26). In Catholic theology Matthias Joseph Scheeben exemplifies this tendency. In the Reformed tradition, God is commonly depicted under the aspect of his sovereignty, while creatures are viewed as totally subject to God's dominion. Karl Barth recognizes three dimensions of faith. Beginning with a certain kind of knowledge *(Erkennen),* faith defers to Christ as Lord *(Anerkennen),* and leads to confession *(Bekennen),* which is the third aspect of faith. The principal aspect, however, is seen as the second: the obedient act of acknowledgment and compliance.[23]

Rudolf Bultmann's dialectical theology bears a certain resemblance to that of Barth. For him faith is an abandonment of all attempts to save ourselves and a total surrender to God as our security. Faith's attitude, for Bultmann, is the radical opposite of "boasting" or self-assertion. It is "the radical renunciation of accomplishment, the obedient submission to the God-determined way of salvation."[24] Faith is a free decision but not, in Bultmann's pejorative sense of the word, a "work."

The equivalence between faith and obedience was strongly asserted by Dietrich Bonhoeffer. "The road of faith," he wrote, "passes through obedience to the call of Jesus. . . . *Only he who believes is obedient, and only he who is obedient believes.*"[25] In the same book Bonhoeffer protested that the formula "justification by faith alone" could easily be misused to make believers feel exempted from having to follow the difficult precepts of the Sermon on the Mount. Grace, he held, is costly, because it cannot be separated from the demands of discipleship. "The word of cheap grace," he declared, "has been the ruin of more Christians than any commandment of works."[26]

In his posthumously published *Letters and Papers from Prison* Bonhoeffer asserted that faith is a total act, involving the whole of a person's life. As a participation in the life of Jesus, the "man for others," faith orients us to live for others.[27]

The common thread uniting the representatives of this fifth category is their conviction that the Word of God comes with a sovereign claim over the whole life of the hearer. Most of them understand obedience not in the sense of carrying out specific commands but in the broad biblical sense *(hypakoe, oboedientia)* as a kind of reverent and submissive hearing. The human person, they would say, is receptive in the process of justification, which depends wholly upon the initiative of God.

Thus broadly understood, obedience need not be taken as excluding belief and trust, both of which are rather implied. The fifth theory, however, places the accent on the believer's total subordination to God's sovereign initiative. This may be accepted as consonant with common Christian doctrine, provided that God's sovereignty is not depicted as detracting from human freedom and initative. Many Christians, especially in the Catholic communion, understand the divine freedom as encompassing and enhancing human freedom and creativity.

## Praxis Model

Yet a sixth variety of the theology of faith is found in some European political theology and in contemporary liberation theology, notably in Latin America. In this type of theology the term "praxis" is taken from Karl Marx and twentieth-century neo-Marxists, for whom it has a technical meaning. It refers to human activities that are directed to overcoming the alienations in present-day society. Revolutionary activity, it is held, is necessary for anyone to avoid being mentally imprisoned in the present oppressive situation, and to discern correctly the path toward a just social order.

In his efforts to oppose the privatization of faith in "bourgeois" society, Johann Baptist Metz has proposed a political theology. His concept of faith is indicated in the following quotation:

The faith of Christians is a praxis in history and society that is to be understood as hope in solidarity in the God of Jesus as a God of the living and the dead who calls all men to be subjects in his presence. Christians justify themselves in this essentially apocalyptical praxis (of imitation) in their historical struggle for their fellow men. They stand up for all men in their attempt to become subjects in solidarity with each other.[28]

Later Metz speaks of Christian faith as a "subversive memory" that recalls the freedom of Jesus and emancipates believers from every kind of enslavement to earthly powers.[29]

Gustavo Gutiérrez, possibly the most prominent of the Latin American liberation theologians, holds, as do many of his colleagues, that the word of God does not come from Scripture or from Christian proclamation except in the context of a concrete situation, that of contemporary society. In Latin America, they maintain, the society is one in which a radical division exists between rich and poor. In this situation, they conclude, Christ is encountered in the voices and faces of the poor. Christ appears as the one in whom God has embraced poverty and in whom he undergoes suffering for the sake of justice. To have faith in Christ therefore implies solidarity with the poor and commitment to the cause of justice. Faith is an acceptance of revealed truth, but truth in the biblical sense is never something purely theoretical; it involves commitment and practice. The word of God, coming to persons in a dehumanizing and oppressive situation, demands a social response, and more specifically a commitment to liberation. Otherwise it could not be a commitment to Christ as the "way."

> To believe is to love God and to be in solidarity with the poor and exploited of this world in the midst of social confrontations and popular struggle for liberation. To believe is to proclaim the kingdom as Christ does—from the midst of the struggle for justice that led him to his death.[30]

Faith in contemporary liberation theology may be characterized, summarily, as "the historical praxis of liberation."[31] It is *historical* because it arises in a concrete social situation; it cannot be abstract, universal, or eternal. It is a *praxis* because it engages the believer in a struggle for social change—a struggle that transforms the believer's whole way of thinking and feeling. Finally, it is a praxis of *liberation* because it is directed to "the freedom with which Christ has set us free" (Gal 5:1). This includes, but is not restricted to, political and economic transformation. Since his earliest writings Gutiérrez has insisted that liberation cannot be complete except in the kingdom of God, which will be established by God himself at the end of history.

Although Gutiérrez's theology of faith is fairly representative of liberation theology, it is not the only view found within the movement. Juan Luis Segundo, as we have seen in Chapter 7, develops a theology of faith as a pure judgment of value without any factual content. He appears to accept something like the fact-value distinction in use among certain nineteenth-century Kantians such as Albrecht Ritschl. Segundo, however, combines this with the assertion that faith must be made historically concrete through the acceptance of a specific ideology, and his own ideology has a rather Marxian tenor. "Faith without ideologies," he asserts, "is dead."[32]

Faith in the liberationist framework is not a purely interior or individual matter. Faith, so conceived, is operative through love (cf. Gal 5:6). It is a participation in a social movement that aims to be "faithful" to God's purposes in history, and thus to eradicate injustice. It adheres to Christ, who, according to prophecy, "will not fail or be discouraged till he has established justice in the earth" (Is 42:4).

Few Christian theologians question the desirability of an active faith that displays itself in works on behalf of a better social order. But many would prefer to define faith more specifically as an interior adherence to the word of God. They would say that it is possible to be a sincere believer, a person of faith, without having any particular commitment to changing the social order. Further difficulties arise when social engagement is understood in terms of a Marxian social analysis. Christian believers can disagree among themselves about whether capitalism, as portrayed from a Latin American liberationist perspective, is the cause of poverty and misery. The concept of faith must be broad enough to include Christians who have different social philosophies.

## Personalist Model

A seventh and final group of theologians object that it is too restrictive to define faith in terms of powers, faculties, and specific modes of action. They prefer to define faith in terms of a new personal relationship conferring a mode of life and being. Maurice Blondel, for example, wrote:

> If faith increases our knowledge this is not first and foremost because it teaches us, through authoritative testimony, certain objective truths, but because it unites us to the life of a subject, because it introduces us, by loving thought, into another thought and another love. . . . That is why faith terminates in the most realistic of the forms of knowing."[33]

The Catholic personalist Jean Mouroux proposed a similar participatory theory. "Christian faith," he asserted, "is specified in its entirety by Christ; it is a participation in the life of a person, in the mystery of his death and resurrection; thanks to this mediation it is a trinitarian faith, and a sharing in the life of the Three Persons."[34]

Similar reflections may be found in the writings of Henri de Lubac. Faith, he holds, "is not only a mode of knowing. It is something completely different from a simple cognition. It is an essentially personal act which, if rightly understood, involves the depths of one's being. It gives a definite orientation to one's entire being. Hence it has been said that faith is a 'total synthesis.'"[35] As de Lubac goes on to say, we do not adhere to God's word as to the testimony of a purely external witness. God is intimately present within us, leading us to assent and to obey. Faith, as a total self-gift, "calls to mind the reciprocal gift of spouses."[36]

Something of the same personalism appears in the writings of Hans Urs von Balthasar, who describes faith as an encounter of the whole person with God who reveals,[37] so that the believer's very existence becomes centered in Christ.[38] "Faith is nothing but the believer's whole existence as buried and rising along with Christ, the Word made flesh."[39]

This participatory theory of faith has a Protestant analogue in the theology of Paul Tillich, who writes: "Faith is a total and centered act of the personal self, the act of unconditional, infinite and ultimate concern."[40] Faith, he says, has repercussions in the cognitive, volitional, and affective spheres, but it precedes the distinctions between these functions. We are driven toward faith by an awareness of the infinite, in which we participate, but which we do not own as a possession.[41] The infinite, present and active within us, gives us the inner restlessness that is the source of faith.

This vitalist or participatory understanding of faith has the advantage of overcoming the fragmentation that can arise from defining faith in terms of special faculties and functions, as the preceding models tend to do. Faith is, after all, a deeply personal relationship to a personal God, who wills to communicate himself in love. It is rooted in a grace that affects the way a person thinks, feels, and wills. But the question may still be asked whether the various aspects of this global relationship ought not to have different names. The Scholastics of old distinguished between the light of faith, the devout inclination to believe, the judgments of credibility and credentity, and, finally, the act of faith, which presupposed all the foregoing. They regarded love, hope, worship, obedience, and committed action as normal consequences, enrichments, or accompaniments of faith, but not as components or constitutive elements.

These Scholastic distinctions, subtle as they were, facilitated the handling of certain real questions that were bound to arise in reflection and analysis. Should we, for example, attribute faith to persons who believe but fail to act in accordance with their beliefs? What, moreover, should we say about persons who are well affected toward revelation but do not actually believe in any revealed truths because revelation has not been credibly proposed to them? It seems possible and necessary, in theology, to break down the global phenomenon of which Tillich and others are speaking into a variety of components, some of which may stand in the absence of others. The various "models" bring out different components.

## Models in Dialogue

The distinctiveness of the seven models may be clarified if we ask about God's part in the genesis of faith. In the propositional model God appears as teacher, whose statements are to be accepted on his authority. In the transcendental model he is an enlightener; he illumines the minds of those who are struggling in darkness. In the fiducial model God is a merciful benefactor, who can be trusted to keep his promises. In the affective, or experiential, model he is a lover who touches the hearts of those who seek him. In the obediential model God is a revered ruler, whose word is a command. In the praxis model, he is the great emancipator, who lends strength to those who struggle against injustice and oppression. In the personalist model, finally, God is the ever-blessed source of life, who draws others into his own glory by enabling them to participate in it.

The tensions between these different approaches make it inevitable to wonder whether theologians who write about faith are all talking about the same thing.

Could there not be several different things to which the name "faith" has been attached? To some degree this is no doubt the case. Those who understand faith as an assent to doctrine are not talking about exactly the same thing as those who understand it as a loving act of self-commitment or as an experience of the divine.

For systematic reasons it may be desirable for a given author to limit the term "faith" to one or another of these aspects. Such a limitation may be required in order to address a particular set of questions or to speak to a particular audience. The biblical authors, inspired as they were, used terms such as *'emunah, pistis*, and their cognates with different shades of meaning, as may be seen by comparing John with the Synoptic Gospels, or Paul with the Pastoral Letters or with Hebrews. Contemporary authors should be allowed a similar range of options, provided that they do not deny the right of other authors to use a similar freedom.

Yet it must be acknowledged that theologians discussing faith have been convinced that they were speaking about the same reality. There is a broad consensus to the effect that faith is the basic act or disposition by which human beings respond to revelation and enter into a saving relationship with God. On closer examination, it is evident that most theologians who stress one aspect or another also recognize, at least in "fine print," the aspects that are more explicit in positions other than their own. It seems safe to hold, therefore, that there is a single, complex reality having different aspects, and that this global phenomenon, as well as certain of its elements, may properly be called faith.

Ideally, faith should take root at the deepest level of the human personality. It should transform believers from within, orienting them in a new way toward God as their creator, savior, and last end. Faith should make a person doctrinally orthodox, trustful, obedient, and socially committed. It should go out to God as one who is to be believed, trusted, obeyed, and loved. I see no reason why faith, without loss of its identity, could not have all these dimensions. Where one or another of these characteristics is lacking, faith must be judged to be mutilated or imperfect.

If this thesis is correct, the different "models" of faith should be seen as complementary, not contradictory. None of them needs to be rejected, but all of them have to be expounded in such a way as to allow them to be supplemented by the others. A mutual critique, leading to adjustments, is appropriate.

## Issues

The divergences between the "models" should not be allowed to obscure the real and virtually unanimous consensus among Christian theologians about many fundamental points. It is quite generally agreed, for instance, that faith is a gift of God, that it rests on revelation, and that it is necessary for salvation. But we shall have to deal also with debated issues such as the following:

- Does faith require, or essentially consist in, an assent to doctrine, and more specifically to propositions that are accepted as divinely revealed? Or is doctrine a purely human effort to translate faith into concepts and speech that inevitably suffer from cultural and historical limitations?

- Does God speak an inner word of love and grace? Does that word come even to persons who receive no outer word of revelation? Is the acceptance of the inner word an act of faith? If so, does faith extend also to the acceptance of an outer word from God? Or is belief in the outer word an additional step, separable from faith itself?
- Can faith exist without a heartfelt trust in the God who reveals and acts? Or does faith consist in trust rather than in an intellectual assent to revelation?
- Does faith rest on an experience of the realities in which we believe? Or does one believe precisely what one does not experience? Does the experience of the divine precede faith, coincide with faith, or follow as a consequence of faith?
- Does faith involve knowledge of the realities in which one believes? Is it possible to believe something and at the same time to know that it is true? Or are faith and knowledge mutually exclusive states of mind?
- Must faith always issue in obedient action, so that the latter is included in the very concept of faith? Or can one believe and at the same time be conscious of failing to obey the God in whom one believes?
- Must the believer, under pain of ceasing to have faith, engage in action on behalf of a more just and loving society? Is liberative social action (orthopraxis) normative for faith, or is it subject to the norm of right thinking (orthodoxy)?
- Does faith involve personal union with God in the depths of the human spirit? Does it have a mystical component?

These and similar questions will have to be discussed as we seek to develop a systematic theory of faith.

## Prospectus

In the chapters that follow an effort will be made to gather up the principal elements of the central Christian tradition and to restate them from the point of view of contemporary Catholic theology. The material will be organized according to headings that have, over the centuries, become classical.

Chapter 9 will deal with the nature and object of faith. It will take up many of the issues raised in the present chapter, since the "models" involve different understandings about what faith really is. We shall have to discuss the motive of faith and the nature of faith's contents, including the relationship between faith and belief and the doctrinal or propositional character of faith. Attention will also be given to the role of the Church as mediator and guarantor of faith, and the corporate, or ecclesial, character of faith itself.

In Chapter 10 we shall take up the rational character of faith, its grounding in evidence and experience. We shall ask whether the revelation needs to be seen as credible, and if so, whether its credibility must be accessible to the eyes of unaided reason. How does religious experience contribute to faith and arise from it? Can one believe without the consoling experience of God's gracious presence?

Chapter 11 will be concerned with four properties that, in addition to reasonableness, are attributed to faith in the standard treatises: supernaturality, freedom, certainty, and obscurity. All five properties, we shall contend, mutually qualify one another, and therefore cannot be rightly understood except in their interrelationships. Taken in isolation, the properties might be seen as mutually antithetical.

Chapter 12 will have as its theme the birth, growth, decline, and possible extinction of faith in the life of the individual. In treating the connection between faith and baptism we shall discuss the appropriateness of baptizing infants, who are apparently incapable of personal acts of faith. We shall then turn to the growth of faith both from a theological point of view and in the light of contemporary psychological investigations. Finally we shall have to deal with the phenomenon of loss of faith and with the question whether such loss is always culpable.

As our last major topic we shall treat in Chapter 13 the salvific power of faith and the reasons for holding, as do Scripture and Christian tradition, that faith is absolutely necessary for eternal salvation. This discussion will lead to a consideration whether the virtue of faith can be possessed by persons who have never heard the Christian proclamation or by those to whom it has not been credibly proclaimed.

The concluding chapter will be a brief statement about the nature and attributes of faith summarizing the main results of the preceding chapters.

## Notes

1. John Locke, *Essay Concerning Human Understanding*, IV.18.2.

2. Gordon D. Clark, *Faith and Saving Faith* (Jefferson, Md.: Trinity Foundation, 1983), 118.

3. Carl F. H. Henry, *God, Revelation and Authority*, vol. 3, *The God Who Speaks and Shows, Fifteen Theses, Part Two* (Waco, Tex.: Word Books, 1979), 487.

4. Germain Grisez, *The Way of the Lord Jesus,* vol. 1, *Christian Moral Principles* (Chicago: Christian Herald, 1983), 477–505, quotation from 493–94.

5. William Marshner, *Reasons for Hope* (Fort Royal, Va.: Christendom College Press, 1982), quotations from 157 and 172.

6. Karl Rahner, "Thoughts on the Possibility of Belief Today," *Theological Investigations*, vol. 5 (Baltimore: Helicon, 1966), 7.

7. Idem, "Faith between Rationality and Emotion," *Theological Investigations*, vol. 16 (New York: Seabury/Crossroad, 1979), 67.

8. Bernard Lonergan, *Method in Theology* (New York: Herder and Herder, 1972), 115.

9. Ibid., 119.

10. Martin Luther, "A Brief Explanation of the Ten Commandments, the Creed, and the Lord's Prayer" (1520), WA 7:215; *Works of Martin Luther*, vol. 2 (Philadelphia: Muhlenberg, 1943), 368.

11. Augsburg Confession, art. 20, no. 26; in *The Book of Concord*, ed. and trans. Theodore G. Tappert (Philadelphia: Fortress, 1959), 45.

12. Philipp Melanchthon, *Apology for the Augsburg Confession*, art. 4, no. 227; *Book of Concord*, 138–39.

13. Ibid., no. 312; *Book of Concord*, 155.

14. John Calvin, *Institutes of the Christian Religion*, Book III, chap. 2, no. 7; ed. John T. McNeill, Library of Christian Classics 20 (Philadelphia: Westminster, 1960), 551.

15. Albrecht Ritschl, *Justification and Reconciliation* (Clifton, N.J.: Reference Book Publishers, 1966) 3:103.

16. Wilhelm Herrmann, *The Communion of the Christian with God* (Philadelphia: Fortress, 1971), 223, 241.

17. Wolfhart Pannenberg, "Response to the Discussion," in James M. Robinson and John B. Cobb, Jr., eds., *Theology as History* (New York: Harper Row, 1967), 273.

18. Idem, "Dogmatic Theses on the Doctrine of Revelation," Thesis 3; in W. Pannenberg and others, *Revelation as History* (New York: Macmillan, 1968), 138; cf. W. Pannenberg, *Faith and Reality* (Philadelphia: Westminster, 1977), 65.

19. Jürgen Moltmann, *Theology of Hope* (London: SCM, 1967), 44.

20. Edward Schillebeeckx, *Interim Report on the Books "Jesus" and "Christ"* (New York: Crossroad, 1981), 50.

21. Idem, *Christ: The Experience of Jesus as Lord* (New York: Seabury/Crossroad, 1980), 78.

22. Idem, *On Christian Faith: The Spiritual, Ethical, and Political Dimensions* (New York: Crossroad, 1987), 66–68.

23. Karl Barth, *Church Dogmatics*, IV/1 (Edinburgh: T. and T. Clark, 1953), 758.

24. Rudolf Bultmann, *Theology of the New Testament*, 2 vols. (New York: Scribner, 1961), 1:316.

25. Dietrich Bonhoeffer, *The Cost of Discipleship* (New York: Macmillan Paperbacks, 1963), 68–69.

26. Ibid., 59.

27. Idem, *Letters and Papers from Prison* (enlarged edition, New York: Macmillan, 1972), 381–82.

28. Johann Baptist Metz, *Faith in History and Society* (New York: Seabury/Crossroad, 1980), 73.

29. Ibid., 90–91.

30. Gustavo Gutiérrez, *The Power of the Poor in History* (Maryknoll, N.Y.: Orbis, 1983), 20.

31. See Avery Dulles, "The Meaning of Faith Considered in Relationship to Justice," in *The Faith That Does Justice*, ed. John C. Haughey (New York: Paulist, 1977), 10–46, esp. 33–37.

32. Juan Luis Segundo, *The Liberation of Theology* (Maryknoll, N.Y.: Orbis, 1976), 181; idem, *Jesus of Nazareth Yesterday and Today*, vol. 1, *Faith and Ideologies* (Maryknoll, N.Y.: Orbis, 1984), 126.

33. Maurice Blondel, art. "Foi," in *Vocabulaire technique et critique de la philosophie*, ed. A. Lalande, 10th ed. (Paris: Presses universitaires de France, 1968), 360.

34. Jean Mouroux, *I Believe* (New York: Sheed & Ward, 1959), 37.

35. Henri de Lubac, *The Christian Faith* (San Francisco: Ignatius, 1986), 145–46. The final phrase is quoted from Maurice Nédoncelle.

36. Ibid., 148.

37. Hans Urs von Balthasar, *The Glory of the Lord*, vol. 1, *Seeing the Form* (San Francisco: Ignatius, 1982), 219.

38. Ibid., 179.

39. Ibid., 197.

40. Paul Tillich, *Dynamics of Faith* (New York: Harper & Brothers, 1957), 8.

41. Ibid., 9.

# 9

# Nature and Object of Faith

## Nature of Faith

The term "faith" is frequently used in a generic sense without any religious or theological significance. Philosophers and others use it to mean the acceptance as true or real of anything that is not immediately evident or demonstrable. In this sense faith is an ingredient in virtually all human knowledge and activity. Whenever I read the newspapers, speak about history or science, and in fact whenever I get on a train, eat a meal, or perform many other ordinary actions, I am implicitly making acts of human or natural—that is to say, non-theological—faith. In so doing I may be following a spontaneous instinct, an acquired habit, or a free, voluntary decision. I may be said to be exercising faith in my senses, in my memory, in the reliability of a machine, or in the competence and integrity of other persons.

The term "faith" is especially appropriate in the case of firm beliefs involving implicit trust in another person or other persons. Faith in this case is closely connected with love and loyalty. The English word "believe" is etymologically connected with the word "love," just as the Latin *credere* implies a gift of the heart *(cordare)*.[1] Faith normally leads to faithful action, which is a matter of "keeping faith" with persons or living up to one's commitments.

When a person is said to have or profess *a* faith, the reference may be to a comprehensive vision that serves to give an interpretation of life as whole, including a scale of values. For convinced adherents, philosophical systems such as Platonism and ideologies such as Marxist Communism serve as faiths of a quasi-religious type.

Faith in the theological sense includes everything connected with the secular meaning of the term. But over and above this, it is a response to God as he acts and manifests himself in the world and in human consciousness. The nearest thing to a normative Catholic definition of the act of faith is provided by the following sentence from Vatican Council II: "The 'obedience of faith' (Rom 16:26; cf. 1:5; 2 Cor 10:5–6) must be given to God who reveals, an obedience by which one entrusts *(committit)* one's whole self freely to God, offering 'the full submission of intellect and will to God who reveals' [Vatican I, *Dei Filius,* chap. 3, DS 3008], and freely

assenting to the revelation given by him" (DV 5). This statement reflects an awareness of the different emphases in Protestant and Catholic theology and an intention
to include the sound elements of each. The dimensions of trust, obedience, and
intellectual assent are here harmoniously integrated into an expression of full personal adhesion. Faith is seen as a welcoming response to God's self-offer, trustful
reliance on his saving help, obedient submission to his sovereign lordship, and
assent to his revealing word.

Faith may be defined not only as an act but also as a stable disposition *(habitus)*. The disposition is a proximate capacity or readiness to perform acts of faith.
Vatican I gave a classic description of faith under this aspect. It is "the supernatural
virtue whereby, inspired and assisted by the grace of God, we believe that what God
has revealed is true, not because of the intrinsic truth of the contents as recognized
by the natural light of reason but because of the authority of God himself, the
revealer, who can neither be deceived nor deceive" *(Dei Filius,* chap. 3, DS 3008).

Vatican I, following Thomas Aquinas and the main scholastic tradition,
emphasized especially the cognitive dimension of faith. But this dimension by no
means excludes those of trust and affectivity. St. Thomas, following Augustine, recognized three dimensions in faith *(S. Th.,* 2-2.2.2). In the first place, he explains,
faith is a reverent submission to God as revealer, an acceptance of the authority of
God as "First Truth" *(credere Deo)*. In the second place, faith is assent to that which
God has revealed, and primarily to God himself as self-revealed *(credere Deum)*.
Third, to have faith is to tend toward God as the one who will bestow eternal blessedness *(credere in Deum)*. According to St. Thomas these three aspects are not distinct acts, but three ingredients in any act of faith. Faith as an assent has both a
formal object *(credere Deo)* and a material object *(credere Deum)*. Insofar as the
assent of the intellect is prompted by the will, which tends toward God as the
supreme good, faith is a dynamic movement *(credere in Deum)*. For St. Thomas,
the formal object of faith is God as supreme truth, for faith, in his view, is an essentially intellectual act.

A modern version of this Augustinian and Thomistic position, more closely
aligned with biblical usage and with the language of Vatican II, would give greater
emphasis to the elements of trust and commitment. It is appropriate to distinguish
three aspects of faith: assent, trust, and commitment (or obedience).[2] Insofar as it
is assent, faith means acceptance of a revealed message on the word of the divine
revealer. Insofar as it is trust, it involves self-surrender into the hands of God and
confidence in God as the savior who is utterly faithful to his promises. Insofar as it
is commitment, it involves an intention to conform one's conduct to the values and
norms established by revelation—to be a "doer" and not simply a "hearer" of the
word (cf. Jas 1:22).

St. Paul associates faith very closely with hope and love but does not totally
equate it with them (1 Cor 13:13). The medieval tradition, reading Paul in the light
of Aristotelian psychology, made sharp conceptual distinctions between the three
theological virtues—faith, hope, and charity *(caritas)*. But the linkage was maintained. Insofar as it proceeds from a will attracted toward God as the goal of life,
faith always contains at least the beginnings of hope and love. But hope and love,
which develop on the basis of faith, have different formal objects. The assent of faith

goes out to God as one whose word is accepted as true and reliable; hope goes out to God as the bestower of blessings that lie beyond human capacities; love goes out to God as supremely good and desirable.

Although the three "theological" virtues bring out different formalities, they overlap and interpenetrate. "Living faith" is always informed by love, and indeed by the highest degree of love, technically called "charity"; it always expresses itself in works of love. "Dead faith" is a deficient form of faith, and should not be the norm. As Juan Alfaro says, "If charity is lacking, faith itself is mortally wounded, and there is an inner tension in the believer that can be resolved only by reconciliation with God or radical separation from him through disbelief."[3]

Comprehensively, then, faith may be understood as an assent within a trusting commitment, or alternatively as a trustful submission involving assent to the God who reveals. Without a measure of trust and commitment, the assent could not arise. In principle, the commitment should be a loving self-surrender to God as preeminently good. A trustful, affectionate submission to God enables one to see reality in a new perspective, to discern God's word, and to accept beliefs that embody that word.

Faith in this sense unites one very closely with God, who becomes, so to speak, the center of the believer's own existence. To describe this ontic or entitative union, however, it seems preferable to speak of grace rather than faith. In the Scholastic tradition grace is well described as an "entitative habit," affecting one's mode of being. Faith, however, is an "operative habit." The virtue of faith and the acts that flow from it seal and intensify the personal union signified by grace.

Faith as a virtue or "habit" is interior to the believer, but tends to express itself in external as well as internal acts. Following St. Thomas (*S. Th.,* 2-2, qq. 2 and 3) some theologians make a helpful distinction between the inner and the outer acts of faith. For Thomas himself faith's inner act is to believe, but in accordance with the perspective of Vatican II one could also include acts of trust and homage, insofar as they are rooted in the stance of faith.

As the outward act of faith, St. Thomas speaks of confession (in the sense of a profession of faith). It would be possible and, I think, desirable, to speak also of obedience and faith-inspired practice as external acts of faith. The labor of an apostle, the death of a martyr, and the work of a Christian artist or social reformer may be seen as expressions of interior faith. Faith normally leads to committed action, by which, in turn, it is signified and reinforced. It is possible, however, to be a sincere believer and still not live up to one's faith. The failure to put one's faith into practice and to abide by its standards is regrettable and reprehensible, but does not necessarily signify that the virtue or "habit" of faith is absent.

## Formal Object

The intrinsic motive (or formal object) of faith is the supreme authority *(auctoritas)* or trustworthiness of God (Vatican I, *Dei Filius,* chap. 3, DS 3008; can. 2, DS 3032). Insofar as faith is assent, it relies on God's supreme knowledge and truthfulness *(veritas, veracitas).* As the Oath against Modernism has it, the believer accepts what God has said "on account of the authority of God, who is supremely truthful" (DS 3542). In other words, faith in its first aspect, as assent, depends on God as the witness who "can never be deceived or deceive" (*Dei Filius,* chap. 3, DS 3008). In its second aspect as trust, faith goes out to God as fully reliable and faithful to his promises. It has confidence in God as the all-powerful and merciful Savior. Finally, in its third aspect as commitment, faith submits to God as the sovereign Lord whose word is on all accounts to be obeyed. It inclines believers to act in conformity with their conviction.

Within the formal object some Scholastic theologians, seeking additional precision, distinguish the *objectum formale quod* (the formal object which is attained, and by reason of which the material object is attained) from the *objectum formale quo* (that by virtue of which the formal object is attained). They hold that the formal object "which" *(quod)* is attained in faith is God himself, the Creator and Lord, and that the formal object "by which" *(quo)* God's authority becomes accessible is God's action in revealing. Thus the formal object, completely stated, is the "authority of the revealing God."

St. Thomas and others who emphasize the intellectual aspect of faith frequently characterize the formal object as the First Truth *(prima veritas).* Thomists frequently express the formal object "by which" *(objectum formale quo)* as "the authority of the First Truth.in revealing" or "the truthfulness of God in speaking."[4]

This intellectualization of faith offers some systematic advantages insofar as it permits a sharper distinction between faith and the other theological virtues, but it also involves a risk of reducing faith to its cognitive dimension. Because in God truth is one with love and power, and because faith is a full personal response, the intellectual aspect (truth, truthfulness) should not be seen in isolation. Personal trust and commitment are intrinsic to faith itself. Thus there are advantages in speaking of the formal object of faith in a general way as the "authority of God revealing" (Vatican I) rather than specifically as First Truth or God's supreme truthfulness.

It is sometimes said that the motive of faith is the "word" of God, and this expression may be accepted if the intention is to designate the authority of God as he addresses his creatures and draws near in revelation. In adhering to God as revealer the believer accepts God as the one whose word is supremely deserving of assent, trust, and obedience. The authority of God who speaks is inseparable from the authority of God's word, but the word as a created reality cannot be the formal object, or motive, of faith.

The "word" of God may be taken in a broad sense to include all the means by which God manifests and communicates aspects of his knowledge, intentions, and will, in such a way that the content can be assented to on his authority. But the term "word" may also be taken in a narrower sense as signifying a conventional sign, oral or written, devised for the purpose of communication. Using "word" in this narrower sense, Vatican II states that revelation occurs through a combination of words and deeds, intrinsically connected with each other (DV 2).

According to the Catholic understanding, the word of God comes to Christians in two basic forms, Scripture and Tradition. Vatican I, for example, speaks of "the word of God written and handed down" (*verbum Dei scriptum et traditum,* DS

3011). Vatican II, clarifying the relations between Scripture and Tradition, taught that they coalesce so as to constitute "one single deposit of the word of God" (DV 10). Inasmuch as Scripture and Tradition embody God's testimony they pertain formally, though of course only instrumentally, to the motive of Christian faith. As authoritative loci, Scripture and Tradition together constitute a created norm whereby the Church discerns what God has revealed. In the final analysis, of course, God alone is the intrinsic motive or formal object of faith. Scripture and Tradition are the channel through which God's authority manifests itself.

We shall later discuss, in connection with the supernaturality of faith, the process by which the believer is enabled to grasp God's authority as the formal object of faith. Some theologians, as we shall see, hold that the formal object must itself be accepted by faith; others hold that it is known by some kind of natural or supernatural intuition that precedes faith.

## Material Object

The formal and material objects of faith are correlative and inseparable. The formal object, as we have said, is that whereby one sees what is to be believed; the material object is that which is believed by virtue of the formal object. It is, in other words, the content of faith.

The principal material object, according to St. Thomas and the Scholastic tradition that follows him on this point, is God himself (*S. Th.*, 2–2.1.1). God discloses himself not simply in his eternal and necessary being, as he is in himself, but especially as he freely chooses to be "for us and for our salvation"—to quote what the Nicene Creed says about the purpose of the Incarnation (DS 125; cf. 150). The truth of revelation therefore is what Trent called "salvific truth" (*veritas salutaris*, DS 1501). It is truth given "for the sake of our salvation," as Vatican II remarked with reference to the inerrant testimony of the inspired Scriptures (DV 11). The material object of faith includes not only what God discloses as factually true, but also what God promises and commands. Thus the material object of faith is closely intertwined with the material objects of hope and love.

God gives an initial revelation of himself in nature. According to Vatican II, "God, who creates and conserves all things through his Word (cf. Jn 1:3), gives a perennial witness to himself in created things (cf. Rom 1:19–20)" (DV 3). This "general revelation"—as it is often called—is given to all human beings and calls for a kind of "general faith," which corresponds to God's permanent self-manifestation through the order of creation. Christianity, however, is principally concerned with the supernatural revelation that God has given in history, and more specifically through the patriarchs, Moses, and the prophets, whereby he prepared the way for the gospel.

This historical revelation came to its unsurpassable climax in Jesus Christ, the incarnate Word, who is the "mediator and fullness of all revelation" (DV 2), and hence also the central content of faith. In his teaching, his behavior, and especially in his death and resurrection, Christ imparts the divine wisdom, manifests God's loving mercy, and gives concrete expression to the new commandment of love.

Christian faith is most fundamentally an acceptance of Christ as the great revelation of God. In relation to Jesus Christ, other "words" of God are preparatory or explanatory. Christ cannot be rightly understood except in the context of the whole history of revelation.

In the Pauline letters the central object of faith is frequently designated as the "mystery" *(mysterion)*, the plan of salvation whereby God unites and redeems all things through the saving work of the incarnate Son (Eph 1:9–10; 3:3, 9–12). Paul and other biblical authors interpret the history of Israel as authentic, abiding, but unfinished revelation. Those who, with the grace of faith, accepted the preparatory revelation were already believers, even though the full and definitive revelation had not come to them. Considered in relation to the fullness of revelation, their faith was deficient inasmuch as it failed to adhere explicitly to Jesus Christ. It reached forward in a vaguely implicit manner to the full revelation of God's plan of salvation in Christ (Rom 16:25–26; Col 1:26–28).

Vatican II recognized the importance of the "mystery of Christ" as a focus for the communication of doctrine. In its Decree on Priestly Formation it directed that seminary studies should be so ordered as to bring out the centrality of the "mystery of Christ," the "mystery of salvation" (OT 14). The Decree on Missionary Activity declared that the mystery of Christ must be proclaimed in such a way that the hearers may be "drawn away from sin and introduced into the mystery of the love of God, who invites them to enter into personal relationship with himself in Christ" (AG 13). This sentence has been understood as a concise modern summary of the central mystery of faith.[5]

The content of revelation became objectively complete with the Christ-event as interpreted by the apostolic Church. Vatican II, following previous Catholic teaching, clearly asserted this. Since the Christian dispensation is "the new and definitive covenant," it follows that "no new public revelation is to be expected before the glorious manifestation of our Lord Jesus Christ" (DV 4). The task of the Church since apostolic times is not to communicate new revelation, but to hand on the revelation already given, to guard it against dilution or distortion, to show its credibility, and to spell out its implications.

Vatican I speaks of "divine and Catholic faith" (*Dei Filius,* chap. 3, DS 3011). Faith may be called "divine" insofar as it assents to the word of God, "Christian" insofar as it takes Christ as "the mediator and fullness of all revelation" (DV 2), and "Catholic" insofar as it accepts what the Church accredits as having been revealed in Christ and transmitted in Scripture and Tradition.


## Faith and the Church

In the creed we profess our faith in the "holy Catholic Church." As one of the articles specified in the creed, the Church may be called a "material object" of faith: we believe that the Church exists as a divinely established community and as a God-given sign and instrument of salvation. This statement, however, does not exhaust the relationship between faith and the Church. The Church is a witness insofar as it credibly and reliably proposes the contents of revelation. Thus the Church pertains to faith not simply as one of many objects but as a principle or organ for discerning what is to be believed. The Church as a whole mediates God's revelation in Christ, and the ecclesiastical magisterium (the teaching office of the Church) has the special function of authenticating the contents of revelation and supervising the transmission of doctrine. Since it is the "pillar and bulwark of the truth" (1 Tim 3:15), enjoying the perpetual assistance of Christ (Mt 28:20) and the Holy Spirit (Jn 14:26), the Church pertains, in an instrumental way, to the formal object of faith. That is to say, it is a divinely appointed means whereby the authority of the revealing God manifests itself.

Besides being a material object of faith and a divinely commissioned witness, the Church is, thirdly, a believer. The revelation of God was delivered not to isolated individuals but to the believing community—initially, the people of Israel and subsequently, the Church as the New Israel. The apostles themselves came to believe within the community that Jesus gathered around himself. The Church is the believing community, and each individual believes only by participating, consciously or unconsciously, in the faith of the Church.

Because the Church is a community, it is made up of many groups and individuals, each having a distinct character and history. They assist one another to gain a complete and balanced appreciation of the full content of the revelation to which all of them adhere. In some sense we may say that the Church itself is the great believer. The believers are united in a single faith, which is that of the Church.

Henri de Lubac, in the course of a learned and inspiring discussion of the faith of the Church, points out that the ancient writers used the term "ecclesiastical faith" to designate the faith of the whole Church, in which individual believers share, each in his or her own measure and style.[6] This ancient usage, which should be gratefully recalled, should not be confused with the modern meaning of "ecclesiastical faith," which will be discussed below.

## Faith and Doctrine

Faith is not in the first instance doctrinal. Most Christians come to faith by hearing or reading the biblical story. Initially faith takes, for them, the form of an adherence to the community that tells the stories and a commitment to worship and behave in ways recommended by the stories. It is often argued that the stories are not intended to communicate speculative truth but only to evoke feelings, attitudes, and behavioral commitments. But even if this be the case, the emotional and attitudinal responses would not be acceptable unless reality were of such a character that such responses were justified. Thus religious faith must have at least an implicit cognitive content.[7]

Although stories, symbols, and behavioral precepts play an important role in Scripture, biblical faith has never been without doctrinal content. It has always included truth claims that could be explicitly stated and authoritatively taught. In ancient Israel the basic article of faith was that "the Lord our God is one Lord" (Dt 6:4). The great deeds of God on behalf of his people were remembered in faith and commemorated in confessional formulas such as those in Deuteronomy 6:21–25

and 26:5–10. In New Testament times the basic content of Christian faith was articulated in brief confessional formulas such as "Jesus is the Christ," "Jesus is Son of
God," and "Jesus is risen Lord." In the course of time the principal contents of faith
were summarized in creeds, and the creeds were further elaborated and explained
by dogmatic declarations to give additional clarity and prevent misinterpretations.
Particular articles of the creed and particular doctrines are not independent objects
of faith; they are to be believed as parts of an organic whole.

Not all church teaching is a matter of faith. Faith, in the theological sense of
the term, extends only to divine revelation. Catholic faith extends to all that the
Church, through its supreme magisterium (the college of bishops and the pope as
head of the college), requires all the faithful to believe as being contained in divine
revelation and authoritatively attested by Scripture and Tradition (DS 3011). Some
modern dogmas such as the Immaculate Conception and the Assumption, which
were not present in the original deposit in any obvious sense, are taught as having
been implicit in Christian revelation from apostolic times. To trace how they are
found in the Scripture and apostolic Tradition is the task of other disciplines, and
need not be attempted in a study of the theology of faith.[8]

Few if any believers explictly know everything that the Church, through its
magisterium, has taught and teaches as divinely revealed. For the ordinary believer,
who is not an expert on the history of doctrine, it suffices to adhere explicitly to the
central truths of Christianity. These are well known from familiar passages in Scripture, from Christian preaching and catechesis, from the creeds (which summarize
the central articles of faith), and from the liturgy (which celebrates the great mysteries of faith in the annual cycle of feasts and seasons). Much of the Church's dogmatic heritage is affirmed by "implicit faith." In saying "I believe what the Church
teaches" the Christian expresses a global assent that includes doctrines of which he
or she might as an individual might not be distinctly aware. Negatively, the Church
member is committed not to reject the definitive teaching of the Church on matters
of faith and morals.

## Propositional Faith?

At this point we may address a difficult question that has been raised in earlier sections: Is faith propositional? The debate has been somewhat confused, partly
because the term "proposition" has been used in different senses. For purposes of
the present discussion, a proposition (corresponding to the Latin term *enuntiabile*)
will be taken as meaning a definite intelligible content that can be expressed in a
declarative sentence. It is, so to speak, a mental utterance involving a specific truth
claim—an assertion that is determinately true or false. A single proposition may be
expressed in a variety of different linguistic formulations, but because human
thought cannot dispense with language, the discussion of propositions cannot be
neatly separated from the discussion of statements of faith.

To clear the ground it may be repeated that the primary language of religious
faith is not, or need not be, propositional. The original proclamation often conveys
the revealed message in figurative and symbolic language. Descriptions or stories

that are factually inaccurate may communicate truths of faith by their evocative power. Reflection is needed to elucidate the revealed meaning in symbolic actions, parables, myths, and legends, and to express this meaning in propositional statements. Even in the creeds the propositional element is only inchoative. It is difficult to specify the literal truth contained in the statements that the eternal Son is "light from light," that Jesus "descended into hell," and that he "is seated at the right hand of the Father." By contrast, modern dogmatic definitions, such as that of papal infallibility, usually employ precise, technical language.[9] The appropriate language of dogma and academic theology, as distinct from worship and proclamation, is propositional. But is it proper to speak of revelation or faith as propositional?

The answer of Thomas Aquinas to the question before us still seems to be acceptable. After explaining that faith is one and undivided in its content (since all truth is one in the divine mind), he points out that the human mind, unable to take in the entire content of faith in a single act, divides that content into articles. But the articles or propositions, he explains, are not, strictly speaking, the objects of faith "for the act of the believer does not terminate in the proposition *(enuntiabile)* but in the reality [signified by the proposition]; for we do not form propositions except to have knowledge of things by means of them, whether in science or in faith" (*S. Th.,* 2–2.1.2, ad 2).

Although propositions are not its true objects, faith may be called propositional inasmuch as its contents can, at least to a large extent, be expressed in propositions, such as articles of the creed and dogmatic definitions. To affirm the propositions is to affirm the faith, and acceptance of the faith, properly understood, prevents the believer from denying the propositions that express it.

In theology, as in other fields of knowledge, the more technical concepts may be unassimilable by some minds, and the formulations are capable of being misunderstood. Just as it is objectively true to say that water consists of hydrogen and oxygen, even though some people may not know the meaning of these terms from chemistry, so it is objectively true, in the judgment of Christians, to say that Jesus Christ is the incarnate Word of the Father, even though this statement may seem unintelligible or false to some hearers. The proposition correctly states the reality, if only from a certain limited perspective.

While respecting the value of propositions, we must not confuse the propositions set forth in creed and dogma with faith itself. The propositions, without being objects of faith, are useful and sometimes necessary instruments for bringing the mind into contact with the realities that are faith's object. In their formal structures they depend on human abstractive powers and conventions of thought and expression that may be tied in some measure to particular cultural and historical situations. The Congregation for the Doctrine of the Faith recognized this element of relativity in its Declaration *Mysterium Ecclesiae:* "Even though the truths which the Church intends to teach through her dogmatic formulas are distinct from the changeable conceptions of a given epoch and can be expressed without them, nevertheless it can sometimes happen that these truths may be set forth by the Sacred Magisterium in words that bear traces of such conceptions."[10]

For the sake of effective communication, the Church may at times have to change the conceptuality and language in which it has been heralding God's revelation. Even when the mental and linguistic formulations are clear and accurate, some members of the Church may have difficulty understanding what is meant. Those who reject the formulations cannot without further ado be judged to have lost the faith. It is possible that, while adhering in their hearts to the realities of faith, they are unable to recognize these realities in the official formulations. The conceptual categories and language may be opaque and confusing to their minds.

## Faith and Belief

In view of the nonidentity between the propositions of faith and the divine reality to which faith goes out, difficult questions arise concerning the relationship between particular beliefs and the encompassing mystery of faith. In earlier chapters we have seen how transcendental theologians such as Lonergan deal with this relationship. In recent English-speaking theology it has become common to distinguish sharply between faith and belief, to the disadvantage of the latter. Roger Haight, for example, maintains that "beliefs may be considered expressions of faith that are distinct from faith itself." He adds that "beliefs are distinct enough from faith that beliefs can be changed even while faith remains substantially the same."[11] Another modern author, Dermot Lane, reflecting a similar point of view, remarks:

> Faith needs beliefs, but is not identifiable with beliefs. Beliefs mediate faith, conceptualize faith and communicate faith. . . . Beliefs are the human expressions of our understanding of the mystery of God and are, to that extent, subjective—that is, they come from the side of man and are not given objectively from above. In contrast, faith can be said to be objective in the sense that it is directed to the transcendent reality of God. Beliefs are historical; they reflect the cultural circumstances of their original definition. As historical, beliefs are also plural and diverse, whereas faith, which perceives truth in the midst of plurality, is one and unifying.[12]

Lane in this passage depends heavily on Wilfred Cantwell Smith, a contemporary Protestant authority on comparative religion, who holds that adherents of different religions, while divergent in their beliefs, are nevertheless one in their faith. Smith seeks to interpret Thomas Aquinas as supporting his position. He paraphrases St. Thomas as holding in effect that the formulations of faith "are human and as it were accidental, historically conditioned, while faith itself, mediated by them, is divine."[13] He goes on to say that for St. Thomas

> Faith is man's relation to transcendent reality, and the mundane objects through which faith is expressed, whatever they be, including, he says, ritual and ceremony, the sacraments, scripture, but also explicitly including propositions, belief, and other intellectual constructs, have to do with faith insofar, and only insofar, as they serve as activating symbols or effective channels of that reality.[14]

If Smith's paraphrase were correct, St. Thomas would have held that beliefs cannot be matters of faith. But he taught, on the contrary, that Christians assent to the contents of the creed because they are revealed by God, the infallible witness; they constitute the material object of faith. The light of faith shines on that which is truly revealed, and on nothing else. The human mind, thanks to that light, apprehends and affirms the material object, and does so with an assent of faith. Although the revealed reality is utterly simple in the divine mind, the believer, having only a human intelligence, assents to that content in a composite manner, breaking it down into a multiplicity of "articles" or doctrines.[15]

What is at issue in this discussion, at least for Catholics, is not a mere matter of textual interpretation or theological opinion. For centuries the Catholic Church has taught that articles of the creed and dogmas of the Church are "revealed truths," and that their contents are to be accepted on the motive of divine and Catholic faith. Vatican I has been cited above to this effect (*Dei Filius,* chap. 3, DS 3011). In defining dogmas, popes and councils regularly assert that the truth in question is to be accepted in faith as a "divinely revealed dogma."[16] Vatican II taught that the dogmatic definitions of bishops in ecumenical councils are to be adhered to with the submission *(obsequium)* of faith (LG 25). When we assent to a dogma we are not merely accepting a human opinion that is subjective and hypothetical; we are submitting to a divinely revealed, objective, irreversible truth.

There is no need to deny the culturally and historically conditioned character of human affirmations, even those that rest on revelation. The dogmatic teachings of the Church, although their truth is divinely certified, are neither pure nuggets of divine truth nor merely human products. They are divinely revealed truths refracted through human minds. While they are true and irreversible in their substantive content, they may undergo reconceptualization and reformulation so as better to convey the revealed truth to new generations.

Many contemporary theologians are rightly concerned with safeguarding the personal and self-involving character of the assent of faith. Faith is a comprehensive term that designates a living adherence to what Newman would call the "idea" of Christianity,[17] and what Vatican II, following St. Paul, called the "mystery of salvation" (OT 4). But specific beliefs, secondary though they may be, are not expendable. Although faith cannot be reduced to an assent to formulated truths (particular "beliefs") it does involve an acceptance of such truths. Belief itself etymologically means more than intellectual assent. To "believe" in someone is to have a personal relation of trust, normally based on respect and affection, but that relation implies an acceptance of what the person avers. It would be a mistake, therefore, to try to separate faith from belief, as though faith were divine and belief purely human.

## Erroneous Faith?

In this connection it must be asked whether the assent of faith can extend to propositions that are not revealed, but are only thought to be such. This problem is especially acute where there is question of assent to error. In some of his early works, St. Thomas held that the virtue or *habitus* of faith, establishing a kind of personal affinity or "connaturality" between the believer and the realities of salvation, would prevent the believer from embracing anything false or opposed to revelation.[18] But in the *Summa theologiae,* which represents his mature thought on the matter, he holds that although the assent of faith extends to nothing false, an uninstructed or poorly instructed believer may assent inculpably, through simplicity of mind, to some error that is in fact opposed to faith (2-2.2.6, ad 2; cf. 1-2.19.5). In such cases, however, the *habitus* of faith, which inclines one to assent only to what is in accordance with right faith, cannot be the source of the false judgment (2–2.1.4, ad 3). The erroneous assent can only be a matter of human faith or conjecture.

The mature position of St. Thomas on this question seems to be both doctrinally sound and concordant with experience. Even Christians and Catholics may be confused about the real contents of the faith they profess. They often do not distinctly know which of their beliefs are matters of faith, for it is not evident from mere introspection whether a given assent is an act of divine faith or an act of human faith or conjecture. Thus one may in good conscience be convinced that something is a matter of divine faith although in fact it is neither revealed nor true. It does not follow, however, that beliefs are merely human constructions rather than matters of faith. As we have seen, revealed truths, when affirmed with the help of the grace of faith, are believed with the assent of divine faith.

Some modern Thomists have introduced further subtleties into the discussion. Relying, it would seem, on the epistemology of Pierre Rousselot and Joseph Maréchal, Jean Mouroux maintains that every judgment is a synthesis of representation and affirmation. In affirmations of faith, he says, the essential is the movement of the subject's whole being toward the reality of the divine, a movement that overflows the limitations of every concept or judgment. In comparison with the Absolute which is the object of the profound intention, the concepts and formulas can often be extraordinarily poor and inadequate. God looks at the heart, at the spiritual striving, which may be true in spite of conceptualizations that are inadequate or even false. This is true, Mouroux says,

> for three reasons, namely, because the essential of any judgment is not the representation but the meaning which one attaches to it; because the "supernatural" in a judgment of faith is not the representation but the meaning—the relation to the First Truth; and, finally, because the weakness of and obstacles to the representation are seldom in any way culpable in the unbeliever seeking the truth.[19]

He then concludes: "For all these reasons the saving movement of the soul, initiated by grace, can pass through formulas, themselves pitifully inadequate, or even glaringly false."[20] Thus an affirmation that contains a material falsehood in its conceptual or verbal formulation could be a true act of faith, and conversely, what appears to be a rejection of the faith could be, at a deeper level, a clumsy expression of faith.

These speculations of Mouroux, which could be matched from the work of a number of contemporary theologians, depend on a highly sophisticated epistemology that the critics do not always understand. According to Maréchal and his school, judgments about matters of spiritual and divine significance spring from a spontaneous movement of the human spirit, aided by grace, at a preconceptual level. Affirmations of faith therefore have a meaning that transcends the objective significance of the mental concepts and verbal formulations, which enter into the judgment as subordinate, material elements. The object of the judgment is vaguely but truly apprehended in the movement of the human mind toward it. In terms of this epistemology one may say not only that errors about the content of the faith may be inculpable and compatible with the virtue of faith—as St. Thomas himself acknowledged—but that the mind may affirm the true object of faith through conceptualizations that are deficient and even distorted.

Experience seems to bear out what these writers are saying. Often in daily life we intend to say something for which we cannot find adequate concepts and language. We express ourselves faultily; we know more than we clearly state, even to ourselves. This tension can arise also in the realm of faith. Dealing as it does with mystery, faith-language is particularly inadequate to its subject matter. Every act of faith has a divinely revealed material object, but that object is refracted in human conceptuality and language; in some cases it may be poorly or incorrectly articulated. Although assent to error cannot itself be an act of faith, faith in God the Revealer can sometimes be bound up with, and expressed through, inadequate or erroneous statements. The deficient formulations do not negate the movement of faith insofar as it is directed to God.

This concession should not lead to complacency regarding error. In principle, divine revelation is intended to give rise to correct doctrine, and it is the mission of theologians and of all concerned with religious education to strive to sift out errors in matters pertaining to faith. In the last analysis it is the task of the ecclesiastical magisterium, assisted as it is with the charism of infallibility, to expose and condemn harmful errors in matters of faith and morals. Divine revelation is intended to give authentic guidance; it tends by its very nature to liberate and redeem the life of the mind. The faithful, though they may fall into inculpable errors in expressing their faith, should instruct themselves and receive instruction according to their ability, making use of the means that God has provided.

## The Question of Ecclesiastical Faith

When popes or councils issue doctrinal definitions with an appeal to their charism to teach infallibly, they may be asserting or expounding the contents of the apostolic faith. In such cases their utterances, as said above, are to be accepted in faith *(fide divina)*. Very frequently, however, the magisterium, without any claim to be teaching a definitive doctrine, is seeking "to aid a better understanding of revelation and make explicit its contents, or to recall how some teaching is in conformity with the truths of faith or finally to guard against ideas that are incompatible with these truths."[21] In such cases the pronouncements, while authoritative, are not binding in the name of divine faith. They require a lesser degree of adherence technically called, in Latin, *religiosum voluntatis et intellectus obsequium* (religious submission of will and intellect). This *obsequium* normally takes the form of a firm, but not irrevocable, assent.[22]

According to the common teaching, there is yet a third type of response to the magisterium, intermediate between divine faith and religious submission. Infallibility extends not only to revealed truth (the primary object) but also to naturally known truths intimately connected with revelation (the secondary object). Certain nonrevealed truths are so closely connected with revelation that they must be accepted if the revealed truth is to be properly affirmed, explained, and defended. When, for example, the Church asserts that a particular pope or council is legitimate, the assertion is not itself a revealed truth, but (it is argued) if the Church could not definitively pronounce on these matters it could not effectively transmit and safeguard the apostolic deposit.[23]

Assuming that infallibility does extend to this secondary object, one must ask what name should be given to the response expected from the faithful. The teaching, not being a revealed truth, cannot be held on a motive of divine faith. For lack of a better term, some authors speak in this connection of a distinct species of faith, called "ecclesiastical faith." This usage of the term "ecclesiastical faith" is not the same as the patristic usage preferred, as we have seen, by de Lubac. It means the kind of assent that is due to the Church as an infallible teacher in matters closely connected with revelation.[24] For purposes of the present discussion this question of terminology is not crucial. Even if there were no such thing as "ecclesiastical faith" in this modern sense, it would not concern us, since our theme in this work is divine faith.[25]

## Faith in Private Revelation

Another question that has been much debated in modern theology is the proper response to private revelation.[26] Such revelation is called "private" to distinguish it from the "public" revelation contained in the Church's deposit of faith. The term "private" should not be understood as meaning that it concerns only the individual who receives it. A few such revelations, for example, the revelations of the Sacred Heart to St. Margaret Mary Alacoque in 1673–1675, have had considerable influence on the piety of the faithful, and even on the liturgy of the Church. Possibly terms such as "special revelation," used by the Council of Trent (DS 1540, 1566) and "particular revelation," used by some theologians in their presentations at Trent, might be more apt, but "private revelation" has wider currency.

Exceptional communications from on high are frequently mentioned in Holy Scripture. Paul in his letters speaks of visions and revelations given to himself (2 Cor 12:1–7), and the Book of Acts reports many such experiences. Prophetic revelations played a significant part in the life of the early Church, as is evident from the *Didache,* the *Shepherd* of Hermas, and the letters of Cyprian. Although somewhat discredited by the excesses of Montanism, revelations of this type continued in the Middle Ages, notably in the case of remarkable religious women such as Hildegard, Catherine of Siena, Catherine of Genoa, and Bridget of Sweden. In the nineteenth and twentieth centuries a number of Marian apparitions have occurred, accompanied by heavenly messages such as those given to Catherine Labouré, the children of La Salette, Bernadette Soubirous, and the children of Fátima.

Private revelations should be clearly distinguished from those that belong to the deposit of faith. They do not propose any new doctrine, though they may call attention to matters that are already part of the Church's doctrine and even perhaps prompt the Church to examine whether some doctrine is contained in revelation. Their import is primarily practical. As Thomas Aquinas observed, the different ages of the Church have never lacked individuals "having the spirit of prophecy, not indeed to produce new doctrines but for the direction of human acts" (*S. Th.,* 2–

2.174.6, ad 3). Pope John XXIII confirmed this position when he declared, on the occasion of the centenary of the apparitions at Lourdes, that the popes "have a duty to recommend to the attention of the faithful—when after mature examination they consider it opportune for the general good—the supernatural lights which it has pleased God to dispense freely to certain privileged souls, not to propose new doctrines but to guide our conduct."[27]

Theologians of the Thomistic tradition, such as Cajetan, Melchior Cano, and Domingo Bañez, have maintained that because these revelations are essentially practical in character, and do not disclose anything new about the mystery of God's intimate life, they are not capable of being accepted on a motive of divine faith. These authors generally hold that the proper response is human faith, which may amount to a moral certitude exceeding mere probability, according to the nature of the case.[28] Yet some Thomists, including Domingo de Soto and the Carmelites of Salamanca, speak in this connection of a kind of practical faith *(fides de agendis)*, differing from dogmatic faith.[29]

The Council of Trent somewhat changed the state of the question by its teaching that individuals may not claim absolute and infallible certitude that they have been justified or are among the elect, unless they have learned this through a special revelation (Session VI, chap. 12, DS 1540; canons 14–16, DS 1564–66). It seems to be here implied that if such a special revelation were given, one ought to believe its content as a matter of divine faith. Following the Council of Trent, theologians such as Andrea Vega, Francisco Suarez, and Juan de Lugo held that a special revelation, when sufficiently proposed, could constitute an object of divine faith for its recipient, and indeed for anyone to whom the fact of the revelation was sufficiently manifest. In the present century Jesuits such as Hermann Dieckmann and Michael Nicolau hold that the immediate recipient may be obliged to make an act of divine supernatural faith in the content of the revelation, but they deny that others who hear about the revelation are so obliged.[30] The divine faith here in question, however, must be distinguished from what Vatican I called "divine and Catholic faith," for the content is not part of the deposit of faith committed to the Church as part of its apostolic heritage.

Church authorities have a responsibility to investigate the authenticity of alleged apparitions, especially when they have pastoral consequences. Bishops and theologians make use of certain general criteria, such as conformity with Catholic doctrine, moral probity, conversion to a better life, and miracles, such as the healings reported at Lourdes. In some cases fraud or delusion can be confidently affirmed, but it is difficult to establish the supernatural origin of true revelations.

Where approval is given, it normally takes the negative form of a declaration that the message contains nothing opposed to Catholic faith and morals, and that therefore the faithful are free to believe it. For example, Pius X, in the encyclical *Pascendi* (1907), reaffirmed a decree of the Sacred Congregation of Rites (1877), which asserted with regard to apparitions such as those of Lourdes: "These apparitions and revelations have neither been approved nor condemned by the Holy See, which has simply allowed that they be believed on purely human faith, on the tradition which they relate, corroborated by testimonies and documents worthy of credence."[31] The type of assent to be given in such cases is well described by Prosper

Lambertini, in his classical treatise on canonizations and beatifications: "While the assent of Catholic faith must not and cannot be given, an assent of human faith may be due, following the rules of prudence, and according to which these revelations are probable and are piously to be believed."[32]

Contemporary theologians are conscious of the social and psychological mechanisms at work in visions and auditions.[33] Such phenomena normally occur in a context of faith and of struggle for the faith. The visionaries tend to be eidetically gifted and emotionally involved. The words and images are normally borrowed from the seers' own memory and past experience. Even an authentic divine revelation is filtered through a human consciousness that influences the choice of words and concepts. One must be cautious, therefore, in what one attributes to God the Revealer. Special caution is required in evaluating accounts given some time after the apparition, whether by the visionaries themselves or by others reporting what was allegedly said.

Lest people become overinvolved in the pursuit of private revelations, it would be well to keep in mind the cautions of St. John of the Cross and of other saints who have warned against the illusions that are likely in such matters.[34] Some recent theologians are likewise on guard against excessive avidity and gullibility. Karl Rahner, after conceding that under certain conditions the immediate recipient of a divine revelation might be permitted or even required to believe it by divine faith, adds:

> Without a miracle such a vision can lay no claim whatever to the assent of outsiders. To reject such a revelation (always conformably to our general human duty of caution, restraint, and reverence) in any case never implies resistance to divine grace, and may rather be part of man's duty to "believe not every spirit; but try the spirits if they be of God."[35]

Even if the Church gives its approval and encouragement, he asserts, a Catholic is not forbidden to have a personal opinion that the approbation was unwarranted.

## Conclusion

The findings of the present chapter may be summarized somewhat as follows. Faith in the theological sense of the term is to be given to God who reveals. Such faith has three main aspects: assent, trust, and obedience or commitment to action. Although an act of faith is not the same as an act of hope or love, some measure of hope and love are involved in every act of faith. Living faith is animated by charity, a love of God for God's own sake.

Faith normally overflows into external acts of confession and practical conduct, but it is possible for the virtue and inner act of faith to exist in the absence of these external manifestations.

The formal object of faith is the authority of God who reveals. Faith goes out to God as truthful, trustworthy, and deserving of obedience. The authority of God makes itself effectively present in God's word, especially as given in Scripture and Tradition.

The primary material object of faith is God himself, our Lord and Savior. But the material object includes all that God has said, especially what he discloses for our salvation through Jesus Christ. Faith is Christian insofar as it accepts Christ as "the mediator and fullness of all revelation."

The Church is one of the material objects of faith, but it is also a divinely commissioned witness and a corporate believer. Christian revelation is reliably transmitted in and through the Church. The individual believes within the community, participating in the faith of the Church.

Faith never exists without a content or material object. Beliefs, therefore, pertain to faith itself. Beliefs can to some extent be formulated in propositions. The assent of faith does not make propositions its object, but goes out to God by means of propositions. The formulations of faith are inevitably affected by cultural and historical conditioning, and must sometimes be changed in order to mediate revealed truth more credibly and effectively.

Faith as a virtue or as an act of the virtue always goes out to revealed truth, never to error. But genuine acts of faith can sometimes be interwoven with faulty human opinions and deficient conceptualizations. Mistaken or confused beliefs, therefore, can be existentially bound up with the acceptance of revelation in faith.

When the Church engages its supreme authority in proclaiming the word of God, its teaching is to be accepted by divine and Catholic faith. No other Church teaching, even though it be infallible, is accepted by divine faith. "Ecclesiastical faith," as the term is used by modern Scholastic authors, has to do with non-revealed doctrine. It is not faith in the full theological sense, and for this reason many authors prefer to avoid the term.

Private revelations, likewise, cannot be objects of Christian or Catholic faith. It is possible, however, that God may so manifest himself to the seer that the latter may be able and required to accept the message on a motive of divine faith. It is doubtful whether third parties can have more than a human prudential certitude regarding private revelations. The withholding of assent from reported revelations may be, and often is, prudent.

## Notes

1. For discussion of the etymologies in several languages see Louis Monden, *Faith: Can Man Still Believe?* (New York: Sheed & Ward, 1970), 16.

2. Avery Dulles, *The Survival of Dogma* (Garden City, N.Y.: Doubleday, 1971), 17–18.

3. Juan Alfaro, "The Dual Aspect of Faith: Entrusting Oneself to God and Acceptance of the Christian Message," in *Man and Man as Believer,* ed. Edward Schillebeeckx and Boniface Willems. Concilium 21 (New York: Paulist, 1967), 53–66, at 58. In Chapter 6, above, Hans Urs von Balthasar has been quoted to the same effect.

4. Réginald Garrigou-Lagrange, *The Theological Virtues,* vol. 1, *On Faith* (St. Louis: B. Herder, 1964), 51–84; idem, *De revelatione per ecclesiam catholicam proposita* (Rome: Ferrari, 1945), 1:410.

5. Karl Rahner, "In Search of a Short Formula of the Christian Faith," in *The Pastoral Approach to Atheism,* ed. K. Rahner. Concilium 23 (New York: Paulist, 1967), 70–82, at 74.

6. Henri de Lubac, *The Christian Faith* (San Francisco: Ignatius, 1986), 228–29.

7. For a noncognitivist view see Richard B. Braithwaite, *An Empiricist's View of the Nature of Religious Belief* (Cambridge, Eng.: Cambridge University Press, 1955). The problem of religious language and its cognitive character has been extensively debated in British

philosophical circles, and is the object of many specialized studies. For a treatment that harmonizes well with my own thinking, see Josef Meyer zu Schlochtern, *Glaube-Sprache-Erfahrung: Zur Begründungsfähigkeit der religiösen Überzeugung* (Frankfurt am Main: Peter Lang, 1978). Ian Barbour, *Myths, Models and Paradigms* (New York: Harper Row, 1974), is also valuable.

8. The fundamental treatise on the general subject of development of doctrine is still John Henry Newman, *An Essay on the Development of Christian Doctrine* (1845; Garden City, N.Y.: Doubleday Anchor, 1960). A modern Catholic work is Jan Hendrik Walgrave, *Unfolding Revelation: The Nature of Doctrinal Development* (Philadelphia: Westminster, 1972). The development of the more recent Marian dogmas is treated in Clément Dillenschneider, *Le sens de la foi et le progrès dogmatique du mystère mariale* (Rome: Academia Mariana Internationalis, 1954).

9. See Vatican I, *Pastor aeternus,* chap. 4 (DS 3074). For other examples see note 16 below.

10. Congregation for the Doctrine of the Faith, *Mysterium Ecclesiae,* AAS 65 (1973): 396–408; quotation from 403; ET, *Declaration in Defense of the Catholic Doctrine of the Church against Certain Errors of the Present Day* (Washington, D.C.: United States Catholic Conference, 1973), 8.

11. Roger Haight, *Dynamics of Theology* (New York: Paulist, 1990), 26–29, 42–44; quotations from 26 and 29.

12. Dermot A. Lane, *The Experience of God: An Invitation to Do Theology* (New York: Paulist, 1981), 59–60.

13. Wilfred Cantwell Smith, *Faith and Belief* (Princeton, N.J.: Princeton University Press, 1979), 89.

14. Ibid., 91.

15. For a critique of Smith see Frederick J. Crosson, "*Fides* and *Credere:* W. C. Smith on Aquinas," *Journal of Religion* 65 (1985): 399–412. Along the same lines, see the section "Faith and Propositions" in Brian Davies, *The Thought of Thomas Aquinas* (Oxford: Clarendon, 1992), 276–77.

16. For examples see Vatican I's definition of papal infallibility (*Pastor aeternus,* chap. 4, DS 3074) and Pius XII's definition of the Assumption of the Blessed Virgin (*Munificentissimus Deus,* DS 3903). Pius IX in defining the Immaculate Conception referred to it as a "divinely revealed doctrine" (*Ineffabilis Deus,* DS 2803).

17. Newman in his *Essay on Development,* chap. 2, sec. 1 (pp. 94–108), explains how the idea of Christianity in the course of time expands into multiple aspects of itself.

18. See Thomas Aquinas, *In 3 Sent.,* Dist. 23, q. 3, a. 3, qc. 2c and ad 2; Dist. 24, q. 1, a. 3, qc. 2, ad 3; Dist. 25, q. 2, a. l, qc. 2, ad 3; *De ver.,* q. 14, a. 10, ad 10.

19. Jean Mouroux, *I Believe* (New York: Sheed & Ward, 1959), 73.

20. Ibid., 73–74.

21. Congregation for the Doctrine of the Faith, "Instruction on the Ecclesial Vocation of the Theologian," no. 23; *Origins* 20 (July 5, 1990): 117–26, at 122.

22. Ibid.; see also LG 25. Theologians today are still discussing whether *obsequium religiosum* can exist when a person, even though unable to achieve intellectual assent, is reverently inclined to accept the teaching of the magisterium. For present purposes there is no need to take sides in this dispute. It suffices that *obsequium religiosum* be clearly differentiated from the *obsequium* of divine faith.

23. The Declaration *Mysterium Ecclesiae,* chap. 3, states: "According to Catholic doctrine, the infallibility of the Church's Magisterium extends not only to the deposit of faith but also to those matters without which that deposit cannot be rightly preserved and expounded" (ET, 5–6). The "Instruction on the Ecclesial Vocation of the Theologian" speaks in this con-

nection of "truths concerning faith and morals, which even if not divinely revealed are nevertheless strictly and intimately connected with revelation" (no. 23, p. 122). The whole question of the so-called secondary object of infallibility is too complex to be adequately treated here. The question is raised simply to make clear that some teachings of the Church, even though promulgated and accepted as definitively binding, are not usually regarded as matters of divine faith. For further details on the "secondary object" the reader may consult standard treatments such as Francis A. Sullivan, *Magisterium: Teaching Authority in the Catholic Church* (New York: Paulist, 1983), 131–38. See also Sullivan's article, "The 'Secondary Object' of Infallibility," *Theological Studies* 54 (September 1993):536–50.

24. The CDF in its "Instruction on the Ecclesial Vocation of the Theologian" (no. 23, p. 122), says that such teachings "must be firmly accepted and held." It does not use the term "faith" in this context.

25. For further discussion see Yves Congar, "Fait dogmatique et foi ecclésiastique," *Catholicisme hier, aujourd'hui, demain,* vol. 4 (Paris: Letouzey et Ané, 1956), cols. 1059–67. Following Garrigou-Lagrange and others, Congar takes the position that dogmatic facts are objects of divine faith—a position contrary to that taken in my text and in note 23.

26. On this question see Yves Congar, "La crédibilité des révélations privées," *Vie spirituelle* 53 (1937): Supplément, 29–43; Karl Rahner, "Visions and Prophecies," in his *Inquiries* (New York: Herder and Herder, 1964), 87–188; Laurent Volken, *Visions, Revelations and the Church* (New York: P. J. Kenedy, 1963); Pierre Adnès, "Révélations privées," *Dictionnaire de spiritualité* 13 (1988): 482–91; Jean Galot, "Le apparizioni private nella vita della Chiesa," *Civiltà cattolica* 136 (1985:II): 19–33; Benedict J. Groeschel, *A Still Small Voice: A Practical Guide on Reported Revelations* (San Francisco: Ignatius, 1993); Augustin Poulain, *The Graces of Interior Prayer* (London: Routledge and Kegan Paul, 1950), 299–399; Antoine Vergote, "Visions et apparitions: approche psychologique," *Revue théologique de Louvain* 22 (1991): 202–25.

27. Pope John XXIII, "Nuntius radiophonicus," February 18, 1959, AAS 51 (1959): 144–48, at 147.

28. See Adnès, "Révélations privées," 488.

29. See Volken, *Visions,* 205.

30. Hermann Dieckmann, *De Ecclesia* II (Freiburg, 1952), 150–51; Michael Nicolau, "De Revelatione christiana," in *Sacrae theologiae summa,* vol. 1, 2d ed. (Madrid, Biblioteca de autores cristianos, 1952), p. 56, no. 56. Rahner, "Visions and Prophecies," 105 and 164, holds that the same obligation would weigh on outsiders, provided that it was sufficiently demonstrated, e.g. by a miracle, that the message was from God.

31. Text in Claudia Carlen, ed., *The Papal Encyclicals* 3 (1903–1939) (Wilmington, N.C.: McGrath Publishing Company, 1981), 96.

32. Prosper Lambertini (later Pope Benedict XIV), *De servorum Dei beatificatione* (Rome, 1747), Bk. II, chap. 32, no. 11, p. 402.

33. Vergote, "Visions et apparitions," 213–16; cf. Rahner, "Visions and Prophecies," 115–57.

34. *Ascent of Mount Carmel,* II.22.5. See above, p. 54.

35. Rahner, "Visions and Prophecies," 88–188; quotation from 164–65. Earlier (note 11, p. 94) Rahner quotes Benedict XIV to the same effect.

# 10

# The Grounding of Faith

Once faith is understood as a firm assent and trustful commitment to God as he reveals himself, it must be asked how the believer is warranted in accepting a given content as the word of God. How is it ascertained that the authority of God lies behind the Christian message?

This question confronts us with the age-old problem of faith and reason. Many authors have held that the decision to believe is justified by prior rational inquiry. Before believing, one perceives evidence that serves as a basis for belief. On this view, faith is justified by reason. An alternative view is that faith is an act of loving trust that has no basis except in revelation. The first position tends toward rationalism, the second toward fideism. After surveying the different answers given to the problem of faith and reason we shall reflect on the different meanings attached to the terms "faith" and "reason" in different theological schools.

Without necessarily denying the role of reason, some authors find it more plausible to ground faith in some kind of exceptional experience of God or of grace. In a later portion of this chapter, therefore, I shall consider the role of experience in contributing to the assent of faith. I shall conclude with some reflections on the continued importance of reason and experience within faith.

## Faith and Reason

Few problems have been more persistently discussed through the centuries than the relationship between faith and reason.[1] The prominence of this problem is due, in great part, to the general acceptance of Greek philosophical categories as the basis for theological reflection during the first millennium and beyond. Greek philosophy, on the one hand, was an effort to achieve certified, permanent, and universal truth by human intellectual effort. It aimed to go beyond opinion and appearances and gain definitive insight into reality itself. Biblical faith, on the other hand, is based upon oracles spoken in the name of God, and accepted on the authority of the speaker—an authority confirmed, in some cases, by miracles.

Already in the New Testament we find the authors struggling to clarify the relationship between Christian revelation and the philosophy or wisdom of the Greeks. St. Paul points out that to the Greeks the message of the gospel appears as foolishness; but the foolishness of God, he adds, is wiser than human wisdom (1 Cor 1:23–25). In other texts Paul warns the faithful not to be misled by "philosophy and empty deceit" (Col 2:8). Yet, notwithstanding these reservations, Paul expresses high esteem for wisdom. God, he says, has made Christ our wisdom (1 Cor 1:30). "Among the mature *(teleiois)* we do impart wisdom—not a wisdom of this age or of the rulers of this age . . . but . . . a secret and hidden wisdom of God" (1 Cor 2:6–7). In the Letter to the Colossians Paul prays that the faithful "may be filled with the knowledge of his will in all spiritual wisdom and understanding" (Col 1:9) and that they may "have all the riches of assured understanding and the knowledge of God's mystery, of Christ, in whom are hid all the treasures of wisdom and knowledge" (Col 2:2–3; cf. Eph 1:17–18). Paul's distinction between a worldly wisdom that is opposed to faith and a holy wisdom that is grounded in faith set the stage for many of the debates that were to follow.

The apologists of Christian antiquity could adopt either of two strategies. When they were polemically engaged with Gnostics who relied too much on Greek speculation, they could, like Tatian and Tertullian, scorn Athens and its rational tradition. But when they were answering accusations of irrationality, they could claim, with Clement and Origen, that Christianity was in perfect accord with Hellenistic wisdom, and that the pagan philosophers were secretly guided by Christ, the divine Logos.

Augustine, with his heavy debt to Neoplatonism, tended to see faith as directing reason and imparting a higher vision of eternal truth. He was followed in the Middle Ages by Anselm and many monastic theologians, who accepted the priority of faith over reason. Bernard of Clairvaux, adhering to this monastic tradition, resisted the nascent Scholasticism of the universities.

Under the influence of the Aristotelian style of dialectics, university theologians in the twelfth century began to use autonomous reason to construct a system of knowledge not dependent on faith. Abelard looked on some traditional formulations of faith as needing to be revised in the light of rational reflection. This line of development was carried to greater lengths by the Averroists, who regarded faith as a merely preliminary and approximative form of knowledge, to be replaced, ideally, by the definitive, rationally grounded wisdom of philosophy. Thomas Aquinas, consciously opposing the Averroists, acknowledged a sphere of purely rational knowledge but held that it could prove nothing contrary to faith. In his view, autonomous reason paved the way for the decision to believe; it could also confirm the truth of some doctrines of faith. Faith, grounded in divine revelation, elevated reason, gave it a broader range of vision, and prevented it from falling into errors to which it would be subject without the guidance of revelation. Theology, for St. Thomas, is a higher wisdom based on the premises of faith.

The Scholastic theologians of the fourteenth and fifteenth centuries, while generally accepting the full heritage of Catholic faith, showed particular interest in exploring the capacities of unaided reason and speculating on what might have been the case in a purely natural order, had God decreed to establish one.

Martin Luther and many of the sixteenth-century Reformers reacted against the academic subtleties of the Scholasticism in which they had been trained. They opted for the priority of faith and often spoke contemptuously of reason. Yet Luther himself, as we have seen, did not reject the idea that reason could operate successfully within faith. Beginning with Philipp Melanchthon, many Lutherans made extensive use of Aristotle in their theology, as did Calvinists such as François Turretin. Richard Hooker and other Anglican theologians placed high value on reason as a gift that could prepare the way for faith.

During the seventeenth century reason was increasingly used as a critical tool to distinguish between truth and error. Benedict Spinoza, one of the most consistent rationalists, adopted a position reminiscent of Averroism. He regarded the Bible as an imaginative depiction of religious truth composed for the benefit of persons incapable of philosophic thought. For John Locke critical reason provided the final criterion to which all affirmations of faith must be subject. This principle was applied by some of Locke's followers, and more generally by Deists, to develop a full-scale critique of the Christian claims and to establish a predominantly or exclusively natural religion.

Immanuel Kant, although he owed much to the rational critique of Christianity, limited the scope of speculative reason and thereby made room for faith as sovereign in the realm of moral values. In this he was followed by Protestant liberal theologians, who erected a dichotomy between speculative truth, which falls within the competence of reason alone, and practical truth, which is based on the axioms of faith. Some nineteenth-century Protestants, strongly committed to the prevailing methods of academic history, attacked the credibility of the gospels.

John Henry Newman, seeking to answer the difficulties of Locke and David Hume, assigned a modest but positive role to reason in the approach to faith. In his view the truths of faith could not be established by formal demonstration, but the way to faith could be opened by tacit or implicit reasoning under the guidance of antecedent desires and expectations. Newman also extolled the wisdom that could flow from sustained reflection upon the truths of faith.

Vatican Council I, reacting against the destructive tendencies of critical reason, sought to reestablish the Thomistic synthesis. While holding that saving faith could not be achieved without the help of grace, the Council emphasized the value of reason in demonstrating the credibility of the Christian religion. Vatican I also recognized the value of theological insights achieved by rational reflection on faith.

In nineteenth-century philosophy, as in earlier rationalism, the powers of reason were frequently exalted to the detriment of faith. Some idealists looked upon reason as a power for synthesizing the whole of knowledge in a unified system of truth. G. W. F. Hegel and others contended that the Christian faith could be retained, with some refinements and reinterpretations, in such a philosophy. Søren Kierkegaard reacted by ridiculing the capacity of reason to verify the truth of faith and to achieve the kind of grand synthesis envisioned by Hegel.

In the mid-twentieth century, theologians such as Rudolf Bultmann and Paul Tillich attempted to maintain the truth of faith as an existential or self-involving type of knowledge. While ceding the realms of science and history to critical or technical reason, they reserved a separate sphere for faith. According to them, both faith and reason were autonomous and sovereign in their respective realms. Wolfhart Pannenberg, turning against existentialism, understands reason as a comprehensive power to synthesize all knowledge, including especially the meaning of history. Faith, in his view, depends upon historical knowledge. Catholics today generally understand faith as an assent to revealed, salutary truth that perfects and supplements, but does not replace or contradict, the knowledge accessible to unaided reason.

On the basis of this historical overview one may construct typologies. Theologians may be divided into three main categories: those who see faith and reason as mutually supportive, those who see them as antagonistic, and those who see them as pertaining to separate spheres. Within the class of those who hold for harmony, a distinction can be made between some who regard faith as the higher form of knowledge, perfecting reason, and others who look upon faith as needing to be perfected by reason. Within the category of those who see the two forms of knowledge as conflicting, some hold that faith should be accepted against reason; others, that reason should be preferred when it conflicts with faith.

These typologies, however, are of limited value because the authors do not share a common understanding of the meaning of either faith or reason. The various views of faith have been discussed in Chapter 8. It makes considerable difference whether faith is seen, for example, as an assent to doctrine, a unitive experience, a heartfelt trust in Christ, or a commitment to a certain style of action. We may at this point presuppose what has been said in Chapter 9 regarding the nature of faith.

A similar variety of views characterizes the discussion of reason.[2] When they speak of reason, different schools of theologians envisage different operations. The Platonists and Augustinians have in mind a kind of contemplative or intuitive reason ("higher reason") that makes contact with eternal truth and sees all reality in relation to that truth. The Aristotelians and positivists are generally referring to discursive or inferential reason ("lower reason"), either deductive or inductive. Some inferentialists are concerned with demonstrating the truth of revelation before the bar of reason; others, with detecting falsehood and reconstructing Christian doctrine on the basis of right reason. Many modern thinkers distinguish between explicit reason, which consciously follows logical rules, and informal or tacit reason, which is guided by what Blaise Pascal called the "reasons of the heart."

The Hegelians, for their part, regard reason as the mind's ability to fashion a comprehensive synthesis of everything that becomes known in the course of the ongoing historical process, a synthesis that anticipates the final consummation of the process itself. Faith, for the Hegelians, is a vague and approximative anticipation of the definitive system achieved by true philosophy.

Reason, moreover, is variously understood by theologians who have in mind different states of human existence. Some understand it as a power belonging to nature in the pure state, others as a capacity of fallen nature, and still others as a faculty illumined and elevated by grace. When Thomists speak of reason in contrast to faith, they are primarily interested in the relation between the natural and the supernatural. Reason is for them a cipher for natural knowledge; faith, for supernatural knowledge. When Lutherans refer to reason they are often talking about the cognitive capacities of fallen human nature apart from God's word of pardon and grace; and when they speak of faith they mean a trusting commitment to God as revealed in Jesus Christ.

The linguistic discrepancies must be taken seriously, since they often reflect real philosophical and theological differences. But because the authors are using different terminologies, some of the conflicts may be more apparent than real.


## Evidence of Credibility

As has been shown in Chapter 9, faith, without being merely cognitive, has a cognitive dimension. It is, under one aspect, an intellectual assent to revelation, and this assent would be irresponsible unless there were sufficient grounds for accepting the revelation as true. Reason is often employed to ascertain whether the alleged revelation is worthy of belief, or (to use the technical term) credible.

In biblical times the problem of credibility was already recognized. Old Testament writers, seeking to discern true from false prophecy, invoke criteria such as miracles, fulfilled prophecies, moral behavior, and compatibility with the rest of revelation (Dt 13:1–5; Jer 28:9–32; Ezek 13:1–7). New Testament authors, while they look on faith as a free gift of God, point to miracles and fulfilled prophecies as grounds for accepting the authority of Jesus and the apostles. The resurrection of Jesus is the centerpiece of New Testament apologetics. In the early centuries, when Christianity became established in the Hellenistic world, apologetics became a well-recognized discipline, and such it has remained down through the centuries.[3]

In modern times some theologians, swayed by philosophical agnosticism, took the "fideist" position that faith is its own ground, and that it cannot and should not appeal to reason. Others, under the spell of rationalism, held that faith must confine itself within the limits of pure reason. The Catholic magisterium in the nineteenth and early twentieth centuries, notably at Vatican I, set forth a moderate position that was opposed to fideism on the one hand and to rationalism on the other. The basic teaching of Vatican I on faith and reason remains normative for Catholics in our day.

The reasonableness of the act of faith has to be reconciled with other attributes to be considered below in Chapter 11, notably its supernaturality, its freedom, and its obscurity. Vatican I was conscious of this problem and proposed the elements of a solution. On the one hand, it stated that the contents of faith are not believed because of intrinsic arguments (i.e., arguments that would directly prove the truth of the doctrines themselves) but because of the authority of God who reveals (*Dei Filius,* chap. 3, DS 3008). On the other hand, the Council maintained that the Christian revelation, and the Catholic Church as the bearer of that revelation, have "evident credibility" by reason of the wonderful dispositions of divine providence in favor of Christ and the Church (ibid.; DS 3013). The Council does not attempt to decide the question whether the truth of revelation can be demonstrated. It contents itself with making three affirmations: first, the truth of revelation cannot be demonstrated by intrinsic arguments; second, its credibility can be demonstrated;

third, the motive of faith is not the force of the arguments but the authority of God who reveals.

Vatican I, then, left open the question whether the truth of Christianity could be cogently proved by indirect or extrinsic arguments, establishing the fact of divine revelation. The Council did not wish to condemn the doctrine of "acquired faith" *(fides acquisita),* as taught by the Scotists, or the "apologetical rationalism" of Miguel de Elizalde and Thyrsus Gonzalez. It left room for the doctrine of "scientific faith" that would be held by Louis Billot and Ambroise Gardeil. But, as we have seen in our historical survey, these theories have fallen increasingly out of favor, at least in our own century. If the fact of revelation could be stringently demonstrated, it is difficult to see how the assent of faith would be free and supernatural. For St. Thomas, at least, evidential knowledge and faith exclude each other. It is rather commonly held today, consistently with Vatican I, that it is not possible to demonstrate the fact of Christian revelation but only the credibility of the claim to revelation. In other words, it is possible to establish by rational argumentation that there are sufficient grounds for a free and reasonable decision to believe that Christianity is a revealed religion.

In its discussion of credibility, Vatican I distinguished between "interior helps of the Holy Spirit" and "external arguments" (*argumenta externa;* ibid.; DS 3009). By the "internal helps" the Council clearly meant the light and inspiration of grace, given to the individual approaching the act of faith. The "external arguments of revelation," which are presented as accessible to reason, are also called "divine works" (*facta divina;* ibid.) By these, Vatican I means signs given in history, particularly miracles and fulfilled prophecies. More specifically, the Council mentions the signs worked through Moses, the prophets, the apostles, and especially through Jesus Christ. Several paragraphs later Vatican I refers to the Catholic Church itself as being "a great and perpetual motive of credibility and irrefutable testimony to its own divine mission" (ibid.; DS 3013). In this connection the Council speaks of the marvelous expansion of the Church, its unity, its durability, its holiness, and its fruitfulness in all that is good. In effect the Council is here claiming that the Catholic Church is a moral or sociological miracle—an exception to the general laws governing human societies. Here again, the Council merely indicates the line of argument, leaving it up to theologians to develop it. Before Vatican I issued this statement, several theologians, including Victor Dechamps and Joseph Kleutgen, both of whom were present at the Council, had propounded this argument.

In summary, Vatican I commended several distinct apologetical approaches as vindications of the reasonableness of faith. It did not press the historical arguments from biblical miracles and prophecies to the exclusion of arguments from the Church as a present reality answering to the inner intimations of the human spirit. Nor did it endorse the latter to the exclusion of the former. The Council put its blessing on both types of argument and made no effort to rank them in order of merit. The text of Vatican I may perhaps be read as implying that a convergent argument based on both sets of data would be the most persuasive.

To assert that the evident credibility of the Christian religion is demonstrable is to say that by using rational arguments it is possible to distinguish faith from gullibility and wishful thinking. Such arguments can satisfy believers that their faith is reasonable and can challenge nonbelievers to take the claims of revelation seriously.

Many authors distinguish between a speculative and a practical judgment of credibility. The first is general and objective; the second, personal and subjective. The first may be expressed by the proposition: "this could reasonably be believed"; the second by the proposition: "it would be prudent for me, here and now, to believe." The prudential judgment is influenced in subtle ways by the individual's temperament, prior experiences, presumptions, aspirations, and hunches—in sum, by Pascal's "reasons of the heart." The faith of the individual is reasonable if sustained by a practical judgment of credibility; it need not rest on speculatively sufficient grounds known to oneself. The judgment of credibility, moreover, need not be distinctly articulated. It may be implicitly present in the act of faith as exercised by a prudent believer.

For the faith of the Church, however, speculative grounds of credibility would seem to be requisite. Unless the Church could give objectively solid motives for believing, its proclamation of the gospel would be defective. It would be hampered in its mission if it could not provide convincing reasons for not dismissing faith as an illusion. Apologists have the task of elaborating speculatively sufficient grounds of credibility, responding to the objections that may arise from time to time. Although these explicit arguments are not needed by all believers at all times, such arguments can on occasion prepare a person's way to faith or prevent a person's faith from being troubled by specious objections.

Vatican I does not clearly distinguish between speculative and practical credibility, but its decrees may be interpreted with this distinction in mind. The emphasis falls primarily on the objective reasonableness of the Catholic faith, in view of the many signs of credibility that God has wrought in its favor. It seems to be implied that any individual must have access to sufficient evidence so that his or her faith is subjectively prudent and is not a "blind movement of the mind."[4]

The external signs of credibility are seen as providential helps enabling believers to assure themselves that they are not deluded. The Council, however, does not teach that every believer needs to rely on these external signs for his or her faith to be reasonable. A given believer, it would seem, might be satisfied with internal criteria such as the wonderful correspondence of the Christian message with one's own aspirations and presumptions. Although Vatican I particularly emphasized the arguments from prophecy and miracle, it did not deny that valid conclusions may be drawn from the inherent features of the Christian message judged in the light of the believer's moral and religious sense.

As Newman and his followers have pointed out, personal factors play an important role in the calculus of credibility. Whether a given message is deemed worthy of belief depends to a great extent on the recipients' antecedent desires and expectations. Religious inquirers commonly presume that divine revelation, if given, will show them the meaning and purpose of their lives, provide norms of conduct, offer deliverance from the burden of guilt, and provide a horizon of hope. These prerequisites are not sufficiently concrete to give advance notice of the specific content of the revelation. Indeed, a revelation will be more credible if its contents are utterly beyond all that human ingenuity would have conjectured. But, once given, the revelation must give meaning, direction, and order to one's life. It must overcome anomie and despair. It must enable the believer to cope with pain, humiliation, and adversity.

These antecedent prescriptions, arising from interior needs, must be supplemented by a posteriori indications that the purported revelation is not a deliberate fraud, a delusion, or an empty myth. In the case of a historical revelation such as Christianity, it will be normal for believers to seek some historical evidence that the reported revelation is from God. Divine signs such as miracles and fulfilled prophecies will be relevant considerations. The testimony of competent witnesses can be an impressive sign, especially if the witnesses exhibit extraordinary joy, peace, energy, conviction, sincerity, and readiness to make sacrifices for their faith.

In historical assessments of this character no one piece of evidence, taken in isolation, will suffice, but the accumulation of many convergent signs can often lead to firm conviction. This will be the case if the truth of the revelation gives the only satisfactory explanation for the presence of so many convergent signs. The cumulative style of argument, developed in the eighteenth century by Joseph Butler, was perfected by Newman in his discussion of informal inference:

> It is plain that formal logical sequence is not in fact the method by which we are enabled to become certain of what is concrete; and it is equally plain, from what has already been suggested, what the real and necessary method is. It is the cumulation of probabilities, independent of each other, arising out of the nature and circumstances of the particular case which is under review; probabilities too fine to avail separately, too subtle and circuitous to be convertible into syllogisms, too numerous and various for such conversion, even were they convertible.[5]

As is also evident from what has been said, the ultimate judgment of credibility will not depend on external signs alone, but rather on a combination of a priori and a posteriori factors. The exact proportion will vary from one individual to another. As Newman perceived, antecedent probabilities may weigh very heavily:

> It is difficult to put a limit to the legitimate force of this antecedent probability. Some minds will feel it to be so powerful, as to recognize in it almost a proof, without direct evidence, of the divinity of a religion claiming to be the true, supposing its history and doctrine are free from positive objection, and there be no rival religion with plausible claims of its own.[6]

Antecedent probabilities, as Newman here points out, do not carry one the whole way, but they are a normal and a powerful ingredient in the process of coming to a decision whether to believe.

## Supernatural Helps

In speaking of the inner assistance of grace and the external arguments of credibility, Vatican I did not settle the question whether the latter are fully convincing without the former. By its statement that God wished to conjoin the external evidence for revelation with the inner helps of the Holy Spirit (*Dei Filius,* chap. 3, DS 3009), the Council seemed to imply that in the actual order grace is at work in the hearts and minds of anyone approaching the decision of faith. On the other hand, the Council did not indicate that the light of grace makes the motives of credibility more convincing than they would otherwise be.

Pierre Rousselot is the chief defender of the thesis that grace casts a new light on the perception of credibility—a light without which the judgment of credibility could not be firm. While grace itself is not perceived, he argued, it gives connaturality with the divine, and such connaturality enables a person to synthesize the signs of God's presence and activity in history. The rationality of faith, for Rousselot, is not weakened but enhanced by the attraction of grace.

The encyclical *Humani generis* (1950) seemed to discountenance the thesis of Rousselot. It taught that the human mind may experience difficulties in forming the judgment of credibility "even though God has provided such numerous and wonderful signs of credibility that the divine origin of the Christian religion could be certainly proved even by the merely natural light of reason" (DS 3876). Although this concessive clause is not an unequivocal rejection of the Rousselot position regarding the necessity of the infused light of faith for the perception of credibility, it was so interpreted by many theologians. Vatican II, however, did not follow up on this teaching of Pius XII. It was silent regarding the evidence of credibility. Thus it would seem that the Rousselot position on this point may still be defended by those who favor it. As we have seen, theologians of the stature of Karl Rahner and Hans Urs von Balthasar accept the fundamentals of the Rousselot position, and in this they would seem to be correct.

To conclude the present discussion, it should probably be added that the assessment of credibility is never a purely intellectual process. In classical analyses such as that of Thomas Aquinas, careful attention is paid to the role of the will as well as to that of the intellect. The approach to faith, it was seen, presupposes a spontaneous orientation to the Absolute Good, which is found in God alone—an orientation that may be strengthened and made more determinate through the leading of grace. A sense of guilt and a yearning for salvation can greatly contribute to the process.

These affective dispositions enter vitally into the assessment of credibility, even though they may not be noticed. If reflected on, they give antecedent grounds for crediting an alleged revelation to the effect that God calls us to himself, that he wills to forgive us and to renew our fallen nature. The aspiration of the will inclines the intellect to search for traces of redemptive revelation. The connaturality established by grace makes it easier for the intellect to perceive the signs of God's loving approach. Far from giving rise to illusions, a deep reverence for God as the transcendent source of all truth puts one on guard against error and facilitates the apprehension of truth. Thus the antecedent desires and anticipations are no mere "subjective supplement" to compensate for the insufficiency of the intellectual evidence, as Gardeil at one point seemed to suggest. Newman, Maurice Blondel, and Rousselot correctly held that affective factors enter into the very process of intellectual discernment. The dawning light of faith exhibits the harmony between the object of faith and the anticipations aroused by grace. The depth, tenacity, and life-giving power of the inclination to believe may be taken as signs that the inclination itself has a divine origin.[7]

## Motives of Credibility and of Faith

One of the most difficult theological questions about faith has to do with the relationship between the motives of credibility and the motive of faith itself. All agree that the motive of faith is the authority of God who reveals. But is the divine authority apprehended in the created signs that point to him or in a pure perception of the uncreated testimony of God? On this point there is a deep cleavage between two schools of thought.

One group, following the general tendency of Juan de Lugo, makes a very close connection between the created and uncreated testimony. Karl Adam, Pierre Rousselot, Jean Mouroux, Guy de Broglie, Felix Malmberg, and others hold that grace, attuning our minds and hearts to the word of God, enables us to discern the meaning of the external signs—miracles, prophecies, and the life and preaching of the Church—and to affirm in faith, "The finger of God is here!" Perception of the signs of credibility plays a constitutive, if only instrumental, role in the act of faith itself, since it is by means of such signs that God communicates his message. In the words of de Broglie: "To dream of a knowledge by testimony that would not be essentially founded in the *signs* which the witness gives of his thought would be to set out on the path of absolute nonsense."[8] On this theory the perception of God's invitation does not demand that the significance of the signs be established by formal logical demonstration. The discernment, while rational in its own way, is spontaneous; it rests on a total estimate of the situation that cannot be analyzed in abstract and discursive terms. To believe is in effect to say to an earthly witness, "You have the words of eternal life" (cf. Jn 6:68).

The other school, represented by Léopold Malevez, Louis Monden, Marie-Dominique Chenu, and practically all Dominicans, maintains that the discernment of the visible signs is merely an extrinsic preparation for faith, and that faith itself has as its sole motive the uncreated testimony of God, recognized by a grace-imparted interior instinct. The person of faith no longer relies upon the signs of credibility that made the approach to faith possible.

St. Thomas himself, in his lectures on the fourth chapter of John, seems to favor the latter alternative. He asserts that the created signs are inducements that draw us toward faith, but that once we do believe, we do so not because of any external signs, but only because of the truth itself.[9]

Réginald Garrigou-Lagrange, a faithful Thomist, finds confirmation of this doctrine in the experience of the mystics. In the "dark night of the spirit," as described by St. John of the Cross, the motives of credibility lose their persuasive force and the soul is forced to rely solely on the uncreated motive of faith, God in himself. Many of the saints, including Blessed Henry Suso, St. Vincent de Paul, and St. Thérèse of the Child Jesus, like John of the Cross, spent long years in a dark tunnel at the end of which they found not light in the ordinary sense but rather a darkness more brilliant than the day. Long before them Gregory of Nyssa wrote of "the divine night in which the beloved comes near but does not appear."[10]

Without totally resolving the disagreement, one may find merit in both positions. To the Thomists it should be conceded that the sole motive of faith is God himself, and that the motive of faith is not the same as the motives of credibility. But the Rousselot school would seem to be correct in holding that no one can adhere to a specific revelation unless that revelation is mediated through some created sign, whether interior or exterior, which is discerned to be from God. Although beginners tend to rely consciously on physical miracles and apologetical arguments, souls advanced in the spiritual life pay less attention to created signs. Caught up in the joint meaning of the signs, they shift their attention to the God who speaks by means of them. They often have the impression of directly experiencing the presence of the unseen God. Rousselot has on this subject a dense paragraph that repays meditation:

> The more responsive the mind is to the promptings of the Holy Spirit, the more easily it will come to assent to the Christian faith by means of signs that are ordinary, everyday signs, in no way "extraordinary" or "miraculous." That is why an incontrovertible tradition, going back to the Gospel itself, praises those who have no need of wonders. They are not praised for having believed without reasons; that would only be reprehensible. But we see in them truly illuminated souls, capable of grasping a vast truth through a tiny clue. Does not experience show that, when the Holy Spirit visits the soul with His consolation, the soul is no longer capable of doubting, as it were, and glimpses manifest signs of the truth in everything? "Think of anything you wish," says the author of *L'Aiguillon d'amour,* "and you will find in it many reasons for loving your Creator." Some saints went into esctasy on viewing a blade of grass. So, too, when it comes to faith. When responding to the divine light, the believer sees all of world history as proving the Church's mission; the most commonplace word or fact floods the soul with certitude and peace. Experiences of this sort cannot be expressed in words. But in defining that there are motives drawn from outward signs, the Church never defined that there exist only motives susceptible of expression. The motives we are talking about, if given expression, might well seem contemptible to those bereft of the Spirit. But the lover recognizes the Spouse "by a single hair of her neck."[11]

When Rousselot speaks of motives that are not susceptible of expression and that would seem contemptible to those bereft of the Spirit, he may be referring to the inability of the mystics, who are swept up in the brilliance of the divine night, to set much store by the conventional arguments of credibility.

## The Experience of Discovery

From the discussion thus far it would seem that informal or tacit reasoning plays a greater role than formal reasoning in the approach to faith. This conclusion may be reinforced from the very nature of religious conversion. Formal reasoning always works within the framework of the already known; it cannot validate a radically new perspective implying a fresh set of principles. Yet this is precisely what is required for religious conversion. Faith, then, is initially achieved by a mysterious process of discovery in which the human mind, impelled by grace, lights upon a truth beyond all that it could logically derive from the data of common experience.

The highly personal process of religious conversion has analogies in scientific discovery. As Michael Polanyi, Arthur Koestler, and others have shown in detail, something akin occurs in the minds of great inventors and innovative theorists.[12] They are driven by a passionate desire to know, by a haunting presentiment that there is a great truth waiting to be found, by the thrill of seeing the clues gradually coalesce into intelligible patterns, and by the joyful release of heuristic tension that follows upon discovery. When the answer comes, says Polanyi, "it arrives accredited in advance by the heuristic craving which evoked it."[13]

An analogous process occurs in religious discovery. The inquirer is deeply troubled but at the same time confident that the unknown answer will disclose itself. Restless searching is often accompanied by ardent prayer. When the answer comes, the discoverer experiences a shock of recognition. The God of grace appears as the Beloved for whom one has been passionately seeking. "I found him whom my soul loves" (Song of Sol 3:4). The convert cries out, as did Augustine, "Late have I loved you, O beauty ever ancient and ever new! Late have I loved you!"[14] Great converts such as Luther, Pascal, and Wesley allude to the ineffable subjective experiences that brought them to adhere passionately to the Christian message. While these leaders are exceptional, their conversions may be thought to illustrate in striking ways the kind of holy encounter that must play a part in every authentic decision of faith.

Because formal reasoning is secondary, many authors prefer to ground faith not so much in reason as in experience, a category closely associated with faith in early modern authors such as Philipp Jacob Spener and August Francke, George Fox and Jonathan Edwards. With Friedrich D. E. Schleiermacher and the nineteenth-century Protestant liberals experience and feeling came to be seen as the very heart of religion, including faith. Rudolf Otto, building in part on Schleiermacher, explored the unique features of experiences he called "numinous." George Tyrrell looked upon faith as an incommunicable personal experience. Karl Rahner spoke freely of the experience of uncreated grace, whereas Edward Schillebeeckx prefers to speak paradoxically of Christian faith as an experience of that which transcends experience.

Conservative and dialectical Protestant theology, committed to the sovereignity of God's word in Christ and in Scripture, is generally wary of the category of experience. Catholics, especially in the climate of baroque and neo-scholastic theology, have kept their eyes fixed primarily on the magisterium, and have been suspicious of appeals to experience. The Holy See reacted sharply against the exaltation of experience in Modernism.

The entire question is complicated by disagreements about the nature of experience. Originally the term meant any process of trial or testing. It gradually came to signify controlled observation or experiment, considered as a source of verified knowledge. Then, in British empiricism, the term was used to mean the perception of concrete phenomena, especially those that impinge on the external senses at a point prior to reflective thought. For William James, who stood fundamentally within the empiricist school, experience consisted of "present data considered in their raw immediacy, before reflective thought has analysed them into subjective and objective aspects or ingredients."[15]

In his *The Varieties of Religious Experience* James identified religion itself with experiences of a particular type. He asked his hearers to accept his definition of religion as "the feelings, acts, and experiences of individual men in their solitude, so far as they apprehend themselves to stand in relation to whatever they may consider the divine."[16] He singled out for special attention certain feelings associated with a quasi-mystical apprehension of a spiritual Presence. His view that the divine could be immediately perceived as an individual, self-evidencing phenomenon, although still defended in some circles, has been widely challenged in recent years by philosophers and theologians of different schools.[17]

Religious experience, like other experience, never occurs in a vacuum. It is shaped in large measure by the cultural, linguistic, and social context in which it occurs. Contemporary authors emphasize the social and participatory factors in experience. Many, with whom I align myself, regard experience as the awareness given in an encounter with some present concrete reality. Experience is a complex event having strictly perceptual, imaginative, and affective dimensions, all of which depend in part on the character of the subject who is undergoing the experience. There is no such thing as a strictly uninterpreted experience, since interpretative factors due to the dispositions and training of the subject will affect the very manner in which the data are initially perceived. The "religious" character of an experience cannot stand apart from the interpretation given to it, normally within a religious tradition.

For understanding the kind of religious interpretation involved in Christian faith, it is helpful to recall that, as transcendental theologians have pointed out, the human spirit has a native orientation to that which lies beyond all mundane and finite phenomena. As Augustine wrote in the first chapter of his *Confessions:* "You have made us for yourself, O Lord, and our hearts are restless till they find rest in you!" Karl Rahner has repeatedly insisted that all human experience is influenced by a pre-empirical orientation of the human spirit to God as absolute mystery. God is never experienced in himself as an object alongside of others, but he is co-experienced, nonobjectively, as the transcendental ground of all intelligible experience. Except perhaps in some rare mystical states, we do not perceive God within us by simple introspection, but we become aware of God's presence when we experience other things in their finitude and transitoriness. We experience ourselves as separated from God and as drawn toward him.[18]

It is not easy to say to what extent this "co-experience" of the divine is natural, and to what extent it is due to grace. The theologian may suppose that God, who wills all human beings to come to eternal salvation, calls everyone by his grace. St. Thomas and his school hold that the believer relies not only on external signs but also on "the interior instinct of God who invites him to believe" (*S. Th.,* 2–2.2.9, ad 3). This inner instinct or attraction could hardly contribute to faith unless it had some perceived effect, even though the believer might have no clear and distinct perception of grace as such. A felt attraction toward the divine, even though it may not be consciously adverted to, is a necessary condition, I believe, for the spiritual experience of the prophets, the mystics, and the founders of great religions. In less conspicuous forms, this attraction is an ingredient in the religious life of anyone who comes to believe.

Human beings, according to Rahner, would be correct in interpreting their own concrete experience, in its highest moments, as "the experience of a supreme, most radical, saving and forgiving presence of the mystery of God communicating himself absolutely." Such experience of grace, he goes on to say, occurs in the most varied forms. "It may, for example, be indescribable joy, unconditional personal love, unconditional obedience to conscience, the experience of loving union with the universe, the experience of irretrievable vulnerability of one's own human existence beyond one's own control, and so on."[19]

To give additional concreteness to these remarks, and to bring them into closer connection with systems of religious belief, some typical forms of religious experience may be recalled. Ian G. Barbour proposes a list of seven common forms, which may be briefly paraphrased as follows:[20]

1. *Awe and reverence.* In his classic of religious phenomenology, *The Idea of the Holy,* Rudolf Otto discusses the *mysterium tremendum,* a "numinous" encounter with an external reality that evokes a combination of fascination and dread. He gives many examples from the Bible and other religious literature.

2. *Mystical union.* The mystics of various religions speak of experiences of bliss and rapture pointing to the ultimate oneness of all things.

3. *Moral obligation.* The transcendent is often manifested by the voice of conscience commanding us to perform or avoid certain actions, by the sense of guilt for our own misdeeds, and by the moral outrage that we feel against the perpetrators of monstrous evils.

4. *Reorientation and reconciliation.* An overwhelming sense of the healing power of love can overcome alienation and enable us to accept ourselves or others.

5. *Interpersonal relationships.* Our encounter with other human persons in dialogue is sometimes interpreted as a form of encounter with what Martin Buber called "the eternal Thou."

6. *Key historical events.* Some events are of such a nature that they provide a framework in which the community can understand its corporate identity and find direction for its ongoing life. For Christians the event of Jesus Christ serves as the center of meaning for all reality.

7. *Order and creativity in the world.* For many believers, the sense of order and design in nature has led to a spontaneous conviction regarding the existence of a wise and provident deity.

These "depth experiences," Barbour observes, are open to a variety of interpretations, but for many the theistic interpretation seems reasonable, even mandatory. The full acceptance of such an interpretation involves conversion, that is to say, commitment to a new way of looking on reality and to a new style of behavior.

Any free adherence to a specific religious interpretation may be called "faith" in a broad sense of the word, but something more is required to constitute faith as the term is being used in this book. For divine faith, the interpretation, while presumably resonating with the believer's personal experience, must be seen as authoritatively given by divine revelation. In principle, this could be a particular revelation received by oneself, but in the case of Christianity the believer consciously adheres to a public revelation that can be traced through the apostolic tradition to Jesus Christ, who was himself divine. Jesus interpreted his own experience and that of the persons to whom he spoke; he reinterpreted the religious heritage given in the Scriptures and traditions of the Jews, and he provided a pattern whereby future believers could interpret their experience.

Faith in the Christian sense, therefore, is not simply a personal interpretation of one's experience. It is an acceptance of a holy and divine revelation as the key to interpreting the meaning and goal of all human experience. When the proffered interpretation makes sense of the enigmas of life and provides an answer to a passionate quest for meaning and fulfillment, the encounter with revelation can unleash a profound religious experience, as occurred in the lives of the eminent converts mentioned above.

## Reason and Experience within Faith

Since this chapter deals with the "grounding" of faith, I have discussed the role of reason and experience only in connection with the approach to faith. The reader should not imagine, however, that when faith is achieved, reason and experience cease to have any function. Faith enriches, and is enriched by, reason and experience.

The act of faith is itself, from a certain point of view, an act of reason—not the *raison raisonnante* of the logician, but the heuristic reason of the discoverer, carried by grace toward the God who has revealed himself. Without the use of reason, one could not find God in the signs that point to him.

With regard to the use of reason within faith, Vatican I taught that reason, assisted by the light of faith, is able to achieve ever greater understanding of the contents and meaning of faith. "When, enlightened by faith, reason inquires assiduously, devoutly, and soberly, it attains by God's gift some understanding of the mysteries and, at that, a most fruitful one" (*Dei Filius,* chap. 4, DS 3016). Hence there can be true progress in knowledge and wisdom and in the understanding of revealed doctrine, both for individuals and for the whole Church (ibid., DS 3020). In this connection the Council explained that faith and reason, far from contradicting each other, give mutual support. Right reason "establishes the foundations of faith," and gives intelligibility to the contents of faith. Faith, on the other hand, "frees reason from errors, protects it, and provides it with manifold insights" (ibid., DS 3019).

The ancient Alexandrian theologians, in the footsteps of Paul and John, rejected the idea of a separation between faith and reason. According to Clement of Alexandria "there is no *gnosis* without *pistis,* and there is no *pistis* without *gnosis,* just as there is no Father without the Son."[21] Newman, as mentioned above, set high store on the wisdom that can be attained by meditation on the contents of faith. Von Balthasar, with many references to Clement and Origen, insists rightly that faith does not merely seek understanding; it already has insight and understanding. By the light of faith believers in some sort "see" what they believe. But they can continually deepen the insight that they have. The increase of knowledge does not lead them out of faith but enables them to grow in that faith.[22]

On some occasions new explorations into the deposit of faith will unveil truths that have been obscured or neglected in recent teaching. The theologian will have to point out that modern formulations, although they may have been current for some time, are inadequate or misleading. Fresh developments may be called for in the light of new information or with the help of new methods. History attests that many of the most creative theologians have been for some time under suspicion for subverting the faith. Their insights have to be tested in the community of faith. Generations are often required to sort out the good grain from the chaff.

Just as reason, after having prepared the way to faith, continues to operate within faith, so too does experience. Faith itself, as an intensely personal act, is under one aspect an experience. As a form of religious experience it is, in the terminology of Jean Mouroux, an act by which one becomes aware of oneself in the presence of God.[23] As an experience faith is integrating, holy, mediated, and dynamic. It is integrating because all the main aspects of the person, individual and social, are involved and integrated in a structured way. It is holy because it brings one into communion with the divine. It is mediated because God is encountered through created signs; and it is dynamic because it embodies a propulsion toward the infinite. The experience of faith is lived out progressively through temptations and struggles that reveal its character as an unmerited gift, and through consolations that point forward to the final fulfillment.

Faith permeates the whole of the believer's experience. The saints, whose lives are most palpably dominated by faith, interpret all that happens to them as an unfolding dialogue with God. Even amid the joys of this world, they are pained by a sense of exile because they cannot look upon God face to face; yet in the midst of suffering they find joy, insofar as it enables them to participate in the sufferings of Christ, whom they love. Thanks to faith, the believer has a new capacity for experiencing grace and experiencing God—not in the crude empirical sense, as though God were an object alongside of others, but in the sense that the perspective of faith allows one to perceive created things as mediations of God's self-communication.

A certain reciprocity therefore exists between experience and faith. We do not have faith because we were previously conscious of experiencing God but because, with the help of grace, we freely accept a divinely revealed interpretation of the world as the clue to the meaning of our own existence. Having so interpreted the world, we become aware of God's presence in created realities, and consequently we experience those realities in a new and different way, in their transparency to God. Faith and experience therefore coalesce.

Faith frequently gives rise to rich, intense, and meaningful experiences. Gregory Baum, in proposing what he calls "A Modern Apologetics," holds that people become Christians and remain Christians when they find that the gospel message explains, purifies and multiplies what he calls their "depth-experiences," a term by which he means "ordinary experiences that are memorable, the source of many decisions and tend to unify human life."[24] Conversely, he says, "If this message—because of the way and the context in which it is announced—fails to explain, purify and intensify the depth-experiences of men, they have no human reasons available to them for becoming Christians."[25]

It is true that experiences of the type that Baum describes often give a satisfying confirmation of faith, but his approach might give the misleading impression that the true value of faith consists in its capacity to generate a continual series of profound and intense experiences. God can give consoling experiences of grace, but he can also allow the soul to proceed, without privileged experiences, by the common light of revelation as mediated through the Church. Often, I would surmise, believers live out their faith-commitment in a quiet manner, if not in a state of aridity. In any case, it would be an error to make religious experiences, or depth-experiences, a criterion by which to judge whether one ought to become or remain a Christian. St. John of the Cross warned against this error when he wrote:

> In order to preserve the purity of his faith, a person should not believe already revealed truths because they are again revealed [by special manifestations to oneself], but because they were already sufficiently revealed to the Church. Closing his mind to them, he should rest simply on the doctrine of the Church and its faith which, as St. Paul says, enters through hearing [Rom 10:17].[26]

## Conclusion

Many authors have sought to ground faith in reason. Rationalists tend to make reason the norm by which faith is judged, whereas fideists maintain that faith, having its assurance only from revelation, cannot be certified by natural knowledge. Catholic theology generally upholds the value of reason in leading to faith and in demonstrating the credibility of revelation. But faith is considered to be superior insofar as divine revelation, accepted in faith, can extend the range of reason and protect reason against errors.

Christian revelation can be presented in such a way that its credibility cannot reasonably be denied. Whether an individual recognizes the credibility and actually believes depends on personal factors. Contemporary apologists, influenced by Newman, often hold that belief is prompted by a cumulative argument in which many convergent signs are seen to merge into a coherent pattern, having a religious meaning. The efficacy of the argument depends to a great extent on the antecedent desires and expectations of the inquirer. The working of grace, which attunes the mind to God, makes it easier to discern the presence of God in the signs that are given in history and in experience.

The motive of faith is God alone. In order to be such a motive, God must be perceived. It is difficult to understand how God, being utterly transcendent, could ever become a direct and immediate object of experience. In any case, God could not communicate a definite message except through created signs, which must be discerned as coming from him. In higher stages of the spiritual life, the believer's attention may be so intently focused on God that the signs are scarcely noticed. The truth of revelation is apprehended in what mystics describe as a luminous divine night.

In coming to faith, believers normally employ a "logic of discovery" in which the mind, pondering the clues, is guided by a hope-filled anticipation of God's self-revelation. The discovery is accompanied by intense joy and satisfaction. An attraction toward the divine appears to be a necessary ingredient in any religious conversion. Faith arises when important areas of human experience are interpreted according to divine revelation. Christian faith consists in an acceptance of God's revelation as the light by which one finds ultimate meaning in one's life and one's world.

Reason operates not only in the approach to faith but also in the act of faith and in the subsequent reflection in which one's understanding of the mysteries of faith is deepened. The movement from simple faith to deeper understanding is not a withdrawal from faith but a growth in faith. Thanks in part to the labor of theologians, the whole Church makes progress in its understanding of Christian doctrine.

Although faith presupposes some measure of religious exerience, experience is not simply a preliminary. Faith itself is under one aspect a religious experience. It casts a new light on all things, enabling them to be perceived in their relationship to God. On occasion faith flowers in intense and consoling experiences of the divine presence, but the Christian should beware of making such peak experiences a norm or condition of faith. God is to be believed because he has spoken and because his word resounds in the Church.

## Notes

1. The concise survey that follows is based for the most part on information detailed above in chapters 1 through 7.

2. The ambiguities in the concept of reason are helpfully discussed in Wolfhart Pannenberg, "Faith and Reason," in his *Basic Questions in Theology,* vol. 2 (Philadelphia: Fortress, 1971), 46–64.

3. See Avery Dulles, *A History of Apologetics* (Washington, D.C.: Corpus, 1971); *Enciclopedia di Teologia fondamentale,* ed. Giuseppe Ruggieri (Genoa: Marietti, 1987), 1:3–400.

4. Vatican I, *Dei Filius,* chap. 3 (DS 3010). In my interpretation I follow Hermann J. Pottmeyer, *Der Glaube vor dem Anspruch der Wissenschaft* (Freiburg: Herder, 1968), 264–65, 272–73. Pottmeyer, in turn, follows Edouard Dhanis in his review of the first edition of Roger Aubert, *Le problème de l'acte de foi,* in *Nouvelle revue théologique* 68 (1946): 26–43, at 29–30. Aubert takes the position that Vatican I did not enter even implicitly into the question of what motives of credibility the individual must have. In his second edition (Louvain: E. Warny, 1950), note 31, 166–67, Aubert reaffirms his position but adds that Dhanis's arguments must be taken into serious consideration.

5. John Henry Newman, *Grammar of Assent* (Garden City, N.Y.: Doubleday Image, 1955), chap. 8, sec. 2, p. 230. The broad currency of cumulative arguments for religious belief in contemporary British philosophy is due in part to the influence of Basil Mitchell, *Justification of Religious Belief* (London: Macmillan, 1973).

6. Newman, ibid., chap. 10, sec. 2, §3, 328–29.

7. This line of thought is developed in Aubert, *Problème*, 2nd ed., 758–76.

8. Guy de Broglie, "L'illumination des signes de crédibilité par la grâce," *Recherches de science religieuse* 53 (1965): 507.

9. Thomas Aquinas, *In Evangelium secundum Joann.*, cap. 4, lect. 5 (Turin: Marietti, 1925), 137–38; quoted above in Chapter 2.

10. Gregory of Nyssa, *In Canticum Canticorum*, PG 44:1001. John of the Cross in his poems speaks of the "guiding night .. more lovely than the dawn" and of the dark cloud that "lit up the night." See his *Collected Works*, trans. Kieran Kavanaugh and Otilio Rodriguez (Washington, D.C.: Institute of Carmelite Studies, 1973), 711 and 719.

11. Pierre Rousselot, *The Eyes of Faith* (New York: Fordham University Press, 1990), 35.

12. See Avery Dulles, "Revelation and Discovery" in *Theology and Discovery: Essays in Honor of Karl Rahner, S.J.*, ed. William J. Kelly (Milwaukee, Wis.: Marquette University Press, 1980), 1–29. Among the foundational works are Michael Polanyi, *Personal Knowledge* (New York: Harper Torchbooks, 1964) and Arthur Koestler, *The Act of Creation* (New York: Macmillan, 1964).

13. Polanyi, *Personal Knowledge*, 130.

14. Augustine, *Confessions*, Book X, chap. 6, trans. Rex Warner (New York: Mentor-Omega Books, 1963), 215.

15. William James, "Experience," from Baldwin's *Dictionary;* quoted by Nicholas Lash, *Easter in Ordinary: Reflections on Human Experience and the Knowledge of God* (Charlottesville, Va.: University Press of Virginia, 1988), 16.

16. William James, *The Varieties of Religious Experience* (New York: Mentor Books, 1958), 42. James places the words I have quoted in italics.

17. In addition to the work of Lash cited in note 15, see the various books of John E. Smith, notably *Experience and God* (New York: Oxford University Press, 1968); also Wayne Proudfoot, *Religious Experience* (Berkeley, Cal.: University of California Press, 1985). I have briefly indicated some possible weaknesses of Jamesian radical empiricism in *Models of Revelation* (Garden City, N.Y.: Doubleday, 1983), 78–83.

18. These ideas, repeated in many of Rahner's essays, are well expressed in his "Experience of the Spirit and Existential Commitment," *Theological Investigations*, vol. 16 (New York: Seabury/Crossroad, 1979), 24–34, esp. 27–29. Rahner here allows for the possibility of mystical experiences in which "the grace of the Spirit is really grasped without the mediation of any categorial, a posteriori object coming from without" (28). This exception becomes bothersome in the light of Rahner's doctrine, expressed in some of his later interviews, that "the Christian of the future will be a mystic or will not exist" and that the individual must enjoy "an immediate, personal experience of God," *Karl Rahner in Dialogue: Conversations and Interviews, 1965–1982*, ed. Paul Imhof and Hubert Biallowons (New York: Crossroad, 1986). Is the by-passing of the categorial here becoming the rule?

19. Karl Rahner, "Faith. 1. Way to Faith," in *Encyclopedia of Theology* (New York: Seabury/Crossroad, 1975), 496–500, at 498.

20. Ian G. Barbour, *Myths, Models and Paradigms* (New York: Harper & Row, 1974), 53–56.

21. Clement of Alexandria, *Stromata*, V.1.3, quoted by Hans Urs von Balthasar, *The Glory of the Lord*, vol. 1, *Seeing the Form* (San Francisco: Ignatius, 1982), 138.

22.  Von Balthasar, *The Glory of the Lord,* 1:131–41, especially 133.

23.  Jean Mouroux, *The Christian Experience: An Introduction to a Theology* (New York: Sheed & Ward, 1954), 15. See the fuller discussion, 15–24 and 331–34.

24.  Gregory Baum, "A Modern Apologetics," in his *Faith and Doctrine: A Contemporary View* (New York: Newman, 1969), 51–90, at 60.

25.  Ibid., 89.

26.  John of the Cross, *The Ascent of Mount Carmel,* Book II, chap. 27, no. 4; in *Collected Works,* p. 201. On this theme see also Robert Sokolowski, "Christian Experience," chapter 11 of his *The God of Faith and Reason* (Notre Dame, Ind.: University of Notre Dame Press, 1982), 133–43.

# 11

## Properties of Faith

Theologians, in accordance with their own systematic orientations, list the properties of faith in slightly different ways. In Catholic theology there is a broad consensus that faith, in addition to its reasonableness, has the following four qualities: it is supernatural; it is free; it is certain; and it is obscure.[1]

### Supernaturality

Although the Bible does not explicitly make the natural/supernatural distinction, Christian theologians, confessions, and councils frequently find the supernatural origin of faith implied in a host of biblical texts; for example, Matthew 16:17 ("Flesh and blood has not revealed this to you . . ."); John 6:44 ("No one can come to me unless the Father who sent me draw him"); John 15:57 ("Without me you can do nothing"); Acts 16:14 ("The Lord opened her heart . . ."); 2 Corinthians 3:5 ("Not that of ourselves we are qualified to take credit for anything as coming from us; our qualification comes from God"); and Ephesians 2:8 ("By grace you have been saved through faith; and this is not your own doing, it is the gift of God").

Christians of the mainline churches have always agreed that faith is a gift of God over and above the gift of being human. In calling faith supernatural they do not mean simply that the revelation to which it responds discloses things that lie beyond the investigative powers of human reason. The virtue of faith is supernatural, more proximately, because the response itself is a gift from God. The act of faith is impossible unless the mind and heart of the believer are interiorly moved by divine grace.

The Second Council of Orange, following Augustine's anti-Pelagian treatises, insisted that faith cannot be achieved by unaided human effort but that it depends on the free and merciful assistance of God. In reply to the "Semi-Pelagian" theologians of Marseilles who held that the beginnings of faith were human achievements and that the increase and consummation are from God, this sixth-century council taught that "not only the increase but the very beginning of faith *(initium fidei)* and the will to believe *(credulitatis affectum)*" come not from our natural powers but from "the gift of grace, that is, the inspiration of the Holy Spirit" (canon 5, DS 375; cf. canon 7, DS 377).

The Council of Trent declared that the prevenient grace of the Holy Spirit is needed for anyone to believe "as is required so that the grace of justification may be bestowed upon one" (Session 6, canon 3, DS 1553). An essential disposition for justification, said the Council, is a free assent "aroused and assisted by divine grace" whereby a person "believes as true that which has been divinely promised and revealed" (ibid., chap. 6, DS 1526). Vatican I, as we have seen, described faith as a "supernatural virtue" *(Dei Filius,* chap. 3, DS 3008). Following Orange II, it affirmed the impossibility of making a salutary act of faith without the illumination and inspiration of the Holy Spirit (chap. 3, DS 3010), and taught that grace was necessary even for an assent of faith not vivified by charity (canon 5 on faith, DS 3035).

Vatican II, with an explicit quotation from Orange II, likewise taught that the act of faith presupposes grace: "For this faith to be accorded, we have need of the prevenient and concomitant grace of God and of the interior helps of the Holy Spirit, who moves the heart and turns it toward God, and gives 'joy and ease *(suavitatem)* to all in consenting to the truth and believing it'" (DV 5, quoting DS 377). The help of the Holy Spirit has traditionally, since Orange II, been characterized in terms of enlightenment and inspiration.

On the supernatural or gratuitous quality of faith there is no real disagreement between Catholics and Protestants. Like their Catholic counterparts, the sixteenth-century Reformers were strongly influenced by the later writings of Augustine, which were quoted or paraphrased by Orange II. In his "Small Catechism," when he takes up the article on sanctification, Martin Luther writes: "I believe that by my own reason or strength I cannot believe in Jesus Christ, my Lord, or come to him. But the Holy Spirit has called me through the Gospel, enlightened me with his gifts, and sanctified and preserved me in true faith. . . ."[2] John Calvin insisted that for the human mind to assent to God's word as true it must be illuminated by the Holy Spirit, and that for the human heart to place full confidence in God's promises, it too must be strengthened and supported by the power of the same Spirit. The Holy Spirit, therefore, is the author and cause of faith *(Institutes,* Bk. III, chap. 2, no. 33).

Theologians of different traditions give different answers to the question why faith must be supernatural. Protestants have tended to emphasize the effects of original sin, which shackle the human spirit in evil so that it cannot rise to the divine unless God cleanses and liberates it. Catholics, without denying the need for remedial grace, tend to put the accent on elevating grace. Even if there had been no Fall, they hold, faith would still be a free gift of God because created nature does not have by itself the capacity to enter into union with God. Faith, as an acceptance of revelation, is an entrance into the horizons of God's own knowledge and an initiation into the divine life.

Thomas Aquinas at one point defines faith as "the habit of mind whereby eternal life begins in us, causing the mind to assent to things that do not appear" *(S. Th.,* 2-2.4.1). Later he explains that "since in assenting to matters of faith a person is raised above his own nature, it is necessary the assent arise from a supernatural

principle moving the person inwardly; and this principle is God" (*S. Th.,* 2-2.6.1).
Once faith is understood as a foretaste of the beatific vision it follows evidently that
it cannot be other than supernatural. Only God can impart, when he chooses, a
share in his own divine life, which lies beyond the capacities and merits of any creature. In opposition to the Semi-Pelagians, St. Thomas holds that the first grace cannot be merited. We are justified by faith, not in the sense that our own activity in
believing merits justification, but in the sense that the movement of faith, produced
in us by grace, is a principle of justification (*S. Th.,* 1-2.114.5).

As will be recalled from the historical survey, Catholic theologians differ
among themselves about whether faith has a supernatural formal object. Although
all agree that faith is supernatural in the sense that it comes as a grace, and that its
formal object is the authority of God who reveals, some deny that the formal object
has to be grasped in a supernatural manner. Many theologians, including Luis
Molina, Juan de Lugo, Juan de Ripalda, and Louis Billot, hold that the believer
submits to the authority of God simply because he is God, and not because he is
author of the supernatural order. According to their view the motive need not be
supernatural. The act of faith is supernatural not because of its motive but because
God by his grace elevates the act. This elevation is "merely entitative" and leaves
the intentionality of the act unchanged.

Francisco Suarez and the Thomists, reasoning from the metaphysical principle
that acts are specified by their formal objects, affirm that faith, as an essentially
supernatural act, must have a supernatural formal object. It has a different modality
from any natural act, for the believer assents to God as he graciously bestows himself, thanks to the inner invitation and illumination of the Holy Spirit. A purely
entitative elevation, according to this school, does not suffice. If grace did not affect
faith in its quality as a conscious act, a person without grace could believe with the
same kind and degree of conviction as one assisted by grace. What, then, would the
assistance do? An entitative elevation that had no assignable effect on the quality
of the act would seem to be vacuous or even unreal. In recent Catholic theology the
Thomist position appears to be gaining ground; the Molinist view is rarely
defended.

As has been seen in Chapter 10, there is a broad agreement, even among theologians who hold for a supernatural formal object, that the presence and operations
of grace cannot be distinctly perceived by mere introspection, except possibly in
certain rare mystical states. In affirming that a given act of faith is supernatural,
therefore, we are making an inference from the experience of the life of faith as
interpreted with the help of Scripture and Tradition, including the teaching of the
magisterium. Thanks to these authoritative guides, we can confidently affirm that
divine grace, raising the mind of the believer to a certain connaturality with the
things of God, makes it possible to "consent to the truth" with "joy and ease"
(Orange II, canon 7, DS 377).

## Freedom

The freedom of faith is not directly treated in Scripture, but it seems to be implied.
In his lament over Jerusalem Jesus protests that he had tried to gather the people

to himself but that they were unwilling (Mt 23:37). In this passage and elsewhere Jesus seems to ascribe the rejection he encounters to the lack of good will on the part of the hearers. More generally, Scripture describes the refusal to believe as culpable and punishable (1 Jn 3:23; Mk 16:16). God, being just, would not blame and punish people for faults they could not avoid.

The question of the freedom of faith became an issue at the time of the Reformation. Reacting against certain quasi-Pelagian tendencies in late Scholasticism, the Lutherans taught that human freedom, insofar as it could enable one to turn to God, was extinguished by the Fall. In his *The Bondage of the Will* Luther vehemently censured Erasmus for having insisted on free will. According to Luther the human will is like a beast of burden placed between two riders. "If God rides it, it wills and goes where God wills. . . . If Satan rides it, it wills and goes where Satan wills; nor can it choose to run to either of the two riders or to seek him out."[3] Salutary faith and justification, for Luther, depend entirely on God's choice and not at all on our own autonomous decision.

Philipp Melanchthon in the *Augsburg Confession* (art. 18) and in the *Apology for the Augsburg Confession* (art. 18), maintained that civil righteousness lay to some extent within the power of our free will, but that spiritual righteousness could only be the effect of grace. The Formula of Concord, summarizing the Lutheran position, declares: "The Holy Scriptures ascribe conversion, faith in Christ, regeneration, renewal, and everything that belongs to its real beginning and completion in no way to the human powers of the natural free will, be it entirely or one-half or the least and tiniest part, but altogether and alone to the divine operation and the Holy Spirit."[4]

John Calvin, as we have seen, restricts faith to the elect (*Institutes*, Bk. III, chap. 2, no. 12). In their case, he asserts, "faith is something merely passive, bringing nothing of ours to the recovering of God's favor but receiving from Christ that which we lack" (ibid., Bk. III, chap. 13, no. 5). He does not seem to look upon the reception of God's word as a human act, but rather as something that the Holy Spirit brings about in a purely passive recipient.

In answer to what were understood as Protestant denials of the role of free will, the Council of Trent affirmed that, while faith is impossible without supernatural assistance, grace does not bring about the saving act of faith without the free consent of those who receive it. Thus human freedom, although weakened by the Fall, is not extinguished (Session 6, chap. 1, DS 1521). It remains in sufficient measure for the adult believer to submit willingly to the grace-given inclination to believe the truth of God's promises in Christ (chaps. 5 and 6, DS 1525–26). Although the grace of God is necessary for any salutary act of faith (canon 3, DS 1553), it is unacceptable to assert "that a person's free will, when moved and aroused by God, gives no cooperation by responding to God's summons and invitation . . . and that it cannot, if it so wishes, dissent but, like something inanimate, can do nothing at all and remains purely passive" (canon 4, DS 1554). According to the Council, therefore, the will in coming to faith is indeed moved by God, but God does not move it coercively, as irrational creatures are moved, but freely, in such a way that it makes its own contribution. The Council did not attempt to solve the theoretical questions that can arise in harmonizing the sovereign efficacy of God's grace with the human capacity to refuse it. These questions are aspects of the more general problem of the relationship between grace and free will, much debated ever since the time of Augustine.

Vatican I repeated the doctrine of Trent that faith is a free submission of the self to God's grace, which is not irresistible (*Dei Filius*, chap. 3, DS 3010). But this council also had to deal with new questions that had arisen in Catholic theology. While making allowance for freedom in the response to grace, Georg Hermes and Alois von Schmid maintained (or were understood to maintain) that the truth of faith can be rigorously demonstrated, especially to the practical reason, in such a way that the intellect, perceiving the force of the evidence, could not withhold the assent of faith *(Vernunftglaube)*. The freedom of faith, for them, would come in at a second stage, in which the believer would make a trustful and loving self-commitment to God *(Herzensglaube)*. In opposition to this and similar theories, Vatican I reaffirmed the freedom of faith as an intellectual assent. It asserted, against Hermes, that the human person, even after appreciating the rational force of the arguments in favor of Christianity, remains free either to assent or not (ibid., canon 5 on faith, DS 3035). Thus faith, whether as assent or self-commitment, is uncoerced. Although the evidence of credibility can prepare the way for the decision of faith, the decision itself is a truly free and personal response to a call that comes from on high.

The freedom of the act of faith was a major theme of Vatican II. The Constitution on Divine Revelation attributes freedom to faith in its two aspects as submission and assent. It describes faith as "an obedience by which one entrusts one's whole self freely *(libere)* to God, . . . willingly *(voluntarie)* assenting to the truth revealed by him" (DV 5). The Declaration on Religious Freedom treats the freedom of faith in the context of the innate dynamism of the human person to seek and appropriate truth in a responsible manner. The dignity of the human person, as well as the nature of faith itself, demand that coercive methods should not be used to secure adherence to religious truth (DH 10). The Decree on the Church's Missionary Activity reaffirms the same principle: "The Church strictly forbids forcing people to embrace the faith, or attracting or enticing them to do so by unworthy techniques. By the same token it strongly insists on everyone's right not to be deterred from the faith by unjust harrassment" (AG 13).

The Council's conception of freedom is concisely set forth in the Pastoral Constitution on the Church in the Modern World:

> It is only in freedom, however, that human beings can turn to what is good, and our contemporaries are right in highly praising and assiduously pursuing such freedom, although often they do so in wrong ways as if it gave a license to do anything one pleases, even evil. Genuine freedom is an oustanding sign of the divine image in human beings. For God has willed to leave man 'in the hand of his own counsel' (Sir 15:14), so that he can seek his creator spontaneously and freely arrive at full and blessed perfection by adhering to God. Hence human dignity demands that the individual act according to a knowing and free choice, as motivated and prompted personally from within, and not through blind internal impulse or merely external pressure. (GS 17)

The Pastoral Constitution goes on to explain that human freedom has been damaged by sin, so that only with the help of divine grace can one fully realize one's innate orientation toward the divine (ibid.).

The Declaration on Religious Freedom guards against the danger of interpreting the freedom of faith as though it meant that faith had to be achieved by autonomous individuals isolated from all religious influences. Faith, as a response to revelation, presupposes that revelation has been presented by credible witnesses. The principle of religious freedom, therefore, cannot be used to exclude the kind of committed testimony that is involved in evangelization and religious education. The Declaration consequently insists on the freedom of the family, private associations, and schools to transmit religious convictions and on the freedom of the Church to proclaim the gospel and teach sacred doctrine with authority (DH 13–14). Religious testimony that invites a free response should not be confused with proselytization in the pejorative sense, which consists in winning converts by false and misleading statements or by appealing to unworthy motives.[5]

From what has been said it follows that there are degrees of freedom in faith. Some measure of psychological or sociological pressure is commonly present, especially in the initial stages of faith. People are likely to believe, in part, because they fear to challenge the dominant outlook of their social group, because they feel constrained by the human authority of parents and teachers, because they superstitiously expect temporal favors, or for other human and imperfect motives. Only gradually, with the assistance of grace, do they arrive at a fully free faith in which God is the sole motive. Made free by the truth itself, believers come to share in "the glorious liberty of the children of God" (Rom 8:20).

The physical freedom of people to disbelieve should not be confused with moral freedom. The act of faith is not purely optional. Vatican II, in its Declaration on Religious Freedom, emphasized this point. "All people are bound [by a moral obligation] to seek the truth, especially about God and the Church, and when they have found it, they are bound to embrace and keep it" (DH 1).

## Certitude and Doubt

From a purely philosophical point of view the certitude of faith might seem contestable. The evidence for Christian revelation is not stringent and, according to many competent authorities, does not suffice to exclude all risk of error. Is it not unreasonable, then, to call for a firm assent to the doctrines of faith?

Some philosophers deny that certitude ought to be required. Richard Swinburne, for instance, points out that in common speech one may be said to believe things that are merely probable—more probable than their contradictories.[6] The Church, in his opinion, has never clarified publicly the kind of belief involved in faith (124, 164). It would be excessive, he holds, to demand belief that each and every article of the creed is more probable than its contradictory. It suffices that the Christian be prepared "to act on the assumption that there is a God who has certain properties and has done certain things and provided certain means of salvation" (166–67). This pragmatic stance does not require belief in the usual sense of the word. "A man may put his trust in something which, on balance, he does not believe to exist" (167).

This philosophical position, however appealing it might sound, runs counter to Scripture and Christian Tradition. In Romans 4:20–21 Paul holds up as a model for Christians the faith of Abraham, who did not waver but was fully convinced that God would be able to do what he had promised. Writing to Christians whose property had been plundered, the author of Hebrews attributes their patience to their knowledge that they "had a better possession and an abiding one" (Heb 10:34). It is not enough to act "as if" one believed, "for whoever would draw near to God must believe that he exists and that he rewards those who seek him" (Heb 11:6). In Hebrews 11:1 the terms "assurance" and "evidence" (*hypostasis* and *elenchos*) are applied to faith, and in 1 John 5:9 the assertion "God's testimony is greater" implies that divine faith, unlike human faith, rests on an absolutely solid foundation.

Theologians of different Christian traditions have agreed that faith is an assured belief. On this point there was no dispute between Protestants and Catholics at the time of the Reformation. Luther and Calvin built the element of certitude into their very definitions of faith. Luther called it "a living, daring confidence in God's grace, so sure and certain that the believer would stake his life on it a thousand times."[7] Calvin defined faith as "a firm and certain knowledge of God's benevolence toward us, founded upon the truth of the freely given promise in Christ, both revealed to our minds and sealed upon our hearts through the Holy Spirit" (*Institutes*, Bk. III, chap. 2, no. 7).

Catholic authoritative teaching is no less insistent on firmness of conviction. Vatican I makes the rather obvious point that what God has revealed must be true, inasmuch as God "can neither be deceived nor deceive" (*Dei Filius*, chap. 3, DS 3008). Faith, to the extent that it accepts God's revelation, must therefore be objectively certain. The subjective certitude (i.e., the firmness of the believer's internal assent) is more difficult to establish, but authoritative teaching on this subject can be found.

Positively, one may argue from the Church's professions of faith. In creeds such as the *Quicumque* (art. 42; DS 76), the profession of Faith of Lateran IV against the Albigensians and Cathari (DS 800), the Bull of Union with the Copts and Ethiopians promulgated by the Council of Florence (DS 1330, 1333), the Tridentine profession of faith (DS 1862), and the Oath against Modernism (DS 3537), the Church has asserted that its own faith is altogether certain and has required the faithful to confess that they "firmly believe" the articles of faith. Negatively, the magisterium rejects the idea that mere probability, let alone merely hypothetical assent, suffices. One of the propositions condemned by the Holy Office under Innocent XI in 1679 was to the effect that faith was compatible "with merely probable knowledge of revelation, and even with the fear that God had not spoken" (Prop. 21, DS 2121).

Theologians, reasoning from the fact that the assent of faith is prompted in us by divine grace (the supernaturality treated above) and that the formal object of faith is the authority of God the Revealer, commonly assert that faith is "most firm" and even "an assent firmer than all others" *(assensus super omnia firmus)*.[8] But, as we shall see, they often qualify assertions of this kind.

In the patristic period Tertullian and Clement of Alexandria celebrated the firmness of faith, as did Basil and Gregory Nazianzen. Pseudo-Dionysius and Maximus the Confessor attributed the singular assurance of faith not to its theoretical grounds but to the union between the human spirit and the divine. Medieval theologians, following Augustine, made much of the affective component in faith. Bonaventure, consequently, was able to say that while faith ranks below scientific knowledge in speculative certitude, it surpasses science in practical certitude or firmness of adherence.

Thomas Aquinas reflected on the certitude of faith in comparison with the certitude of wisdom *(sapientia)*, scientific knowledge *(scientia)*, and understanding *(intellectus)*. In this connection he distinguished between objective and subjective certainty:

> Certainty can be considered in either of two ways. In one way, from the cause of certainty, and in this way that which has a more certain cause is said to be more certain. And in this way faith is more certain than the other three [intellectual virtues], for faith rests on the divine truth, while the three others mentioned rely on human reason. In the other way certainty may be considered from the point of view of the subject, and then that which more fully satisfies the human intellect is held to be more certain. And in this way, because the things of faith are above the human intellect, whereas the objects of the other intellectual virtues are not, faith is in that respect less certain. But because anything is judged simply speaking according to its cause, and in a qualified sense [*secundum quid*] according to the disposition of the subject, therefore faith is simply speaking more certain, but the others are in a qualified sense more certain, i.e., with regard to us. (*S. Th.,* 2-2.4.8c)

Without questioning St. Thomas's conclusion, one may observe that in our day people asking about the certitude of faith are generally interested in the subjective aspect. St. Thomas may be read as supporting the view that from the point of view of the believer faith is less than absolutely certain.

In other texts St. Thomas gives a further explanation of this qualified certitude. Accepting Augustine's definition of faith as "to consider with assent" *(cum assentione cogitare)*, he points out that the definition contains two components that point in different directions (*S. Th.,* 2-2.2.1). The first component, assent *(assentio)*, means firm intellectual adherence to a determinate position, as distinct from mere opinion, which is a tentative or inconclusive adherence, with fear of the opposite. Faith resembles scientific knowledge insofar as it is firm. But the ground of the certitude is not the same as in scientific knowledge, for in the case of faith the mind does not have conclusive evidence that eliminates the possibility of the opposite. A further difference between faith and scientific knowledge comes from the obscurity of faith's content. The mind does not clearly apprehend what it is assenting to.

It may seem problematic that in faith the mind adheres firmly in spite of the lack of stringent evidence. Ultimately Thomas Aquinas and his disciples account for this apparent anomaly in terms of grace attracting the will and illuminating the practical judgment to the effect that a given individual (more precisely, I myself) should here and now believe. On this ground they can respond to the dilemma: If the evidence of credibility were not strong enough to preclude doubt, a firm assent could not be reasonable; but if it did preclude doubt, the assent would be necessary rather than free.

The idea of free certitude, although initially puzzling, has real plausibility. In merely human affairs we often hesitate to assent where the rational grounds, though not weak, are complex, especially where the authority of witnesses is involved. If the testimony does not please us, we easily find excuses for not believing. The influx of the will may be needed to overcome our undue reluctance. In the supernatural assent of faith, the will, freely submitting to the attraction of grace, gives special force to the assent following upon practical judgment to believe.

The second component in Augustine's definition, *cogitare*, is connected, according to St. Thomas, with the nonevidential character of the assent, a property that faith shares with mere opinion. *Cogitare* is difficult to translate into English, because the obvious word "think" does not convey the point that Aquinas is here making. "Doubt," on the other hand, would be misleading because it would suggest the lack of certitude. A better translation, in my estimation, is "consider."[9] Josef Pieper has made a careful study of the matter:

> What is meant is searching investigation, probing consideration, conferring with oneself before deciding, being on the track of, a mental reaching out for something not yet finally found. All of these processes, taken together, may be subsumed within the term "mental unrest."[10]

This "mental unrest" is not doubt in the usual sense, but it includes a consciousness of the courage needed to make the commitment of faith. Even though one may see good and sufficient reasons for being a believer, the assent does not follow automatically from the evidential grounds. Often enough the grounds are highly personal and cannot be clearly explained to oneself, let alone to others. By its very nature faith is subject to challenge. The intellectual difficulties make it apparent that faith is a free submission to the attractions of grace. We believe things that we cannot really understand and do so, to some extent, in spite of appearances to the contrary. We can at any time envision how, having freely come to faith, we could freely cease to believe. In other words, we can see that faith is faith.

John Henry Newman clearly affirmed the certitude of faith, but he did so in terms that reveal his awareness of the complexities. In his Oxford University Sermons he called faith "a reaching forth after truth amid darkness," but added that the search issues in "the absolute acceptance of a certain message or doctrine as divine." It "starts from probabilities, but it ends in peremptory statements, if so be, mysterious, or at least beyond experience. It believes an informant amid doubt, yet it accepts his information without doubt."[11] In his *Apologia* he recognized that the believer may be perplexed by innumerable difficulties, but that "ten thousand difficulties do not make one doubt. . . . Difficulty and doubt are incommensurate."[12]

In his reflections on faith and doubt, Paul Tillich asserts that every act of faith calls for daring and courage, and includes, in principle, the possibility of failure. "The risk to faith in one's ultimate concern is indeed the greatest risk man can run."[13] Again he writes: "There is no faith without an intrinsic 'in spite of' and the courageous affirmation of oneself in the state of ultimate concern."[14] This consciousness of risk, Tillich holds, is not the same thing as skeptical doubt, which would prevent the full personal commitment of faith, or methodological doubt, which would put the commitment in brackets. But it can be called doubt, Tillich holds, in a certain sense, which he calls "existential doubt." By this he means an acceptance of the insecurity inseparable from faith.

The assent of faith, then, can coexist with a realization that faith is a risk and that it hovers over an abyss of nonevidence. In some cases this realization can cause a kind of dizziness and anxiety. Some Catholic authors, going beyond Aquinas and Newman, vividly describe the kind of questioning or doubt that can arise within faith. Ida Görres, for example, depicts a kind of "blinded faith" which she regards as not uncommon in recent decades:

> Authentic unbelief is proud of itself and is irritated by or laughs at the spectacle of the simple believer; it confirms in their doubt those who weaken; it ridicules those who bear or represent the Church, and rejoices in their imperfections and mistakes.

> That manner of unbelief which I would prefer to call blinded faith, or blindfolded faith, behaves quite differently. It continues walking at the modest pace of the ordinary Christian. It does not show its distress. How many among us lead this life? There are priests grappling with the intimate obscurities which devour them; nuns for whom, in the secret of their souls, everything seems to have lost all meaning; the parish assistant who with fearless courage maintains and fortifies in the faith those who are entrusted to his care. There are lay people who get accustomed to the idea of being in a rabbit-hutch, for whom the liturgy has become a scandal, who at Mass only notice the priest's routine, his mediocre sermon, and the pretensions of the choir, but who nevertheless not only never miss Mass, but what is more, as often as they can, give it their time, their sleep, and their strength. In this way they unfailingly bring others to the faith, strengthening them in it, teaching them to pray, to be steadfast for the good; forgiving injuries, combating their own faults with all their strength, they act as models of goodness, patience, self-control and generosity to others. God shines through them. But they themselves do not see this. God strengthens them without comforting them. Those around them see more clearly than they do. "When she has left, there still remains a bright spot where she was sitting," writes the friend of a woman who thought herself to be an abyss of darkness.[15]

Johann Baptist Metz, in a similar vein, writes of a dialectical coexistence between belief and unbelief, such that the same person may be *simul fidelis et infidelis*. "Our discussion of unbelief in the believer . . . is not, as some think, dangerous mysticism or intellectual toying with unbelief. Rather does it lay bare the questionableness of our existence in faith at any time, and it teaches us to repeat, not in mere imitation or false pretense, the biblical words: 'I do believe; help my unbelief' (Mk 9:23)."[16]

These testimonies, describing the experience of certain highly introspective believers, find echoes in the experience of others who may at one time or another pass through a crisis of faith. But it should not be thought that believers are normally in a state of anxiety and stress. Many of the faithful rest peacefully in their commitment, assisted by the Holy Spirit who "gives joy and ease in consenting to the truth." Even when temptations and struggles are felt, they cannot derogate from the firmness of faith itself. Faith must be a firm assent, or it is not really faith.

It should be added, however, that a person who makes a firm and serene commitment of faith may have real questions about whether a given proposition is to be held as a matter of faith. Only a very few propositions can be singled out as having the kind of certification that calls for firm assent. While giving certitude about some matters, faith leaves the believer free to question whatever is not clearly contained in God's word or necessarily bound up with that word.

Catholics are required in principle to affirm with certitude the articles of the creed, the defined dogmas of the Church, and doctrines constantly and universally taught in the Church as matters of divine and Catholic faith. But they are not bound to accept, under pain of infidelity, everything taught by the magisterium. Most of the doctrines of the Church are taught noninfallibly and are, as the phrase goes, reformable. About these "nondefinitive" teachings, the Catholic is entitled, for adequate reasons, to have doubts. Such doubts are not sins against faith, but are held within faith, since the doctrines in question do not clearly belong to God's revelation in Christ.[17]

## Obscurity

The obscurity of faith is closely connected with its freedom and affects the mode of its certitude. This obscurity can be understood in either of two ways. In the first place, faith is obscure if the truth of the content is neither immediately evident nor capable of being stringently demonstrated by intrinsic arguments. Second, it is obscure if its object or content, even when grasped, exceeds the comprehensive powers of the human mind. Christian faith is obscure in both senses. The believer accepts, on the authority of God the revealer, truths that cannot be immediately perceived or stringently demonstrated on the basis of what is immediately evident. Furthermore, the content of faith includes strict mysteries, such as the Trinity, the Incarnation, the real presence of Christ in the sacraments, and the elevation of the human spirit through divine grace. Truths such as these remain obscure because they are beyond the normal range of human cognitive powers. Of these mysteries we can speak only haltingly, since we lack comprehensive knowledge of the subject matter and have to rely on inadequate analogies from ordinary experience. It is not surprising, therefore, that we cannot fully understand how it is possible for one and the same God to exist as three divine persons, or how Jesus Christ can be fully God and at the same time fully a man. These and other contents of revelation offer endless food for reflection but can never be mastered by human thought.

The Bible has many passages that refer to the mysteriousness of God. A classic text is the scene in Exodus in which Moses asks the Lord, "I pray thee, show me thy glory" (Ex 33:18). God replies that no one can see him and live, but he allows Moses to watch from a cave as the glory of the Lord passes by, and to gaze on the back of the Lord as he departs. Isaiah and other prophets, in their inaugural visions, encounter God as one who is ineffably holy (Is 6:1–5; cf. Jer 1:4–10 and Ezek 1:1–28). When Job is puzzled by the dealings of Providence, God from the whirlwind instructs him regarding the need to submit blindly in faith (Job, chaps. 38–41). The allusions to the constellations and the strange beasts in these chapters magnificently convey what Rudolf Otto calls "the wholly incomprehensible character of the eternal creative power" which "can yet stir the mind to its depths, fascinate and overbrim the heart."[18]

In the New Testament Paul declares that while we are away from the Lord we walk by faith, not by sight (2 Cor 5:6–7). In this life, he says, we see through a mirror dimly, whereas we hope to see God face to face in eternity (1 Cor 13:12). The famous text that faith is "the evidence (conviction, *elenchos*) of things unseen" (Heb 11:1) is usually interpreted as meaning that faith, insofar as it gives conviction, takes the place of evidence, which is lacking.[19] The mysterious character of revelation is emphasized in the early chapters of First Corinthians. Paul claims to impart "a secret and hidden wisdom of God" (1 Cor 2:7). It is secret not simply because it was unknown before God revealed it but because, even after revelation, it cannot be received except by those who possess the Holy Spirit, "for no one comprehends the thoughts of God except the Spirit of God" (1 Cor 2:11).

In patristic times the mysteriousness of Christian revelation and the obscurity of faith were thematically taught by Gregory of Nyssa and John Chrysostom against the Eunomians. In the Middle Ages Bernard and the monastic theologians asserted these points against some of the early Scholastics, such as Abelard. In a letter of admonition to the theology faculty of the University of Paris (1228), Pope Gregory IX quoted from his predecessor, Gregory the Great, the aphorism, "Faith has no merit if it rests on the experience of human reason."[20]

The mysterious character of the divine was deeply appreciated by Luther, who maintained that theology must contemplate God through suffering and the cross, symbolized by God's "back side" in the incident from Exodus. Faith, he said, must endure being constantly contradicted by reason and experience; it finds God hidden under the forms of weakness and helplessness.[21] Criticizing the skepticism of Erasmus, Luther, in the early sections of *The Bondage of the Will*, concedes that there are many things hidden in God that surpass our knowledge; he concedes also that there are many passages in Scripture that we, in our ignorance, find hard to understand, but he asserts that the great mysteries of revelation, such as the Trinity and the Incarnation, are brought to light in the Scriptures and are no longer hidden away. Christians have clarity in believing that things *are* so, even though Scripture does not tell us *how* they are so, a point we do not need to know. The gospel itself, Luther claims, is plainly disclosed. From Paul he quotes, "Even if our gospel be veiled, it is veiled only to those who are perishing. In their case the god of this world has blinded the minds of unbelievers" (2 Cor 3:15).[22]

In other places Luther asserts that "we must believe even those things that are hidden."[23] By this he seems to mean that we cannot explain how it is possible for things to be as faith says that they are. Luther, therefore, does not deny that faith involves an element of obscurity. The question of clarity and obscurity did not become an issue between Catholics and Protestants in the Reformation.

In modern times theologians affected by Deism sought to minimize or eliminate the mysterious elements in Christianity, leaving only what coincided with the clear concepts of natural religion. Rationalists attributed the obscurity of faith to the deficiency of symbolic, as contrasted with rational, thought. Some Hegelians believed that the Christian doctrines, though obscure in their present form, were capable of being translated into clear philosophical concepts. Several nineteenth-century Catholic theologians (Georg Hermes, Anton Günther, Jakob Frohschammer) were characterized as semi-rationalists because, while conceding that the mysteries of Christian faith could not become known except through faith, they maintained that believers, reflecting on the truths of faith in the light of reason, could come to see their intrinsic intelligibility, so that faith could yield to rational understanding.

Semi-rationalism was rejected by several documents in the reign of Pius IX, and again, more definitively, by Vatican I. According to Vatican I "divine mysteries by their very nature so exceed the created intellect that, even after they have been communicated and received in faith, they remain covered by the veil of faith itself and shrouded as it were in darkness, as long as in this mortal life 'we are away from the Lord; for we walk by faith, not by sight'" (*Dei Filius*, chap. 4, DS 3016; quoting 2 Cor 5:6–7).

It is debated among Catholic theologians whether faith and evidential knowledge are mutually exclusive. As we have seen, Paul several times contrasts the faith-knowledge that we have in the present life with the vision to which we look forward. On the other hand, Paul also speaks of faith as "abiding" (1 Cor 13:13), even though what is imperfect will have passed away (13:10). Thus Hans Urs von Balthasar and others, inspired by the Alexandrian doctrine of *gnosis*, argue that in heaven we shall believe what we see, and see what we believe.[24] Even on earth, it can be held, we are in some fashion able to see, thanks to faith, the content of what we believe, for, as Augustine said, faith sees with the eyes of love. This "seeing" of what we believe is of course dependent on the free and supernatural stance of faith, and thus differs from the kind of seeing that simply acknowledges what imposes itself on the mind.

The conflict of opinions on this point is perhaps more apparent than real. When Thomas Aquinas and his followers insist that faith is an assent to things unseen, they understand "seeing" as a form of cognition that is coerced by the sensory or intellectual evidence, once this evidence is attentively considered. Faith, they hold, cannot be evident since it is a free commitment in which stringent evidence is lacking. But St. Thomas does not deny that the "light" of faith discloses more than we could naturally apprehend. At one point he writes, "The light of faith causes us to see the things that are believed."[25] He also maintains that living faith brings with it the spiritual gifts of understanding and wisdom, thanks to which one can intellectually penetrate the meaning of what one believes.

## Conclusion

In Chapter 10 one property of faith, its reasonableness, was examined. The assent was seen to be *reasonable* because there are sufficient signs to convince the intelligent inquirer that it would be prudent to believe. Once these signs are apprehended by the added light of grace, which intensifies the desire and expectation that a redemptive revelation will be given, the full commitment of faith may be warranted.

In the present chapter it has been seen that faith has four additional properties. It is supernatural, free, certain, and obscure.

Faith is *supernatural* in the sense that the act and virtue of faith cannot be acquired by merely human effort, but must be received as an unmerited gift of God.

This is true not only of a developed and mature faith, but even of the beginning of faith.

The act of faith is *free* because it follows upon a conscious choice prompted from within. Imperfect acts of faith, while enjoying a measure of freedom, may be determined in part by psychological and sociological pressures. Faith attains its full freedom as it divests itself of unworthy fears and attachments and spontaneously cleaves to God as the supreme font of all truth and goodness.

Faith is *certain* in the objective sense because its content is from God, who can neither be deceived nor deceive. It is subjectively certain because the signs of credibility are synthesized under the light of a divinely given inclination to believe. Even though the assent is subjectively certain, the lack of cogent evidence leaves room for a certain mental dissatisfaction or unrest within faith.

Faith is *obscure* because its content is neither immediately evident nor strictly demonstrable, and also because it adheres to mysteries that exceed the comprehensive powers of the human mind.

These five attributes of faith must be taken in unison, since they intrinsically qualify one another. Those who accept the supernaturality and obscurity but deny the freedom and reasonableness of faith misunderstand its certainty and fall into a one-sided fideism or supernaturalism. Those who opt for freedom and rationality without supernaturality and obscurity are prone to a type of Pelagianism that reduces faith to the level of natural knowledge. The certainty of faith must be understood as both supernatural and free, as both reasonable and obscure.

In short, no one of the properties of faith can be properly interpreted in isolation from the other four. A balanced appreciation of all five is necessary if the epistemological uniqueness of faith is to be maintained.

# Notes

1. In his treatise "De fide," Iosephus A. de Aldama establishes that faith is obscure yet certain (thesis 6), free (thesis 7), and supernatural (thesis 8). For the reasonableness of faith he refers to the treatise on fundamental theology. See *Sacrae theologiae summa*, vol. 3, 3d ed. (Madrid: Biblioteca de Autores Cristianos, 1956), 749–80.

2. Martin Luther, "Small Catechism. III, The Third Article," in *The Book of Concord*, ed. and trans. Theodore G. Tappert (Philadelphia: Fortress, 1959), 345.

3. Idem, *Bondage of the Will*, LW 33:65–66.

4. "Solid Declaration," 2:25, *Book of Concord*, 526.

5. For a description of "proselytism" in the pejorative sense, see the statement adopted by the Central Committee of the World Council of Churches on "Christian Witness, Proselytism, and Religious Liberty," reprinted in *A Documentary History of the Faith and Order Movement, 1927–1963*, ed. Lukas Vischer (St. Louis: Bethany, 1963), 183–96.

6. Richard Swinburne, *Faith and Reason* (Oxford: Clarendon, 1981), 3–8.

7. Luther, "Preface to the Epistle of St. Paul to the Romans," LW 35:370.

8. See, for example, de Aldama, "De fide," no. 90, p. 760.

9. One might also translate *cogitare* by "ponder," as does T. C. O'Brien in the new Blackfriars translation of the *Summa theologiae*, vol. 31 (London: Eyre & Spottiswoode, 1974), 59.

10. Josef Pieper, *Faith and Belief: A Philosophical Tract* (Chicago: Regnery, 1963), 45–46. In the German original, *Über den Glauben: Ein philosophischer Traktat* (Munich: Kösel, 1962), 61–62, Pieper referred to "das forschende Untersuchen, das suchende Bedenken, ein Mit-sich-zu-Rate-Gehen vor der Entscheidung, ein Auf-der-Spur-sein, ein denkende Trachten nach etwas noch nicht entgültig Gefundenem—was alles miteinander mit dem Namen 'Denk-Unruhe' einigermassen adäquat benannt sein dürfte."

11. John Henry Newman, *Fifteen Sermons Preached before the University of Oxford 1826–43* (London: SPCK, 1970), Sermon XV, no. 34, p. 298.

12. Idem, *Apologia pro vita sua*, Part VII (Garden City, N.Y.: Doubleday Image, 1956), 317.

13. Paul Tillich, *Dynamics of Faith* (New York: Harper & Brothers, 1957), 17.

14. Ibid., 21.

15. Ida Görres, "The Believer's Unbelief," *Cross Currents* 11 (1961): 51–59, at 57.

16. Johann Baptist Metz, "Unbelief as a Theological Problem," *The Church and the World*. Concilium 6 (New York: Paulist, 1965), 59–77, at 73–74.

17. The differing degrees of binding force in different types of Church teaching are pointed out by the Congregation for the Doctrine of the Faith in its "Instruction on the Ecclesial Vocation of the Theologian," *Origins* 20 (July 5, 1990): 117–26. For a more detailed treatment see the statement of the United States bishops, "The Teaching Ministry of the Diocesan Bishop: A Pastoral Reflection," *Origins* 21 (January 2, 1992): 473–92. I have discussed this point in *The Craft of Theology: From Symbol to System* (New York: Crossroad, 1992), 105–8.

18. Rudolf Otto, *The Idea of the Holy* (New York: Oxford University Press, 1958), 80.

19. John Chrysostom, expounding Hebrews 11:1, writes: "Faith, then, is the seeing of things not plain (he means), and brings what are not seen to the same full assurance with what are seen," *In epist. ad Hebr. homiliae* 21:2; PG 63:151; in *Select Library of the Nicene and Post-Nicene Fathers of the Christian Church*, vol. 14, ed. Philip Schaff (Grand Rapids, Mich.: Eerdmans, 1956), 462–63.

20. Gregory IX writes: "Fides non habet meritum, cui humana ratio praebet experimentum," Letter "Ab Aegyptiis argentea," 1228 (DS 824). He is here quoting Gregory I, *In Evgl. hom.*, Bk. II, hom. 26, no. 1; PL 76:1197.

21. See Paul Althaus, *The Theology of Martin Luther* (Philadelphia: Fortress, 1966), esp. chap. 5, "The Theology of the Cross," 25–34.

22. Luther, *Bondage of the Will*, LW 33:25–28.

23. "It is incomprehensible that God suffered—something that even the angels do not sufficiently understand, and wonder at. Therefore we too must believe even those things that are hidden *(arcana)* . . . Even though these things seem foolish and absurd to reason, still we have to believe the word and be aware that at this point the rules of logic *(regulae dialecticae)* fall silent," Luther, Disputation *de Poenitentia*, May 23, 1541; WA 39[II]: 279.

24. Hans Urs von Balthasar, *The Glory of the Lord*, vol. l, *Seeing the Form* (San Francisco: Ignatius, 1982), 131–41. See the very nuanced discussion of this point in von Balthasar's *Explorations in Theology*, vol. 2, *Spouse of the Word* (San Francisco: Ignatius, 1991), 64–73; also above, Chapter 6.

25. "Lumen fidei facit videre ea quae creduntur," Thomas Aquinas, *Summa theologiae* 2-2.1.4, ad 3. Some codices, however, change the sense by a marginal gloss adding two words: "facit videre ea quae credunter *esse credibilia*" (". . . causes us to see *that* the things believed *are credible*").

# 12

# Development of Faith

Now that the nature, grounds, and properties of faith have been investigated, it will be in order to discuss the history of faith in the life of the individual. In the present chapter we shall consider whether infants can have faith, how faith arises in adults, how it grows, or diminishes, or is lost.

## Baptized Infants

The faith of baptized infants represents a special case, involving difficult problems that do not arise in the case of adults. The infant, by definition, is one incapable of reflective personal acts, including the act of faith. Theologians have long debated whether infants could have faith, and if so in what sense.

In dealing with this thorny question Augustine maintained that baptism is essentially the sacrament of faith. In receiving the sacrament, therefore, one cannot but receive faith. "So, then, although the child has not yet that faith which resides in the will of believers, the sacrament of that faith makes him one of the believers. And, as the answer is given [by the sponsors] that they believe, so they are called faithful because they receive the sacrament of faith, even if they do not assent to the faith by a mental act. . . . If [the baptized infant] departs from this life before attaining the use of reason, he is freed by this Christian remedy, through the loving recommendation of the Church, from that condemnation 'which by one man entered into the world' (Rom 5:12)."[1] Augustine has usually been understood as teaching that baptized infants have faith and are saved not by reason of their own action but thanks to the faith of their sponsors or that of the Church, which is imputed to them.[2]

In the early Middle Ages some theologians held that baptism removes the stain of original sin from the souls of infants, and confers a certain participation in Christ's priestly office (the sacramental "character"), but does not confer sanctifying grace and the virtues.[3] Peter Lombard, after setting forth this opinion, suggested to the contrary that infants might receive grace and the gifts as a habitual possession but not as capable of being exercised *("in munere, non in usu"),* so that when they later attained the use of reason they could exercise these gifts, and would be culpable if they failed to do so.[4] Lombard's position became dominant by the thirteenth century. Thomas Aquinas, responding to the earlier opinion, writes:

> This opinion is evidently false for two reasons. First, because infants, like adults, are made members of Christ in baptism, and hence must receive an influx of grace and virtue from the head. Secondly, because if the opinion were true, infants who died after baptism would not attain eternal life; for, as is written in Rom 6:[23], "the grace of God is eternal life." And thus it would not profit them for salvation to have been baptized.

> The cause of the error was that [these theologians] did not know how to distinguish between the habit and the act, and so, seeing the infants incapable of acts of the virtues, they thought that they in no sense had the virtues after baptism. But this inability to act does not befall infants from lack of the habit, but from a bodily impediment, just as those who are asleep, even though they have the virtues habitually, are prevented from the acts by their sleep.[5]

The Catholic magisterium, while tolerating the earlier view, has leaned increasingly toward the position of Peter Lombard and Thomas Aquinas. Innocent III, in a letter to Ymber of Arles (A.D. 1201), simply expounded the two positions without deciding between them.[6] The Council of Vienne (A.D. 1312), after noting the two opinions, added:

> We, considering the general efficacy of Christ's death, which through baptism is applied in like manner to all the baptized, choose, with the approval of the sacred Council, the second opinion, which says that sanctifying grace *(gratiam informantem)* and the virtues are conferred in baptism on both infants and adults, as more probable and more in harmony with the words of the saints and of modern doctors of theology.[7]

Martin Luther wrestled long and hard with this question. In early works such as "The Babylonian Captivity of the Church" (1520) he held that in baptism little children are justified vicariously by the faith and confession of the sponsors, who answer in the child's name the questions asked in the baptismal liturgy.[8] Later, however, he took the position that baptized infants must believe for themselves. At one point he asserted that since children do not have reason "they are more fitted for faith than older and more rational people who always trip over their reason and do not wish to push their swelled heads through the narrow gate."[9] In his "Large Catechism" he continued to maintain that baptized infants have faith, but held that their faith was not a necessary condition of the validity of the baptism: "Baptism does not become invalid even if it is wrongly received or used, for it is bound not to our faith but to the Word." In the case of infant baptism, "we bring the child with the purpose and hope that he may believe, and we pray God to grant him faith."[10]

John Calvin took up the question of the faith of infants in his treatise of baptism. Confronted by the objection that infants should not be baptized because they are incapable of repentance and faith, he replied: "Infants are baptized into future repentance and faith, and even though these have not been formed in them, the seed of both lies hidden within them" (*Institutes*, IV.16.20).

The Council of Trent, in its thirteenth canon on baptism, apparently directed against the radical wing of the Reformation (the Anabaptists), declared:

If anyone says that little children, because they make no act of faith, should not after the reception of baptism be numbered among the faithful; and that, therefore, when they reach the age of discretion, they should be rebaptized; or that it is better that their baptism be omitted than that they be baptized while believing not by their own faith but by the faith of the Church alone: let him be anathema.[11]

This text concedes that baptized infants can make no personal acts of faith, but it teaches that they are not justified without faith. What counts in their case is the faith of the Church, by which they are held to believe.

In its Decree on Justification, Trent taught that "no one is ever justified without faith," but it did not say that this means the individual's personal faith. In the course of a discussion of the faith of adults,[12] Trent asserted that at the moment of justification the three theological virtues (faith, hope, and charity) are simultaneously infused.[13] Although this assertion has often been interpreted as if it applied to the justification of infants through baptism,[14] it could, without violence to the text, be restricted to the case of adults. The Council does not clearly reject the earlier view that a justified infant could lack the virtue of faith.

Vatican I did not directly address the question of the faith of baptized infants; it simply repeated Trent's statement that no one has ever been justified without faith (*Dei Filius*, chap. 3, DS 3012). An amendment was offered stating more specifically that faith is necessary for all who have attained the use of reason, but the Deputation on Faith rejected it on the ground that the text referred to the virtue, not the act of faith.[15] Bishop Konrad Martin, reporting for the Deputation, explained: "As we all know, this faith as a virtue is also in baptized infants, for faith is infused through the sacrament of baptism."[16] Thus the Deputation on Faith revealed its preference for the more recent opinion that baptized infants have the infused habit of faith.

It must be recognized, however, that whatever faith infants receive in baptism is not exactly the same as the habit of faith in an adult. The infant's faith does not come from having heard the proclamation of God's revealed word; the infant is incapable of personal acts of faith. The Rite for the Baptism of Children approved by Pope Paul VI in 1969 declares in its Introduction that children or infants cannot have personal faith, but are baptized in "the faith of the Church," a faith in which they must later be formed.[17] Accordingly a contemporary Catholic theologian, Edward Schillebeeckx, writes:

St. Thomas teaches that in children the faith of the Church makes up for the absence of their own religious intention. This means that when the sacrament is administered by the Church to a child the communion of saints, in heaven as well as on earth, gathers itself around him in union with Christ to beg God, through the ritual prayer of the sacrament, to bestow grace on him. Hence the one sacrament, as it were in the second phase of its realization, actually gives the child the grace which was prayed for. This clearly brings out once again the dogmatic and liturgical meaningfulness of an active and prayerful participation of the whole parish community in the administration of baptism.[18]

Setting aside certain idiosyncratic statements of Luther, we may say that all parties to the debate agree that infants, although unable to make personal acts of faith, cannot be saved without faith. They depend on the faith of the Church, which is expressed by the sponsors at baptism. Even if, as the preferred opinion has it, baptized infants receive the virtue of faith, they do not possess it in the same way as adults. In adults, as we shall see, the virtue arises from acts of faith performed in response to the hearing of the word of God. The faith of infants, since it is not yet in a condition that permits it to proceed into act, is by comparison deficient.

## Birth of Faith in Adults

The act of faith, according to Catholic teaching, does not occur without any previous preparation. It presupposes that the revealed object has in some way been presented to the consciousness of the believer. Once this presentation has been made, there follows a process of deliberation: one considers whether or not to believe. During this period the intellect considers the credibility of the alleged revelation, while the affections are attracted or repelled by the apparent desirability or undesirability of believing.

The preliminaries of the act of faith have been treated by many authors under the rubric of the *initium fidei* (beginning of faith). Whatever this term may have meant in the fifth century, it later came to mean the process leading up to the first act of faith.[19] The Second Council of Orange, as we have seen, insisted that the very beginnings of faith *(initium fidei)* and the will to believe *(credulitatis affectus)* are the work of grace, so that it is impossible to perform any act pertaining to eternal salvation without the illumination and inspiration of the Holy Spirit (DS 375, 377; 396–97). It is common doctrine in the Catholic Church that every step positively leading up to the supernatural assent of faith and to justification must be made with the assistance of the Holy Spirit, who enlightens the mind and inspires the will. The grace of God, however, does not coerce the assent. Thus the human powers of will and reason are engaged in the process, as the Councils of Trent and Vatican I insisted.

Scholastic theologians such as Ambroise Gardeil constructed elaborate systems in which they tried to distinguish the respective contributions of nature and of grace. They generally maintained that, although the human mind and will are intrinsically capable of appreciating the natural credibility of Christian revelation and the natural desirability of believing, the approach to faith is never accomplished by unaided nature; the whole process is in fact assisted by the grace of God, who wills that all come to the truth. For the utterly firm assent and commitment of faith, a strictly supernatural grace is absolutely required.

In conformity with the decrees of Orange II, Catholic theologians agree that nothing prior to faith can strictly (or "condignly") merit the grace to make a supernatural act of faith. Some maintain, however, that the grace of faith may be "congruently" merited in the sense that when people do what lies within their power, God cannot fittingly deny the grace needed for justification. Without establishing a strict entitlement, congruent merit, according to this theory, makes it appropriate for God, in his goodness, to give the required help. To merit in the strict sense, one would have to be in a state of supernatural friendship with God, for which faith would be an essential prerequisite.

The dispositions especially conducive to faith are supernatural in the sense that they rest on the grace of God. Prevenient grace can induce people to repent of their sins, to desire God's pardon, and to hope that God will give them revelation and faith. Dispositions such as these do not cause the act of faith, or strictly merit the grace to believe, but they render it more likely that the gospel, when duly presented, will be believed.

Baptism is par excellence the sacrament of faith. The New Testament describes baptized Christians having been enlightened (Heb 6:4; 10:32). In the rite of solemn baptism the presentation of the lighted candle to the baptized with the words, "Receive the light of Christ," signifies the bestowal of the light of faith. It should not be assumed, however, that faith comes into existence only at baptism. In the normal case of adult baptism the candidate already possesses faith, at least in some measure. In asking for faith, as the ritual prescribes, the candidate may be understood as asking for a deeper and richer faith within the Church as the community of faith.

## Increase of Faith

The Church prays in the liturgy, "Almighty and eternal God, give us an increase of faith, hope, and charity. . . ."[20] The idea of an increase of faith is well founded in the New Testament. In the Gospels Jesus rebukes some of his hearers, including Peter and other apostles, for being persons of "little faith" (Mt 6:30; 8:26; 14:31, 16:8; 17:20; Lk 12:28). Conversely, he praises various individuals (such as the centurion and the Syro-Phoenician woman) for the greatness of their faith (Mt 8:10; 15:28; cf. Lk 7:9). The disciples pray to Jesus, "Increase our faith" (Lk 17:5).

To express the growth that he desires in the faith of his Corinthian converts, Paul uses the analogy of a child becoming capable of taking solid nourishment, and not only milk (1 Cor 3:1–2). He speaks of the possibility of having a faith so great as to move mountains, and of the insufficiency of such faith unless it be accompanied by charity (1 Cor 13:2). In Romans 12:6 Paul teaches that God assigns different measures of faith to different individuals. Paul is conscious that Christians may be "weak in faith" (Rom 14:1). He longs to see the Thessalonians again in order that he may "supply what is lacking in your faith" (1 Th 3:10). He tells the Philippians that he is eager to visit them again "for your progress and joy in the faith" (Phil 1:25).

Once it is granted that faith can increase, the question arises as to the respects in which it increases. Thomas Aquinas distinguishes three aspects of growth: faith may increase through a more complete and explicit knowledge of the things to be believed, the material object of faith; it may increase in that the assent becomes more certain and steadfast; and it may increase in the sense that one believes with greater devotion or trust (*S. Th.*, 2-2.5.4). Schematizing this division, we may say that faith can be perfected either extensively, by more explicit awareness of the contents to be believed, or intensively, by firmer assent, livelier trust, or fuller commitment.

The first of these aspects seems obvious enough. In its cognitive aspect (sometimes called *notitia*), faith may be related to its object only in a vague and implicit manner, or it may include a relatively complete and accurate awareness of the revealed mysteries. Classical theologians such as Thomas Aquinas maintained that there was a progress in the history of God's revelation to his people from the patriarchs, through Moses and the prophets, to the apostles, through whom the mystery of Christ was fully revealed. Thus the articles of faith underwent an increase throughout the stages of salvation history (*S. Th.,* 2-2.1.7). Since the apostolic age the contents of faith have not increased, but councils and popes have from time to time formulated the contents of Christian faith more explicitly in order to ward off heretical misinterpretations (*S. Th.,* 2-2.1.9, ad 2 and 2-2.1.10).

Vatican I, after warning that the advance of knowledge could not reverse the meaning of dogmas already taught as matters of faith, affirmed that the whole Church, as well as its individual members, should grow in understanding of the faith with the passage of time (*Dei Filius*, chap. 4, DS 3020). In this passage it suggested that dogma develops over the centuries. In a similar vein, Vatican II taught that through the assistance of the Holy Spirit the whole Church grows in the understanding of what is handed on, both the words and the realities they signify. "Thus, as the centuries advance, the Church constantly moves toward the fullness of divine truth until the day when the words of God will reach their fulfillment in the Church" (DV 8).

A similar increase in knowledge of the contents of faith can occur in the case of individual Christians. In Hebrews 5:11–14 the author distinguishes between a childish faith that grasps only the rudiments and a mature faith that can appropriate more advanced teaching. Six examples of the rudiments, presumably from the catechesis of the day, are then listed: repentance from dead works, faith, instruction about baptisms and laying on of hands, the resurrection of the dead, and eternal judgment (6:1–2). The kind of instruction about priesthood given in the following chapters of the same letter may serve as an example of more advanced teaching. In our own day, Christians may be considered to have a relatively educated faith if they are familiar with the general outlines of Scripture, the principal doctrines of the Church, and the common teaching of theologians about the main points of faith. This knowledge is conveyed through catechesis, sermons, and participation in the liturgy.

In its subjective aspects, faith may increase according to the three dimensions mentioned in Chapter 9: assent, trust, and fidelity. Faith is more perfect to the extent that the intellectual assent is prompt and firm, to the extent that the believer has confidence in God and his word, and to the extent that the believer is committed to live up to the requirements of faith. In the Synoptic Gospels, Jesus makes the distinction between having little faith and having great faith, principally on the basis of the trust people show in his power to act in God's name. Other New Testament passages, as we have seen, put the accent on firm conviction that the creedal claims are true and on faithful obedience to the word of God. The Letter to the

Hebrews, after recalling the heroic fidelity of the saints of old, reminds Christians that they have not yet resisted to the point of shedding their blood (Heb 12:4). Full commitment involves the readiness to make sacrifices, including that of life itself.

It was noted in Chapter 11 that the freedom of faith is subject to growth. In young or immature believers, faith is often coerced to some extent by fear, by hope of temporal favors, or by human respect for parents, teachers, and companions, whose authority can seem to overshadow that of God. Faith achieves greater freedom and purity as believers gain a better understanding of true doctrine and enter into living communion with God. This freedom does not weaken the believer's bonds with the Church and its members, but strengthens these bonds with supernatural motivation. A living and personal faith liberates believers from human fears and manipulation.

According to the New Testament, faith may be expected to flower in wisdom and understanding. Paul frequently prays that his converts may advance in these gifts (Col 1:9; 2:2–3; cf. Eph 1:9, 17–18). Among the mature he claims to impart wisdom, though not the wisdom of this world (1 Cor 2:6). Taught by the Holy Spirit, believers may be able to penetrate the deep things of God (1 Cor 2:10), to judge all things (1 Cor 2:15), and eventually to comprehend with all the saints the breadth, length, height, and depth of the love of Christ "which surpasses knowledge" (Eph 3:18–19).

Vatican II, in its Dogmatic Constitution on Divine Revelation, espoused a dynamic view of faith. "The Holy Spirit," it declared, "constantly perfects faith by his gifts, to bring about an ever deeper understanding of revelation" (DV 5). The Dogmatic Constitution on the Church taught that the Holy Spirit arouses and sustains in the people of God a sense of the faith, whereby they penetrate more deeply into the meaning of faith and apply it more fully to life (LG 12).

The intellectual growth of faith was a favorite theme of the Alexandrian fathers. Beginning with Clement and Origen, they spoke of progress from simple faith, as submissive trust in the word of another, to *gnosis*, an enlightened belief that grasps by spiritual experience the inner meaning and reality of what is believed. They made it clear that *gnosis* is not a substitute for faith, but is faith itself perfected by understanding. Reviving this Alexandrian position, Hans Urs von Balthasar insists that faith is never entirely devoid of *gnosis*, since to believe is already to see something by the light of grace. He agrees with the ancients that *gnosis* must not be understood in the Hegelian sense as reduction to a self-evident idea, or as an immediate mystical encounter, but rather as steadfast contemplation in which the true significance and inner consistency of the data of faith are perceived.[21]

The relationship between faith and understanding was much discussed by the medieval Scholastics. Thomas Aquinas explains how faith, as an infused supernatural virtue, is perfected by the gifts of the Holy Spirit, especially the gifts of understanding and knowledge. Unlike the virtues, which have their proper principles in us, the gifts dispose us to be moved externally by the Holy Spirit (*S. Th.*, 1-2.68.1). Whereas faith is an assent to God's revelation, understanding goes beyond it by penetrating the meaning of that to which we assent and by grasping the content through a kind of spiritual insight (*S. Th.*, 2-2.8.6). Knowledge, as a gift of the Holy

Spirit, gives ready discernment and sure judgment about the things that are to be believed (*S. Th.,* 2-2.9.1).

The gift of wisdom, according to St. Thomas, is in some ways perfective of faith, insofar as, like faith, it inheres in the intellect. In his system, however, wisdom has a close affinity with the virtue of charity, for it involves a "connaturality" with the things of God, as does charity, which results from the vital indwelling of the Holy Spirit. Wisdom *(sapientia)* implies a taste *(sapor)* for the divine. Because of this element of affectivity, wisdom is causally in the will, while remaining, like faith, formally in the intellect. Wisdom enables one to judge rightly about divine matters by virtue of connaturality or union with God. "Faith assents to divine truth as it as grasped by faith, whereas the judgment that is according to God's own truth pertains to the gift of wisdom. And therefore the gift of wisdom presupposes faith" (*S. Th.,* 2-2.45.1).

John Henry Newman, who was greatly devoted to the Alexandrian fathers, held that "faith is the elementary grace which is required of all, especially of hearers." Wisdom, on the other hand, "belongs to the perfect." It is an orderly and mature development of thought that enables us to obtain, with the assistance of the Holy Spirit, "a right judgment in all things."[22] In one of his sermons Newman explains that Mary's faith "did not end in a mere acquiescence in Divine providences and revelations; as the text [Lk 2:19] informs us, she 'pondered' them."[23] This pondering, continued collectively in the Church, leads to a development of doctrine, as truths implied in the original idea of faith are made explicit. In still other texts Newman holds that faith is perfected "not by intellectual cultivation, but by obedience."[24] Obedience, he writes, makes the conscience keen-sighted and sensitive. "The more we *do,* the more shall we trust in Christ."[25]

The various dimensions involved in the growth of faith are compactly summarized in the final paragraph of one of Newman's sermons:

> Let us ever make it our prayer and our endeavour, that we may know the whole counsel of God, and grow unto the measure of the stature of the fulness of Christ; that all prejudice, and self-confidence, and hollowness, and unreality, and positiveness, and partisanship, may be put away from us under the light of Wisdom, and the fire of Faith and Love; till we see things as God sees them, with the judgment of His Spirit, and according to the mind of Christ.[26]

Although human means should not be neglected, the increase of faith, like its beginning, is always the work of grace. It is the task of God, who begins the process, to bring it to completion (cf. Phil 1:6). The Second Council of Orange (canon 5, DS 375) explicitly taught that the increase of faith cannot come except from God. The essential is, as Paul recognized, "that Christ may dwell in your hearts through faith" (Eph 3:17). Vital insertion into the divine life through Christ assures that faith will not wither but will grow in its several dimensions. Just as Christian faith normally takes root through incorporation in the Church, the increase of faith normally depends on the regular listening to the word of God, participation in the sacraments, and the support of a believing community. These means of grace should lead to personal prayer and contemplation, deeper spiritual experience, and greater personal responsibility for one's own faith.

## Psychology of Faith Development

Can a believer's progress in faith be correlated with age, temperament, and psychological maturity? A generation ago, authors such as Romano Guardini and Pierre André Liégé pointed out that the form of faith differs according to the psychological characteristics and age of the believer. They distinguished between the faith of childhood, adolescence, adulthood, and old age. The child lives in a small, protected world, in which it seems easy to relate to the invisible and the transcendent. But that world is made up of an ambiguous mixture of myth and mystery, which must later undergo the criticism of awakening reason. In adolescence the world of myth and authority is challenged, and faith must be reconstructed to make room for the youth's new-found independence, energy, enthusiasm, and boundless hopes. The faith of the adolescent, however, is too often confused with a naive expectation of transforming the world according to one's own ideals. In maturity faith has to face up to the harshness of reality and the experience of repeated failures. As it matures, faith takes the shape of fidelity, discipline, and perseverance in the face of struggle and disappointment. In old age a person's energies wane, and the risk of cynicism or skepticism arises. But if faith can learn to become more detached and to nourish itself on the consciousness of eternity, it can regain, on a higher level, the simplicity characteristic of childhood.[27]

In recent years moral and religious growth have been intensely studied by developmental psychologists such as Jean Piaget, Lawrence Kohlberg, and Erik Erikson. The most ambitious attempt to spell out the stages of faith development is that of James W. Fowler, notably in his *Stages of Faith*.[28] He distinguishes six stages. The first three correspond to childhood and early adolescence, in which the individual becomes increasingly identified with the group. Stage 4 ("individuative-reflective faith") characteristically occurs in late adolescence, when the believer consciously chooses a set of beliefs and commitments. The fifth, "conjunctive faith," comes with experience of one's own limitations and with greater exposure to contrary points of view; it involves "epistemological humility in the face of the intricacy and richness of mystery."[29] Fowler has no distinct stage corresponding to the faith of the elderly as described by Guardini and Liégé. His sixth stage represents the ideal, rarely verified in fact. It involves a decentering of the self, participation in the Ultimate, and the ability to love and value from a centering point located in the Ultimate.[30]

Fowler tries to give an analysis acceptable to readers of any religion or no religion (292).[31] To a great extent, he believes, this can be done by adopting Tillich's concept of faith as "ultimate concern" (4) and H. Richard Niebuhr's vision of faith as "the search for an overarching, integrating and grounding trust in a center of value and power sufficiently worthy to give our lives unity and meaning" (5). With Wilfred Cantwell Smith, Fowler holds that faith is "generic, a universal feature of human living, recognizably similar everywhere despite a remarkable variety of forms and contents of religious practice and belief" (14).

While emphasizing the formal aspects of faith rather than its contents, Fowler finds it impossible to follow Piaget and Kohlberg in identifying the structural features of faith with the formal, logical structures of reason (272). As a theologian, he recognizes the crucial importance of the contents of faith, by which he means the believers' "centering values, their images of power or the master stories they take as descriptive of reality" (273). Faith at Stages 5 and 6, he concedes, will take essentially religious forms (293).

Fowler's system is an intriguing combination of empirical and theological assertions. He professes to be dealing with faith not as a divine gift (justifying or saving faith) but as a generic human phenomenon—an individual's relation to a center of meaning, trust, and loyalty. Faith in this sense is not necessarily religious. It is a mode of existence that gives form and coherence to human life. Development, in Fowler's writings, generally means the unfolding of one's human potential in ways that bring about greater maturity and socialization. Fowler sometimes warns his readers that "the stages are not about salvation" and that he is "not allowing judgments about the truth, adequacy, or orthodoxy of the content or substance" of a person's faith to to be determinative.[32]

In spite of these disclaimers, Fowler is convinced that his theory "can be integrated into and made accessible to Christian theological perspectives and norms, and employed in reshaping the life and mission of Christian churches."[33] Elsewhere he writes: "Human development toward wholeness is, I believe, always the product of a certain *synergy* between human potentials, given in creation, and the presence and activity of Spirit as mediated through many channels."[34] Thus it would seem that progress to a higher stage is correlated with growth in grace.

In the end, I believe, Fowler cannot separate his theory of faith-development from his own religious stance. Since no one can be religious in general (292), and since different religions have different doctrines and scales of value, it seems inevitable that the appraisal of faith at these higher stages must become intertwined with the appraiser's own religious convictions. Fowler's own appraisal reflects the outlook of a particular theological school, that of the authors cited above. From these mentors he takes over the idea that no one can be without faith. He follows them in opting for a wide separation between faith and belief. He speaks a great deal about centers of value, very little about doctrinal truth. "Creeds and doctrines," he holds, "are formulations of the reflective faith of persons in the past"; they are "invitations and stimuli for *contemporary* experiments with truth" (295).

He describes Stage 6 in predominantly Christian categories, borrowing Niebuhr's conceptions of "radical monotheism" and the Kingdom of God (204–11). The theory of faith development therefore interlocks with a faith-conviction that God is sovereign and free. "In the biblical tradition," Fowler declares, "God is recognized as sovereign reality—as creator, ruler, and as redeemer of *all* being" (302). The growth of faith depends in part upon the revelatory actions of God, which are free and unpredictable. Fowler therefore concedes that faith cannot be rightly understood as a merely developmental matter (303).

Theological commentators generally acknowledge that the maturation expressed in Fowler's first four steps corresponds to a normal development from childish faith to a faith that is freely and personally affirmed, though there are risks as well as opportunities in each passage to a higher stage. The critical faith typical of later adolescence (Stage 4) can be a positive or a negative phenomenon, depending on whether it means a more personal participation in the faith of the Church or an individualistic self-distancing from that faith. The transition to Stage 5, again, is theologically ambiguous. Those who come to recognize the intricacy of mystery can retreat from confessional faith into a vague agnosticism or they can advance beyond merely conceptual forms of faith toward a richer apprehension of meaning.

Fowler's sixth and highest stage calls for similar reservations. As he describes it, it might well represent the experience of the saintly prophet heralding an authentic vision of God's coming Kingdom. But some critics raise serious objections. A Catholic religious educator, Paul Philibert, remarks: "Fowler's conception of the end-term of development as probably leading to lonely prophetic martyrdom rather than to mutually enlivening commmunity raises some underlying questions." Is Fowler, he asks, reinforcing the individualism, competitiveness, and isolation characteristic of North American society?[35]

A Methodist psychologist, H. Newton Malony, has a different objection:

> Finally, there is the question whether religious maturity can be equated with that openness, uncertainty, and tolerance for lack of final answers which is implied in Fowler's Stage 6. Although Fowler contends that Stage 6 includes commitment, one gets the distinct impression that "Universalizing Faith" implies a judgment that all faiths are implicitly equal and are to be judged pragmatically in terms of whether they are beneficial for a given individual or not."[36]

Modern empirical psychology, like other sciences, can be serviceable for the theology of faith. If nature builds on grace, as the axiom has it, faith has a better chance of achieving its goal in a healthy mind. Psychological immaturity or neuroses can inhibit the spiritual growth that, by right, ought to occur. In the words of a distinguished priest-psychologist,

> Faith requires and also creates basic trust and fidelity. If the ego's capacity for trust is impaired, the movement to faith is more difficult. But the energizing capacity of grace can shore up the ego's impairment and renew those basic sources of trust in and through faith. In doing so, grace and faith touch every stratum of the mind and affect all parts of the psychic structure.[37]

There is no automatic correlation between faith and psychological maturity. Although Scripture admonishes believers to give up childish ways (1 Cor 13:11; 14:20), it also indicates that they must become like little children in order to excel in faith (Mt 18:4; 19:14 and parallel texts). The young are often most generous and open to the initiatives of grace; the mature may become set in their ways and resistant to conversion. Being well adjusted to the world, they may feel little need to rely on God.

Although grace has a healing influence, it rarely overcomes all personality defects. Some saints appear to have had a deep and lively faith in spite of persisting emotional disorders. Psychological health and maturity, conversely, do not by themselves assure a robust and developed faith. The true growth of faith depends principally on theological factors, including, most importantly, the grace of Christ and the gifts of the Holy Spirit.

## Decrease and Loss of Faith

Faith, as we have seen, is a grace that can be either accepted or refused. Just as faith can be born and increase, so also it can decrease and die. History and experience provide many instances in which faith has apparently diminished or even ceased to exist. Such regressions are manifested by confessions of unbelief or by the absence of the signs of genuine and lively faith. Various factors that might weaken or imperil faith may here be mentioned.

Faith, as we have seen, can continue to exist in a person who loses the virtue of charity.[38] But faith is defective when unaccompanied by charity for, as Trent puts it, such faith fails to unite one perfectly with Christ and make one a living member of his body.[39] "Unformed" or "dead" faith, according to St. Thomas, is not even a virtue, for it does not suffice to make the believer a good person nor does it attain the proper goal of faith, which is spiritual union with God (*S. Th.*, 2-2.4.5). When the believer does not love God for God's own sake, the acts of faith become less intense and satisfying. The "joy and ease in assenting to the truth" (DS 377) that come from grace are no longer experienced. The greater one's love for God, the stronger will be the motivation to submit one's mind to God as faith requires. As Juan Alfaro says:

> Faith reaches its fullness as faith when it is love of God, made present in love of man. If charity is lacking, faith itself is mortally wounded, and there is an inner tension in the believer that can be resolved only by reconciliation with God or radical separation from him through disbelief. The believer, as a whole human being, truly accepts the Word of God in action alone by living the Christian life, which is not a result of faith but its authentic working-out in man; in his actions, man gives his full assent to the fact that the mystery of Christ is real.[40]

It seems evident that the sinner, having freely chosen to live in opposition to the precepts of Christ, the gospel, and the Church, will experience an inclination to repudiate the faith that condemns this manner of life. People tend to disbelieve teachings that run counter to their preferred patterns of behavior.

The causes of disbelief are not entirely within the control of the individual. Through contact with a secularized environment, habitual association with unbelievers, non-Christian education, and indiscriminate reading, a person may find plausible grounds for rejecting or questioning what has been presented as revealed truth. It is quite true that, as Newman put it, a thousand difficulties do not make a doubt, but intellectual and emotional difficulties, especially when they accumulate, can become occasions for doubt, and thus undermine the security that faith should have. Until the difficulties are resolved, they constitute a threat to faith.

Because faith is a complex reality, loss of faith has different dimensions. Concentrating on the intellectual aspect, traditional theology distinguishes between two species of infidelity or unbelief: heresy and apostasy. Heresy is the rejection of one or more truths of faith by a baptized person who still professes to be a Christian. Apostasy is the total repudiation of Christian faith.[41]

With regard to heresy it must be further asked whether the person continues to adhere to the norm of faith, which for Catholics is the revelation of Christ as attested by Sacred Scripture, by apostolic Tradition, and by the magisterium. If this norm of faith continues to be accepted, an erroneous opinion can easily be corrected when the individual's attention is called to the discrepancy between the deviant opinion and the authoritative teaching. St. Thomas speaks of uneducated persons who are confused about the true teaching of the Church or who have been misled by others. "If they do not obstinately cling to false doctrine, and if they err out of ignorance *(ex simplicitate)*, they are not held to blame" and should not be called heretics (*S. Th.,* 2-2.2.6, ad 2). In modern terminology, such persons are not formal heretics but material heretics. Since "heresy," properly speaking, is a sin against faith, those who err out of ignorance are not heretics in the strict sense of the term.[42]

More serious is the case of those who deny certain doctrines because they do not accept the Catholic rule of faith. According to Thomas Aquinas the formal object of faith is "the first truth as this is made known in Scripture and the teaching of the Church that proceeds from the first truth" (*S. Th.,* 2-2.5.3c). He therefore maintains that "anyone who does not hold as the infallible and divine rule of faith Church teaching that derives from divine truth as handed down in Scripture, does not have the habit of faith" (ibid.). Lacking the basic attitude of faith, such as person cannot believe anything at all on a motive of faith. "A heretic in respect to one article of faith does not adhere to the other articles by faith but by some sort of opinion that suits his own will" (ibid.).

In view of St. Thomas's own distinction between culpable and inculpable heresy, these judgments may not be applied in an unnuanced way to individuals, especially in the world of our day. Living in a pervasively Catholic environment, the Angelic Doctor tended to write as if only obstinate persons could deny the Church's authority as an infallible teacher. In the more ecumenical atmosphere of our time, it seems evident that one can be a sincere Christian without accepting the full Catholic rule of faith. Protestants, for example, can make acts of Christian faith on the basis of Scripture while rejecting the claim of the ecclesiastical magisterium to issue dogmatic definitions that are binding in faith.

So far as Catholics are concerned, it does seem that if they flatly denied something that the Church clearly teaches as a dogma of the faith, it would be inconsistent on their part to accept other doctrines on the authority of the Church as teacher. Having denied the authority of the Church even in this one instance, they would have ceased to believe as Catholics. But it would be rash to judge that such persons do not have any faith at all, and that they are not submitting their minds to God, the first truth. Perhaps they are convinced of the divine authority of Scripture, the creeds, and the teachings of the so-called "undivided Church" of the first few centuries. Possibly they believe with divine faith what they find in these sources, but feel unable to accept certain obligatory teachings of the modern Church as coming from God. If they were better instructed, such persons might be able to overcome their objections. But in the meanwhile they must be accepted for what they are: Christian believers who stand in the Catholic tradition without accepting the full dogmatic heritage of their own Church.

At this point we begin to touch on the status of Catholics who leave the Church.

Vatican I made some authoritative comments on this point. It stated in chapter 3 of its Constitution on Faith, *Dei Filius*, that "those who have adhered to Catholic truth through the heavenly gift of faith . . . [and] have received the faith under the teaching authority of the Church, can never have any just cause for changing their faith or calling it into doubt" (DS 3014). In canon 6 (DS 3036) this last phrase is spelled out more fully with reference to the theories of Georg Hermes and others that it would be proper for Catholics to suspend their faith provisionally, and subject it to methodic doubt, in order to ascertain the objective grounds of credibility and in this way rebuild their faith in a more solid form. This rejected theory rested on the supposition that genuine faith could be achieved by a sheer exercise of reason—a supposition that several councils have emphatically denied.

Granted that this procedure of methodic doubt is unacceptable, it must be asked whether Vatican I, in *Dei Filius* as quoted above, taught that the loss of Catholic faith on the part of those raised within the Church is always culpable. As has been noted in our historical survey, the commentators do not all agree. The majority, however, follow Theodor Granderath and Jean-Michel-Alfred Vacant in holding that the Council here teaches only that the Catholics here described (those who have arrived at faith under the teaching authority of the Catholic Church) cannot have *objectively* valid reasons for abandoning their faith.[43] But the context suggests that this abandonment of the Catholic faith will be contrary to the solicitations of grace. God, according to the Council, "wills that all should come to the recognition of the truth (1 Tim 2:4), and confirms with his grace those whom he has brought from darkness into his wonderful light (cf. 1 Pet 2:9) so that they may persevere in that same light, for he does not desert those who have not deserted him" (DS 3014).

Vacant cites an opinion to the effect that an uninstructed Catholic might be induced by persons of great authority to abandon the Catholic faith and join a heretical sect without personal sin.[44] Nothing in the acts of Vatican I, he says, indicates that the Council wanted to condemn this opinion. In view of the relatively large number of Catholics who have in the course of time joined other religious bodies or given up religion altogether, this hypothesis is not far-fetched. It seems best to affirm the general theological principle that divine grace draws people to the truth, and to leave the judgment of individuals up to God, who alone can scrutinize the depths of the human heart and assign the exact measure of responsibility.

In cases where there seems to be a total abandonment of faith in revealed religion, a particular problem arises. According to the Council of Trent, the virtue of faith, once possessed, is not lost by any mortal sin but only by a sin of infidelity.[45] Have we, then, the duty to conclude that all who have ceased to believe in God and revelation have seriously sinned against faith itself and that they will suffer eternal condemnation unless they are reconverted? This might be the required conclusion if we could be certain that they had indeed abandoned faith altogether, but this certainty does not seem humanly attainable. We may have here a case of faith reduced to its minimum, hardly capable of being formulated, yet not entirely extinct. The virtue of faith might somehow survive without the explicit content normally required for acts of divine faith. When the lapsed Christian comes before God's throne for judgment, God may be able to find authentic embers even in this vestigial faith. Further light on this question may be shown by closer analysis of the faith necessary for salvation, the theme of our next chapter.

## Conclusion

The act of faith should not be conceived as something that occurs only once, as though it were nothing but a decision made at the moment of conversion. Each act of faith is one of a continuing series of acts, a process in which growth can and should occur. The virtue of faith, correspondingly, is not just a static foundation for the spiritual life but an intrinsic element of that developing life.

The beginnings of faith are expressed and sealed by baptism, which incorporates its recipients into the life of the Church, the community of faith. Infants, who lack personal faith, receive grace from the faith of the Church and are thus prepared to make acts of faith, if they freely wish to do so, when they acquire the use of reason. When adults approach an acceptance of the faith, the grace of God enlightens their minds and inspires their wills so that they can see the content of faith as fully credible and attractive. Faith matures when believers allow their lives to be permeated by it, listening devoutly to the word of God, partaking of the sacraments, and striving to act according to the ideals and principles of faith.

As faith develops under the aegis of the Holy Spirit, it ordinarily becomes more joyful, serene, and free. Through the gifts of wisdom, understanding, and knowledge believers penetrate more deeply into the true meaning of revelation, view the world from the point of view of faith, and gain right judgment in applying the principles of faith to their conduct.

It is normal for faith to take different forms according to the age and temperament of the believer. Serious psychological deficiencies may limit the freedom and strength of a person's faith, but personal maturity does not by itself assure the presence or growth of faith. Faith tends to bring the believer beyond childish self-centeredness and to foster strong and mature commitments. The growth of faith is primarily due to the grace of God, which can achieve wonderful results even in unpromising human subjects.

Since the content of faith is never possessed by evidential knowledge, faith is always, in some measure, precarious. Temptations come from within insofar as human nature in its fallen condition is swayed by alien principles. The world is an external source of temptations against faith since it tends to resist Christ and the gospel. The security of faith comes not from the believer's mind and will, or from the social environment, but from God, who ordinarily works through the means of grace he has established. For the reception of the gift of faith, and for perseverance and growth in faith, it is ordinarily necessary to pray for grace and to have recourse to the word of God, the sacraments, and persons who exemplify Christian holiness.

Since faith is a free response to grace, it is capable of being lost. To all appearances, some who once believed have become unbelievers. But the apparent unbeliever may be, perhaps even unconsciously, a searching believer who fails to recognize the doctrines and formulas of faith as expressions and explanations of divine revelation. Such a failure of perception may be culpable or inculpable. In the last analysis only God can judge the question of culpability just as he alone can be sure whether faith is truly absent.

# Notes

1. Letter 98, to Bishop Boniface, in Augustine, *Letters*, vol. 2 (New York: Fathers of the Church, 1953), 138. The words in brackets are my own additions.

2. Augustine, *De peccatorum meritis et remissione* 1:25; CSEL 60:35–37 and PL 44:129–31. Thomas Aquinas, in *Summa theologiae.*, 3.69.6 ad 3, quotes a similar text from Augustine and adds: "And so infants believe, not through their own act but through the faith of the Church, which is communicated to them; and grace and virtue are conferred upon them in virtue of that faith [of the Church]."

3. A. Michel, "Vertu. Les vertus infuses," DTC 15:2759–74, at 2761.

4. Peter Lombard, *Sententiae*, Bk. IV, Dist. 4, chap. 7 (Collegium S. Bonaventurae: Ad Claras Aquas, 1916), 2:771–72.

5. Thomas Aquinas, *Summa theologiae.*, 3.69.6c.

6. Innocent III, "Maiores Ecclesiae causas," DS 780.

7. Constitutio "Fidei catholicae," DS 904; translated in *Decrees of the Ecumenical Councils* ed. Norman P. Tanner (Washington, D.C.: Georgetown University Press, 1990), 361 (lines 19–24). The decrees of the Council are written in the name of Pope Clement V.

8. Luther, "The Babylonian Captivity of the Church," LW 36:73–74.

9. Luther, "Homily on the Gospel for the Third Sunday after Epiphany, Mt 8:1ff," (1525), WA 17$^{II}$, 72–88, at 84–85; cf. Paul Althaus, *The Theology of Martin Luther* (Philadelphia: Fortress, 1966), 366.

10. Luther, "Large Catechism," Part IV, Baptism; in *The Book of Concord*, ed. and trans. Theodore G. Tappert (Philadelphia: Fortress, 1959), 443, nos. 53 and 57.

11. DS 1626; ET in *Decrees*, ed. Tanner, 686:15–19.

12. Session 6, chap. 5 (DS 1525)

13. Session 6, chap. 7 (DS 1530).

14. For an example of this interpretation see Francisco Sola, "De Sacramentis Initiationis christianae," in *Sacrae theologiae summa*, vol. 4, 3d ed. (Madrid: Biblioteca de Autores Cristianos, 1956), no. 96, p. 177.

15. Jean-Michel-Alfred Vacant, *Études théologiques sur les Constitutions du Concile du Vatican*, vol. 2 (Paris: Delhomme et Briguet, 1895), 126.

16. *Actuum et Decretorum S. Conciliorum recentiorum. Collectio lacensis*, vol. 7 (Freiburg: Herder, 1890), 178.

17. *The Rites of the Catholic Church* (New York: Pueblo, 1976), 188.

18. Edward Schillebeeckx, *Christ the Sacrament of the Encounter with God* (New York: Sheed & Ward, 1963), 141.

19. See above, Chapter 2, note 31.

20. Opening Prayer, Thirtieth Sunday in Ordinary Time. This prayer is quoted by Trent in session 6, chap. 10 (DS 1535).

21. Hans Urs von Balthasar, *The Glory of the Lord*, vol. 1, *Seeing the Form* (San Francisco: Ignatius, 1982), 136–41.

22. John Henry Newman, *Fifteen Sermons Preached before the University of Oxford, 1826–1843* (London: SPCK, 1970), Sermon 14:2, 279.

23. Ibid., Sermon 15:2, 312.

24. Ibid., Sermon 12:36, 250.

25. Idem, *Parochial and Plain Sermons*, II.14 (San Francisco: Ignatius, 1987), 327.

26. Idem, *Fifteen Sermons* . . . , Sermon 14:48, 311.

27. Romano Guardini, *The Faith and Modern Man* (New York: Pantheon, 1952), 93–109; idem, *The Life of Faith* (New York: Paulist, 1963), 72–89; Pierre André Liégé, "The Ages of Faith," in *Theological Library*, vol. 4, *The Virtues and States of Life*, ed. A. M. Henry (Chicago: Fides, 1957), 34–37.

28. James W. Fowler, *Stages of Faith: Psychology of Human Development and the Quest for Meaning* (San Francisco: Harper Row, 1981).

29. Idem, "Faith and the Structuring of Meaning," in *Faith Development and Fowler*, ed. Craig Dykstra and Sharon Parks (Birmingham, Ala.: Religious Education Press, 1986), 15–42, at 30.

30. Ibid., 31.

31. References in parentheses are to *Stages of Faith*.

32. James W. Fowler, "Foreword," *Christian Perspectives on Faith Development: A Reader*, ed. Jeff Astley and Leslie Francis (Grand Rapids, Mich.: Eerdmans, 1992), xi–xiv.

33. Ibid., xiv.

34. Idem, *Becoming Adult, Becoming Christian: Adult Development and Christian Faith* (San Francisco: Harper & Row, 1984), 74.

35. Paul Philibert, in "Review Symposium" on Fowler's *Stages of Faith*, *Horizons* 9 (1982): 118–22, at 122. Fowler in his response, 123–26, rejects the charge of individualism.

36. H. Newton Malony, "The Concept of Faith in Psychology," in *Handbook of Faith*, ed. James Michael Lee (Birmingham, Ala.: Religious Education Press, 1990), 71–95, at 94. As a preferable alternative to Fowler's position Malony proposes (84–89) the analysis of André Godin, who makes a sharp distinction between functional religion, which reaches out to God as a means of fulfilling instinctive wishes, and Christian faith, which submits to the will of God as revealed in Jesus Christ. See André Godin, *The Psychological Dynamics of Religious Experience* (Birmingham, Ala.: Religious Education Press, 1985), esp. 195–203.

37. William W. Meissner, *Life and Faith: Psychological Perspectives on Religious Experience* (Washington, D.C.: Georgetown University Press, 1987), 149.

38. Council of Trent, Session 6, chap. 15 (DS 1544) and canon 28 (DS 1578).

39. Ibid., Session 6, chap. 7 (DS 1531).

40. Juan Alfaro, "The Dual Aspect of Faith: Entrusting Oneself to God and Acceptance of the Christian Message," in *Man as Man and Believer*, ed. Edward Schillebeeckx and Boniface Willems. Concilium 21 (New York: Paulist, 1967), 53–66, at 58.

41. "Heresy is the obstinate denial of, or obstinate doubt concerning, some truth that is to be believed with divine and catholic faith, on the part of one who has been baptized. Apostasy is the total repudiation of Christian faith. . . . " Code of Canon Law (1983), canon 751.

42. Note the word "obstinate" in canon 751, cited above.

43. Roger Aubert, *Le problème de l'acte de foi*, 2d ed. (Louvain: Warny, 1950), 218–19; Hermann J. Pottmeyer, *Der Glaube vor dem Anspruch der Wissenschaft* (Freiburg: Herder, 1968), 341–47.

44. Vacant, *Études théologiques* 2:165–66, 178–79. He cites Theodor Granderath, *Constitutiones dogmaticae sacrosancti Oecumenici Concilii Vaticani . . . explicatae* (Freiburg im Br.: Herder, 1892), p. 61.

45. Council of Trent, Session 6, chap. 15 (DS 1544); cf. canon 28 (DS 1578).

# 13

# Faith and Salvation

## Necessity of Faith

Nearly all the mainline churches, including the Catholic Church, have consistently taught that divine faith is necessary for justification in the present life and for salvation in the life to come. Many biblical texts assert this.

The Gospel of Mark, in its canonical conclusion, represents the risen Jesus as saying: "He who believes and is baptized will be saved; but he who does not believe will be condemned" (Mk 16:16). In the Gospel of John, Jesus instructs Nicodemus on the necessity of rebirth through water and the Holy Spirit as a condition for entering the kingdom of God (Jn 3:5). In this connection Jesus asserts: "He who believes in him [the Son] is not condemned; he who does not believe is condemned already" (Jn 3:18; cf. 3:36). The idea that belief in the Son is required for eternal life reappears in John 5:24, John 8:24, and in many other Johannine texts.

The Book of Acts is permeated by the conviction that faith is needed for the forgiveness of sins and salvation (Acts 10:43; 16:30–31; 26:17–18). The theme of justification by faith runs like a refrain throughout the letters of Paul, especially Romans and Galatians. He frequently declares that human beings are made righteous not by performing "works of the law" but by faith in Christ (e.g., Rom 3:28; Gal 2:16). The Letter to the Hebrews contains the firm declaration: "Without faith it is impossible to please God" (Heb 11:6).

Following texts such as these, the Council of Trent taught that without faith "no one has ever come to justification" (Session 6, chap. 7, DS 1529) and faith is "the beginning of human salvation, the foundation and root of all justification" (Ibid., chap. 8; DS 1532). Vatican I stated: "Since, therefore, 'without faith it is impossible to please God,' and enter into fellowship with his sons and daughters, it follows that no one has ever achieved justification without faith, and that no one who fails to persevere in faith to the end, will attain eternal life" (*Dei Filius*, chap. 3; DS 3012). Vatican II contains no formal treatment of the connection between faith and salvation, but in many texts it alludes in passing to the absolute necessity of faith for the attainment of eternal salvation (LG 14 and 24; AA 6; PO 4; AG 7 and 8). No theory that calls into question the necessity of faith for salvation can be viable in Catholic Christianity.

To show by theological reasoning why faith is necessary is a more delicate task. Thomas Aquinas, in the first article of the *Summa theologiae* (1.1.1) appeals to the philosophical premise that human beings, as free and rational, must knowingly move themselves toward their last end. But since that end exceeds the capacities of nature, it can only be known to them through revelation accepted in faith. Without faith, therefore, human beings could not rightly order themselves to the end for which God has destined them.

In his treatise on faith in the *Summa theologiae* St. Thomas adopts a slightly different approach (2-2.4.1). Interpreting the text, "Faith is the assurance *(hypostasis)* of things hoped for" (Heb 11:1), he follows the Vulgate by translating the term *hypostasis* as *substantia*. He then interprets the term as meaning the beginning *(inchoatio)*, the first installment. Since eternal life consists in the intuitive vision of God, the beginning of eternal life in us involves an anticipation of what we hope to see. Faith is, as it were, the seed that will eventually flower into the beatifying vision. By faith we obtain a real participation in the divine self-knowledge, and thus a fore-taste of the eternal vision for which we hope. St. Thomas here writes: "Understood in this way, faith is the 'substance of things hoped for' because the first beginning of the things for which we hope is in us through the assent of faith, which virtually contains all the things we hope for. For we hope to receive blessedness by a clear vision of the truth to which we now adhere by faith, as is apparent from what was said above about beatitude" (cf. *S. Th.,* 1-2.3.8; cf. 4.3).

In Scripture the connection between faith and salvation is presented particularly in terms of trust. Isaiah and the Psalms make it clear that Israel cannot hope for protection from death and destruction except by putting its trust entirely in the one who alone is capable of overcoming all enemies, namely the true God who revealed himself to Abraham and Moses. "If you will not believe," says the Lord through Isaiah, "surely you shall not be established" (Is 7:9). The Psalmist is confident that the Lord will deliver him from all enemies:

> I love thee, O Lord, my strength.
> The Lord is my rock, and my fortress, and my deliverer,
> my God, my rock, in whom I take refuge,
> my shield, and the horn of my salvation, my stronghold.
> I call upon the Lord, who is worthy to be praised,
> and I am saved from my enemies.
>
> (Ps 18:1–3)

Nowhere in the Bible is it suggested that the salvific power of faith derives from the value of faith as a merely subjective act. Faith can save if, and only if, it clings to, and pins all its hope on, the one true God, for he alone has both the power and the will to grant salvation. Those who look to the God of Abraham and of Jesus Christ for salvation will indeed be saved; but those who look elsewhere are on a road that does not lead to salvation at all. To put one's ultimate trust in any other person or agency, whether a graven image, a false deity, a nation, an army, or a secular ruler, is to lack faith in the biblical and theological sense of the term.

In the New Testament Jesus characterizes his word as the solid rock upon which a wise man builds his house (Mt 7:24–27). Paul and other New Testament writers explain that the salvific power of faith comes from God or Christ as the content of the revelatory word. Abraham was justified not simply because he believed, but because he believed in the "God who gives life to the dead and calls into existence the things that do not exist" (Rom 4:17). If Christians are saved through faith in Christ, this is because Christ has died for their sins and was raised up for their justification. Since the salvific value of faith depends totally upon its object, the faith of Christians would be a deception unless Christ had really risen from the dead (cf. 1 Cor 15:12–19).

From all this it follows that faith cannot arise unless the one true God has revealed himself, and that anyone who lacks access to revelation is not in a position to make an act of saving faith. For the early Christians, and indeed for Christians of all but the most recent times, this has been a powerful motive for missionary activity. Paul, the great missionary of the primitive Church, expressed this motivation by a series of rhetorical questions:

> "Every one who calls upon the name of the Lord will be saved." But how are men to call upon him in whom they have not believed? And how are they to believe in him of whom they have never heard? And how are they to hear without a preacher? And how can men preach unless they are sent? As it is written, "How beautiful are the feet of those who preach good news!" (Rom 10:13–15)

Having shown that faith in the gospel leads to salvation, the New Testament writers had to explain how the patriarchs and prophets of the Old Testament, who lived before the advent of the Savior, could have come to salvation. They consistently give one answer to this question: The saints of the old dispensation looked forward in hope to the coming of the Savior; they believed in him as the one who was to come. Thus Jesus is reported as saying to his adversaries: "If you believed Moses, you would believe me, for he wrote of me" (Jn 5:46); and again: "Your father Abraham rejoiced that he was to see my day; he saw it and was glad" (Jn 8:56). For Jesus and the early Christian community, the Mosaic books, the Prophets, and the Psalms have Christ as a central theme (e.g., Mk 12:35–37; Lk 24:27, 44–45; 1 Cor 10:4; Heb 1:5–14). The long catalogue of the heroes of faith in the eleventh chapter of Hebrews treats them as adhering to promises of which Christians have seen the fulfillment. "God had foreseen something better for us, that apart from us they should not be made perfect" (Heb 11:40).

## Faith of the Unevangelized: Bible and Magisterium

A further question arose regarding the pagans, those who never received the revelation given to Abraham and his progeny. On this question the New Testament speaks less clearly, but there are hints that a saving relationship to God is a possibility even for them. The Letter to the Hebrews requires that anyone coming to salvation have faith in a twofold object: It is necessary to believe that God exists and that he rewards those who seek him (Heb 11:6). This passage does not indicate whether such belief presupposes revelation, but the author very probably looked upon all knowledge of divine things as a gift of God, and in that sense as revelation. Paul, for his part, speaks now and again of God revealing himself to all peoples through the order of nature (Rom 1:19–20; cf. Acts 14:15–17; 17:22–31) but, it must be confessed, Paul's intention is to show why the Gentiles are guilty for having failed to believe and to worship God, rather than to show how they can be saved. At one point, Paul refers to a kind of revelation of God's law through the voice of conscience, written on human hearts (Rom 2:14–16). Although obedience to this law could in principle be justifying, Paul seems to think that in fact it serves to make the pagans culpable for their disobedience. As a result all human beings, whether Jews or pagans, stand in need of redemption through faith in Christ (Rom 3:9–25). Paul appears to be convinced that in the present time of grace there is no other way to salvation (Rom 3:25–26; cf. Acts 14:16; 17:30).

The magisterium of the Church has gradually clarified its position regarding the possibilities of salvific faith for the unevangelized. From patristic times until our own century the axiom "Outside the Church no salvation" was often stated in terms that seemed to make explicitly Christian and Catholic faith an absolute condition for salvation. For example, the Council of Florence in its Decree for the Jacobites (1442) asserted: "[The Holy Roman Church] firmly believes, professes, and preaches that none of those who exist outside of the Catholic Church—not only pagans but also Jews or heretics and schismatics—can become sharers of eternal life; rather, they will go into the eternal fire 'that was prepared for the devil and his angels' [Mt 25:41] unless, before the end of their lives, they are joined to that same Church" (DS 1351).[1]

This position was nuanced in the mid-nineteenth century. In an allocution given on the occasion of the definition of the Immaculate Conception of the Blessed Virgin in 1854, Pope Pius IX reminded the assembled bishops of the error of thinking that Catholics "can well hope for the eternal salvation of all those who have in no way lived in the true Church of Christ." But then he added that God in his justice and mercy will never impute guilt to those who innocently err. We must not presume to judge the limits of invincible ignorance, "taking into account the great variety of peoples, lands, native talents, and so many other factors."[2]

In an encyclical of 1863 the same pope again repudiated the extremes of rigorism and latitudinarianism. He wrote:

> It is once again necessary to recall and censure the very serious error in which some Catholics are unfortunately involved, that of believing that it is possible to attain eternal life although living in error and in a state of alienation from the true faith and from Catholic unity. This view is utterly contrary to Catholic teaching.
>
> You know also that people who are invincibly ignorant of our holy religion, provided that they sincerely keep the precepts of the natural law, who are prepared to obey God, and who live honorable and upright lives, can, by the efficacious power of the light and grace of God, attain eternal life; for God, who fully beholds, scrutinizes, and knows the minds, hearts, thoughts, and dispositions of all, in his supreme mercy will by no means permit anyone who is not guilty of voluntary fault to suffer eternal punishments.[3]

Under Pius XII the salvation of "nonbelievers" was discussed in connection with the necessity of belonging to the true Church in order to be saved. The encyclical *Mystici corporis* (1943), after declaring that the Catholic Church alone is the Mystical Body of Christ, spoke of the possibility of belonging to it not by formal membership but "by a kind of unconscious desire and intent" (*inscio quodam desiderio ac voto*, DS 3821). The pope seemed to imply that this latter type of belonging, even though it did not give the full benefits of incorporation in the visible organization of the Good Shepherd, might suffice for salvation in the case of persons inculpably ignorant of the true faith. In 1949 the Holy Office, in a letter to the Archbishop of Boston, declared that an "implicit intent" *(implicitum votum)* could suffice, provided that it was accompanied by supernatural faith and perfect charity (DS 3870–72). These texts, while not dealing directly with the kind of faith required for salvation, implied that explicit faith in Christ and the Church would not be necessary in the case of the unevangelized.

Vatican II touches on our problem in a variety of texts. At several points it implies that faith in Christ is in some sense necessary for salvation. The Dogmatic Constitution on the Church, after asserting that Christ is the one and only way of salvation, adds that faith and baptism are requisite, and that membership in the Church is also indispensable, at least for those who know that God has made the Church necessary (LG 14). The same Constitution states that the Church is obliged to preach the saving truth of the gospel and thereby draw its hearers to faith (LG 17). In the Decree on the Apostolate of the Laity, the Council declares that salvation is to be achieved through the grace of Christ and through belief in him (AA 6). The Decree on Priestly Ministry quotes Paul to the effect that faith depends on hearing, and hearing on the word of Christ (PO 4). The Decree on the Church's Missionary Activity holds that all must be converted to Christ as known through the preaching of the Church, but then it adds a significant qualification: "God, in ways known to himself can lead those who through no fault of their own are ignorant of the gospel, to that faith without which it is impossible to please him" (AG 7).

Other texts reinforce this last point. In a passage that makes no mention of faith, the Dogmatic Constitution on the Church asserts that divine providence grants "the helps that are necessary for salvation to those who, through no fault of their own, have not attained to the express recognition of God, yet who strive, not without divine grace, to lead an upright life" (LG 16). Still more positively, the Pastoral Constitution on the Church in the Modern World asserts that grace works in a hidden way in the hearts of all. Inasmuch as all are divinely called to salvation, "we are obliged to hold that the Holy Spirit offers everyone the possibility of sharing in this paschal mystery in a manner known to God" (GS 22). While these texts do not exclude the possibility that God might give everyone the opportunity to arrive at explicit belief, they seem to suggest that implicit faith in Christ, and indeed in God, could suffice.

## Faith of the Unevangelized: Theological Theories

As our historical survey of the theology of faith has shown, theologians have propounded a number of different theories with regard to the salvation of "unbelievers." The following selection may serve to recall and explain some of the principal options.

*1. Explicit Faith in Christ.* The axiom "Outside the Church no salvation" was originally used against Christian heretics and schismatics, but after the establishment of Christianity as the official religion of the Roman Empire, the axiom was directed also against Jews and pagans. Gregory of Nyssa and John Chrysostom took the position that the gospel had been preached to the whole world and that therefore non-Christians were culpable before God if they failed to embrace the true faith. This view was taken up in the West by Ambrose and Augustine, and promoted in a very rigorous form by Fulgentius of Ruspe. The medieval theologians for the most part differed from Fulgentius and the extreme Augustinians by holding that God seriously willed all human beings to be saved. They tried to reconcile this with the traditional view that since the promulgation of the Christian message, no one could be saved without explicit belief in the central mysteries of the faith, including the Trinity and the Incarnation.

Thomas Aquinas may be regarded as representative. In his early commentary on the *Sentences* and in his *De veritate* he maintains that if someone were brought up in a situation in which there was no possibility of learning the central articles of faith, and if that person faithfully observed the principles of the moral law, "God would either reveal to him by internal inspiration the things that it was necessary to believe, or would direct a preacher of the faith to him, as he sent Peter to Cornelius, Acts 10" (*De ver.* 14.11 ad 1; cf. *In III Sent.* Dist. 25, qu. 2, a. 7, sol. 1, ad 1). St. Thomas seems here to presume that in his day practically every human being was in a position to learn the principal mysteries of faith. As an example of invincible ignorance he therefore proposes not an inhabitant of a populous region but the imaginary case of "a boy brought up in the forest or among brute beasts."

In the *Summa theologiae*, whether for the sake of brevity or as a result of further reflection, he makes no mention of special providences on behalf of inculpable unbelievers. He contents himself with saying (*S. Th.,* 2-2.2.7c):

> After the time of grace revealed, both leaders and simple people are bound to have explicit faith in the mysteries of Christ, especially with regard to those points that are commonly celebrated and publicly taught in the Church, such as the articles of the creed concerning the Incarnation, discussed above.

The early Protestants, following the strict Augustinian school, were even more pessimistic than the medieval Catholics regarding the possibilities of salvation for the unevangelized. Martin Luther in his "Large Catechism" stated very forthrightly: "For where Christ is not preached, there is no Holy Spirit to create, call, and gather the Christian church, and outside it no one can come to the Lord Christ. . . . But outside the Christian church (that is, where the Gospel is not) there is no forgiveness, and hence no holiness."[4] John Calvin was no less absolute. Those who are deprived of the capacity to hear the word of God, he states, are among the reprobate, whom God "created for dishonor in life and destruction in death, to become the instruments of his wrath and examples of his severity" (*Institutes*, III.24.12).

In the Catholic tradition the Jansenists, likewise denying the universality of God's salvific will, affirmed that all inhabitants of unevangelized regions were predestined to damnation. In our historical survey we have mentioned Antoine Arnauld as a proponent of this position. His restrictive view remained widespread in the eighteenth century. As late as the mid-twentieth century Leonard Feeney, S.J., and his followers at St. Benedict Center in Cambridge, Massachusetts, proclaimed that no one could be saved without joining, or explicitly intending to join, the Roman Catholic Church. Feeney's pessimistic position was, however, rejected by the Roman Congregation of the Holy Office, which asserted, as already mentioned, that a merely implicit desire to join the Catholic Church, if accompanied by faith and informed by perfect charity, could suffice.[5]

This first option seems to be trapped in a dilemma. It must either deny the reality of God's universal saving will or else invoke miracles as a regular feature of the economy of salvation. Although a miraculous presentation of salvific knowledge might be the solution in rare cases, such as St. Thomas had in mind, it can hardly be understood as a regular feature of God's providence for the immense portion of the human race who have not been evangelized. Human beings ordinarily acquire information through sensory experience and testimony, not through direct supernatural revelation. If the knowledge required for salvation is inaccessible to the unevangelized, they have no possibility of salvation, and it appears that they cannot be included in God's saving plan. Thus it becomes difficult to defend Catholic doctrine of God's universal salvific will, which was in fact denied by the rigorist Augustinians, including the Jansenists. Although damnation need not be understood as subjection to tormenting fires, it seems unlikely that a God who is all-powerful and all-loving would place the majority of the human race in a position in which they were unable to attain the blessedness to which (according to Church teaching) all human beings are called (GS 22).

*2. Supernatural Elevation of Natural Knowledge.* As mentioned in our historical survey, a more liberal view emerged in the sixteenth century, after the voyages of discovery had made their impact on the European consciousness. Juan de Ripalda and others advanced, with subtle distinctions, the hypothesis that it might be possible for pagans to come to justification by accepting the naturally knowable truths of religion, provided that this acceptance were supernaturally elevated and illuminated by grace. Such a grace-enlightened acceptance of religious truth could be called faith in the broad sense *(fides late dicta).*

Ripalda's solution, when originally proposed, was considered rather bold because it ran up against a long tradition that required faith in the stricter sense of the word, that is to say, acceptance of some definite content on the basis of positive revelation. The Holy Office in 1679 condemned the thesis that "*fides late dicta* from the testimony of creatures or some such motive suffices for justification" (DS 2123). It is not clear that the condemnation extends to the theory of Ripalda, who explained that he was speaking in a hypothetical manner about what God could do if he so willed.[6] Nor is it entirely clear why the proposition in question was condemned. Possibly the Holy Office wished to disapprove of the theory that a purely natural faith could be salvific, even without supernatural elevation, or that faith in the broad sense could suffice even for persons who were in a position to make explicit acts of faith in God as known by Christian revelation.

The idea that God might use the order of creation as a means of testifying to his existence, his power, and his goodness has an excellent biblical background, for example, in Acts 14:17 and Romans 1:19–20. This idea reappears in the documents of Vatican II. The Constitution on Divine Revelation teaches that "God offers to humankind a lasting testimony to himself in created things" (DV 3), and the Pastoral Constitution on the Church in the Modern World states that "all believers of whatever religion have always perceived the voice and manifestation of God in the utterance of creatures" (GS 36). Although the Council did not say so, it would seem possible that such a revelation through the order of creation might serve, when elevated by grace, to ground an act of justifying faith. Further discussion would be needed to clarify how such an act of faith would be related to Christ as redeemer.

*3. Limbo.* Augustine and his disciples held that unbaptized infants would inevitably go to hell and suffer at least moderate pains on account of original sin. Following Anselm, medieval authors such as Peter Abelard, Peter Lombard, and Thomas Aquinas modified that Augustinian position by their doctrine that the torments of hell would be inflicted only for personal sin, so that anyone dying with original sin alone would suffer no positive pains but only the privation of the beatific vision. With later theologians such as Francisco Suarez the doctrine of a limbo of children, in which natural happiness would be enjoyed, came to be widely accepted, especially among Jesuits.

The existence of limbo has never been formally taught by the Church. The Pelagian doctrine that unbaptized infants would go to a place of beatitude without entering heaven was in fact condemned by the Council of Carthage of 418 (DS 224). The nearest thing to an approval of limbo is the statement of Pius VI, in the bull *Auctorem fidei* (1794) condemning as false and rash "the [Jansenist] doctrine which dismisses as a Pelagian fable the place in hell that the faithful sometimes call the 'limbo of children,' in which the souls of those who die with no guilt except that of original sin are punished with the pain of loss without pain of sense" (DS 2626). The Jansenists are here rebuked not for their denial of the existence of the "limbo of children" but for attacking the defenders of the theory as heretics. A number of catechisms adopted the limbo solution, but *The Catechism of the Catholic Church*, approved by John Paul II in 1992, omits all mention of limbo and declares that there are grounds for hoping that there may be a path of salvation open to unbaptized infants (no. 1261). Nothing is said about whether this path of salvation requires that these infants at some point make personal acts of faith or whether they somehow benefit from the faith of others.

The doctrine of limbo could have applications not only to infants but to adults. From early times theologians had speculated that the holy men and women of Old Testament times, between their death and the advent of the Redeemer, had been temporarily consigned to limbo. In his *Divine Comedy* Dante Alighieri depicted virtuous pagans of antiquity, such as Plato, Aristotle, and Virgil, together with more recent figures such as Avicenna and Averroes, as dwelling permanently in a place of relative light, in which their only punishment was a continual desire for the vision of God, unrelieved by hope. Except perhaps for his identification of the inhabitants of limbo, Dante's position is fairly typical of medieval theology.

Early in the sixteenth century the doctrine of a limbo of adults was given a more optimistic turn in response to questions raised by the recent voyages of discovery. Claudius Seyssel, archbishop of Turin, maintained that all who, by the light of unaided reason, followed the precepts of the natural law without having access to revealed truth, would be able to attain a purely natural beatitude, corresponding to the state of pure nature.[7]

In the early twentieth century Louis Billot, S.J., added a new dimension to the theory of the limbo of adults. In opposition to Seyssel's thesis regarding the natural beatitude given to virtuous pagans, he held that anyone who reached moral maturity would either achieve supernatural salvation or suffer eternal damnation. He maintained, however, that an immense multitude of pagans, by reason of the irreligious or superstitious climate in which they were raised, were "moral imbeciles," incapable either of serious sin or of merit. Such persons, he argued, would go to limbo with the unbaptized infants.[8] Billot's theory rested in part on his conviction that any capacity to perceive moral obligation presupposes a clear and explicit knowledge of God as lawgiver and of the content of God's law. Although the existence of some "moral imbeciles" may be admitted, the very broad extension that Billot gave to this category has not appealed to Catholic theologians.

The idea of limbo as a permanent state of natural blessedness is a pure hypothesis that has no foundation in Scripture. The Gospels speak of only two classes, the sheep and the goats, the saved and the damned. The hypothesis of a limbo intermediate between heaven and hell is hard to reconcile with the doctrines that all inherit original sin, that "Christ died for all," and that "the ultimate calling of humanity is one and divine" (Vatican II, GS 22). The theory of a limbo of adults is particularly fragile. In accordance with the teaching of Vatican II summarized earlier in this chapter, Catholic theologians generally reject the hypothesis that an adult would be left without access to the faith that would be absolutely required for eternal salvation. Depending on how they responded to that offer of faith, all would be either saved or damned.

*4. Primitive Revelation.* Following certain suggestions of Juan de Lugo and other theologians of the seventeenth century, Félicité de Lamennais and the French traditionalists of the nineteenth century proposed still another solution, which appealed to Johann Sebastian von Drey, Johann Adam Möhler, and others of the Tübingen school.[9] According to this view God gave a primitive revelation to Adam, which was passed down by tradition among the descendants of Seth. This tradition, which entered a new stage after the Great Flood, survives to some extent in a variety of religions. By accepting the revealed tradition with the help of grace, adherents of nonbiblical religions can make true and supernatural acts of faith. In the early twentieth century the Viennese cultural anthropologist, Wilhelm Schmidt, S.V.D., contended that the monotheism still found among primitive peoples was traceable to primitive revelation.

Traditionalism as a theological system, which made all knowledge, or all religious knowledge, dependent on revelation as its source, was rejected by the Holy See in the nineteenth century. But there is nothing unorthodox in the idea of a primitive revelation transmitted by tradition. The idea has, however, lost credibility in view of modern scientific studies about the antiquity of the human race. It seems historically unlikely that people living in modern times could receive their religious knowledge from revelations given to Seth or the sons of Noah and passed down by tradition.[10] Some theologians attempt to salvage the concept of primitive revelation by saying that God has always been revealing himself to human beings,[11] but this is to substitute a theory of universal revelation for the theory here under examination.

5. *Dynamism of First Moral Act.* Jacques Maritain and a number of Thomists in the mid-twentieth century developed a new theory on the basis of a rather obscure text in the *Summa theologiae* (1-2.89.6). Here St. Thomas stated that a child, on first achieving the use of reason, either orders itself to the right end or does not. In the former case the child is justified, and in the latter case it commits mortal sin. Maritain, reflecting on this text, held that the moral option for the right end involves a vital, nonconceptual knowledge of God. Taking this text from the *Summa theologiae* in conjunction with another on the need for grace in order to love God above all things (*S. Th.,* 1-2.109.3), Maritain went on to say that fallen human beings cannot rightly order themselves to their last end without the help of grace. He concluded, then, that when a child is faced by its first moral option, grace will in fact be given and that a virtuous response will be therefore elevated to the supernatural level. In this elevated act God will be sought as Savior. If it accepts the inner impulse of grace, the mind will be adhering to God's testimony, and thus making an act of faith that is formal and actual even though devoid of conceptual content. Faith therefore penetrates the immanent dialectic of the first act of freedom. Maritain went on to assert that this "lived" faith, as a practical or existential knowledge of God, can coexist with theoretical ignorance of God. It is even possible for a person who thinks of himself or herself as an atheist to be adhering to the reality of God known in a vital, preconscious manner.[12]

If a fundamental moral option can be made at the dawn of reason, there is no reason, in principle, why it could not be made at some later point in a person's life. The moral experience of being confronted with a crucial choice and of accepting the light and guidance that come from above could be characterized as an implicit act of faith.

Even before Maritain, other modern Thomists, such as Ambroise Gardeil, M.-M. Labourdette, and M.-J. Nicolas, used the Thomistic theory of the first moral act to indicate how faith can be present among persons who have not received any positive revelation through historical channels. Such persons, these authors maintain, could have faith by reason of a grace-illuminated initial adherence to God as their last end.[13]

This theory, insofar as it can appeal to the authority of Thomas Aquinas, makes an important contribution. It brings out the value of nonconceptual knowledge through what Aristotle and Aquinas called "connaturality." But the theory is hard to reconcile with the insistence of many authors, including St. Thomas, that saving faith is a response to actual revelation, and not merely to an interior illumination. While conceding that grace may stir up what has traditionally been called the "intention of faith," many theologians continue to ask whether or how this subjective orientation can serve as a substitute for the faith that comes from hearing.

6. *Final Option.* In the early 1930s Canon Palémon Glorieux, followed by a number of other Catholic theologians, maintained that to die was a finally decisive act, and that at the moment of death God would give a special opportunity to cooperate with grace. This could well involve a supernatural illumination that would enable unbelievers to make, or refuse to make, a salutary act of faith, even if they had not previously become aware of God's positive revelation in history. At the moment when the soul comes to the point of no return it could make a definitive choice, whether for or against God, that would seal its fate for eternity.[14]

Ladislas Boros, a recent herald of the "final illumination" theory, wrote a book in defense of the following thesis: "Death gives man the opportunity of posing his first completely personal act; death is, therefore, by reason of its very being, the moment above others for the awakening of consciousness, for freedom, for the encounter with God, for the final decision about his eternal destiny."[15] It is not necessary, Boros maintains, to postulate any limbo for imbeciles and for infants who die without baptism. "In death the infant enters into full possession of its spirituality, i.e. into a state of adulthood that many adults never reach during their lifetime. The result of this is that no one dies as an infant, even though he may leave us in infancy."[16]

The "final option" theory can be very persuasively defended. If it be assumed that grace is operative with its illuminative power in the crucial options of any person's life, it seems logical to suppose that this might be eminently the case at the moment of death, as the moment when the soul passes to its definitive stage and as the last moment at which the divine mercy can be exercised before the fate of the individual is sealed. If the theory holds for adults as they come to the end of their earthly journey, it might also be applied to infants who die without baptism, thus suggesting a solution to a problem that has long vexed theologians.

The theory of the final option suffers from many of the same objections as that of the first moral act. Unless some positive revelation were given as the content of the act of faith, the illumination would not supply what many theologians deem essential for saving faith. Besides, like the theory of the first moral act, this theory lacks any empirical foundation. People who die in their sleep, or by a sudden accident, show no sign of making a final option of any kind. It is difficult, moreover, to conceive of a "moment of death" intermediate between this life and the next, as the authors of the theory describe it. Some theologians have expressed concern that the theory of the final option unduly depreciates the meaning of life in the body, and that it might induce people to postpone their conversion, on the supposition that abundant grace would be offered at the moment of death. At least it needs to be said that if adults make final choices at the moment of death, those choices will presumably be in conformity with the pattern of their previous life.

7. *Supernatural Existential.* Still another proposal has been framed by Karl Rahner and other transcendental theologians. As has been seen in our historical survey, they hold that God's grace is given as offer to all human beings at every moment of their lives. This offer of grace is, in Rahner's terminology, "a supernatural existential." Even prior to its acceptance, grace gives a new horizon to human consciousness, so that our relationship to God is perceived in a different way than it would

be in a purely natural order. To accept ourselves as we really are, that is to say, as ordered toward the vision of God, is to accept grace, and this acceptance, in its cognitive dimension, is an act of faith. According to Rahner, the equivalence between faith and the acceptance of God's universal offer of grace supplies a satisfactory explanation for the possibility of salvific faith for all human beings, as the doctrine of God's universal savific will requires. In Rahner's words:

> Salvific activity without faith is impossible, and faith without an encounter with God revealing himself personally is a contradiction in terms.
>
> In the concrete, then, there remains no other conceivable possibility but a faith which is simply the obedient acceptance of man's supernaturally elevated self-transcendence, the obedient acceptance of his transcendental orientation to the God of eternal life. As an a priori modality of consciousness, this orientation has the character of a divine communication.[17]

One asset that Rahner finds in his theory is that it accounts for the possibility of salvation even of persons who regard themselves as atheists. Like Maritain, in the article analyzed above, Rahner distinguishes between two kinds of theism or, alternatively, atheism. He calls them "transcendental" *(transzendentale)* and "categorial" *(kategoriale)*. By "categorial" knowledge of God he understands "the objective, conceptual, and articulated interpretation of what we know of God in a subjective and unreflective way."[18] A "transcendental" affirmation of God is present when the human spirit accepts its inner orientation to the ultimate source and goal of all being. It is quite possible, he points out, to be a theist and a believer on the transcendental level while rejecting, on the categorial level, what one erroneously imagines God or Christ to be. What counts for salvation is the free acceptance of the subject's transcendental orientation toward God in the depth of the human heart.[19]

As already indicated in our historical survey, Rahner's theory of the "supernatural existential" has a wide following in contemporary Catholic theology. Even though the theory has never been formally embraced by the magisterium, it can claim to be in harmony with certain texts of Vatican II and other recent Church teaching. Many critics, however, complain that the theory seems to make explicit faith unimportant for salvation, and that it is hard to reconcile with the biblical and traditional understanding of the salvific importance of Christian proclamation. These objections do not necessarily invalidate the theory, but until they are satisfactorily answered the theory must be regarded as vulnerable.

*8. Non-Biblical Religions.* Under this heading we must make allusion to a vast body of literature that cannot here be discussed in detail. In the past fifty years or so a number of theologians, Protestant, Catholic, and Orthodox, have grappled with the question whether nonbiblical religions—those which are not derivative from Judaism or Christianity—can be mediators of faith and salvation to their adherents.

In the early 1960s Karl Rahner broke new ground in several essays in which he suggested that salvation history was not confined to the biblical religions, but was materially identical with the history of the human race. Divinizing grace, and thus transcendental revelation, were offered to all peoples and at all times. In the course of history the various peoples objectified their experience of the transcendent in diverse religions, each of which which serves to express and mediate grace, even though, because of human sinfulness, these religions are necessarily ambiguous. Rahner viewed these religions as "anonymously Christian" inasmuch as they were unconsciously oriented to Christ, the final and unsurpassable expression of God's saving will.[20]

A disciple of Rahner, Heinz Robert Schlette, proposed in 1963 that the non-Christian religions could be seen as ways of salvation and indeed as "ordinary" ways, in contrast to Christianity, which should be understood as the "extraordinary way of salvation."[21] Members of other religions, he held, could be saved thanks to a "tacit, implicit faith which does duty for the explicit Christian faith that is not within their power."[22]

About the same time an Indian priest, Raimundo Panikkar, who was likewise influenced by Rahner, published the first edition of his *The Unknown Christ of Hinduism*.[23] In this and many subsequent works Panikkar develops the thesis that the mystery of Christ is present, though in different ways, both in Christianity and in the other great religions. In the Church the mystery of Christ is overtly and explicitly believed, whereas it is at work in other religions in an implicit, concealed manner. In some of his writings Panikkar adopts the radical distinction between faith and belief proposed by Bernard Lonergan, Wilfred Cantwell Smith, and others.[24] Adherents of nonbiblical religions, he says, differ from Christians and from one another in their beliefs, but all have faith in one and the same mystery, which Christians hold to have become incarnate in Jesus Christ.[25] This one incarnation, however, does not exhaust the mystery, which is capable of making itself present elsewhere than in Jesus. One aim of interreligious dialogue is to exhibit the presence of the same mystery, the mystery of the transcendent Christ, in the various religions.

According to Schlette's and Panikkar's approach, then, adherents of non-Christian religions may attain saving faith not simply by reason of an interior encounter with God in the depths of their consciousness, but through their own religions. Even without hearing the gospel, they can be saved through the implicit relationship to Christ that is given in those religions.[26]

Other authors go beyond Rahner, Schlette, and Panikkar. In Anglican and Protestant circles the works of Maurice Wiles and John Hick, who reject Christocentrism in favor of a theocentric model of religion, are widely read. The Catholic missiologist Paul F. Knitter rejects the salvation-history model in favor of a symbolic model heavily influenced by Jung. He writes:

> Myth-symbols save. Historical facts do not. . . . It is only when we are grasped by and find ourselves responding with our whole being to a symbol, myth, or story that we are encountering the divine, touching and being touched by "the Ground of Being," and experiencing grace.[27]

Denying that Christ works "mystically, cosmically, anonymously within all religions," Knitter has proposed to move from a christocentric to a theocentric model for the theology of religions.[28] Criticizing his own earlier positions, he has more recently made a further move from theocentrism to "soteriocentrism." What unites the religions in common discourse and praxis, he declares, is not how they conceive of Christ or of God but rather how they promote salvation *(soteria)*.[29]

Theories that seem to put Christ on a par with other savior figures, so that faith in them can be as salvific as faith in Christ, are widely perceived as unacceptable in the Catholic tradition. In an address to the college of cardinals (April 4–7, 1991), Cardinal Jozef Tomko, prefect of the Congregation for the Evangelization of Peoples, warned against certain deviations that were widespread, he said, in India. Among these he mentioned the idea that "the Logos can appear in other religions and be hidden in other historical figures," so that the founders of other religions might be called "saviors in whom the infinite mystery of God is at work or is historically incarnated."[30]

It would probably be premature to attempt to give a firm judgment on the presence of revelation and faith in nonbiblical religions, for the debate is still in progress. Not everything, however, is in doubt. In Catholic teaching it is clear that there can be no salvation except in Christ "for there is no other name under heaven given among men by which we must be saved" (Acts 4:12). The savior is not simply the heavenly Christ, as a mythic figure, but the incarnate Son. "There is one mediator between God and men, the man Christ Jesus, who gave himself as a ransom for all" (1 Tim 2:5–6). Christians have faith (and not simply "belief") in Jesus Christ as divine savior.

It is debatable, moreover, whether any non-Christian religions are objectively revealed by God, so that an assent to their content can be an act of divine faith. Nothing in Scripture seems to suggest that God regularly reveals himself through nonbiblical religions, or that people can attain salvation by making acts of faith in the stories and doctrines of such religions. At most Scripture allows that pagan religion leaves room for an "unknown god" who is the true God of Christian faith (Acts 17:23).

Vatican II, recognizing the complexity of the question, refrained from pronouncing on whether the other religions contain revelation and whether they are ways of salvation. It spoke vaguely of the religions as growing out of "a certain perception of that unseen force which is present in the course of things and in the events of human life, and sometimes even an acknowledgement of a supreme deity or even of a Father" (NA 2). It did not, however, assert that this perception was more than natural or that this acknowledgement amounted to justifying or saving faith. Avoiding these questions, the Council contented itself with saying:

> The Catholic Church rejects nothing that is true and holy in these religions. It looks with respect on those ways of acting and living, and those precepts and doctrines which, though often at variance with what it holds and expounds, frequently reflect a ray of that divine truth that enlightens everyone. Yet it unceasingly proclaims, and is bound to proclaim, Christ who is "the way, the truth, and the life" (Jn 14:6), in whom all people find the fullness of religious life and in whom God has reconciled all things to himself. (NA 2)

Ten years after the Council, Paul VI taught clearly that Christianity is the ordinary way of salvation and that the proclamation of the gospel is the duty of Christians.[31] Supporting the opinion of distinguished theologians such as Jean Daniélou,

Henri de Lubac, and Hans Urs von Balthasar, the pope took the position that non-Christian religions offer only "natural religious expressions" of human striving for union with God. Only Christianity, he held, can establish "an authentic and living relationship" with the divine.[32] The implication would seem to be that these religions do not provide the possibility of saving faith. Members of these religions might indeed be saved, but not precisely through their religions. It is doubtful, however, that in this passing statement the pope intended to settle the theological debate.

Pope John Paul II goes beyond his predecessors in praising the religious life of non-Christians. Beginning with his first encyclical, *Redemptor hominis* (1979), he has repeatedly alluded to the presence of the Spirit of truth among followers of the other religions.[33] Alluding to the Day of Prayer for Peace held at Assisi in 1986, he declared in an address to the Roman curia on December 22, 1986, "Every authentic prayer is under the influence of the Holy Spirit."[34] Then in his encyclical on missionary activity, *Redemptoris missio* (1990), he stated that the Church's relationship with the other religions is dictated by a twofold respect: "Respect for man in his quest for answers to the deepest questions of his life, and respect for the action of the Spirit in man."[35] Like Paul VI, John Paul II refrains from speaking of non-Christian religions as revealed or as "ways of salvation."

It seems entirely possible that God in his supernatural providence intends other religions besides Judaism as preparations for the gospel, and that their founders hold a position in salvation history for nonbiblical peoples in some way resembling (though not completely parallel to) that of the patriarchs and prophets for Israel. If one accepts Rahner's theory of the "supernatural existential," it becomes highly probable that these other religions are expressions and mediations of supernatural faith, secretly oriented to Christ the universal Savior. But in the framework of Catholic Christianity it seems evident that other religions could not offer grace and salvation unless Christ, the divine Savior, were at work in them.[36] These religions may be thought to provide helps for salvation to the extent that they assist their adherents to reach out to Christ, the mediator of all saving truth.

## Conclusion

The biblical and traditional teaching must be allowed to stand: Faith is essential for salvation. God does not wish to save us unless we lovingly welcome the word by which he manifests himself and invites us to follow the path that he has marked out for us. According to Christian faith God's word is one: Jesus Christ, the eternal Word. The human race is likewise one. It has one destiny, the salvation offered in Christ. He is the sole Redeemer, and all who have saving faith are partakers of his grace.

Faith, then, is essentially oriented toward Christ, the mediator and fullness of all revelation. The ancient Israelites looked forward in hope, amid shadows and confusions, to the decisive act by which God would inaugurate his kingdom. Through their faith they were partakers of the blessings that were to be given through the Son. The saving history of Israel reaches its culmination in Christ, and is not theologically intelligible apart from him. The great heroes of faith of the Old

Testament did not receive in their life on earth what had been promised to them, but God was not unfaithful to his promises. "God had foreseen something better for us, that apart from us they should not be made perfect" (Heb 11:40).

An apparent exception to the rule of salvation by faith has already been discussed in Chapter 11. It was there seen that baptized infants, even before they make any personal acts of faith, are counted among the faithful by reason of the faith of the Church, in which they participate through baptism.

Theologians have speculated since patristic times about the ultimate fate of unbaptized infants. A possible solution has been found in the doctrine of a "limbo of children" in which they would enjoy some kind of natural blessedness. But this hypothesis has been falling out of favor. Theologians today are more inclined to the view that such infants are included in God's salvific plan. Although nothing on this subject is revealed, it is possible that unbaptized infants may be granted an opportunity to make an act of personal faith at the moment of death or that they may be made beneficiaries of the faith of the Church. All we can know for certain is that God will provide for them in a manner consonant with his justice and mercy.

Since the sixteenth century many theories have been proposed to explain how adults who have never heard the proclamation of the gospel, or who have not heard it proclaimed in ways that they could find credible, might still have faith. Does God illuminate the first moral act at the dawn of human reason? Does he give the unevangelized some special enlightenment or revelation at the moment of their death? Is Christ secretly at work in nonbiblical religions and quasi-religious ideologies? Does his grace elevate the natural religious knowledge available through the order of creation? Does he invite the human spirit into communion with himself by an unfailing "supernatural existential"? These and other theories have real plausibility provided that they are not set forth as alternate plans of salvation apart from Christ, the one mediator. No one can be saved by sincerity, by good faith, or by any other subjective dispositions, even with the elevation of interior grace, apart from the objective deed by which God enters human history.

Reversing Knitter's dictum, it might be better to say: "Myth symbols do not save. Historical facts do." The salvific fact par excellence is the paschal mystery— Christ crucified and raised for our salvation. The finest subjective attitudes would be of no avail unless there were a correlative reality to which they were oriented. Faith has saving power insofar as it reaches out to, and derives efficacy from, the redemptive action whereby God in Christ reverses the history of sin and draws humanity toward its true end.

"If I be lifted up I will draw all things to myself" (Jn 12:32). This "all" may be taken as including everyone who, by God's grace, searches devoutly for the one true Redeemer and rejoices when and if that Redeemer shows his face.

## Notes

1. Earlier official documents to the same effect would include the 1215 declaration of the Fourth Lateran Council *Firmiter credendum* (DS 802) and the 1302 bull of Boniface VIII *Unam sanctam* (DS 870). The history of the question, with special reference to official Cath-

olic teaching, has recently been traced in Francis A. Sullivan, *Salvation Outside the Church?* (New York: Paulist, 1992).

2. Pius IX, Allocution "Singulari quadam" (DB 1647, not reprinted in DS); quoted in part by Sullivan, *Salvation*, 113.

3. Pius IX, "Quanto conficiamur moerore," DS 2866. My translation differs slightly from that in *The Papal Encyclicals*, vol. 1, ed. Claudia Carlen (Wilmington, N.C.: McGrath, 1981), 369–73, at 370.

4. Luther, "Large Catechism," Part II, art. 3, nos. 43 and 56; in *The Book of Concord*, ed. and trans. Theodore G. Tappert (Philadelphia: Fortress, 1959), 416, 418.

5. Sacred Congregation of the Holy Office, Letter to Archbishop of Boston, August 8, 1949; text in DS 3866–73. The position of Leonard Feeney and his disciples, which occasioned this letter, is reported and criticized in Sullivan, *Salvation*, 134–36.

6. See Louis Capéran, *Le problème du salut des infidèles*, rev. ed., vol. 1 (Paris: Beauchesne, 1934), 342–43. Additional references are given above in Chapter 3, note 54.

7. See Ibid., 1:222–25.

8. Louis Billot, "La Providence de Dieu et le nombre infini d'hommes hors de la voie normale du salut," *Études* 161–76 (1919–1923), nine articles. Cf. Capéran, *Problème du salut*, 1:512–31, 2:34–40; Riccardo Lombardi, *The Salvation of the Unbeliever* (Westminster, Md.: Newman, 1956), 21–24; Maurice Eminyan, *The Theology of Salvation* (Boston: Daughters of St. Paul, 1960), 22–23.

9. See Capéran, *Problème du salut*, 443–59; also Josef Rupert Geiselmann, *The Meaning of Tradition* (New York: Herder and Herder, 1966), 39–80.

10. As Karl Rahner puts it, "In view of the spatial extension and especially the temporal duration of the history of the human race as we know it today, we can no longer seriously assume without making arbitrary postulates that all men have been in contact with concrete, historical, verbal revelation in the narrowest sense, and hence with the explicit tradition of a primeval revelation in paradise or with the biblical revelation in the Old or New Testaments, and that they must have been in contact [with it] in order to be able to believe and thus achieve their salvation." *Foundations of Christian Faith* (New York: Crossroad, 1982), 152.

11. E.g., Heinrich Fries, "Primitive Revelation," *Encyclopedia of Theology* (New York: Seabury, 1975), 1468–71.

12. Jacques Maritain, "La dialectique immanente du premier acte de liberté," *Nova et vetera* 20 (1945), 218–35, reprinted in his *The Range of Reason* (New York: Scribner's, 1953), 66–85.

13. See Eminyan, *Theology of Salvation*, 65–71.

14. Lombardi, *Salvation of the Unbeliever*, 234–66, and Eminyan, *Theology of Salvation*, 80–95 survey the positions of Glorieux and others of this school. Eminyan returns to the same theme in his *The Mystery of Salvation* (Valletta, Malta: Malta University Press, 1972), 172–76. See also George J. Dyer, *Limbo: Unsettled Question* (New York: Sheed & Ward, 1964), 117–22.

15. Ladislaus Boros, *The Mystery of Death* (New York: Herder and Herder, 1965), ix.

16. Ibid., 110.

17. Rahner, *Foundations of Christian Faith*, 152.

18. Karl Rahner, "What Does Vatican II Teach about Atheism?" in Karl Rahner, ed., *The Pastoral Approach to Atheism*. Concilium 23 (New York: Paulist, 1973), 7–24, quotation from 17.

19. Ibid., 19.

20. See Karl Rahner, "History of the World and Salvation-History," *Theological Investigations*, vol. 5 (Baltimore: Helicon, 1966), 97–114; "Christianity and the Non-Christian Religions," ibid., 115–34; idem, *Foundations of Christian Faith*, 311–21.

21. Heinz Robert Schlette, *Towards a Theology of Religions* (New York: Herder and Herder, 1966), 80–81.

22. Ibid., 92.

23. Raimundo Panikkar, *The Unknown Christ of Hinduism* (London: Darton, Longman Todd, 1964).

24. See above, Chapter 7, "Faith and Belief."

25. See, for instance, the long introduction to the revised edition of Panikkar's *The Unknown Christ of Hinduism: Towards an Ecumenical Christophany* (London: Darton, Longman, and Todd, 1981). For a recent restatement see Raimon Panikkar, "A Christophany for Our Times," *Theology Digest* 39 (1992): 3–22.

26. For the positions of Rahner and Panikkar see the helpful survey in Jacques Dupuis, *Jesus Christ and the Encounter of World Religions* (Maryknoll, N.Y.: Orbis, 1991), especially pages 127–30, 147–51, 184–90. Dupuis is generally favorable to the Rahner school, but he rejects Panikkar's separation of faith from belief. There is no Christic mystery, he holds, "dissociable from Jesus of Nazareth—a Christ of faith without the Jesus of history" (190).

27. Paul F. Knitter, "Jesus-Buddha-Krishna: Still Present?" *Journal of Ecumenical Studies* 16 (1979): 651–71, quotation from 657. Cf. Avery Dulles, *Models of Revelation* (Garden City, N.Y.: Doubleday, 1983), 189–92 for further discussion of this and other texts of Knitter.

28. Knitter, *No Other Name? A Critical Survey of Christian Attitudes toward the World Religions* (Maryknoll, N.Y.: Orbis, 1985), 125–30, 152–57, 165–67.

29. Idem, "Toward a Liberation Theology of Religions," in *The Myth of Christian Uniqueness: Toward a Pluralistic Theology of Religions*, ed. John Hick and Paul F. Knitter (Maryknoll, N.Y.: Orbis, 1987), 178–200, at 187.

30. Jozef Tomko, "On Relativizing Christ: Sects and the Church," *Origins* 20 (April 25, 1991): 753–54; quotation from 754.

31. Paul VI, *On the Evangelization of Peoples*, no. 80 (Washington, D.C.: United States Catholic Conference, 1976), 63.

32. Ibid., no. 53, pp. 36–37. In taking this position, the pope may have been following what he understood to be the dominant view at the synod of Bishops, which had dealt with evangelization in its 1974 meeting.

33. John Paul II, *Redemptor hominis*, no. 6 (Washington, D.C.: United States Catholic Conference, 1979), 17–18.

34. Idem, Address to Roman Curia, December 22, 1986, text in *Origins* 16 (January 15, 1987): 561–63, at 563.

35. John Paul II, *Redemptoris missio*, no. 29; text in *Origins* 20 (January 31, 1991): 541–68, at 550.

36. Ibid., no. 5, p. 544. Here the pope explains that Christ is the one mediator and that any other mediation of grace or of salvation can only be a participation of his mediation.

# 14

# Concluding Synthesis

Amid the welter of questions, theories, and controversies about faith the reader could easily lose track of the main stream of concordant affirmation, which has been relatively constant down through the centuries, and may be recapitulated here by way of a conclusion. This final chapter will take the form of a summary of the principal points of this central tradition, viewed in the perspectives of the present author. The following brief, thesis-like propositions presuppose the more detailed exposition given in the previous pages.

## The Nature of Faith

*1. Faith, in the broad, anthropological sense of the term, is a constant feature of human cognition and existence.* All conviction that cannot be reduced to self-evidence through immediate experience and deduction rests upon a free and trusting commitment that may be called faith in this generic sense. Thus I may be said to have faith in what I know from books about history and science, faith in what is reported through the news media, faith in the fact that the sun will rise tomorrow, faith in the honesty of my banker, and faith even in the reliability of my own senses. This is what some authors call "human" or "philosophical" faith as opposed to "divine" or "theological" faith, which is based on the word of God. In spite of rationalist claims to the contrary, purely human faith may under certain conditions have a firmness surpassing mere probability. The convergence of the signs or the force of the testimony may exclude all prudent doubt.

*2. Faith in the theological sense (which alone concerns us in this book) is a self-surrender to God as he reveals himself.* By making himself discernibly present in human history by signs and symbols, God calls men and women to participate in his own divine life. Faith in its full and integral reality is more than a merely intellectual assent or an act of blind trust. It is a complex act in which assent, trust, obedience, and loving self-commitment are interwoven.

*3. Faith is a religious act.* It involves an adoring submission of one's whole self to God as supreme lord of all things. In faith I abandon the self-centeredness of my normal vision and consent to look at reality from God's perspective. I transfer my concern from narrow self-interest to the God on whom I depend and who is to be unconditionally esteemed, trusted, and loved for his own sake. The intrinsic motive of faith, the "authority" of God, is God himself in his wisdom, truthfulness, holiness, power, and fidelity. These divine attributes, though conceptually distinct, are all identical in God.

*4. Faith presupposes revelation.* I could not submit to God's vision and plan for me, or respond to his call, unless he emerged from his silence, manifested himself, beckoned to me, and spoke a word of truth that I could recognize as coming from him. Whether such a word is in fact forthcoming depends upon God and is not predictable from a merely human point of view. It may be presumed that if God does speak, his word will come through signs and symbols given in history and through the insights of privileged interpreters; for human life generally rises to its higher levels through socially and historically transmitted memories of striking events and through the guidance of spiritually perceptive persons.

## Attributes of Faith

*5. Faith is free.* If it were an involuntary submission to a divine force, faith might be objectively good but it would have no religious or moral value. Unlike revelation, which is God's act, faith is the believer's own act—a conscious choice to welcome and respond to God's gracious initiative. The freedom of faith may be limited in particular cases by social and psychological pressures upon the believer. Faith grows in freedom to the extent that it takes God alone as its motive. In the last analysis, it is divine grace that sets the believer free.

*6. Faith is supernatural: it is borne by grace.* By myself I would not be capable of radically changing the horizons of my own vision and putting the center of gravity of my existence outside myself. For me to take God's word as the norm of truth and his goodness as the goal of my being, God must first manifest himself and draw me to himself. I cannot claim any entitlement to this benefit. For anyone who wishes to acquire faith or grow in it, it would be fitting to pray for the needed grace. Although never forced on believers, faith is a gift: it is "infused" into the mind by God.

*7. Faith is experiential.* For those who view the universe in the perspectives of faith, everything is experienced in a different way. Although God's grace is not distinctly perceived, its presence is apprehended by its holy effects, including interior light, consolation, and a sense of union with God. Even amid suffering and disappointments the believer enjoys an inner peace and joy that are not of this world. With the help of grace the believer is attuned to the message of salvation and accordingly finds joy and ease in assenting to the truth.

*8. Faith is cognitive.* Based on revelation, faith is not just an attitude of docility, a pious wish, or a feat of constructive imagination. Although not reducible to belief, faith includes belief as a fundamental and essential ingredient. As a believer, I cannot be satisfied with behaving as if certain things were true; I must recognize that what God is held to have disclosed is actually true. Otherwise faith could not be a firm conviction or a trustful self-surrender, nor could it provide a solid ground for total self-commitment. Deprived of its cognitive character, faith would lose its essential attributes.

*9. Faith is sapiential.* Faith surpasses and on some points rejects purely human wisdom, which takes no direction from revelation. Although it may appear as foolishness to its "cultured despisers," faith provides a wisdom of its own. It enables the believer to see reality from God's perspective, so that in its light many enigmas of life become meaningful. Faith therefore gives rise to knowledge and understanding. With the help of the Holy Spirit, faith flowers into wisdom, a loving contemplation of the things of God as perceived by the light of grace.

*10. Faith has a doctrinal component.* Although it may be initially communicated by means of symbols and metaphors, God's revelation has a content that can, to a certain extent, be spelled out in propositions that capture its true meaning. God at times gives prophets and inspired writers the grace to formulate in declarative sentences particular truths that believers are to accept. The doctrines of revealed religion are not just words, but are meanings conveyed by human statements. The true object of belief, strictly speaking, is neither the verbal formulations nor even the propositions but rather the realities signified by the words and propositions: most importantly, the three-personed God himself as our creator, our ruler, our savior, and as the goal toward whom we move.

*11. Faith is reasonable.* The ground for the assent of faith is prepared by an exercise of reason, which makes inferences from naturally accessible data, including the signs given in history and in one's personal experience. Human reasoning can reach the conclusion that it would be prudent to assent to the revelation as coming from God. It can also overcome the force of various objections. But purely rational arguments accommodated to all human minds do not by themselves bring about the full conviction required for faith. Unwavering assurance cannot be achieved unless the arguments are synthesized in the light of a grace-given desire for, and heartfelt anticipation of, a redemptive revelation. Theologically it seems probable that the approach to faith is assisted at every stage by the grace of God, who impels and invites sincere inquirers to find him in his word.

*12. Faith is and should be critical.* Far from suppressing the capacity for intelligent judgment, the attitude of faith requires deep reverence for truth and calls for discernment. Faith would not be true to its own nature unless it were passionately concerned to keep itself free from error and superstition, submitting purely to God's own word. Faith must therefore be on guard against self-deceptive projections, frauds, and delusions.

*13. In principle, faith is firm.* Its motive is the authority of God the revealer, whose word is utterly dependable. Thanks to the signs that have been given and the interior grace that assists in the discernment of God's authentic word, the believer can achieve full assurance. A hesitant and qualified assent would not bring about the total submission and commitment that the word of God requires.

*14. Faith is obscure.* It lays hold of its object not directly but through signs and testimonies that present the object only in partial and inadequate ways. The believer is painfully conscious of perceiving "in a mirror, dimly." The God who communicates himself infinitely surpasses all that believers can infer from the indications given. The saving plan of God includes mysteries that are to some degree impenetrable by the human mind. Recognizing God's utter transcendence, the believer does not expect that the deep truths of revelation will be reducible to "clear and distinct ideas."

*15. Faith is vulnerable.* Because it comes about through a grace-borne free assent, faith cannot be a matter of self-evident truth, nor can it be achieved by strict deduction from that which is objectively evident. The believer can be, and often is, conscious of being able to doubt and disbelieve. The most fundamental difficulties against faith are perennial: they come from the fact that faith is faith, a free reliance on the word of another. Faced by such difficulties, the believer will sometimes have to grapple with involuntary doubts. Only through an act of will, prompted by the inclination of grace, can faith retain its clarity of vision and its serenity.

## The Life of Faith

*16. Faith comes from hearing.* In the normal case faith is a response to the good news of what God has done for the sake of human salvation. In the case of historical religions, faith takes the form of an accumulated body of revealed doctrine, established through a succession of privileged recipients. The individual adherent of a revealed religion must hear the external word of proclamation, although the "interior word" of God's gracious self-communication is also required for faith.

*17. By exception faith may arise without hearing.* God can bestow the gift of faith on some who have not heard the proclaimed word. This is notably the case with baptized infants, who are received into the body of Christ before they are able to make personal acts of faith. Participating in the faith of the Church, baptized infants are said in some theological traditions to have "inchoative faith" or the "seed" of faith.

*18. Can unbaptized infants be saved without faith?* Revelation appears to be silent on the point, but theologians often conjecture that they too are included in the divine plan of salvation. In some way known to God, they may possibly be saved through the faith of the Church. Perhaps they are given an opportunity to make a personal act of faith at the moment of their death. In view of the universal effects of the Fall and the universal scope of God's redemptive action in Christ, it seems unlikely that anyone is destined for a purely natural state of beatitude, such as the "limbo of children" was thought to be.

*19. Faith is foundational.* It gives a decisive orientation to the believer's life, setting it on a new basis and providing a new scale of values and principles—those that God in his wisdom is pleased to impart. The passage into faith involves a conversion. Moving beyond the horizons of ordinary human experience and reflection, the believer lovingly welcomes the larger, mysterious world graciously disclosed by God, who is all-knowing.

*20. Faith inwardly transforms the believer.* It gives meaning and purpose to human life, overcoming aimlessness, boredom, and the sense of futility. Sustained by a sense of personal union with God, the believer enjoys a profound inner peace and joy that worldly misfortunes cannot destroy. Faith gives rise to prayer, adoration, hope, love, and other interior acts. Faith and love, when they exist together, reciprocally shape each other. The believer is in a position to love more purely and unselfishly than the nonbeliever; the lover believes with greater ease and joy than the one who does not love.

*21. Faith has exterior as well as interior acts.* It has an inner tendency to flow over into acts of confession, obedience, and service. Unless some obstacle arises, believers give testimony to their faith in word and deed—a testimony that may culminate even in acts of martyrdom. Acknowledging God's supremacy, believers wish their lives to be ruled by him. Regenerated by God's merciful love toward themselves, they engage in works of love and mercy toward others.

*22. Faith strengthens human community.* It gives an unwavering center of loyalty, undergirding trust, truthfulness, and commitment. In so doing faith offers a remedy against cynicism, suspicion, greed, and selfishness. It motivates its adherents to care for the weak and helpless and to contribute to the fashioning of a universal community of peace and justice, a civilization of love.

*23. Faith is subject to growth.* The faith of the Church as a whole achieves more explicit formulations of revealed truth with the passage of centuries. The faith of individuals can grow as believers advance in explicit knowledge of the contents of revelation, as they gain firmer conviction, as they trust more fully in God's mercy and goodness, as they liberate themselves from superstition, and as they turn more to God himself as the sole motive for believing and the sole source of true security. The spiritual gifts of wisdom, understanding, and knowledge bring faith to its full stature. The normal growth of faith is sometimes impeded by mental or psychological defects, but God's grace is able to compensate for human weaknesses. Indeed, grace sometimes manifests itself by its wonderful achievements in persons who are lacking in worldly wisdom, education, and other natural gifts that are capable of engendering pride and self-satisfaction.

*24. Faith is sometimes stunted.* It may be accompanied by ignorance, superstition, anxiety, and fear. It does not always lead to confident and loving self-surrender. The minimal faith that remains in the absence of charity and other virtues is sometimes called "dead" or "unformed" faith. Residual faith may take the form of a sincere belief that God exists, that he has spoken, and that his word is true. Such beliefs, although they constitute a bare minimum, should not be despised. They are fruits of grace and provide a scaffolding that is capable of supporting, and even calls for, generous self-commitment.

*25. Faith faces challenges.* Authentic faith finds itself in competition with false and inadequate faiths. At all times people have been tempted to place their final trust in natural forces, military and political power, wealth, or other created agencies, as well as in spurious revelations. Secularism, which centers human trust and aspirations on things that can be touched and seen, is an acute temptation in the present age. The achievements of human science and technology seem to promise many of the satisfactions that religion has been thought to offer. Often the shock of human disaster is needed to expose the unreliability of natural forces and human ingenuity, and to redirect attention to God, who alone is wholly good and totally trustworthy.

*26. Faith can be lost.* Because faith is a free response, not coerced either by the rational evidence or by the gifts of grace, it can be renounced. In the circumstances of today's world, faith is especially imperilled by the climate of secularism, the erosion of traditional sociological supports, the rapidity of cultural change, the aggressive propagation of alternative belief-systems, and the bewildering variety of contemporary options. Confronted by the instability of tradition and the multiplicity of present choices, the believer can easily fall into a state of indecision and agnosticism that eschews final commitments. In a given case distrust, suspicion, or even despair, may seem to have prevailed. But what appears to human eyes as a loss of faith may in fact be a searching faith that has not succeeded in recognizing where revelation is to be found. In the last analysis, only God can judge whether a given individual possesses supernatural and living faith.

## The Universal Call to Faith

*27. Faith is necessary for salvation.* Without God's offer and its free acceptance, human beings cannot share in the divine life. Responding to God's word and to his invitation to communion, faith brings about a deep union with God. It clings to him as the sole source of all grace and salvation. By establishing a right relationship with God ("justification") faith sets the believer on the path to eternal life. Salvation in the full sense is the ultimate fruit of faith. Eternal life will be the lot of those who believe, who strive to put their faith into practice, and who persevere in faith to the end.

*28. Faith is a constant and universal possibility.* In destining and calling human beings to union with himself, God has written into the human heart a restlessness that cannot be appeased except by God's loving presence and self-manifestation. In view of this divine call, all human beings have an innate inclination to seek God's word. If they follow up this inclination by a persevering search, they will not be disappointed. Although not all have faith, and although those who have it at one time may lack it at another, God's universal salvific will may be expected to make some measure of faith attainable always and by all. In some cases the objective signs of revelation may be few and indistinct, but God's word, as it comes through creation, history, and experience, illuminated by the light of grace, is always sufficient to sustain a genuine, though inchoative, act of faith.

*29. Faith may be expressed and nurtured by non-Christian religions.* In view of the omnipresence of God's revealing word and the universal possibility of faith, it may be presumed that non-Christian religions, even though they lack the fullness of revelation, contain expressions and vehicles of genuine faith. To determine how extensive these sound elements are, and to what extent they are vitiated by the effects of sin and superstition, is the task of theologians who specialize in the study of these religions. Without conducting an assiduous investigation of this kind the systematic theologian is not in a position to form specific judgments on the value of other religions.

## Christian Faith

*30. Even before the time of Christ, faith was at work in Israel as the people of God's choice.* The Christian Church has canonized the Scriptures of ancient Israel and has recognized them as containing revelation, as providentially preparing for Christianity, and hence as permitting, by anticipation, a faith that is in some sort Christian. The New Testament depicts Abraham, Moses, the psalmists, and the prophets as speaking in an obscure way (hidden, no doubt, even to themselves) about Christ and the Church. Because the Holy Spirit was leading them, they spoke better than they knew.

*31. According to Christian belief, faith reaches its full and divinely intended stature in Christ.* In his relationship of trustful obedience to his Father, Jesus makes himself the model and paradigm of all faith. Commending his spirit to his Father, he passes willingly through the darkness of suffering and death, allowing himself to be stripped of all natural and human supports. As the supreme instance of obedient self-surrender crowned by victory, Jesus brings to completion the movement of sacred history that may be traced through the Hebrew Scriptures. The whole pattern of sacred history holds together in Jesus Christ, in whom it reaches its summit and consummation. Even though Jesus, as the incarnate Son, did not have faith in the same sense that other human beings do, he exemplifies in an eminent manner the obedience and trust that are constitutive of faith.

*32. Faith finds its most adequate expression in Christianity.* Coming into its own through the resurrection of Jesus and the descent of the Holy Spirit, Christianity discloses, as no other religion or philosophy does, the inner nature of God, the goal of human life, and the path that leads to everlasting life. Christian faith consists in a warm welcome of the good news of what God has done for humanity in Christ. Transporting the believer into a new relationship of intimate friendship with God the Savior, the gospel is rightly called salvific.

*33. Christian faith can enrich, and be enriched by, other belief-systems.* According to Christian conviction, God's revelation in Christ completes and crowns not only Judaism but also whatever is true and salvific in other religions and quasi-religious ideologies. To give specificity to this principle, and to determine in exactly what sense it applies to particular belief-systems, serious dialogue with these other communities is needed.

*34. The church is the home of faith.* To render Christian faith accessible to all nations and all generations, God has established the Church as a socially organized community of faith. Through its Scriptures, creeds, and authoritative teaching, as well as its liturgy and forms of life, the Church continually transmits its faith to new members. Christians believe from within the Church, as participants in a divinely constituted community of faith. The corporate faith of the Church gives the social ambience in which the faith of individuals can endure and flourish. As a sign or sacrament, the Church makes Christ vividly present in the world, expressing the faith of its members and inviting others to share that faith. The sign is frequently obscured by the weaknesses and infidelity of the members, who thereby raise stumbling blocks to faith.

*35. Christianity is a future-oriented faith.* Because it looks forward to the consummation of all history and the establishment of God's definitive reign, Christian faith is, in a striking way, fiducial. It involves an acceptance of God's promises and a confidence in God's power and will to keep those promises. It goes out to Jesus Christ as the redeemer who will return in glory and gather into his kingdom all who have awaited him in faith.

*36. Faith, as we experience it, is provisional; it supplies for a vision that is yet to be given.* Final salvation consists in a clear vision of God, who cannot be known in the present life except under the veils of faith itself. In eternity the blessed will know God not on the testimony of others, or indirectly through signs, but directly, as he is in himself. Even though the divine mystery is inexhaustible, so that no finite mind can ever be capable of comprehensively knowing it, the saints in heaven will pass beyond that deficient mode of knowledge which, in humanity's present state of pilgrimage, goes by the name of faith.

# Index of Personal Names

# Subject Index